China's provinces in reform

China's provinces are all considerable social, economic and political systems in their own right, and most are the size and scale of a European country in population, land area and social complexity; under other circumstances they might well be regarded as separate states, rather than component parts of a single, unitary system. Despite their distinct identities and importance to the country's social, political and economic development, China's provinces only recently became a major focus of inquiry with the introduction of reform and decentralisation.

This volume is the first of a series examining each of China's provinces in reform and deals with Guangxi, Hainan, Liaoning, Shandong, Shanghai, Sichuan and Zhejiang. It is concerned with the impact of economic reform on social and political change within each of the provinces. The issues revealed by this study are not only the determinants of provincial politics of central–provincial relations in China, but also wider concerns about the impact of economic modernisation on social and political change. The seven cases presented here highlight the effects of economic growth on class formations, regional development within each province and emergent political cultures, particularly those related to questions of local identity.

China's Provinces in Reform is the first of a series that will provide an authoritative and comprehensive survey of China's regional politics. As such it will be essential reading for all those concerned with the impact of the reform era.

David S.G. Goodman is Director of the Institute for International Studies, University of Technology, Sydney.

China's provinces in reform

Class, community and political culture

Edited by David S.G. Goodman

London and New York

First published 1997
by Routledge
11 New Fetter Lane, London EC4P 4EE

Simultaneously published in the USA and Canada
by Routledge
29 West 35th Street, New York, NY 10001

© 1997 Selection and editorial matter, the Institute for International Studies, UTS;
© individual chapters, the contributors

Typeset in Times by
Solidus (Bristol) Limited
Printed and bound in Great Britain by
TJ International Ltd, Padstow, Cornwall

British Library Cataloguing in Publication Data
A catalogue record for this book is available from the British Library

Library of Congress Cataloguing in Publication Data
A catalogue record for this book has been requested

ISBN 0–415–16403–6 (hb)
ISBN 0–415–16404–4 (pbk)

Contents

Maps

Tables

Contributors

Feng Chongyi is Lecturer in China Studies at the Institute for International Studies, University of Technology, Sydney. He is the author of *Peasant Consciousness and China* (Chung Hwa Book, Hong Kong, 1989), *Bertrand Russell and China* (Sanlian Shudian, Beijing, 1994) and (with David S.G. Goodman) *China's Hainan Province: Economic Development and Investment Environment* (University of Western Australia Press, 1995). He was formerly Associate Professor of History, Nankai University, Tianjin.

Jae Ho Chung is Assistant Professor in Chinese Politics in the Department of International Relations at Seoul National University, Korea. He has contributed to *The China Quarterly, Studies in Comparative Communism* and *Pacific Affairs* and co-edited *The Emergence of East Asia: Bilateral Dynamics of the Region and Multilateral Issues of APEC* (1995) and *Provincial Strategies of Economic Reform in Post-Mao China* (1997).

Keith Forster teaches at Southern Cross University. His research interests lie in the contemporary politics and economics of China, and he has published widely on these subjects. He has published *Rebellion and Factionalism in a Chinese Province: Zhejiang, 1966–1976* (Sharpe, New York, 1990) and (with Dan Etherington) *Green Gold: The Political Economy of China's Post-1949 Tea Industry* (Oxford University Press, New York, 1993). He taught at Hangzhou University for three years during the late 1970s and has made extensive research trips to Zhejiang every year since 1988.

David S.G. Goodman is Director of the Institute for International Studies, University of Technology, Sydney. His most recent publications include (with Richard Robison) *The New Rich in Asia: Mobile phones, McDonalds and Middle-Class Revolution* (Routledge, London, 1996), (with Gerald Segal) *China Deconstructs: Politics, Trade and Regionalism* (Routledge, London, 1994) and *Deng Xiaoping and the Chinese Revolution* (Routledge, London, 1994).

Hans Hendrischke is Director of the Access China Centre, Macquarie Graduate School of Management, Macquarie University. He has provided China-related consultancy to major manufacturers and financial institutions, and worked as a foreign business manager for a large leasing company pioneering financial cooperation with China. His research is on economic and political reforms in China.

Lijian Hong is a lecturer in the Department of Asian Languages and Studies, Faculty of Arts, Monash University. A native of Sichuan, he was formerly a Research Fellow at the Institute of Political Science, Sichuan Academy of Social Sciences. He is a graduate of Wuhan University and the Australian National University. His publications in English and Chinese cover several aspects of Chinese politics.

J. Bruce Jacobs is Professor and Head of Department of Asian Languages and Studies and Director of the Centre of East Asian Studies at Monash University. He has published widely in English and Chinese on Chinese and Taiwan politics, society, history and economics.

Margot Schueller is an economist at the Institute of Asian Affairs in Hamburg. She has lived, studied and worked in Liaoning. Her recent works include articles on the Chinese financial system and on the prospects for the economic relationship between China and the European Union. She has co-edited a book on China's integration into the world economy – *Weltwirtschaftsmacht China* (Institut für Asienkunde, Hamburg, 1995).

Preface

The political and economic development of the People's Republic of China since the start of the reform era in 1978 has drawn increased attention to the provincial-level of the system. In *China Deconstructs: Politics, Trade and Regionalism* Gerald Segal and I emphasised the changing regional nature of the Chinese state under the dual pressures of domestic reform and increased international economic integration. The project to examine *China's Provinces in Reform* follows directly on from that earlier work. It has been organised by the Institute for International Studies, University of Technology, Sydney and is designed to examine the impact of economic reform and growth on social change and internal politics within each of the provinces in the People's Republic of China. The aim is to produce a series of studies, each of which analyses the development of a specific province from a provincial perspective.

Each provincial study will deal centrally with the contemporary political economy of a specific province: how economic modernisation has impacted on society (or societies) and the political consequences, potential or otherwise. Economic development, personal relationships between and among elites, and historical background may all be important issues, as is the sociological pattern of communal development, but it is the bigger picture interaction between the economy, society and politics which is intended as the primary focus.

The Institute for International Studies at University of Technology, Sydney has organised a series of annual workshops in China where participants in the project to examine *China's Provinces in Reform* can meet to discuss their work with each other and with other interested academics from China and around the world. This volume results from the first workshop held at Suzhou University in Suzhou, Jiangsu Province during October 1995. Some thirty participants attended the Suzhou Workshop and their contributions to the discussion and to the final shape and form of this volume is greatly acknowledged. In addition to the contributors to the project whose papers appear in this volume, those include Peter T.Y. Cheung, James Cotton, John Fitzgerald, Linda Chelan Li, Robin Napier, Sarah Pfitzner, Richard Rigby, Vorakdi Mahatdhnanobol, Andrew Watson and Yao Xianguo.

Organising a project of this kind has been an expensive undertaking. The Institute for International Studies, University of Technology, Sydney, is very grateful to the Neverfail SpringWater Company Proprietary Ltd of Sydney, Australia, for its support and sponsorship.

Similarly, the workshop at Suzhou University and the organisation of the project in general could not have been undertaken without the efforts of a number of people whose assistance must also be gratefully acknowledged. The Institute for International Studies, University of Technology, Sydney, is pleased to acknowledge the cooperation offered by the Office of International Affairs at Suzhou University, under the leadership of Chen Yuping. At University of Technology, Sydney, the staff of the Institute for International Studies – and in particular Anna Bryant and Yiyan Wang – have provided considerable organisational support to both project and workshop.

Professor David S.G. Goodman
Institute for International Studies, UTS
Sydney
September 1996

Abbreviations

ACFTU	All-China Federation of Trade Unions
BZ	Bonded Zone
CCP	Chinese Communist Party
COA	Coastal Open Area
COC	Coastal Open City
CPI	Consumer Price Index
ETDZ	Economic and Technical Development Zone
FEC	Foreign Economic Commission
FETC	Foreign Economic and Trade Commission
FTC	Foreign Trade Commission
FYP	Five-Year Plan
GDP	Gross Domestic Product
GLF	Great Leap Forward
GNP	Gross National Product
GVAO	Gross Value Agricultural Output
GVIAO	Gross Value Industrial and Agricultural Output
GVIO	Gross Value Industrial Output
GVSP	Gross Value Social Product
ImExCom	Import, Export and Trade Commission
MOFERT	Ministry of Foreign Economic Relations and Trade
NHIDZ	New and High-tech Industrial Development Zone
NIE	Newly Industrialising Economy
NMP	Net Material Product
NPC	National People's Congress
PLA	People's Liberation Army
PPC	Provincial People's Congress
PRC	People's Republic of China
RMB	Renminbi (People's Currency)*
SEZ	Special Economic Zone
SOE	State-Owned Enterprise
SPC	State Planning Commission
TLZ	Tourism and Leisure Zone
TVE	Township and Village Enterprise

UNDP   United Nations Development Programme

Note

*1 *yuan* (dollar) rmb [Renminbi = People's Currency] = US$8.4 (1996).

1   China in reform

The view from the provinces

David S.G. Goodman

China's provinces, or rather the provinces, autonomous regions and municipalities at the immediate sub-central level of the People's Republic of China
(PRC), are considerable social, economic and political systems in their own
right. Most are the size and scale of a European country in population, land
area and social complexity, though most are self-evidently not as big in land
area as Tibet, or as large in population numbers as Sichuan's 120 million and
more. Under other circumstances many might well be regarded as nation-
states, rather than component parts of a single, unitary state, or even units of
'local government' as is often misleadingly the case. In terms of their position
in the administrative hierarchy they are perhaps best regarded as at a
genuinely intermediate level that mediates the sometimes conflicting demands
of national and local politics.[1]

The differences and interactions between and among China's provinces
have long been a defining characteristic of that country's politics, not least
since in almost all cases their boundaries have been created by the dominant
'circulations of people, goods and ideas' over some two thousand or more
years.[2] As a result it would be reasonable to expect comparison only with
similar continental systems – the USA, the former Soviet Union, India,
Indonesia, and possibly Australia and Canada – rather than single, unitary
states. That this is often not the case is as much a function of the neuroses of
the Chinese state since the late Qing,[3] as it is of the inability of Western
academics to fully understand and conceptualise the scale of China. The need
for generalisation of a fairly complex environment, often at the behest of
media articulation or to aid governments, is only part of the problem. Lack
of access to or information about the range of experience in provincial China
has perhaps been more fundamental.

Despite earlier attempts, Western attitudes to the PRC really started to
change only with the advent of the reform era.[4] The stimulus was largely the
introduction of a widespread policy of decentralisation, and its more
immediate and obvious consequences. Reform has clearly altered the
relationship between centre and province, not least as central government has
moved from a policy of control through direct management of the economy
to one based on macro-economic controls. In the process, fiscal relationships

between the centre and the provinces have changed dramatically, with the latter gaining control of a higher proportion – in some cases, a dramatically higher proportion – of their revenues.[5]

At its most sensational, the higher profile for the provincial-level in China's politics has led some, but by no means all, commentators to speculate about the continued coherence of the Chinese state.[6] However, to a large extent this is a problem of perspective: greater publicity for and discussion of provinces and provincial differences does not necessarily entail political disintegration. Reform was always bound to affect each province differently. An essential axiom of economic reform has been the drive to encourage each province to develop its comparative advantage. Natural resources, location and the political skills of provincial leaderships have all been important determinants of the specific development of provinces during the reform era.[7]

The project to examine *China's Provinces in Reform* is concerned not so much with the ways in which provinces have responded to the opportunities presented by economic reform, nor the changing relationships between centre and province,[8] but in the ways those economic reforms have influenced social and political change within each province. If it is axiomatic that different provinces respond differently to the prospects of the reform era, then it must necessarily follow that social and political change cannot be identical in each province, though there may of course be common patterns and commonalities between and among provinces. However, to date there have been remarkably few attempts to identify or conceptualise the dimensions of provincial variations in policy and performance, before the reform era let alone since 1978.[9]

At its simplest the analysis of each province represents the attempt to disaggregate overgeneralisations about China's development in the reform era. However, the provincial analysis of social and political change in China has the potential to reveal even more in a comparative perspective. At issue are not only the determinants of provincial politics or central–provincial relations in China, but also wider concerns about the impact of economic modernisation on social and political change. Of course there are limits to the range of outcomes that may result at provincial level within China. Nonetheless the variety of different economic, social and cultural environments, and different rates, sequences and processes of modernisation offer interesting possibilities for examining various hypotheses in the social sciences about the interconnections of economic, social and political change.

China's reform era is commonly approached from one of three broad historical perspectives on the dynamics of social and political change: the experience of Western Europe in the early part of the nineteenth century that gave birth to notions of capitalism and liberal-democracy; the implosion of communism and the subsequent political disintegration that characterised much of the former Soviet Union and Eastern Europe in and after 1989; and the transformation of authoritarianism that has been the hallmark of much of East Asia, but particularly Japan, South Korea and Taiwan since the 1970s.

None of these can be a precise predictor for China's future, or indeed for the future development of any individual province. While the development of the PRC shares common features with each of those historical experiences, it also has significant differences.[10] At the same time, each bequeaths a series of questions which provide a useful framework for the observation and analysis of social and political change in contemporary China, though not all may apply in detail to every province. In particular, they highlight the impact of economic modernisation on the changing role of the state and the locus of political power; on the development of identities and political communities; and on reform and openness, to the outside world and to new ways of operating.

CAPITALISM, LIBERAL DEMOCRACY AND THE STATE

The prospect of state socialism in China becoming or being replaced by some form of capitalism and liberal democracy is hotly debated. There are of course two different axes to this debate: a discussion of what constitutes capitalism often independent of what constitutes liberal democracy. At one extreme of the capitalism part of the debate there are the arguments of those who see any move away from Maoist orthodoxy as the embrace of 'capitalist restoration'.[11] At the other there are those who reject any notion of capitalist development where the forces of industrialisation are not independent of the state.[12] In between there are arguments about the role of the state in forms of late and directed capitalism.[13]

The discussion of the prospects for liberal democracy are similarly complex. There are those who argue that human and civil rights are not universal, and those who maintain the opposite. There are those who argue that the conditions are not appropriate for liberal democracy at this point in time, and those who fundamentally disagree.[14] More even than in the discussion of capitalism there is often considerable confusion between description and prescription.

It seems virtually self-evident that China is not in the process of a bourgeois revolution, as that term is usually understood. Apart from any other considerations, the state created by the revolution of the late 1940s and early 1950s remains in place, though there have been changes in its roles and structures which are central to any analysis of China's political economy. Less confrontational and less cataclysmic changes may or may not prove no less revolutionary in the longer term, but it is likely to be a much longer term and the more immediate concerns become those of detailing and understanding changes in the locus of political power, and in particular the current transformations in the state.

In economic management, particularly of industry, there has been considerable structural change as the state sector's share of production has decreased, and that of the collective sector and to a lesser extent the private and foreign-funded sectors has increased. The precise impact of these changes remains unclear not least because of their inherent variety. Ownership categories are no longer as specific as they were under more orthodox state socialism, and reform has seen a proliferation of practices and experimentation in industrialisation.[15] At the same time, even a cursory glance at statistical compilations reveals significant differences among and within provinces.[16] Hainan Province, for example, has a small collective sector and relatively few private enterprises; Zhejiang Province on the other hand has a collective sector reported to produce over half the province's value of industrial output. Within provinces the differences may even be more extreme. Some localities – even at the level of county or city – apparently favour the development of either collective or private enterprises almost to exclusion, though in practice the effective differences between these two categories of enterprise may be considerably less. Thus, for example, in Guangdong Province, Zhongshan reports a large collective sector and almost no private sector; whereas the opposite is true in Chaozhou.[17]

A key point in discussion of these structural changes in the PRC economy is the extent to which the state or the party-state continues to control the agenda not only of economic management but also of politics in general. This is of course less easy to identify or measure than changes in economic management, not least because as is often the case economic managers and policy-makers may operate in more than one role, particularly in a situation of rapid change. Nonetheless, where there are – or more probably, where there appears to be the start of what might be – concentrations of political power and authority that are not part of the state, these are likely to attract attention, particularly from a comparative perspective.

Concerns with the manifestations (or otherwise) of civil society reflect just one such comparative perspective on potential countervailing forces in China's politics.[18] A number of studies have highlighted the social space to have emerged with economic reform between various social organisations and the state, or the ways in which social groups may start to organise in their own and potentially independent (of the state) interests.[19] While these observations must be central to accounts of change in China, they do not inevitably lead to descriptions of nascent liberal democracy let alone civil society, which is itself almost an essentially contested concept (and possibly a cultural solecism) in a Chinese context. Moreover, the concepts of civil society and liberal democracy may indeed overlap – through such characteristics as freedom of association and expression – yet they may also conflict.[20] As the recent experience of several parts of Eastern Europe and the former Soviet Union demonstrates, a developed civil society may impede rather than assist the emergence of political society and liberal democracy.[21]

PROVINCIALISM, IDENTITY AND COMMUNITY

Equally as hotly debated as the prospects for capitalism and liberal democracy in China is the discussion of the continued cohesion of the unified state. For some, the dramatic implosion of ruling communist parties and the emergence of new localisms in the former Soviet Union and Eastern Europe in and after 1989 are the political spectres at China's economic feast, particularly when added to an apparent history of centrifugalism.[22] Others have emphasised the predominance of the 'state idea' of China in most of the territory of the PRC (Xinjiang and Tibet are the exceptions that may prefer independence but in the process prove the rule in the rest of the PRC);[23] the economic imperatives that reinforce a single China (which paradoxically do not currently include a high degree of national economic integration);[24] as well as the social and cultural differences between China on the one hand and the former communist party states of the former Soviet Union and Eastern Europe, on the other.[25]

There are three distinct but interrelated dimensions to the debate about political disintegration in China. There are arguments over the Chinese Communist Party's (CCP) long-term future in the leadership of China as an institutionalised communist party state; the continuation of the PRC as a unified political system; and the maintenance of a unitary state. Despite the CCP's belief that all three are inseparable, that is no necessary equation. Though it is less likely, the PRC can remain a unified political system even were the CCP to suffer the fate of its counterparts in Eastern Europe. Even less likely, it may also even remain a unitary state under those conditions, assuming the emergence of another at least equally as effective centralising political force. Moreover, the equation of unity with uniformity is by no means immutable, though it has been part of China's political culture for the last two centuries. There are many political systems where unity is based on social and political diversity, including various forms of federalism where governmental functions may not be solely vested in a single level or form of government. Indeed, federal systems are most often found in multi-cultural societies, those with a large territorial area, or those where political divisions are acute.[26]

These observations highlight the importance of political traditions, identities and communities, all of which may well be variable within as well as among provinces. There is already considerable evidence that the CCP's political traditions and its social roots differ from province to province. The CCP has an organised tradition of political support in those provinces – Liaoning, Jilin, Shanghai for example – that were the major beneficiaries of state investment, particularly into heavy industry. If the examples of Eastern Europe are any guide, the CCP could look for continued support in those areas even in an era of competitive elections. In addition, the social roots of the CCP in some provinces go back well before 1949. There are many peasant communities in the former base areas of North China who though otherwise barely politicised still have strong identification with the CCP because their families considered themselves *tubalu* – recipients of land from the CCP Eighth Route Army during the Sino-Japanese War. Under the impact of pressures for reform and rapid economic modernisation it would be reasonable to expect manifestations of the CCP's provincial presence and traditions of these kinds. Similarly in provinces such as Guangdong, where the CCP's roots are considerably shallower, it is hardly surprising that the Governor of the Province and the Provincial People's Government are regarded within the province as senior to the Secretary and other members of the CCP Provincial Committee.[27]

One of the intellectual difficulties with arguments that posit a disintegrating China because of increased provincialism is that they assume a necessary contradiction between provincial and national interests, as well as between identification with the province and identification with the country as a whole. However, traditionally there was always an integrative hierarchy of identification: village to county to province to China.[28] Indeed, it is perhaps more remarkable that local and provincial cultures can be both so highly developed and differentiated – in terms of language, traditions and beliefs – yet remain so strongly self-identified as at the centre of Han China.[29] Political identities at provincial (or indeed more local levels) within the PRC may already exist or may gradually emerge that resist or even oppose incorporation, as for example in both Tibet and Xinjiang where separatist movements are already relatively active. However, as in those cases there has to be some evidence and demonstration of separatist or different political identities: they cannot be assumed.

Concerns with political identity at the provincial level may also focus attention not so much on the potential conflict between provincial and national interests as on disaggregating the competing identities and communities within provinces. Rapid economic modernisation may also increase the degree of political integration as well as economic integration within each province, not least by widening the circle of those politically active. In the process it may even create rising expectations of political participation. Simply put, more activity means a higher potential risk of political conflict, and conversely a need for attention to integrative mechanisms. There may be potential conflict based on either class or some other social formation, on locality, or on community. In Zhejiang, for example, there is some evidence of tension between the cadres long associated with the establishment state sector enterprises on the one hand, and the entrepreneurs and managers of the newer collective sector enterprises on the other.[30] Guangdong's politics at provincial level are shaped by the interplay of groups from the province's six major sub-districts.[31] In Hainan, the boundaries of the province's competing political communities are the result of language, social location, economic activity and political history. In general, the resolution of these conflicts and the integration of communities and political groups is central to the formation and operation of each provincial political system.

OPENNESS, REFORM AND INSTITUTIONAL CHANGE

There is a considerable consensus among Western commentators on the likelihood that China will follow the example of its East Asian neighbours, matching economic success with the transformation of authoritarian politics. Underlying such views of China's future is an argument whose logic is almost inescapable. Faced by the economic success of its East Asian neighbours in the late 1970s and its own relative failure the PRC deliberately and explicitly followed their example and adopted a new export-oriented growth strategy based on technology imports and international economic integration. Starting in the 1980s each of those East Asian neighbours has liberalised its authoritarian politics and developed a more open political system as a result of both changed leadership perspectives and increased social demands. It thus seems logical to predict similar processes occurring in the PRC, not least since by any standard those trends are already under way – China's politics by the 1990s are considerably more open than they were at the start of the reform era.[32]

There is some wishful thinking involved in these predictions. The CCP has frequently stated that the 'peaceful evolution' of the PRC into a liberal democracy is part of the general capitalist conspiracy it faces in international politics. Even so, many people inside and outside the CCP, as well as inside and outside the PRC are keen to ensure the incremental and undramatic transformation of China's authoritarianism under the pressures of rapid modernisation. There are very real concerns that economic growth and development may impact adversely on China's political economy and create chaos and political instability. However, the key problem for analysis – particularly for the more detached Western commentator – lies in explaining how these various processes may be negotiated and the adverse prospects avoided.

In the political systems of the former Soviet Union and Eastern Europe, reform and openness – to new and different ideas from other countries, as well as domestically – came to be equated as governments moved from concerns with control to attempts to regulate. Those who have commented on the subversive nature of these processes have also highlighted the differences between the former Soviet Union and Eastern Europe on the one hand and East Asia on the other. Openness ultimately led in every case in the former Soviet Union and Eastern Europe to the failure of reform and an urgent need for revolution. In East Asia in contrast, reform and openness have developed simultaneously and in a more measured way that in general seems to lead to adjustment rather than confrontation.[33]

Observation of the impact of reform and openness on individual provinces involves identification of the processes of and consequences from the import of new ideas and practices, not only from outside the country but also from other provinces, particularly as the pace of reform quickens within the PRC. In addition, it also involves the identification of the response of that province's institutions and their adaptation to that new environment of reform and openness. The nexus between these two phenomena is crucial for understanding the process of transformation and particularly for assessing the prospects of sustained incremental change as opposed to more dramatic outcomes, given that reform and openness are driven by both social demand and political leadership.

In the reform era openness has become associated with economic phenomenon. The permeability of the Guangdong–Hong Kong border, for example, has been driven by economic conditions on either side of that border, rather than by political activity in either Hong Kong or Guangdong. On the contrary, the extent of economic integration despite the two governments' attempts to restrain involvement during the late 1980s was quite remarkable. Similarly, and even more remarkable was the extent of Taiwan investment in both Guangdong and Fujian at the same time, while the Taiwan government strongly urged caution and alternatives.[34] Moreover, these instances of openness have come to be seen as precursors of a more general pattern: a series of economic integrations that links different parts of the PRC with countries, states and territories in East and Southeast Asia. Economic integration of this kind has had considerable impact on the economic development of Shandong, Jiangsu, Zhejiang and Guangxi, as well as Guangdong and Fujian in the 1990s.[35]

However, it is far from clear that all provinces concentrate only on economic openness, even though other kinds of activities may be presented as such. Since the mid-1980s many provinces have moved to establish relationships with counterpart sub-national authorities in other parts of the world. At that time sister-state relationships with provinces in Japan and states in the USA became widespread. Provincial government offices have been established abroad, and successful people-to-people exchange programmes implemented. While the funds to support such activities are often somewhat hard to obtain and inadequate, political will is frequently more important in developing this kind of openness. In at least one case, that of Shanxi, the provincial government has even established its own scholarship scheme to send young scholars abroad for higher education and training.

It is perhaps somewhat premature to attempt to assess the impact of openness, and indeed reform in general, on provincial political institutions. That is after all, a principal aim of the entire project to examine *China's Provinces in Reform*. Nonetheless, some possible dimensions of change have already been suggested. For example, some have seen the birth of new forms of corporatism in the reform era,[36] and though those observations did not result from an analysis of provincial-level politics, it is entirely possible that they may be particularly apposite in provinces where the All-China Federation of Trade Unions (ACFTU) has a specific political importance, as for example, Shanghai or Liaoning.

Provincial politics have certainly become provincialised in a number of ways during the reform era. Dramatically compared to the period of the PRC before the 1980s, there is now usually room for a large proportion of provincial natives in any provincial leadership group. Where before the reform era this was the exception, and usually allowed only in national minority areas, since 1980 it has increasingly become the norm (except in

Hainan). Moreover, the practice of personnel localisation has expanded to ensure that most of those who come to be leaders of party and government at provincial level have a large number of years of experience in the province, regardless of their nativity, and this too represents a marked break with the pre-reform past.[37]

The provincial media are now larger in number, wider in capacity, and deeper in their coverage of provincial affairs than before 1980. There are now more newspapers, magazines, publishing outlets, radio and television channels that focus on the province. The expansion of television services in particular has had a dramatic impact on the way people live. In most urban areas in most provinces, the provincial evening television news has become an institution. Quite apart from the effect this may have on the television audience, it would also be surprising if it did not also exert some influence on provincial politicians. In many cases provincial politicians not only ensure the timing of their most important to-be-publicised activities in order to catch the evening news bulletins, but also they have modified their political style to appeal to their provincial constituency. Main highways are presented as improvements in communications within the province; trees are planted similarly in order to improve the province's environment. There is a public emphasis on province and locality that was not there before. These changes in political style and culture may be almost imperceptible, but they may also offer important clues to social development and the practice of politics at provincial level.

REFORM AND SEVEN PROVINCES

The project to examine *China's Provinces in Reform* is thus designed to consider the impact of economic reform and growth on social change and the internal politics of provinces as single systems within the People's Republic of China. The seven case studies presented in this volume make no claim to be either comprehensive or representative but rather to be the first stage in what can only be a long process of data accumulation and analysis for the varied environments of China's thirty-one provinces. In addition to highlighting the specific story or themes of each province, each case study has also addressed the need to outline the history of the province before the reform era, the nature of economic reform in the province and its impact on the social structure, as well as in turn the results for provincial politics. In particular each attempts to move its analysis beyond the provincial-level to consider the dynamic of sub-provincial and intra-provincial politics and their interactions. In this process particular attention has been placed on the significance, where appropriate, of class, community and locality. Each case study is accompanied by a map, statistical profile and some references to sources on and about the province.

The seven case studies presented here cover a fair spectrum of the variety of China's provincial conditions. Guangxi and Hainan are South China provinces though until recently more peripheral in the development boom of the South in general, and Guangdong in particular, than either would probably choose. Guangxi's border trade with Vietnam has been perhaps its most remarkable feature in the reform era, though as Hans Hendrischke draws out in his chapter, other provinces – and particularly Sichuan – have built on Guangxi's role as a potential entrepôt. While Hainan's provincial existence is a major feature of the reform era, its ability to build on its new-found status appears hampered by domestic considerations and in particular conflicting visions of the Hainan identity.

In the northeast of China Liaoning remains a wealthy province despite its justified characterisation as a bastion of heavy industry and state socialism. Reform in Liaoning has led to economic restructuring, but more slowly and with more widespread social consequences than elsewhere in China, notably South China. The Liaoning workforce is not only more industrialised but also noticeably more politicised, and one of the consequences for the reform era highlighted by Margot Schueller is to focus attention on questions of class consciousness. Economic restructuring clearly has as much potential to lead to the organisation and articulation of working-class politics as the initial processes of industrialisation.

South China may have seen the start of the rapid economic growth that is now taken as a characteristic of China's reform era but in the 1990s it is East China which carried the baton forward. Shanghai and Zhejiang present very different economic, social and political environments, yet both have been at the forefront of recent changes. Bruce Jacobs in his chapter draws out the importance for Shanghai of national policy settings, and the fundamental impact of preferential policies for the municipality in 1992. These have already started to turn Shanghai into a world city and in the process has led to far-reaching structural changes in Shanghai society, though remarkably leaving the local population unpoliticised.

Keith Forster's portrayal of Zhejiang provides an almost complete contrast. Change there has been largely driven from the bottom up, often against the reluctant wishes of the provincial leadership, and in the process has undoubtedly led to greater political openness if not wider politicisation. Remarkably, Zhejiang's development has come more through domestic (within China as well as within Zhejiang) than through international connections. Despite its apparent international advantages – as a coastal province, personal and family connections between Zhejiang and Taiwan, proximity to Shanghai, plentiful water and agricultural produce – Zhejiang's development has looked inward. The economic changes of Zhejiang's reform era have, as in Shanghai, been driven by agencies of the state, but whereas growth in Shanghai has been led by large-scale state enterprises, in Zhejiang the local government economy has led the way.

Also on China's eastern seaboard, though some considerable distance from Shanghai – economically and politically, as well as physically – Shandong Province, like Zhejiang, has clearly been a province that has responded more enthusiastically to the policies and practices of the reform era than it did to the inappropriate economic development strategies of the Mao-dominated era. Jae Ho Chung in his analysis of the impact of reform on Shandong highlights the inherent regional variations within a province. The disaggregation of politics within single provinces is an important part of the project to examine *China's Provinces in Reform* but the bigger difficulty for Shandong is not just that there are disparities in economic development, but that there is also abject poverty as well as conspicuous economic success, and the gap between the two has increased and may even increase further. The Shandong authorities, and indeed central government, have responded with attempts to alleviate the worst excesses of an unbalanced development strategy, but it remains possible that these disparities in wealth and development potential may present continuing political difficulties.

The remaining case study is that of Sichuan Province, in China's southwest. Sichuan's economy has long been both productive and a strategic contributor nationally, particularly in the field of agricultural produce. However, under the PRC its development has been hampered by its relative isolation from the mainstream of national economic activity and its leaders' relationships with Beijing. The impact of reform on Sichuan has been to redefine the provincial perspectives on national politics. As Sichuan increasingly comes to feel that it not only missed out during the Mao-dominated era but also is in danger of doing so again with the introduction of market-oriented reforms, questions are being asked about past and present leadership mismanagements, as well as the significance of differing economic and political interests within the province. Lijian Hong in his analysis of Sichuan in reform examines several instances – particularly the fate of the Third Front Project, the development of the Three Gorges Dam, and the elevation of Xiao Yang to the provincial leadership – that highlight the province's sense of disadvantage, unease about the mismanagement of its politics, and growing differences within the province.

None of China's provinces is typical, though of course there may be shared or common features in a number of provinces that make it possible eventually to talk about a number of patterns. That is one of the explicit aims of the project to examine *China's Provinces in Reform* of which this volume is but a first step. Even so there are some themes revealed in these seven case studies of the impact of provincial economic development.

Despite the emphasis on provincial variation which lies at the heart of the reform era in China, and on which this volume is based, and the emphasis on the process and outcomes of reform, each of the case studies presented here highlights the importance of policy and policy settings to the provincial environment. Even where the CCP's policy has met the most resistance, ambivalence or lack of understanding – Zhejiang, Sichuan, Hainan – reform required that prior sanction.

The examination of the reform process and its outcomes in each province draws particular attention to the social impact on class and community. Greater openness at the provincial level not only highlights new perspectives on provincial identities, but also allows the questioning of those identities and challenges established notions of what constitutes the political community. Sometimes these differences may be clearly related to class or similar social categories – renewed working-class consciousness in Liaoning is an obvious example – or sometimes they may be equally as clearly related to geographical identities – as in the case of Chongqing and Chengdu's disagreement over the importance of the Three Gorges Dam project to Sichuan's future. However, they may also and more usually result from a complex mixture of reasons with both class and community components. The cases of Hainan and Shandong presented here are both somewhat acute examples. In Hainan, class, social status, economic activity, access to political power and community all tend to mutual reinforcement. In Shandong there is a close relationship between poverty (and wealth too for that matter) and location.

NOTES

1 On the role of the provincial-level in the PRC as the key level of mediation between national direction and local interests, see David S.G. Goodman, *Centre and Province in the PRC: Sichuan and Guizhou, 1955–1965*, Cambridge University Press, 1986, especially pp. 13ff.

2 On this central principle of political geography, see Jean Gottmann, 'The political partitioning of our world: an attempt at analysis', *World Politics* 4 no. 4 p. 512 and *The Significance of Territory*, University of Virginia Press, Charlottesville, 1973; and for its consequences for China, J.B.R. Whitney, *Area, Administration and Nation-Building*, University of Chicago, Department of Geography Research Paper no. 123, Chicago, 1970. On provincial diversity before the modern era in China see in particular Susan Naquin and Evelyn S. Rawski, *Chinese Society in the Eighteenth Century*, Yale University Press, New Haven, CT, 1987, especially pp. 138ff.

3 See for example, and most powerfully, John Fitzgerald, '"Reports of my death have been greatly exaggerated": the history of the death of China', in David S.G. Goodman and Gerald Segal (eds) *China Deconstructs: Politics, Trade and Regionalism*, Routledge, London, 1994, p. 21.

4 Perhaps the most notable earlier attempt both to generate information about the provincial-level and to suggest that its existence was of more than passing significance was the project commissioned by the US Department of State at the instigation of Edwin A. Winckler. A history of each province from 1949 to 1975 was produced by a series of scholars, but unfortunately never published.

5 Peter Ferdinand, 'The economic and financial dimension', in David S.G. Goodman (ed.) *China's Regional Development*, Routledge, London, 1989, p. 38; Christine Wong, 'Central–local relations in an era of fiscal decline: the paradox of fiscal decentralisation in Post-Mao China', *China Quarterly* no. 128, December 1991, p. 691; Wang Shaoguang, 'Central–local fiscal politics in China', in Jia Hao and Lin Zhimin (eds) *Changing Central–Local Relations in China: Reform and State Capacity*, Westview, Boulder, CO, 1994; and Dali L.Yang, 'Reform and the restructuring of central–local relations', in David S.G. Goodman and Gerald Segal (eds) *China Deconstructs: Politics, Trade and Regionalism*, Routledge, London, 1994, p. 59.

6 Outside China the most sensational of such accounts has been W.J.F. Jenner *The Tyranny of History*, Allen Lane, London, 1992. Within China the topic has

become a quite fashionable topic for writers of non-fiction: for example, Qin Xiangyin and Ni Jianzhong (eds) *Nan Bei Chun Qiu: Zhongguo huibuhui fenlie* [The History of the North versus the South: Will China disintegrate?], Renmin Zhongguo chubanshe, Beijing, 1993. See also, Maria Hsia Chang 'China's future: regionalism, federalism, or disintegration', *Studies in Comparative Communism* XXV no. 3 September 1992, p. 211. For counter-veiling views see *inter alia* David S.G. Goodman and Gerald Segal (eds) *China Deconstructs: Politics, Trade and Regionalism*, Routledge, London, 1994.

7   Peter T.Y. Cheung and Jae Ho Chung (eds) *Provincial Strategies of Economic Reform in Post-Mao China: Leadership, Politics and Implementation*, 1997, explores these phenomena and their interactions.

8   These issues have already been relatively well dealt with by other authors and in other publications during the 1990s. See, for example, Jia Hao and Lin Zhimin (eds) *Changing Central–Local Relations in China: Reform and State Capacity*, Westview, Boulder, CO, 1994; and Linda Chelan Li, *Shifting Central–Provincial Relations*, 1997.

9   This point is emphasised by Jae Ho Chung, 'Studies of central–provincial relations in the People's Republic of China', *China Quarterly* no. 142, June 1995, p. 487.

10 David S.G. Goodman, 'Transformations in the Chinese State: historical perspectives on reform', *Journal of the Oriental Society of Australia* 25/26 1993–4, p. 55.

11 Most obviously Michel Chossudovsky, *Towards Capitalist Restoration? Chinese Socialism after Mao*, Macmillan Education, London, 1986.

12 See, for example, the somewhat naive account of capitalist development in David S.G. Goodman, 'China: the state and capitalist revolution', *Pacific Review* 5 no. 4, 1992, p. 350.

13 A recent, brilliant summary and analysis of these views may be found in Linda Weiss and John M. Hobson, *States and Economic Development: A Comparative Historical Analysis*, Polity Press, Cambridge, 1995.

14 This debate is summarised in A. Nathan, 'Is China ready for democracy?', *Journal of Democracy* 1 no. 2, Spring 1990, p. 50; 'China's path from communism', *Journal of Democracy* 4 no. 2, April 1993, p. 30; and A. Nathan and Tianjian Shi, 'Cultural requisites for democracy in China: findings from a survey', *Daedalus* 122 no. 2, Spring 1993, p. 95.

15 Kevin Lee, *Chinese Firms and the State in Transition: Property Rights and Agency Problems in the Reform Era*, M.E. Sharpe, New York, 1991; Victor Nee, 'Organisational dynamics of market transition: hybrid forms, property rights, and mixed economy in China', *Administrative Science Quarterly* 37, no. 1; and David S.G. Goodman, 'Collectives and connectives, capitalism and corporatism: structural change in China', *Journal of Communist Studies and Transition Politics* 11 no. 1, March 1995, p. 12.

16 Table 1.1 provides data on GVIO (Gross Value Industrial Output) by ownership sector, by province, for the provinces discussed in this volume.

17 Table 1.2 provides data on GVIO by ownership sector, for selected districts of Guangdong.

18 'Public sphere/civil society in China?', *Modern China* 19, no. 2, April 1993.

19 For example: Gordon White, 'Prospects for civil society: a case study of Xiaoshan City', in David S.G. Goodman and Beverley Hooper (eds) *China's Quiet Revolution: New Interactions Between State and Society*, Longman, Melbourne, 1994, p. 194; Michel Bonnin and Yves Chevrier, 'The intellectual and the state: social dynamics of intellectual autonomy during the Post-Mao era', *China Quarterly* no. 127, p. 569; David Kelly and He Baogang, 'Emergent civil society and the intellectuals in China', in Robert F. Miller (ed.) *The Development*

Table 1.1 Provincial GVIO by ownership system, 1994 (% of provincial GVIO)

Province	State sector	Collective sector	Private sector	Foreign-funded sector
All provinces	34.1	40.9	11.5	13.6
Guangxi	42.9	26.4	22.1	8.5
Hainan	49.7	13.3	10.3	26.1
Liaoning	42.8	33.0	14.2	10.0
Shandong	24.5	54.8	12.7	8.0
Shanghai	42.4	22.6	0.5	34.6
Sichuan	37.1	34.8	19.5	8.6
Zhejiang	16.1	56.4	17.7	9.9

Source: Percentages calculated from data in State Statistical Bureau, *Zhongguo tongji nianjian 1995*, Zhongguo tongji nianjian chubanshe, 1995, Tables 12-5 and 12-6

Table 1.2 Districts in Guangdong: GVIO by ownership system, 1990 (% of district GVIO)

District	State sector	Collective sector	Private and foreign-funded sectors
Guangzhou	59.7	23.3	17.1
Foshan	27.9	45.1	26.9
Chaozhou	22.2	26.9	50.9
Zhongshan	23.0	59.0	18.0

Source: Percentages calculated from data in State Statistical Bureau, *Zhongguo chengshi tongji nianjian 1990*, Zhongguo tongji nianjian chubanshe, 1990, p. 200

of Civil Society in Communist Systems, Allen & Unwin, Sydney, 1992, p. 24; and Thomas B. Gold, 'The resurgence of civil society in China', *Journal of Democracy* 1 no. 1 p. 18.

20 Philippe C. Schmitter, 'On civil society and the consolidation of democracy: ten general propositions and nine speculations about their relation in Asian societies', paper delivered to the Institute for National Policy Research, Taipei and International Forum for Democracy, National Endowment for Democracy Conference on *Consolidating the Third Wave Democracies: Trends and Challenges*, Taipei, August 1995.

21 See, for example, Aleksander Smolar, 'Civil society in Post-Communist Europe', and Michael McFaul, 'Prospects for democratic consolidation in Russia', papers delivered to the Institute for National Policy Research, Taipei and International Forum for Democracy, National Endowment for Democracy Conference on *Consolidating the Third Wave Democracies: Trends and Challenges*, Taipei, August 1995.

22 For example, W.J.F. Jenner, *The Tyranny of History*, Allen Lane, London, 1992.

23 David S.G. Goodman and Gerald Segal, *China without Deng*, HarperCollins, Sydney, 1995, especially pp. 56ff.

24 See, for example, Dali L.Yang, 'Reform and the restructuring of central–local relations', and Anjali Kumar, 'Economic reform and the internal division of labour in China: production, trade and marketing', in David S.G. Goodman and Gerald Segal (eds) *China Deconstructs: Politics, Trade and Regionalism*, Routledge, London, 1994, p. 59 and p. 99 respectively.
25 Most obviously, where the Chinese state and its provincial and regional structures have evolved over some two thousand years, the 'disintegrated' regimes of the USSR and Eastern Europe were all twentieth-century constructs. In addition, where the USSR and the states of Eastern Europe experienced steady economic decline from about 1950 through to the late 1980s, China had an average annual growth rate of 6 per cent in estimated GNP from 1952 to 1978 (despite often serious fluctuations year-on-year) and approximately 10 per cent from 1978 to the present.
26 Canada is an example of federalism based on a multi-cultural society; Australia, a federal state based on distance and size of territory; and Switzerland, a federalism (despite nominally being a confederation) based on acute political divisions.
27 David S.G. Goodman and Feng Chongyi, 'Guangdong: Greater Hong Kong and the new regionalist future', in David S.G. Goodman and Gerald Segal (eds) *China Deconstructs: Politics, Trade and Regionalism*, Routledge, London, 1994, p. 181.
28 Dorothy J. Solinger, *Regional Government and Political Integration in Southwest China 1949–1954*, University of California Press, Berkeley, 1977, pp. 19ff.
29 Leo J. Moser, *The Chinese Mosaic: The Peoples and Provinces of China*, Westview Press, Boulder, CO, 1985, especially pp. 256ff.
30 David S.G. Goodman, 'China: the state and capitalist revolution', *Pacific Review* 5 no. 4, 1992, p. 350.
31 David S.G. Goodman and Feng Chongyi, 'Guangdong: Greater Hong Kong and the new regionalist future', in David S.G. Goodman and Gerald Segal (eds) *China Deconstructs: Politics, Trade and Regionalism*, Routledge, London, 1994, p. 179.
32 See, for example, Andrew Nathan, 'China's constitutionalist option' and Minxin Pei, '"Creeping democratization" in China?', papers delivered to the Institute for National Policy Research, Taipei and International Forum for Democracy, National Endowment for Democracy Conference on *Consolidating the Third Wave Democracies: Trends and Challenges*, Taipei, August 1995.
33 Barry Buzan and Gerald Segal, 'Defining reform as openness', in Gerald Segal (ed.) *Openness and Foreign Policy Reform in Communist States*, Routledge, London, 1992, especially pp. 2–3, and pp. 217ff.
34 Asia Research Centre, *Southern China in Transformation*, Australian Government Publishing Services, Canberra, 1992, pp. 11ff.
35 This was of course the point of departure for David S.G. Goodman and Gerald Segal (eds) *China Deconstructs: Politics, Trade and Regionalism*, Routledge, London, 1994.
36 See, for example, Anita Chan, 'Revolution or corporatism? Workers in search of a solution', in David S.G. Goodman and Beverley Hooper (eds) *China's Quiet Revolution: New Interactions Between State and Society*, Longman, Melbourne, 1994, p. 162.
37 David S.G. Goodman, 'Political perspectives', in David S.G. Goodman (ed.) *China's Regional Development*, Routledge, London, 1989, p.27.

Guangxi Zhuang Autonomous Region

GENERAL

GDP [Gross Domestic Product] (billion *yuan* renminbi [RMB])	124.20
GDP annual growth rate	16.00
as % national average	135.59
GDP per capita	2,763.85
as % national average	73.60
Gross Value Agricultural Output (billion *yuan* renminbi)	53.70
Gross Value Industrial Output (billion *yuan* renminbi)	138.10

POPULATION

Population (million)	44.93
Natural growth rate (per 1,000)	18.84

WORKFORCE

Total workforce (million)	23.36
Employment by activity (%)	
primary industry	68.00
secondary industry	11.50
tertiary industry	20.50
Employment by sector (% of provincial population)	
urban	8.93
rural	43.07
state sector	6.47
collective sector	6.36
private sector	2.69
foreign-funded sector	0.13

WAGES

Average annual wage (*yuan* renminbi)	4,468
Growth rate in real wage	6.10

PRICES

CPI [Consumer Price Index] annual rise (%)	26.00
Service price index rise (%)	29.20
Per capita consumption (*yuan* renminbi)	960
as % national average	55.27
Urban disposable income per capita	3,981
as % national average	113.87
Rural per capita income	1,107
as % national average	90.66

FOREIGN TRADE AND INVESTMENT

Total foreign trade (US$ billion)	3.04
% provincial GDP	21.10
Exports (US$ billion)	1.29
Imports (US$ billion)	1.75
Realised foreign capital (US$ million)	850.46
% provincial GDP	5.90

EDUCATION

University enrolments	57,945
% national average	55.23
Secondary school enrolments (million)	1.77
% national average	94.61
Primary school enrolments (million)	6.32
% national average	131.40

Notes: All statistics are for 1994 and all growth rates are for 1994 over 1993 and are adapted from *Zhongguo tongji nianjian 1995* [Statistical Yearbook of China 1995], Zhongguo tongji chubanshe, Beijing, 1995 as reformulated and presented in *Provincial China* no. 1 March 1996, pp. 34ff.

Guangxi Zhuang Autonomous Region

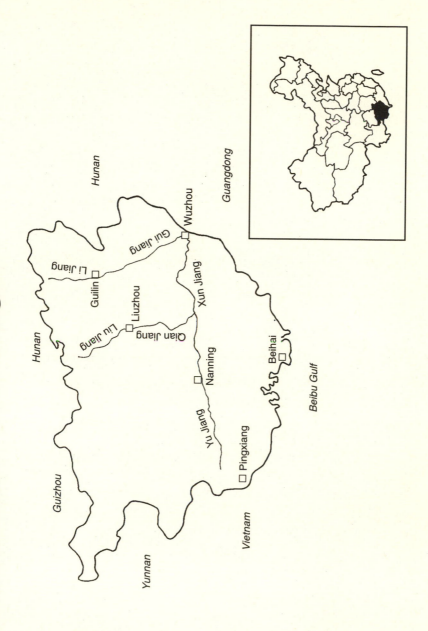

2 Guangxi

Towards Southwest China and Southeast Asia

Hans Hendrischke

By virtue of its geographical position, Guangxi has always formed a natural link between Southwest China and Southeast Asia. Border trade across land and sea has a long historical tradition. However, during most of the history of the People's Republic of China, Guangxi's situation has been defined by political, strategic and military considerations rather than by traditional economic links. Guangxi was in an isolated position, as it faced a real border towards Vietnam and an invisible one towards the rest of China. While its border to Vietnam was open for military supplies, it was for a long time under the threat of a war that could have spilled over into Guangxi. Only a few years after the end of the Vietnam War, Guangxi's border with Vietnam became a war zone that was left heavily mined and inaccessible for more than a decade. As a result it attracted very little investment.

Guangxi had been one of China's poorest provinces in 1949 and remained in that position during the following decades. It has a large impoverished minority population and developed very little for thirty years after 1949. Instead, it depended on central government subsidies to balance its budget, support its impoverished areas and provide aid to Vietnam. In its political outlook, it had adapted to a political climate that provided political solidarity and become used to the centrally planned economic structures that maintained the flow of subsidies.

The reforms from the end of 1978 onwards therefore came as a shock to the Guangxi Zhuang Autonomous Region. It came at the same time as the Chinese–Vietnamese border war, of which Guangxi carried the main burden in personal and material terms, and the necessity of which was hard to explain. Guangxi was not prepared for the changes in political leadership and direction, and it stood to lose out economically from the dismantling of the structures on which it had depended for so long. Almost two decades on, Guangxi is generally assumed to have taken up its role as one of the provinces that have the dual advantage of being both a border and a coastal province. Guangxi has made international headlines with its burgeoning border trade and is attracting investment from Chinese and overseas investors.

Little has been written on Guangxi since Dorothy Solinger's book on provincial integration in Southwest China during the early 1950s.[1] There are big gaps in research on the impact of the Vietnam War and the Cultural Revolution on Guangxi and on its recent reform era history. These lacunae cannot all be rectified here, but an attempt is made to map out the political process accompanying the economic transition from a planned to a market environment in this province. (In 1958 Guangxi Province became the provincial-level Guangxi Zhuang Autonomous Region.)

The general aim is to examine the social and political consequences of overall changes in the economic system. Usually such processes are analysed only at the central-level and for the provincial-level a natural proclivity to embark on economic reforms is assumed. Supported by Chinese propaganda and research, this assumption feeds into the hypothesis that provincial economic self-interest will lead to centrifugal tendencies. While the disintegration of China remains a fashionable topic, more serious research has pointed to the possibility that provincialisation in China might even result in stronger national integration.[2] The fact that Guangxi is neither a typical border province, coastal province nor poor inland province makes its development less predictable and therefore an interesting case to reverse the usual direction of analysis and look at provincial policy changes and political conflicts with the centre that developed in response to the larger economic change. The first section of this chapter considers the political transition from the pre-reform leadership. The second section addresses how underlying economic issues were resolved between the provincial and central levels. The third section delineates the political conflicts that evolved around Guangxi's new economic orientation towards Southeast Asia and Greater Southwest China.

POLITICAL TRANSITION

The analysis of the political and institutional constraints under which an economic reform process unfolded in Guangxi shows three major steps in the process of transition from a policy driven, planned economy to a market oriented economy. Guangxi went through a political transition that included coming to terms with the Cultural Revolution, tentative economic reforms and, finally, the start of a reformed economy. At the end of this process, Guangxi found itself in a situation where former constraining factors, such as its geographical situation, had turned into potential advantages. This transition is not an automatic process, but one that is defined by a new relationship between province and centre, new inter-provincial links and a new attitude to foreign relations.

The political legacy of the Cultural Revolution

Guangxi is a good example of a province that had to be coerced into the reforms by the central leadership. While the Guangxi leadership paid lip-service to the reform programme put forward by the centre, their reluctance to embark on reforms had a political as well as an economic dimension.

Politically, the reform process in Guangxi was hampered by the personal influence of cadres who owed their political allegiance to the Cultural Revolution and whose influence later stalled the introduction of economic reforms during the latter half of the 1980s. The political links of these cadres with the pre-reform central leadership had ensured a substantial flow of subsidies to Guangxi to the degree that the provincial economy had become dependent on them and resisted their abolition. For over a decade, the centre kept intervening in Guangxi's political and economic affairs, until the reform policies were firmly on track.

The following account relies on published[3] and unpublished sources[4] which give a critical retrospective from the later reform-oriented viewpoint of the party. As this is the most relevant perspective for this analysis, these sources are preferred to an empirical data-based approach. They depict the Autonomous Region as throughout the early 1980s struggling to resolve the problems left over from the Cultural Revolution. The central leadership interfered in this process through working groups, detailed instructions and in other ways. Its main concerns were initially political, but soon turned to the lack of economic initiative emanating from the province. From 1985 onwards, the provincial leadership was under pressure to improve its economic performance. Again the centre intervened through various means, including personal visits by top officials. Only by the turn of 1991–2 had a more stable situation emerged under which economic reforms finally took off.

At the end of the Cultural Revolution, Guangxi's leading cadre was Wei Guoqing, a Guangxi native and member of the largest non-Han minority Zhuang (after whom the Guangxi Zhuang Autonomous Region is named) as well as an old revolutionary, experienced soldier and political hardliner. His successors were Qiao Xiaoguang from 1977 to 1979 and Qin Yingji from 1979 to 1983, who were old revolutionaries of a similar background to Wei Guoqing. The leading cadre who held office from 1983 onwards through most of the reform decade was Wei Chunshu, also a member of the Zhuang national minority, as required for this position under its autonomous status.

The generation of revolutionary elders continued to hold considerable power over the leadership of Guangxi, as they remained in important positions. Wei Guoqing remained a member of the Politburo of the CCP until 1985 and retained the position of Vice-Chairman of the Standing Committee of the National People's Congress (NPC) in Beijing until his death in 1989. Qiao Xiaoguang continued to hold a position on the Central Committee of the CCP until 1987 and then moved to the Central Committee's Advisory Commission. Qin Yingji remained in Guangxi and moved to the position of Chairman of the Political Consultative Conference of Guangxi which gave him much power over provincial matters until his death in 1992. Another old revolutionary, Gan Ku, held the position of Chairman of the Autonomous Provincial People's Congress, and succeeded Wei Guoqing as a member of the Standing Committee of the National People's Congress. These leaders were all from a revolution-centred political orientation. Wei Chunshu, who was relatively young and who could have made a turnaround in the political situation owed his loyalties to Qin Yingji, by whom he had been promoted. The other major members of his government were too weak to break away from the influence of the previous generation of leaders. Foreign business and investment was under Chen Ren, an administrator with little experience in this area who also carried little influence beyond the provincial borders. Wei Chunshu's Party Secretary was Chen Huigang, a young engineer and intellectual in his forties, who lost his position after only four years and moved to a less influential position in the Autonomous Provincial Political Consultative Conference.

Support in Guangxi for the radical political line had been strong in the years following the demise of the radical leadership at the centre. The political phenomena that were criticised in later party documents included continuing propaganda for the 'Whateverists', adherence to Hua Guofeng's political and economic programme and participation in the artificial personality cult surrounding Hua Guofeng. On the eve of the crucial Third Plenum in 1978, Hua Guofeng was asked to provide new calligraphy for the title of the *Guangxi Daily*. The lack of support and political preparation for the change in course was later seen as the provincial leadership's major political mistake in the period before the Third Plenum of 1978. The ideological campaign to establish 'practice as a criterion of truth', designed to weaken the influence of Maoist thinking in the party, for example, was pursued only reluctantly. More importantly, the rehabilitation of old cadres who had been persecuted under the Cultural Revolution was not vigorously enforced. Those cadres who demanded political change during the provincial CCP Congress in August 1978 were later themselves attacked.

Later assessments admit that there remained considerable political support for the radical political programme while reform policies were seen as 'revisionist', implying strong political opposition even after the official national introduction of reform. This political opposition found its organisational expression in opposition to the rehabilitation of cadres. Even the relatively discrete language of heavily edited party documents reveals the extent of political tensions that remained. In 1983, the CCP Central Committee approved a report by the Guangxi CCP Committee on the further resolution of problems remaining from the Cultural Revolution in Guangxi. In its instructions to the Guangxi Party Committee the CCP Central Committee acknowledged that the Autonomous Region was especially besieged by unresolved political problems.

When in March 1983 in a personnel reshuffle Wei Chunshu took up his office as Governor, the CCP Central Committee demanded from the new party committee that the rehabilitations should be concluded by the end of the year, and it decided to send a working group to oversee this process. In April, the working group of the CCP Central Committee was sent to Guangxi to assist the provincial leadership in addressing the problems and helping the central leadership to form an opinion. In July 1983, the provincial party leadership had to report to the Central Party Secretariat in Beijing and received 'important instructions' from Xi Zhongxun, Song Renqiong and Qiao Shi on how to 'settle the scores' from the Cultural Revolution. The provincial leadership was obviously not able to satisfy the CCP Central Committee, as in January 1984, another 'important instruction' was issued by Hu Yaobang, Xi Zhongxun, Song Renqiong and Qiao Shi in their party functions. The next 'important instruction' followed shortly after, when Zhao Ziyang visited Guangxi in June 1984. Only three months later, Song Renqiong travelled to Guangxi where he gave another important speech on the same problem. The whole process of coming to terms with the Cultural Revolution officially lasted from the beginning of 1983 until mid-1985, when the provincial party committee issued a concluding report.

This concluding report declared Guangxi a political disaster area during the Cultural Revolution because of the severe factionalism and the high number of deaths incurred during political struggles. According to this report, most deaths had not resulted from armed conflict during the violent period of the Cultural Revolution, but were the result of political persecution after the establishment of Revolutionary Committees at provincial levels and below. This factional struggle had become especially virulent in the years 1975 and 1976, when individuals were attacked and prosecuted for minor issues. And yet those involved in factional killings and persecutions had been brought into leadership positions including the province's CCP Committee. The responsibility for these developments was seen to lie with the provincial party leadership of that period.[5] After 1978 these same people remained in their positions, although some purges did take place, as for example, in 1984 when three former deputy chairmen of the Guangxi Revolutionary Committee were expelled from the CCP.[6] However, the 1985 report insisted that leading cadres of the Provincial CCP Committee were not aware of the personnel situation and had not taken measures against those involved in the killings. It was noted that they had been excluded from the legal system, which meant that inheritance questions could not be resolved, and which in turn had resulted in public complaints and some popular unrest.

From the available documents it is obvious that provincial resistance to post-1978 political guidelines remained strong even after the 1983 report was issued. Leading cadres did not see themselves at fault and attacked the working groups sent by the centre in letters to the CCP Central Committee.

After 1985 the focus of the provincial leadership shifted to economic issues which had remained in the background during the political campaign. The provincial leadership acknowledged that the Autonomous Region had had to pay a considerable price for their allegiance to an outdated policy and to a generation of cadres whose authority was flawed by their previous conduct, unwilling to relinquish their influence.

Economic reconstruction had officially been adopted as a major task at a working conference of the province's party committee that followed the CCP Central Committee's reform plenum in December 1978. This working conference in January 1979 was to change the previous emphasis of economic policies. Instead of focusing attention on steel and grain production, the new focus was to be on products in which Guangxi enjoyed natural advantages, such as non-ferrous metals, agricultural crops and agricultural sideline production. While this was made as a verbal commitment, Guangxi for two years was slow to introduce agricultural reforms by not establishing the responsibility system for farmers until the second half of 1981.[7] Other examples of tardy reform quoted disapprovingly by later documents were the slow progress in enterprise reform, disregard for collective enterprises, and in distribution a preference for state allocation over trade. On one occasion in 1988 Gu Mu travelled to Guangxi to deliver a 'severe criticism' of the provincial leadership for their failure to utilise central funds allocated to Beihai City for the purpose of attracting foreign investment.[8]

Although after 1985, the leadership of Guangxi was officially committed to its reform course, conflicts with the centre continued. This situation improved in 1990, when Cheng Kejie followed Wei Chunshu in the leadership of the Autonomous Region. At the time of his appointment, he had already served as Wei's deputy, albeit with not much power of his own. His professional background was that of a railway engineer from Liuzhou City. He had later become mayor of the provincial capital of Nanning and then Deputy Chairman of the Autonomous Region under Wei Chunshu. In 1990 he was also joined by a new secretary of the CCP committee, Zhao Fulin.

Another of Cheng Kejie's leading cadres was Lei Yu, a Han and Deputy Chairman of the Autonomous Region, which requires only its Chairman to be of Zhuang nationality. Lei Yu was transferred to Guangxi in 1992 with a national reputation from his period in Hainan where he had been instrumental in opening the island to foreign trade and had apparently become involved in a large-scale car smuggling case that led to his recall from that province.[9] Lei Yu was put in charge of Guangxi's foreign trade and investment and credited with the successes that the province had in attracting major foreign investors. Lei Yu's attitudes towards Guangxi's previous policies of relying on the centre were reflected in the following statement:

> Under the previous system of controlled revenue and expenses, we depended on money from above for new projects. If there was no money, we did not embark on the project. This is easily understandable, because it is a result of this system. Now the situation has changed. If we continue to depend on national allocation and national funding for all we do and for our projects, and don't embark on them if we don't get funding, then we will never get on top. If Guangxi wants to get ahead and develop a bit faster, and if every place really wants to get ahead more quickly and not only say so, then we have to rely on ourselves and not wait for and lean on others.[10]

Lei Yu is also quoted in his emphasis on the sense of urgency that the new leadership could exploit:

In the past we have missed several opportunities for development because we were not able to exploit them well. If we are unable to grasp the present opportunity as well and let it pass in vain, then Deng Xiaoping could be right in saying that we will be at pains to explain to the people why we are failing one opportunity after the other. Why are we always behind when everybody else is developing? What I am saying is true, history will not forgive us. We need a strong sense of crisis and responsibility to speed up the construction of Guangxi and really face up to the responsibility of making Guangxi the sea passage for Southwest China.[11]

Under Cheng Kejie, political change was finally achieved. When Cheng took over, Wei Guoqing had already died and other members of the old guard – such as Qin Yingji who later died in 1992 – either had retired or were close to retirement. Cheng Kejie was more trusted by the central leadership and was able to score big personal successes when his supporters in the central leadership involved him in the new reform policies that started in 1992. Reforms until that time were still predominantly initiated by the centre. The turn-around came in 1992 when Guangxi became actively involved in the border trade and Greater Southwest China issues, starting to pursue its own interests in these areas.

Guangxi was among the leftist provinces that made the transition to the reform era late and slowly. Guangxi had historically been very close to the centre in terms of its policies. To some degree this was the result of its strategic position that gave the military a strong interest in Guangxi. Guangxi's leadership for a long time into the 1980s remained committed to a more conservative line that would lead them to follow restrictive central policies rather than the more liberal economic approach that was increasingly followed by neighbouring Guangdong Province. Guangdong, of course, was given more leeway than Guangxi in this respect, but Guangxi hardly made any approaches on its own to expand its economic autonomy.

The reform breakthrough

The breakthrough for economic reforms in Guangxi came in 1992 as a result of central initiatives. The CCP Committee of the Guangxi Planning Commission had received advance notice of Deng Xiaoping's planned trip to South China and his intention to give a boost to the national economy.[12] Under the deputy director of the Planning Commission, Liu Guangyin, a twenty-one-strong delegation visited eleven cities in Guangdong Province. The result of this visit was a report to the Provincial Party Committee and to the Provincial People's Government 'Learning from the East Wind in the South to Enliven the Great Land of Guangxi', which recommended a change of economic policies to an outward directed economic strategy and more rapid economic development for the province.[13] The Party Secretary and the Chairman of the Autonomous Region used this report to organise their own delegation to visit

Guangdong. After their visit, they issued a joint report 'Report on a study tour to Guangdong'. This report also proposed a change to a more active economic policy for Guangxi. More specifically, this report proposed that the emphasis on openness be directed to the coastal ports, the so-called 'Golden Triangle' of Beihai, Qinzhou and Fangchenggang. Second priority was given to the development of the Jianghe area, adjoining the Jianghe, Guangxi's river transport connection with Guangdong Province; and third priority to the development of the interior industrial areas of Guangxi around Liuzhou, Yulin and the tourist region of Guilin.[14]

A second reform push for the post-1990 leadership came with the decision to hold the Southwest China Conference in Beihai. The provincial leadership had originally not even been involved in the decision-making process about where to organise this conference which was to include participants from the State Council, the provinces of Yunnan, Sichuan, Guizhou, Guangdong, Hainan and Guangxi, as well as the cities of Chengdu and Chongqing. When news about the planned conference reached Guangxi in early 1992, the provincial Governor Cheng Kejie travelled himself to Beijing to meet with Vice-Premier Zou Jiahua and to make a formal application to host the conference in Guangxi. The decision by Zou Jiahua to give the conference to Guangxi was a personal success for Cheng Kejie.[15]

As a result of this conference, Guangxi became a more active participant in the plan to create a link between Southwest China and Southern China which was the subject of a CCP Central Committee decision in May 1992. A month later, the State Council formally decided to give special open status to Nanning and to some of Guangxi's border areas, including Pingxiang and Dongxing. Finally, in October 1992, Beihai became one of China's officially designated holiday and tourism destinations.[16]

In the course of 1992, the provincial leadership prepared three plans for the economic development of the province: 'Guangxi's planning concept for the regional development of parts of the Southwest and South China's regions and provinces', 'Planning outline for the opening of Guangxi as a South China Sea province' and 'Guangxi Zhuang Autonomous Region's key support for 29 poor counties in the Eighth Five-Year Plan (draft)'.[17] Much of this planning was undertaken by the younger cadres of the CCP organisation's planning bureaucracy.[18]

In retrospect, it is obvious that Guangxi's economic reform started in earnest only in 1992. Deng Xiaoping's trip to South China provided the new provincial leadership with the opportunity to push ahead with its political and economic reform programme. They were then able to muster political support from the central government for their plans and to integrate Guangxi in the general reform process with which it had lost contact since 1978. In this, they benefited from several favourable circumstances. Since the old leadership had gone into retirement internal political opposition to reforms had weakened. Economically the centre supported the province in its increasing border trade with Vietnam now that political obstacles had ceased to exist; and the concept of a Greater Southwest China Region promised to bring Guangxi a degree of prosperity that could not be achieved in isolation.

ECONOMIC DEVELOPMENT AND SOCIAL INTEGRATION

Guangxi's economic situation is generally characterised in terms of rank poverty and dependence on central subsidies. This was traditionally the case and in the public perception continues to such a degree that it is regarded as an embarrassment by people from Guangxi. Though there is irrefutable empirical evidence that Guangxi has in fact been disadvantaged, the perception of overall poverty is misleading. Guangxi consists of two major economic regions, which especially since the start of the reform period have faced very different conditions.

Leaving aside the varieties and diversified local mixtures of the non-Han nationalities all over the province, one can broadly distinguish a southeastern region (adjacent to Guangdong Province) and a northwestern region (on the borders with neighbouring Yunnan and Vietnam). The southeast of Guangxi has the general advantages of better factor endowment; the northwest comprises the areas of Hechi and Baise where the majority of the 8 million people are officially still regarded as 'poor' by any standard. The northeast is also the area where according to popular folklore Party Secretary Hu Yaobang broke into tears when he visited a family whose members had to share one pair of trousers and had to take turns to leave their house in cold weather because they shared only one coat.

During the 1950s the division of Guangxi along those lines was considered before the Guangxi Zhuang Autonomous Region was established in its present form in March 1958. Under the egalitarian policies of the following decades, intra-provincial differences did not come to the fore and were consciously suppressed. The emphasis on per capita figures used to illustrate Guangxi's plight also has the function of creating a unified economic image of a province that is in fact economically divided.

The division of the province between the southeast and the northwest is along geographic lines and only secondarily has an ethnic dimension. In 1994, 17.2 million people, corresponding to 38.6 per cent of Guangxi's total population, belonged to the ethnic minorities, the largest of them the Zhuang with 14.8 million people.[19] The majority of the Zhuang are distributed among the four areas of Hechi, Baise, Nanning and Liuzhou, and are thus to be found on both sides of the economic divide that runs through Guangxi.

The majority of Guangxi's 8 million population who live below the poverty line are concentrated in Hechi and Baise in the mountainous northwestern areas of the province.[20] The inhabitants of these areas are mainly Zhuang and other national minorities, interspersed with pockets of Han population. These areas have continuously depended on welfare subsidies. On the other side of the divide is the southeastern and eastern part of Guangxi with a predominantly Cantonese-speaking Han population.

Between these areas lies a belt stretching from Nanning to Liuzhou and west of Guilin that has a mixed Han and Zhuang population. In terms of living standards and economic integration, this belt is closer to the developed southeastern parts of Guangxi.

Economic reforms have brought these intra-provincial differences out into the open. Following the rationale of letting some get rich first in Guangxi would mean that the southeastern region should be assigned priority in development because it has superior land and climatic conditions, and offers better road and water transport links to Guangdong Province and Hong Kong. A crude first attempt at a provincial development strategy suggested that within Guangxi the southeastern region could develop economic ties with the industrial belt of western and central Guangdong.[21] However, this strategy failed to address the problems faced by the poorer areas in Guangxi's northwest.

The way in which Guangxi's economic policies were tuned to the needs of these poorer areas was by relying on central financial subsidies. The continuous reliance on subsidies was justified for a number of political and economic reasons. The main political reasons were Guangxi's exposed situation on the Vietnamese border which by the late 1970s required Guangxi to be able to maintain political stability and military readiness along the border. For both reasons, the national minorities along the border had to be integrated. The economic justification for subsidies was that Guangxi was in fact one of the poorest provinces of China in terms of industrial potential and general development and that into the 1990s nearly one-fifth of its population still lives below the poverty line.

With reform, previous policy settings and Guangxi's economic policies in general came increasingly under challenge. The provincial leadership in the 1980s had already lost the trust of the central leadership and was increasingly losing its economic basis. Subsidies were harder to obtain as the central fiscal situation tightened; relations with Vietnam started to improve, relaxing the tensions along the border; and neighbouring Guangdong was surging ahead in economic growth and wealth. The provincial leadership had been reluctant to grasp reform in the 1980s, but when it accepted the challenge in the early 1990s, it was soon confronted by new dilemmas.

Guangxi's subsidised economics

Guangxi in 1949 was one of the poorest and most backward provinces of China. It had only a few small industrial enterprises accounting for 14 per cent of its gross output value (of both agriculture and industry) with agriculture accounting for the remaining 86 per cent. Half of the rural population was classified as poor peasants or farm labourers.[22] Because of this large proportion of impoverishment, Guangxi's per capita figures for agricultural output continued to be below the national average. In 1950 they reached 65.38 per cent of the national average and in 1952 only 59.31 per cent.[23] During the

First Five-Year Plan Guangxi was not able to make up for its economic disadvantages. Guangxi was not allocated one single project among the 156 major national investment projects from 1953 to 1957. The only medium-sized project was a sugar factory in Gui county. Consequently, Guangxi was never able to catch up with the more advanced provinces.

Only during the repeated periods of radical politics did Guangxi seem able to improve its economic base. During the Great Leap Forward Guangxi embarked on a forced industrialisation programme that, though not sustainable, laid the foundation for later industrial development. Capital construction expenditure in 1957 had reached 47.9 per cent of local financial revenue, in 1958 it had climbed to 74.5 per cent and in 1960 to 113.5 per cent.[24] A major population shift further burdened the economy. From 1957 to 1960, the industrial workforce increased from 760,000 to 1,380,000 persons and the urban population from 520,000 to 2,270,000.[25] The view in Guangxi is that by the end of the Second Five-Year Plan Guangxi was no longer able to keep pace with general economic development and progressively lagged behind in per capita terms.[26]

During the implementation of the 'Third Front' investment policy of the late 1960s and early 1970s investment funds were channelled into inaccessible areas to make China less vulnerable in case of a major war and Guangxi finally became a major beneficiary of central largesse. Investment under this policy especially benefited the northwest area of Guangxi. Central investment funding for Guangxi from 1966 to 1976 amounted to 7.5 billion *yuan* compared to 5.6 billion *yuan* of central investment during the preceding seventeen years.[27] However, internal party evaluations still indicate that Guangxi continued to be disadvantaged. Under the Fifth Five-Year Plan from 1976 onwards, Guangxi obtained investment in some middle and small-scale projects which made a certain although not decisive impact on its economy.

Guangxi had thus not been able to improve its overall position as one of the poorer provinces of China. Its starting point in 1949 had been very low and it never managed to attract central investment to the degree that its economic situation was radically altered. The province profited most under periods of radical mobilisational policies. It was during these periods that Guangxi was integrated most into the national economy, but this type of integration was more political than economic, in that the latter was limited to fiscal integration which came in the form of subsidies from the central budget for the province's poverty-stricken, largely national minority areas.

A report prepared by the Guangxi CCP Committee in October 1984 drew a bleak picture of the economic situation of the province. With Guangxi's population accounting for 3.6 per cent of the total national population, the value of its fixed asset investment stood at 1.7 per cent of the national total, its industrial output value at 2 per cent and its financial revenue at 1.1 per cent of the respective national totals. Industrial output value had even declined by 0.2 per cent from 1978.[28] The per capita figures quoted in the document illustrated the bleak situation even better. Industrial and agricultural per capita output value stood at 55 per cent of the national average and was the second worst among the five autonomous regions and the fourth worst among all provincial-level units. Industrial output value per capita reached only 42 per cent of the national average which made Guangxi the second lowest autonomous region and the third lowest of all provincial-level units. Finally, in terms of financial revenue on a per capita basis, Guangxi was the lowest of the autonomous regions and reached less than one-third of the national average.[29] Guangxi's poverty in 1983 was further illustrated by the fact that in forty-eight counties the average annual income was less than 100 *yuan* and that 7 million people had less than 400 pounds of rice or food grains a year. Such poverty accounted for one-fifth of Guangxi's total population and up to 1983 those at or below these levels were not able to safeguard their basic necessities.[30]

While Guangxi had not received what it considered its fair share of central investment, it had long been maintaining a dependence on financial subsidies from the central government. These subsidies did not flow into large economic construction projects, but into the poor areas in Guangxi. When in 1980 the fiscal relationship between the provinces and the centre changed to revenue-sharing and fiscal contracting,[31] Guangxi and the other autonomous regions were exempted from these policies. Their budgets continued to be under central control, requiring central monitoring of expenditure and revenue. In return, they were guaranteed a continuing stream of subsidies.[32] Guangxi had all along relied on central subsidies, among other things to balance its budget, which had been in deficit since 1957.[33] However, under the new policies Guangxi soon came to see itself as disadvantaged in comparison to those other provinces which could retain a much higher proportion of their revenues.

Central subsidies to Guangxi increased in absolute figures during the 1980s, but showed a declining ratio to provincial fiscal revenue, as Table 2.1 indicates.[34]

At the same time, Guangxi kept raising its contributions to the central budget from sectors such as banking, insurance, power generation, railways,

Table 2.1 Guangxi's subsidies from central government, 1978–93

Year	Central subsidy income (million yuan RMB)	Ratio to fiscal revenue (%)
1978	681	47.6
1980	503	40.9
1985	1,290	63.9
1990	1,807	38.6
1991	1,508	27.0
1992	1,578	25.8
1993	1,696	17.7

non-ferrous metals and foreign trade to an extent that was said to largely exceed the subsidies.[35] The argument was raised that the province might be better off if it were allowed to keep its revenue and forgo the subsidies. An additional argument for this was that the reliance on subsidies had given Guangxi a negative image.[36]

By 1984, the Provincial Party Committee had realised that their former support for the radical leadership in reporting success rather than problems to central government had produced the unintended consequence that their demands for funding were not heard. In 1982 and 1983 Guangxi received the lowest capital allocation of all provinces calculated on a per capita basis.[37] In comparison to the other four autonomous regions and the three provinces of Qinghai, Guizhou and Yunnan (all of which also have a high proportion of national minorities in their populations) Guangxi received the lowest allocation of central financial subsidies. From Guangxi's perspective the subsidies received were less than one-third of the 60 *yuan* (1983) that the other comparable provinces received on a per capita basis.[38] Guangxi argued that it received the lowest subsidies on a per capita basis among the eight provinces with a large minority population.

As subsidies were reduced, a number of conflicts arising between the province and the centre simply resulted from changing administrative structures which forced the provincial leadership to adapt to new procedures. Once economic autonomy developed its own dynamics there was bound to be some friction. These problems were not therefore specific to Guangxi, as they would have appeared in similar form in all other provinces embarking on economic reforms. The specific problem for Guangxi was that the price that had to be paid for central subsidies turned out to be high in terms of the lost revenue for the province on which the centre could lay claim. The increasing reduction in subsidies meant that Guangxi was less and less able to pursue its previous egalitarian policies. While it is doubtful that these had in fact improved the overall economic situation of the poor minority areas, there can be no question that the central policies that Guangxi was now forced to adopt meant that its activities had to be concentrated on its relatively well-off coastal and southeastern areas.

From subsidies to special rights

The economic incentives that the centre offered to Guangxi in return for the declining role of subsidies were primarily related to integrating the province into the international economy. In 1984 Beihai became one of the fourteen coastal open cities (COCs) which were entitled to grant special rights to foreign investors. In 1985, Guangxi's foreign trade system was granted the right to retain 50 per cent of export earnings;[39] in 1988 further cities along the coast were granted special rights for attracting foreign investment.[40]

The special rights given to the city of Beihai allowed it to double the size of its basic economic indicators within three years. However, the policies that were designed to make Beihai into a centre of foreign investment and economic activity, such as tax concessions, the right to sell imported consumer goods into China's domestic market and right to raise domestic capital, did not fully produce the expected results and especially did not satisfy the central leadership. In 1988, Gu Mu travelled to Beihai to severely criticise provincial leaders for their inability to make use of the favourable policies offered to them. The most striking example was that of US$30 million originally made available for investment purposes, not more than US$2.9 million had been used by 1988.[41]

In the aftermath of this visit, the provincial leadership started to acknowledge that they had simply not made use of the opportunities offered to them:

> The lesson from the fact that the opening policies for our province have by far not produced the expected result can be summarised in the one point that we have still not fully used the central policies. We have not been able to make use of the special rights of our autonomy to give more content to the opening policies given to us by the centre and to broaden their range.[42]

In contrast to Guangdong which had demonstrated the advantages of pursuing provincial interests, observers in Guangxi noticed that their province had never dared to assert its own interests in its relations with central government bureaucracy in Beijing:

> The reason that our province is getting too little per capita subsidies from the centre is that when the base figures for fiscal contracting were set, our autonomy rights were not used to report clearly and in full our history and our present situation. During the process of contracting we were also not able to be direct and frank enough to ask the centre to grant us flexible procedures of 'giving nothing and receiving nothing'. In one sentence, when the centre set its fiscal policies towards the minority regions, we did not make use of our influence as a minority region and therefore did not receive the support and attention due to us.[43]

In this analysis the centre had offered Guangxi alternative policies to make up for the disadvantages that it would face during the transition away from the planned economy. However, Guangxi's leadership had lost the economic initiative because it had lost contact with the centre by disregarding its political signals and policies. It was seemingly not able to adapt to the new economic environment.

There was however an additional dimension. For the provincial leadership, this whole issue of making use of central incentives was a matter of provincial development strategy. It was argued that the policies promoted by the centre further disadvantaged the already backward regions in the province. There were critical views as to what on a nation-wide basis had been achieved under these policies during the second half of the 1980s and at what costs. The main concern was the increasing income differentiation and economic polarisation between Guangxi's two major regions.

The worsening of intra-provincial differences became a major concern. For the Seventh Five-Year Plan the provincial leadership made equalisation one of their major policies in contrast to the central policies of more flexible development and greater local initiative. The provincial leadership tried to pursue their policies under adverse circumstances where they were no longer able to enforce them. At the end of this period, they summarised their failure as a result of lacking planning authority, underdeveloped market conditions, uncontrolled local interests and other factors.[44]

By the mid-1980s, conflict between Guangxi and the centre had shifted from politics to economics, where it became manifest in two different and conflicting aspects of development strategy. Guangxi's leadership, while reluctant to pursue the economic policies propagated by the centre with their emphasis on coastal development, was not able to propose alternative similarly successful policies which depended on earlier strategies of administrative overall planning and intervention. The central policies of increasing provincial revenues while reducing subsidies proved to be more advantageous for the province than the previous reliance on central subsidies.

In spite of complaints about the negative effects of the new central policies, by the early 1990s there was already no alternative. For the Eighth Five-Year Plan, Guangxi accepted a strategy of differentiated provincial development that would allow the coastal and more advantaged regions to develop faster, even at the cost of less development for the poorer areas.

NEW ECONOMIC ORIENTATIONS

By 1992, Guangxi was being offered new alternatives. A new generation of provincial leaders under Cheng Kejie was finally able to assert its position and improve relations with the centre. However, this did not mean that continued discussion of provincial development strategies was halted. The underlying issue of intra-provincial inequality remained and had to be addressed in order to guarantee economic and social stability for the province. This issue reappeared in different guise with the question of Guangxi's border trade with Vietnam. By that time, Guangxi was offered two new areas of activity for the province's economic development: the economic region of Greater Southwest China, and the prospect of border trade with Vietnam and Southeast Asia.

Guangxi as part of Greater Southwest China

The regional integration of Southwest China started in the early 1950s. At that time integration served political and military ends rather than economic purposes.[45] It could even be argued that regional political integration coincided with economic isolation for different parts of Southwest China, as the different regional economies were constrained in their interaction by the autarky policies imposed by the centre.

The actual initiative for a Greater Southwest economic region is often ascribed to Vice-Premier Zou Jiahua by Guangxi sources. It seems clear that Zou Jiahua made the decision to hold the major conference for planning regional integration when in Guangxi.[46] The decision appears to have been made after a personal visit by Cheng Kejie, who offered the possibility that such an event could be presented as an important political success. The idea of establishing regional economies in China is, however, older and the reasons for the large number of visits by central leaders to Guangxi were probably not even related to Guangxi. The two issues closer to their heart at that time were the controversial decision to build the Three Gorges Dam that would cut off Sichuan Province from its sea access via the Yangtze River, and the normalisation of relations with Vietnam.[47] Sichuan needed to be guaranteed continued access to the sea, and relations with Vietnam could now be augmented by economic links. Guangxi happened to be at the crossing point of those two developments. This would explain the amount of attention that was suddenly focused on Guangxi.

During the Southwest China Conference held in Beihai in July 1992 Vice-Premier Tian Jiyun explained the importance of Greater Southwest China to the national development strategy, and placed its development in its larger international context:

> Southeast Asia and South Asia with over one billion people are huge potential markets. One cannot rely on the insufficient strength of just one province to enter this market. Southwest China can acquire huge economic strength by rational division of labour, mutual supplementing and combining efforts in opening up.[48]

Southwest China could become a region with substantial economic potential, and Guangxi's role was to provide the access routes for this new regional economy:

> It is of major importance to our socialist modernisation that we extend the advantages for development of Guangxi's position on the Beibu Gulf to the interior and link up Guangxi's access routes to the outside world through its ports and border crossings with the resources of our Southwest. Through deeper opening and reforms we will rapidly change the backward state of the Southwestern province.[49]

Central Committee Document no. 4 which was drafted after the conference confirmed Guangxi's role in providing the access routes for Southwest China.[50]

The main focus of this regional integration has been on infrastructure, such as railway, highway, railroad and port construction. One of Guangxi's main efforts has been directed at securing funds for infrastructure projects from its provincial partners. However, there are additional aspects of the proposal that illustrate how the centre has tried to steer the provincial government into economic and administrative integration. According to interviews in Guangxi, there have been both central and provincial policies to facilitate inter-provincial exchange. At the central level, a division of labour has been suggested for the smaller provinces. Yunnan, for example, is to concentrate on the tobacco industry, Guizhou on fruit, and Guangxi is to specialise in sugar production.

This specialisation has not been binding for the provinces and does, in the final analysis, also not commit the centre too strictly. Guangxi, for example, as the province with the largest sugar-refining capacities in China continues to face difficulties in securing its own sugar supplies from overseas. Although the central monopoly on sugar imports, previously held by the China National Cereals, Oils and Foodstuffs Import and Export Corporation had been removed in the early 1990s, sugar import licenses are still required. Buyers in Guangxi who need raw material for their sugar refineries have no special access to these licences, but have to purchase them on the domestic market where they face tough competition from speculators.[51]

Administrative integration is also encouraged through a central policy that allows the provincial administrations of one province to set up branches in another. Mutual investment is also encouraged and provincial policies are flexible enough to even channel tax revenue from an enterprise back into the province from where the investment originated. Actual economic integration in terms of trade levels and intensity of economic exchange has obviously not yet progressed to a significant level, at least not to the degree that interviewees in the provincial trade department in Guangxi in 1995 had statistics on their sales volumes available for partner provinces as opposed to the domestic market in general.

Regional integration was most effective during the economic boom of 1992–3 when investors from other provinces streamed into Guangxi. Guangxi's port cities, especially Beihai, attracted a large volume of funds from neighbouring provinces including not only Sichuan, Guizhou, and Yunnan, but also provinces from further afield, such as Jilin.[52] Sichuan is generally mentioned as the largest source of inter-provincial investment, followed by Hainan, Shandong and Beijing. The limited anecdotal evidence clearly suggests that this inter-provincial investment, mainly in real estate, was not confined to the southwestern provinces.

The experience gained from the investment boom had an impact on how the government in Guangxi later tried to use regional integration to its own end. The short boom had demonstrated that Guangxi's geographical advantages were able to attract investment, once restrictions on the province's trade activities were relaxed. The question was how much authority the centre was willing to cede to the southwest regional economy that it was not willing to cede to individual provinces. This was an essential issue for Guangxi because it impinged on its potential to engage in border trade and to attract outside investment, and was one of the lessons learnt during the boom. Again there seemed to be differences of opinion between the centre and the province regarding foreign trade and other rights. An example was the new administration building for an intended tax-free zone near Beihai port which had been built by provincial authorities, but which in early 1995 had to be closed and fenced off pending a final central decision on its legal status.

Guangxi's integration into Greater Southwestern China is a long-term project that could change the whole province once all the infrastructure measures have been successfully put into place. The rationale that a single province may be too small to solve its own problems, let alone develop links with overseas countries and regions seems convincing in the case of provinces that are among the poorest in China. In 1995 regional integration across provincial borders appeared to be an experiment; for the centre to explore how provinces could be persuaded to cede some of their powers and finances to one another; for the provinces to test how much power the centre was willing to grant to lower levels. The idea of a greater economic region was used as a testing ground where neither side would lose too much. The centre maintained control over inter-provincial exchange and the provinces were not restricted by an administration that resembled a 'super-provincial' integrative power structure. It will be interesting to see if this new push at the regional level for economic integration since 1992 develops its own political and administrative dynamism.

GUANGXI'S BORDER TRADE WITH VIETNAM

As Brantly Womack pointed out in the only study so far of the topic, border trade between China and Vietnam has been little researched because of the deliberate dearth of information.[53] There is no advantage in releasing information – the governments on both sides would not benefit directly, no foreign investment could be attracted – and participants generally prefer that their trading activities go unreported. Since Womack's report, border trade has gone through a peak in 1992–3 and has subsequently suffered from a slump induced by China's macro-economic retrenchment policies and other developments. These events have thrown a new light on the whole question of border trade, indicating that it has a significance much wider than the local. Apart from the development of border trade itself, it is necessary to examine the problems that became contentious issues in discussions between central and provincial governments, as well as for the Guangxi authorities.

There is a long tradition of border trade between Guangxi and Vietnam along the land border as well as along the coast. Links are facilitated by common language in some areas, but more by long-established custom. Cross-border contacts are also facilitated by the contacts that developed between the ruling elite in Guangxi and the Vietnamese who during the war lived and received their education in Guangxi and who are now moving into leadership positions in local government and in Hanoi. The claim by officials in Guangxi that they have links with high-level Vietnamese cadres dating back to their school and university days in Nanning during the Vietnam War are hard to prove empirically, but should not be discounted. It is even said that these links were not disrupted during the Sino-Vietnamese conflict and the border war in 1979. While these links have helped to facilitate cross-border trade, they can also be a source of friction between Guangxi and the centre.

Border trade had, of course, stopped during the border war and afterwards it was impeded by political obstacles and by the mining of the border between Guangxi and Vietnam. The recovery was very gradual and only from 1989 onwards did Guangxi authorities begin to talk about 'border trade'. Chinese sources tend to regard the normalisation of bilateral relations as the major watershed in the development of border trade and support this view with the published trade figures. There is however sufficient evidence to doubt the reliability of the published (and unpublished) figures, even beyond the doubts that Womack raised. For one, the figures that the Guangxi Border Trade Administration used in 1995 did not match the figures published in the more recent editions of the *Guangxi Statistical Yearbook*. The figures that were published in earlier, pre-1992 issues of the *Guangxi Statistical Yearbooks*[54] are obviously only partial figures and can be disregarded. Second, anecdotal evidence suggests that the border trade boom in 1992-93 was much stronger than suggested by all available figures. The most recent figures obtained from the Guangxi Border Trade Administration in April 1995 are reported in Table 2.2.[55]

These figures differ considerably from the estimates given in US dollars by Womack: they show fluctuations that are based on differences in the exchange rate.[56] They also differ from the figures on border trade that were published in the *Guangxi Statistical Yearbooks* for 1993 (p. 250) and 1994 (p. 322) for the years 1992 and 1993 respectively. These figures suggest that border trade in 1992 was 3,192 million *yuan* (US$588.93 million) and 2,867 million *yuan* (US$498.7 million) in 1993.[57] These figures from the latest statistical yearbook are worth consideration because they are much higher than other reports and show a decline from 1992 to 1993 which is also suggested by other evidence. However, it is futile to regard any of these sets of figures as an accurate reflection of actual trade volumes, as border trade and smuggling are so closely connected. The estimate that smuggling amounts to about one-third of total trade is probably far too low.[58] Personal impression suggests that

Table 2.2 Guangxi's border trade, 1989–94

Year	Million yuan RMB	Million US$
1989	450	95.34
1990	760	161.02
1991	2,200	410.45
1992	2,600	479.70
1993	2,600	452.17
1994	2,640	

border trade must have been much more important during its boom period in 1992–3.

Personal impressions from a recent visit to Guangxi (April–May 1995) are that border trade in the speculation and investment drive that followed Deng Xiaoping's visit to Southern China in spring 1992 was at the heart of a short-lived but very significant boom in Guangxi's economy. Especially affected were the port cities on the coast, most strongly Beihai, but also Nanning and other cities. According to accounts heard in Nanning, Beihai and other port cities, several generations of real estate speculators and investors had followed each other within months. Beihai's whole urban area was subdivided into development plots that were clearly evident wherever one travelled. Large-scale real estate development was started and completed to varying degrees. When the boom collapsed in mid-1993 the last wave of investors mostly from other provinces was caught in a wave of insolvencies. The signs of these insolvencies were ubiquitous in the shape of investment ruins and half-finished building. It was a lesson in regional geography to hear who owned the various buildings and marked plots spreading over the whole city. There was literally no piece of land in Beihai that had not been affected by the boom. This made the downturn all the more dramatic. The port was nearly empty, as were the hotels where travellers during the boom reportedly could sell a night's accommodation on the black market if they had to leave before their reservation had expired.

These ups and downs are related to specific government policies and regulations, but behind the official policies lie other motives which are not publicly documented, as there are conflicts of interests between the central government and the provincial level. According to Chinese accounts, trade along the Sino-Vietnamese border was encouraged by the Chinese side from September 1983 onwards by establishing unofficial border crossings for market activities and family visits. Altogether nine such posts were established. In 1987 Vietnam started to relax its policies on border traffic. After September 1988, exchange was further facilitated when Guangxi and Vietnamese authorities agreed to set up twenty-five border trade posts, and thirty-two Chinese state-owned companies were entrusted with wholesale trade.[59] Up to 1992, the number of kinds of goods traded increased from 100 to 1,000. Financial income from border trade for the border town of Pingxiang was reported to have increased from 4.98 million *yuan* RMB in 1988 to 12.66 million in 1989, 19 million in 1990 and 24.84 million in 1991.[60]

Border trade became an official designation from 1991 onwards, when the Chinese started to use this term. Up to October 1991 Chinese officials had to travel to Vietnam under their company titles and not as functionaries of any government entity. In 1991, the Office of the State Council issued Order no. 25 – 'Views on how to promote prosperity and stability in border provinces through active development of border trade and economic cooperation' – in order to encourage border trade.[61] In November 1991 relations between China and Vietnam were normalised.

The big change came in 1992, after Deng Xiaoping's trip to South China to which the Guangxi CCP Committee responded with the policy slogan 'Let's all engage in border trade, let's all use preferential policies'. The ensuing boom was based on the availability of finance and would not have happened without it, but essentially, three factors contributed to the momentous changes of 1992. Relations with Vietnam had just been normalised, the formation of a Southwest China economic region had become necessary with the decision to build the Three Gorges Dam (cutting Sichuan off from its sea access through the Yangtze River) and Guangxi's poor political relationship with the centre had finally been rectified. The central leadership had both initiated and pursued these plans carefully over several years. The core central leadership had visited Guangxi in the preceding years – among them Jiang Zemin in 1990 – or visited it in 1992.

The combination of border trade with regional economic integration in the southwest created important incentives in the economic climate of 1992. From Guangxi's side, both of its traditional economic concerns were taken care of. Border trade would benefit the poorer areas adjacent to the Vietnamese border, while southwest regional integration would contribute to the development of its port and international trading facilities and would bring outside investment into the province. Investors from Southwest China and indeed from all over China were attracted by the special economic zones that were created along the border and the coast and the various incentives these offered. From the centre's perspective, the new relationship with Guangxi's leaders meant that these policies would not be carried out reluctantly or sabotaged by the provincial leadership.

In July 1992 the centre approved special coastal city status for Nanning and special economic status for the two border towns of Pingxiang and Dongxing. The provincial government approved several local investment projects in these localities to support their development.[62] The provincial party committee and government established a local bureaucracy to administer border trade. In the following months, more and more special areas were established along the border and the coast. Altogether there were six central-level open ports or crossings, eight provincial-level ones and twenty-five small border trade posts and border markets.[63] Within months, literally hundreds of companies had sprung up that were engaged in border trade.[64]

As long as the boom lasted, Guangxi could reap the benefits from this economic activity along its land and sea borders. Both developmental concerns were taken care of: the northwestern interior regions profited to some degree as well as the coastal regions in the southeast. In a way, the two issues became merged as small-scale border trade and international trade flowing through Guangxi were not clearly differentiated. A separation of provincial and central interests occurred when the boom started to cool down in mid-1993. The reasons for this were the macro-economic retrenchment policies which restricted real estate speculation and investment all over China; and concern on the Vietnamese side that Chinese imports and Chinese trade activities started to upset the local economy in the North, leading to restrictions and tariffs on the flow of goods. Finally, Beijing's central authorities were also concerned that border trade had become a loophole for Chinese importers to circumvent Chinese customs regulations.

The real estate boom collapsed without specific intervention from the centre when funding dried up. Real estate prices in Beihai, for example, in 1995 reportedly stood at 10 per cent of the level they had reached during the boom period. The concerns of the Vietnamese side were primarily taken care of by central and provincial government institutions which tried to develop more industrial cooperation with Vietnam to replace the focus on trade. This issue and the question of customs became another area of contention between Guangxi province and the central government.

The centre started to restrict activities by defining border trade in much narrower terms than before. Border trade during the boom had expanded to include the exchange of goods such as tropical fruit and raw materials from places as far away as Indonesia and North China. The line between border trade and smuggling was very thin in circumstances where these transactions were effected on a US dollar basis, or where they involved goods under import restriction, such as motor vehicles. Guangxi had profited from these exchanges as an entrepôt, and had in turn benefited from this role through investment flows into Guangxi by provinces, especially Sichuan, eager to secure a foothold in the seaports of Beihai, Qinzhou and Fanchenggang.

The terms under which the centre from 1993 on allowed the continuation of border trade were basically to restrict it to cross-border barter exchange and to coastal traffic on vessels of 2,000 tons or less. One could speculate that this was the type of border trade that might have developed without the short-lived boom, but as a result of the unexpected boom Guangxi had woken up to the potential of its geographical position. Within the provincial leadership there were two positions which again reflect in some way different development strategies. One was to pursue border trade within the available framework and to expand it as far as possible. For this position the limits on barter trade and local exchange were restrictions that were not in line with the autonomous status of the province, granted precisely because of its special circumstances. To put it simply, the 'small' border trade that from a pre-1992 perspective would have provided a noticeable improvement in the economic situation along the border, was from the post-boom perspective an undue central restriction on activities for border provinces that have little other economic potential to rely on.

The other position was to place the main emphasis on foreign investment and foreign trade to enhance the entrepôt role that benefits the coastal areas. In 1995, this was an unresolved situation where transgressions were seemingly tolerated as long as they did not too obviously contravene China's national interests towards Vietnam or give rise to too much provincial independence with respect to national policies.

However far these local positions might have differed on the details of border trade, the developments of the past years have added a new dimension to provincial–central relations in Guangxi. The political leadership as well as those representing trade and business interests in Guangxi have realised not only that their economic potential even for border trade lies in their business links with other Chinese provinces, but also that under current circumstances they will have to rely on the centre in order to be able to activate these links.

CONCLUSION

Guangxi has been a disadvantaged province left behind in living standards, investment volumes and economic development throughout most of the People's Republic of China. One disadvantage was its location on Vietnam's borders while a war raged that could easily have spilled over into the neighbouring province. This is one possible explanation for the high degree of politicisation during the Cultural Revolution. However, the result of that politicisation was that Guangxi made the transition into the reform period very slowly and very late.

Another disadvantage in Guangxi's neighbourhood is the very active economy of Guangdong to its east. Links between Guangdong and Guangxi were so close that during the 1950s even the division of Guangxi was being seriously considered with Guangxi's eastern, Cantonese-speaking portions becoming part of Guangdong Province. Guangxi's eastern sections – including the relatively developed coastal regions – has very different economic interests from the poorer northwest of the province.

The third disadvantage facing the province is the high proportion of its population who are impoverished minority nationalities. This was a historical burden as the minority regions of Guangxi have been impoverished for a long time and remain in need of economic support. Related to this is the issue of autonomy. Autonomous status was granted to the province in 1958, but in practical terms, it did not give much additional authority to the provincial government and party and therefore remained largely symbolic.

It was in the late 1980s and during the 1990s that Guangxi finally came out of its relative political isolation and only then started to realise the economic advantages of its geographical position. In spite of its coastal position Guangxi is not a province that accepted the challenge of reform early or easily. Reforms started much later than in other provinces. Guangxi's leadership had been more committed to the radical line of the pre-reform leadership and had to be forced into the reform era by central intervention. Once this transition was under way, Guangxi suddenly found itself in the middle of an economic boom that linked it much closer to China's other provinces than ever before, but at the same time brought conflicts with central government over a range of reform policies.

For Guangxi, the sudden entry into the reform period has completely changed its economic and political environment. The market economy has exposed the intra-provincial differences between its developed and under-developed regions and has forced its policy-makers to find a balance between different and conflicting development strategies. The central government, on which the provincial pre-reform leadership had so heavily relied, was suddenly no longer able to deliver the large subsidies on which Guangxi's economy depended to a considerable degree. The autonomous status given to Guangxi as a sign of special consideration for its minorities turned out to be of very little use when practical concessions were demanded from the central government.

Relations with China's provincial economies and with Guangxi's Southeast Asian neighbours have also been affected by the way the province entered the reform era. For all its negative reverberations, the 1992–3 boom provided Guangxi with a glimpse of a possible future. On the one side it had an open border with the developing economy of Vietnam which was much more receptive to its goods than the saturated international markets and in addition opened trade links to other Southeast Asian countries. On the other side, there was a domestic market that both provided customers and investment capital. Seen from Guangxi, there were very few problems or conflicts during that period.

Guangxi's political situation has been transformed as a result. The conflict between its provincial development strategies continues to exist, but what used to be alternative concepts of where to direct planned investment, now have become more subtle differences between promoting international trade and investment or emphasising cross-border links. In its relationship with the centre, there is still a link between subsidies and autonomous status, but the tendency is for subsidies to increasingly disappear from a market environment where they are too much of a burden. At the same time Guangxi's autonomous status will have to be substantiated if it is in some way to make up for the loss of subsidies.

The imperative for Guangxi's regional integration had basically been political in nature for most of the history of the People's Republic of China. However, during the boom period of 1992–3 it suddenly became an economic reality with waves of speculative funds pouring in from neighbouring provinces. This process of inter-provincial integration is now back in the treadmills of a bureaucratic routine of high-level mutual visits and resulting communiqués about a few more regionally funded projects. While the short boom has not much changed the slow movement towards long-term integration, it has introduced an element that will accompany this process as a practical vision of the forces that could be unleashed by a more comprehensive market-based integration. The major issue of concern to all southwest provinces, and most of all Guangxi, is that they have to agree with the centre on the integration of their increasingly independent economies in national and regional markets. For Guangxi it seems that the opening to the outside makes economic sense only if it is complemented by an opening to the inside, that is the inter-provincial domestic market.

However, this political analysis should not distract from the present economic reality. Guangxi's economy has hardly ever been as vibrant as it had become by 1995. Looking less towards Guangdong and Hong Kong, Guangxi has found its own role between Southwest China and Southeast Asia. Guangxi has already become the bridge between China on the one hand, and Vietnam and other Southeast Asian countries on the other. Its role as an entrepôt and sea access for Sichuan and China's southwest region as a whole will only increase its potential role in Southeast Asia.

NOTES

1 Dorothy J. Solinger, *Regional Government and Political Integration in Southwest China, 1949–1954: A Case Study*, University of California Press, Berkeley, 1977.
2 David S.G. Goodman, 'The politics of provincialism: economic development, conflict and negotiation', in David S.G. Goodman and Gerald Segal (eds) *China Deconstructs: Politics, Trade and Regionalism*, Routledge, London, 1994, pp. 11f.
3 Dangdai Zhongguo congshu bianjibu, *Dangdai Zhongguo de Guangxi* [Guangxi in contemporary China] 1, Dangdai Zhongguo chubanshe, Beijing, 1992, ch. 5.
4 *Guangxi dashiji* [Guangxi Chronicle] no publisher, Nanning, 1987.
5 *Guangxi dashiji*, op. cit., p. 99.
6 Dangdai Zhongguo congshu bianjibu, *Dangdai Zhongguo de Guangxi*, op. cit., 2, p. 559.
7 *Guangxi dashiji*, op. cit., p. 104.
8 Yu Pimin, 'Guanyu woqu yong hao zizhifa he kaifang zhengce de sikao' [Thoughts on how our province should make good use of the autonomy law and opening policies], *Guangxi minzu yanjiu* no. 1, 1989, p. 11.
9 Feng Chongyi and David S.G. Goodman, 'Hainan: communal politics and the struggle for identity', Chapter 3 in this volume.
10 Zhang Dongmei and Zhang Yuanxin, 'Yangqi shi xiang dahai de fengfan – Guangxi chao zhong de jiduo lianghua' [Hoist the sails towards the great sea – some beautiful flowers in Guangxi's tide], in Yu Fanglin *et al.* (eds) *Guangxi chao* [Guangxi's Tide], Guangxi renmin chubanshe, Nanning, 1993, pp. 147–78.
11 Zhang Dongmei and Zhang Yuanxin, op. cit., p. 177.
12 Zhang Dongmei and Zhang Yuanxin, op. cit., p. 147.
13 Zhang Dongmei and Zhang Yuanxin, op. cit., p. 151.
14 Zhang Dongmei and Zhang Yuanxin, op. cit., p. 153.
15 Zhang Dongmei and Zhang Yuanxin, op. cit., pp. 154–8.
16 Zhang Dongmei and Zhang Yuanxin, op. cit., p. 163.
17 Zhang Dongmei and Zhang Yuanxin, op. cit., p. 164.
18 Zhang Dongmei and Zhang Yuanxin, op. cit., p. 164.
19 Guangxi nianjian she (ed.) *Guangxi nianjian 1995* [Guangxi Yearbook 1995], Guangxi nianjian she, Nanning, p. 421.
20 *Guangxi nianjian 1995*, op. cit., pp. 136–7.
21 Wu Junli, 'Guangxi jingji fazhan zhanlue chuyi' [Initial thoughts on Guangxi's economic development strategy], *Guangxi shifan daxue xuebao (zhexue shehui kexue ban)* 29, no. 1, 1993, pp. 11–14.
22 Ma Biao *et al.* (eds) *Guangxi chanye jiegou yu jingji fazhan zhanlue* [Guangxi's Sectoral Structure and Economic Development Strategy], Guangxi kexue jishu chubanshe, Nanning, 1992, p. 3.
23 Ma Biao *et al.* (eds), op. cit., p. 7.
24 Ma Biao *et al.* (eds), op. cit., p. 13.
25 Ma Biao *et al.* (eds), op. cit., p. 13.

26 Ma Biao *et al.* (eds), op. cit., pp. 10f.
27 Ma Biao *et al.* (eds), op. cit., p. 19.
28 *Guangxi dashiji*, op. cit., p. 129.
29 *Guangxi dashiji*, op. cit., p. 128.
30 *Guangxi dashiji*, op. cit., p. 128.
31 Yang Dali, 'Reform and the restructuring of central–local relations', in David S.G. Goodman and Gerald Segal (eds) *China Deconstructs*, op. cit., pp. 59–98.
32 Yu Pimin, op. cit., p. 10.
33 Guangxi Zhuangzu zizhiqu tongjiju, *Guangxi tongji nianjian 1994* [Guangxi Statistical Yearbook 1994] Zhongguo tongji chubanshe, Beijing, p. 112.
34 Guangxi Zhuangzu zizhiqu tongjiju, op. cit., p. 111.
35 Yu Pimin, op. cit., pp. 10f.
36 Yu Pimin, op. cit., p. 11.
37 *Guangxi dashiji*, op. cit., p. 129.
38 Yu Pimin, op. cit., p. 10.
39 Jin Yifei (ed.) *2000 nian de Guangxi: mai xiang ershiyi shiji de yanjiu* [Guangxi in the Year 2000: Research on the March into the Twenty-First Century], Guangxi minzu chubanshe, Nanning, 1988, p. 470.
40 *Guide to Investment in Guangxi*, Foreign Investment Promotion Commission of Guangxi Zhuang Autonomous Province, 1994.
41 Yu Pimin, op. cit., p. 11.
42 Yu Pimin, op. cit., p. 11.
43 Yu Pimin, op. cit., p. 11.
44 Ma Biao, op. cit., p. 237.
45 Dorothy Solinger, op. cit., pp. 241ff.
46 Li Changjiang, 'Yiye chunfeng hua qian shu: xi kan Guangxi de touzi re' [One night of spring winds lets a thousand flowers bloom: a pleased looked at Guangxi's investment fever], in Yu Fanglin (ed.), op.cit. p. 188.
47 Feng Jing, 'Guangxi: Southwest China's access to the sea', *Beijing Review* 38, no. 30, 24 July 1995, pp. 14–18.
48 Du Xin and He Ping, 'Guangxi: Daxinan de chuhai tongdao' [Guangxi: a passage to the sea for Greater Southwest China], *Liaowang* no. 1, 1992, reprinted in Yu Fanglin *et al.* (eds), op. cit. pp. 132f.
49 Du Xin and He Ping, op. cit., pp. 132f.
50 Du Xin and He Ping, op. cit., pp. 132f.
51 Interviews in Guangxi in April–May 1995.
52 Li Changjiang, op. cit., p. 193.
53 Brantly Womack, 'Sino-Vietnamese border trade: the edge of normalization', *Asian Survey* XXXIV, no. 6, June 1994, pp. 495–512.
54 *Guangxi tongji nianjian* 1990 and 1991, *op. cit.*, p. 381.
55 Guangxi Zhuang zizhiqu bianjing jingji maoyi guanliju [Guangxi Border Trade Administration].
56 Womack, *op. cit.*, p. 500.
57 *Guangxi tongji nianjian*, *op. cit.*, 1993 (p. 250) and 1994 (p. 322).
58 Womack, *op. cit.*, p. 500.
59 Zou Zhang (ed.) *Bianjing maoyi yu touzi zhinan* [Guide to border trade and investment], Zhongguo wuzi chubanshe, Beijing, 1993, pp. 23–4.
60 Zou Zhang (ed.), *op. cit.*, p. 24.
61 Guangxi Zhuangzu zizhiqu bianjing jingji maoyi guanliju, *Fazhan zhong de Guangxi bianmao* [The Developing Border Trade of Guangxi], mimeographed document, no publisher, no place, June 1994, p. 6.
62 Guangxiqu zhengfu nongcun fazhan yanjiu zhongxin 'bianmao' ketizu 'Fazhan bianjing maoyi, zhenxing difang jingji' [Develop border trade, enliven the local economy], in Guangxiqu zhengfu nongcun fazhan yanjiu zhongxin (ed.) *Gaige*

– kaifa – zou xiang shichang – Guangxi nongye de xiwang [Reform, Opening, Towards the Market – Hope for Guangxi's Agriculture], Guangxi renmin chubanshe, Nanning, 1995, p. 537.

63 Guangxi Zhuangzu zizhiqu bianjing jingji maoyi guanliju, *op. cit.*, p. 1.

64 Huang Yushou, 'Feiteng de bianjing maoyi' [Booming border trade], in Yu Fanglin (ed.), *op. cit.*, p. 263.

REFERENCES

Dangdai Zhongguo congshu bianjibu (ed.) *Dangdai Zhongguo de Guangxi* [Guangxi in Contemporary China] 2 volumes, Dangdai Zhongguo chubanshe, Beijing, 1992.

Feng Jing, 'Guangxi: Southwest China's access to the sea', *Beijing Review* 38, no. 30, 24 July 1995, pp. 14–18.

Guangxi nianjian she (ed.) *Guangxi nianjian* [Guangxi Yearbook], Guangxi nianjian she, Nanning, various years.

Guangxi Zhuangzu zizhiqu tongjiju (ed.) *Guangxi tongji nianjian* [Guangxi Statistical Yearbook], Zhongguo tongji chubanshe, Beijing, various years.

Guangxi Zhuangzu zizhiqu tongjiju *et al.* (eds) *Guangxi gongye sishi nian* [Forty Years of Guangxi's Industry], Guangxi renmin chubanshe, Nanning, 1990.

Guangxiqu zhengfu nongcun fazhan yanjiu zhongxin (ed.) *Gaige – kaifa – zou xiang shichang – Guangxi nongye de xiwang* [Reform, Opening, Towards the Market – Hope for Guangxi's Agriculture], Guangxi renmin chubanshe, Nanning, 1995.

Foreign Investment Promotion Commission of Guangxi Zhuang Autonomous Region, *Guide to Investment in Guangxi*, Foreign Opening Administrative Office of Guangxi Zhuang Autonomous Region, Nanning, 1994.

Jin Yifei (ed.) *2000 nian de Guangxi – mai xiang ershiyi shiji de yanjiu* [Guangxi in the Year 2000 – Research on its March towards the Twenty-First Century], Guangxi minzu chubanshe, Nanning, 1988.

Ma Biao *et al.* (eds) *Guangxi chanye jiegou yu jingji fazhan zhanlue* [Guangxi's Sectoral Structure and Economic Development Strategy], Guangxi kexue jishu chubanshe, Nanning, 1992.

Dorothy J. Solinger, *Provincial Government and Political Integration in Southwest China, 1949–1954*, University of California Press, Berkeley, 1977.

Sun Keyong (ed.) *Guangxi chanye jingji yanjiu* [Research on Guangxi's Production and Economy], Guangxi shifan daxue chubanshe, Guilin, 1990.

Qin Lixun, *Fazhan Guangxi jingji zonghengtan* [A Comprehensive Talk on Developing Guangxi's Economy], Guangxi minzu chubanshe, Nanning, 1990.

Carlyle A. Thayer, 'Sino-Vietnamese relations: the interplay of ideology and national interest', *Asian Survey* XXXIV, no. 6, June 1994, pp. 513–28.

Brantly Womack, 'Sino-Vietnamese border trade: the edge of normalization', *Asian Survey* XXXIV, no. 6, June 1994, pp. 495–512.

Ye Shunzan, 'Guangxi cities: new strategies for in-between provinces', in R. Yin-Wang Kwok, William Parish and Anthony Gar-On Yeh with Xu Yueqiang (eds) *Chinese Urban Reform: What Model Now?*, M.E. Sharpe, New York, 1991.

Yu Fanglin *et al.* (eds) *Guangxi chao: Bagui dadi gaige kaifang de lilun he shixian* [The Guangxi Tide: Theory and Practice of Openness and Reform], Guangxi renmin chubanshe, Nanning, 1993.

Yu Pimin, 'Guanyu woqu yong hao zizhifa he kaifang zhengce de sikao' [Thoughts on how our province should make good use of the autonomy law and opening policies], *Guangxi minzu yanjiu* no. 1, 1989, pp. 10–15.

Hainan Province

GENERAL

GDP (billion *yuan* renminbi)	33.10
GDP annual growth rate	11.90
as % national average	100.85
GDP per capita	4,644.41
as % national average	123.97
Gross Value Agricultural Output (billion *yuan* renminbi)	17.00
Gross Value Industrial Output (billion *yuan* renminbi)	16.50

POPULATION

Population (million)	7.11
Natural growth rate (per 1,000)	20.77

WORKFORCE

Total workforce (million)	3.36
Employment by activity (%)	
primary industry	60.90
secondary industry	5.63
tertiary industry	12.80
Employment by sector (% of provincial population)	
urban	18.86
rural	28.33
state sector	13.67
collective sector	5.86
private sector	4.42
foreign-funded sector	0.46

WAGES

Average annual wage (*yuan* renminbi)	4,488
Growth rate in real wage	4.40

PRICES

CPI annual rise (%)	26.70
Service price index rise (%)	37.40
Per capita consumption (*yuan* renminbi)	1,149
as % national average	66.15
Urban disposable income per capita	3,920
as % national average	112.13
Rural per capita income	1,305
as % national average	106.88

FOREIGN TRADE AND INVESTMENT

Total foreign trade (US$ billion)	2.76
% provincial GDP	71.87
Exports (US$ billion)	0.953
Imports (US$ billion)	1.81
Realised foreign capital (US$ million)	936.09
% provincial GDP	24.37

EDUCATION

University enrolments	11,719
% national average	70.58
Secondary school enrolments (million)	0.30
% national average	100.07
Primary school enrolments (million)	1.10
% national average	144.90

Notes: All statistics are for 1994 and all growth rates are for 1994 over 1993 and are adapted from *Zhongguo tongji nianjian 1995* [Statistical Yearbook of China 1995], Zhongguo tongji chubanshe, Beijing, 1995 as reformulated and presented in *Provincial China* no. 1 March 1996, pp. 34ff.

Hainan Province

Guangdong

Qiongzhou Strait

Beibu Gulf

Haikou

Yangpu

Nandu

Jiang

Wanquan River

Qionghai

Basuo

Tongza

Wuzhi
Mountain

Sanya

South China Sea

3 Hainan
Communal politics and the struggle for identity

Feng Chongyi and David S.G. Goodman

One of the more remarkable features of the reform era has been the establishment of Hainan Province and its development as a Special Economic Zone (SEZ). The announcement of Hainan Province in 1988 was the establishment of the first new provincial-level unit to be created in the People's Republic of China since the Cultural Revolution, and effectively since 1952.[1] Largely as a result of preferential policy from Beijing and even allowing for the fairly low point of departure, Hainan Province has experienced high economic growth rates as well as a high rate of foreign investment. A *laissez-faire* economy has emerged which has experienced some spectacular scandals, including a well-known apparently officially sanctioned speculation in the resale of foreign vehicles to the mainland during 1984.[2]

Despite Hainan's reputations as China's 'new frontier' and a kind of 'wild tropical south' – which certainly have some justification – in many ways it is the achievement of provincial status that has been the most startling feature of its development in the reform era. The creation of a Hainan Province would appear to be the fulfilment of a long-cherished local desire for greater autonomy. Throughout the twentieth century there has been a fairly strong movement in Hainan for separate status within China: that Hainan should be a separate province in its own right, and not, as was the case before 1988, a part of Guangdong Province and subordinated to Guangzhou. It is not that Hainanese have not regarded themselves as Chinese – this has not been a movement for independence – but rather a feeling that the interests of Hainan are not necessarily best served by the island's administrative subservience to Guangdong Province.

There is much to support a quasi-colonial interpretation of Hainan's relationship to Guangdong Province and the mainland before 1988. Rich in strategic resources – notably iron ore, rubber, timber and salt – before 1988 its economy was almost purely extractive with no processing or manufacturing industry. Hainan had productive mines, but no iron and steel industry; huge rubber plantations but no associated enterprises; vast cultivated forests but no timber-processing industry. In a scenario familiar to any student of underdevelopment Hainan's agricultural and mineral production all went to supply the rest of China and its economic pattern was determined from and largely by either Beijing or Guangzhou. Thus although Hainan is sub-tropical, almost no tropical crops, other than rubber, were cultivated there in any significant quantity before 1988. Instead, Hainan's peasants were required to cultivate rice in excess in order to feed the large additional numbers of mainlanders who came to the island with the establishment of the PRC. After 1949 Hainan's politics became and remained dominated by cadres from the mainland, and particularly Guangdong, who supplanted the relatively numerous and well-organised (from well before 1949) local Hainanese communists.

However, the achievement of provincial status has brought neither political stability to Hainan, nor solved the problems arising from tensions between Hainanese and other Chinese. The decade to 1995 saw four major leadership changes, accompanied by organisational and policy discontinuities, with the latter in particular related to the island's development strategy. In spite of the remarkable economic growth and liberalisation of the provincial era, many of the issues that dominated the pre-1980s era have remained, become more acute, or taken on new forms. One source of uncertainty has been the ambiguities in the relationship between Hainan's leadership and superior authorities on the mainland. For over a decade no leader of Hainan has been able to successfully manage that relationship, with events elsewhere in the Chinese political system having a disproportionate and deleterious effect, not least on their careers within a relatively short period.[3]

Another, equally as fundamental, source of uncertainty in provincial Hainan is the tension among the island's different communities, and their competing visions of Hainan's identity and autonomy. In the post-1949 era a strong sense of history, ethnic identity, linguistic difference, as well as fairly specific positions in Hainan's economic geography and the island's political economy have combined to create five largely self-identifying and self-contained communities. Each of these communities has deep social roots as well as a view of how the island province should develop.

Hainan in 1995 had a population of approximately 7 million. There are five readily identifiable and fairly homogeneous communities – four of about 1 million people each and one of about 2 million – as well as several minor communities. These communities have been shaped almost completely by the experiences of the post-1949 period, and their impact on the inter-generational transfer of attitudes and values. Each would regard itself as Hainanese, but in different ways and with varied consequences.

The year 1949 is a clear dividing marker of community for many on Hainan. Among those families who can claim Hainanese nativity as of 1949 there are two major and several smaller communities. The largest is the about 2 million Hainanese, native-born speakers of Hainanese who are the descendants of fairly constant Han migration to Hainan over several centuries. The other major native (as of 1949) community are the million Li, the largest group of the island's earliest non-Han inhabitants. The smaller communities include half a million speakers of *Lingaohua* (similar to *Zhuangyu*); 400,000 speakers of *Zhanzhouhua* (a variety of Cantonese); 100,000 speakers of *Junhua* (similar to Southwest Mandarin); and about 60,000 Miao (most of whom live with and have been partially assimilated by the Li) and other non-Han peoples. The non-native (as of 1949) communities include about 1 million 'Old Mainlanders', those who first came to Hainan during the early 1950s; and 800,000 or so 'New Mainlanders', those attracted in and since the 1980s by economic reform. The final readily identifiable community is that of the million or so Overseas Chinese: those who returned from Southeast Asia in the 1950s and 1960s, and their families; as well as the families of Overseas Chinese dependants.

Hainan's provincial era has to some considerable extent been determined by the interactions among and between the island's five major communities. It may not be that social and political tensions, or the imperatives of the wider environment, will result in any movement for or realisation of any greater Hainan independence or autonomy. Nonetheless, an understanding of the development of competing elites and social trends is a necessary basis for interpretations of Hainan's future, not least as the contest for the definition of that future increases.

THE SEARCH FOR PROVINCIAL STATUS

In both the imperial period and during the twentieth century Hainan's experience has been dominated by its quasi-colonial relationship with the mainland. Hainan's political and economic development was determined elsewhere often out of interests self-evidently at odds with those of Hainan and its population. Most obviously that was the case in the twentieth century with the subordination of a successful local Hainan communist movement to mainland interests, and after 1949, a deliberate policy of economic under-development to ensure the supply of the island's primary production to the mainland.

Crucially, policies designed to ensure Hainan's political and economic dependence on Guangdong and the mainland were implemented and the colonial message reinforced through the importation of large numbers of non-native migrants from the mainland. As was the case in the colonies of other earlier imperial powers, policy and direction were not only determined elsewhere (in this case, predominantly Guangzhou) but leadership was exercised by officials who came to the island on relatively short appointments, did not speak the local language, and whose points of political reference were far removed from Hainan. Moreover, as in French colonies, the regime was bolstered by substantial popular migration, so that after the mid-1950s about one-third of the island's population growth was families who as of 1949 had not been on Hainan. Unsurprisingly, there has been considerable resentment among the native Hainanese population and communities.

Hainan under the Empire

Well before 1949, let alone 1988, Hainan had developed reputations for separateness and multi-culturalism. Throughout the Imperial period it was regarded not only as a place of exile and migration but also one of rebellion. Indeed the two were at least partially connected, since the frequent Li rebellions led the Empire to send new troops and pacifying forces, as well as their families and camp followers to restore and maintain order.[4] Successive waves of migration, from either Imperial strength or Imperial weakness – when migrants also came to Hainan seeking refuge from disorder – shaped Hainan's social composition. Though the migrants all regarded themselves as Han Chinese, they nonetheless rapidly assimilated elements of local culture and came to regard themselves as Hainanese.

The original aboriginal people on Hainan have been called the Li by the Han Chinese since the Tang Dynasty. There is widespread disagreement among anthropologists about their origins. Some believe that the Li were a tribe of the 'Southern Yue' who migrated to the island from the area of Guangdong and Guangxi during the Neolithic Age. Others argue that the Li are a South Pacific community because they share common characteristics in lineages, and customs such as decorative body tattoos and picture-weaving.[5] As the Han Chinese moved into Hainan they occupied the northern and the eastern plains areas, and drove the Li into the centre and western – and more mountainous – areas of the island.

In addition to the Li, there are another thirty-seven officially recognised ethnic minorities on the island, notably the Miao and the Hui. There are about 60,000 Miao, who are the descendants of a special unit of soldiers sent from Guangxi by a Ming Dynasty Emperor to put down a rebellion of the Li. Ironically, they were forced to live alongside the Li in the mountain areas, and eventually came to adopt Li customs and religion.[6] The less than 7,000 Hui are Austronesian-Chamic-speaking Muslims of Arabian origin, who migrated to Hainan from Vietnam in the twelfth century. They live in seclusion in two villages in the south of the island near Sanya, maintaining their religion and lifestyle, and rarely marrying outside of their villages.[7]

Imperial rule of Hainan started during the Western Han Dynasty (206 BC to AD 24) and Hainan was formally incorporated into the Empire in 110 BC, when the Hanwu Emperor established Zhuya Jun and Daner Jun as the island's two prefectures. Since then thousands have migrated to the island from the mainland as refugees particularly in the thirteenth century when the Song Dynasty fell to the troops of Genghis Khan, and in the seventeenth century when the Ming Dynasty was conquered by the Manchus.

Han Chinese on Hainan have their own distinct culture. They speak Hainanese, similar to southern Fujianese languages but entirely different from Mandarin. The island's proximity to Southeast Asia, and their intensive communications and interactions, have led to some Malay and English vocabulary being incorporated in the daily speech of Hainanese villagers.[8]

While the Li have been assimilated to some extent by the Han, the Han Chinese on Hainan have come to share some of the religious beliefs of the Li.[9] Moreover, Hainan is popularly well known for its defiance, heretical views and 'exile culture': characteristics consistent with Hainan's physical distance from the mainland and political distance from the Emperor.

Hainanese are very conscious of their distance from Beijing, and indeed mainland and mainstream China. In their minds, distance explains all the differences between Hainan and mainland China. Hainanese popularly believe that Chinese central government always, whatever its complexion, discriminates against the island. In their view, relations between Hainan and the capital have rarely been harmonious.

Central rule over Hainan was very uncertain until the sixth century when Lady Xian – a powerful tribal chief of the Southern Yue[10] – persuaded chiefs of the Li tribes to accept tutelage. In the Tang Dynasty, five prefectures were set up on the island, including Qiongzhou at the northern end and Yazhou at the southern tip, hence the island's abbreviated name of Qiongya. The present name of the island is Hainan, literarily the island in the south over the sea, and is derived probably from *Hainandao*, the hierarchically highest administrative unit set up on the island by the Qing Dynasty in 1730.

Under the Empire when those who lived in South China were generally regarded as 'southern barbarians' by central government and northerners, Hainan was regarded as 'the remotest corner of the earth' – suitable only for the exile of criminals. In the eighteenth century a high-ranking official of the Qing Dynasty reported to the Emperor that Hainan island was so barbarous and far away that 'it was a waste of money to build cities, schools, government offices, and granaries there'.[11]

In reply, Hainanese like to stress their cultural achievements, particularly in the highest Imperial examinations. Despite the obvious impediments to participation, there were 105 successful candidates from Hainan during its 1,300-year Imperial history: 2.6 per cent of the national total, disproportionately high given that Hainan's population was only half a per cent of the national total.[12] Two Ming Dynasty officials of Hainan origin are particularly famous in China even today. One is Qiu Jun, head of the Ministry of Rites (in charge of education and the selection of officials), head of the Ministry of Revenue and teacher of the Emperor. Among his other achievements in history, philosophy and economics, he is believed by many to be the first in the world to advance the labour theory of value.[13] The other is Hai Rui, famed for being an exceptionally upright official as well as the subject of the play that had a central role in the emergence of the Cultural Revolution.[14]

The CCP in Hainan before 1949

When the People's Liberation Army (PLA) came to 'liberate' Hainan in 1950 it enjoyed the substantial assistance of the local Qiongya Column of the Chinese Communist Party and its 25,000 guerrillas.[15] Hainanese communists were and have remained proud that the Qiongya Revolutionary Base Area was the only CCP base area anywhere in the country that had a sustained presence from 1927 right through to 1950. In fighting against both Nationalist and Japanese forces, usually without any help from or contact with the CCP central leadership, the local communists in Hainan lost more than 20,000 people.[16] However, the significance of the Qiongya Column and its pre-decessors is not simply its heroism but its localism, and the conflicts that resulted with mainland CCP organisations.

A communist organisation in Hainan was founded by native Hainan communists in June 1926. The first Secretary was Wang Wenming, a native Hainanese who had joined the CCP in 1924 when he was a student at Shanghai University. In June 1927 as the Nationalist–Communist United Front broke down, Wang Wenming was joined by Yang Shanji, another native Hainanese who had joined the CCP at Moscow Eastern Labour University in 1924, and they established the Qiongya CCP Special Committee, followed shortly after by the 'Qiongya Punitive Revolutionary Army'. By the end of 1927 the local CCP had established several bases, with 17,000 members organised in 400 branches.[17]

From the late 1920s through to 1949 directives from the CCP Central Committee or the Guangdong Provincial Committee proved disastrous to the Hainan communists, and relationships were never good between the local Hainan cadres and their mainland superiors. In July 1929 the Hainan Special Committee was decimated when it moved to the urban areas under an order from the CCP Guangdong Provincial Committee. However, Wang Wenming defied the order and established a new base in Murui Mountain, where he was succeeded on his death from disease in January 1930 by Feng Baiju. Feng Baiju organised the Independent Division of the Red Army – with its own military hospital and military school – and the much-feted Red Detachment of Women.

Attempts to seize Haikou, the island's capital in 1930, under orders from the CCP Guangdong Committee, and the witch-hunt against 'Anti-Bolsheviks' in 1932 under direction from the CCP Central Committee, further weakened Feng Baiju's base. By early 1933 under sustained Nationalist pressure, Feng Baiju was down to his last twenty-six cadres. War with Japan saw Feng Baiju's base redesignated as the 'The Fourth District Independent Team of Guangdong People's Self-defend Regiment against Japan' (for which they were paid 800 *yuan* per person per month by the Nationalist government), and later (in March 1939) as 'The Qiongya Independent Guerrilla Regiment of Guangdong Province', and still later (in late 1944) as 'The Qiongya Independent Guerrilla Column of Guangdong Province'.

Feng's forces grew rapidly and received substantial support, particularly from Overseas Hainanese, who even organised their own 'Qiongya Overseas Chinese Home-going Service Regiment' – over 240 people who joined the communist guerrillas. The communists also won over the Li, whose support was essential to survival in the mountains. In 1943 the Li and the CCP combined in an anti-Nationalist government revolt. Baisha County in the heart of the Wuzhi Range was secured as one of the largest base areas. By the end of the Sino-Japanese War the Qiongya Column was responsible for a base area covering half of Hainan's population.

Despite the success of the local CCP organisation, in its negotiations with the Nationalists nationally the CCP was preparing to sacrifice its southern bases, including Hainan. In February 1946 the Qiongya Column received orders to send some 2,000 cadres to Shandong and to otherwise demobilise. There was considerable reluctance from the Qiongya Column to comply, and in August and again October, Feng Baiju and his troops were ordered to withdraw to Vietnam.[18] Faced by effectively local intransigence the CCP Central Committee had no choice but to permit the Qiongya Column to continue on its own.

In 1949 the Qiongya Column's maintained presence aided the CCP's national aspirations. The presence of the Qiongya Column had earlier made Taiwan a more attractive proposition to the Nationalists looking for an offshore base. Moreover, when the CCP forces decided to invade Hainan, the Qiongya Column was able to provide invaluable support to the military operation, given the difficulties of crossing the Qiongzhou Straits (between Hainan and the mainland) and attacking an island protected by some 100,000 Nationalist troops, a fleet and air forces. Interestingly, not least in terms of later developments, at the end of the Hainan Campaign in April 1950 the Qiongya Column and its cadres were popularly welcomed as the leading 'liberators' rather than the PLA troops. Alongside the pictures that were hung of Marx, Engels, Lenin and Stalin, people in Hainan added a picture of Feng Baiju. Many were more familiar with Chairman Feng than Chairman Mao.[19]

The movement to establish a Hainan Province

In and after 1949 many Hainanese hoped that a Hainan Province separate from Guangdong would be established, permitting greater autonomy. Even in 1949 it was not an overly radical idea. It had been suggested by Pan Chun during the late Qing, and by Sun Yat-sen during the early Republican Period. Chiang Kai-shek also made arrangements to establish a Hainan Province, but its Preparatory Committee collapsed with the Nationalist government defeat of 1949.[20]

With the establishment of the PRC Feng Baiju and the local CCP movement might have thought that their proposal to establish a Hainan Province might be well received. However, the CCP Central Committee's accommodation of the Hainanese guerrillas – Feng Baiju had been appointed as Hainan's leading CCP cadre – rapidly disappeared in a welter of mutual suspicion and mistrust. Increasing numbers of Hainan's local cadres were replaced by members of the 'Great Southbound Army' and its supportive Southbound Work Team, sent from the mainland to control Hainan at Beijing's direction. Resentment led to open complaints by local communists during the Hundred Flowers Movement of 1957, and even an armed uprising in Lingao County in late 1957, which in turn led to the repression of Feng Baiju's so-called 'independent kingdom' and the removal from office of most native cadres above the county level.[21]

The failure of the movement to establish a separate Hainan Province proved entirely counter-productive. Hainan's abundant natural resources proved no comparative advantage once the island was out of favour with the state. During 1950–80 Hainan's economy was exploited almost solely to the benefit of the mainland. There was little attempt from either central or Guangdong governments, where no Hainanese worked in key positions, to develop processing industries or infrastructural projects on Hainan. All strategic resources – iron ore, rubber, timber, and salt – were directly controlled by Beijing or Guangdong and output was allocated to other parts of China for the development of industry elsewhere. Hainanese for their part were required almost exclusively to cultivate grain, particularly rice, to feed the mainland immigrants and the mainland population, rather than the tropical crops more suited to the environment. In industry, Hainan's productive iron mines (unlike the rest of Guangdong Province) developed no local iron and steel industry; its rubber plantations and forests had no associated processing industries or enterprises; and its 1,528 kilometres of coastline had only one harbour for a ship greater than 10,000 tonnes, and that (at Basuo) built exclusively for the transport of iron ore from Shilu to the mainland.

During 1952–80 total state investment in Hainan was only 4.3 billion *yuan* RMB, less than one-tenth of state investment in Shanghai's Baoshan Iron and Steel Plant. Moreover, most state investment in Hainan went into the extraction of rubber, iron ore and other raw materials for the mainland, leaving little to develop the infrastructure of the local economy. In 1980, the level of economic development in Hainan remained very low: the gross value of industrial and agricultural output was only 1.7 billion *yuan* RMB, less than a well-developed county on the mainland. There was only one small airport for both military and civilian use, suitable only for the small An-24 aircraft, with four flights a day to Guangzhou and Zhanjiang; more than half Hainan's factories in the light industrial sector were completely unautomated; and Hainan's urban population was less than 9 per cent of the total, the same as in the 1950s.[22]

Almost unannounced the island suddenly became one of the central government's special projects during the reform era. In 1980 the State Council authorised Hainan's local government to utilise the same policies granted to the Shenzhen and Zhuhai SEZs in their economic relations with the rest of the world. In 1983 the State Council and the Central Committee of the CCP jointly published 'A Summary of the Forum on Speeding Up the Development of Hainan Island' which made Hainan a *de facto* SEZ. Hainan was afforded preferential treatment by the central government more for political than economic reasons. One was a strategy to unify the PRC and Taiwan peacefully. Within China there had been an understandable tendency to compare Hainan and Taiwan, since they were the country's only two large islands. Hainan's backwardness was clearly an embarrassment to Beijing in the comparisons of the 1980s. During the 1940s Taiwan's level of economic development had been only slightly higher than that of Hainan. By the 1980s the per capita Gross National Product (GNP) of Taiwan was about twenty times higher than that of Hainan, despite the latter's richer natural resources and much smaller population.

The Guangdong Provincial Government appointed Lei Yu to lead Hainan in August 1982. Through a largely successful high-profile campaign he attempted to improve Hainan's infrastructure and educational facilities within five years. However, he rapidly came to realise that the lack of capital, and of an adequate institutional framework, specifically the absence of provincial status, were brakes on what could be achieved. His attempts to solve the lack of capital were to lead to his downfall and the further shelving of plans for a Hainan Province. The 1983 Forum on Hainan's development adopted policy including provision for the island to import state-controlled consumer goods, including cars and household durables. These imported goods could not be resold to the mainland, but there was no regulation that forbade Hainan selling 'secondhand' goods to the mainland. In early 1984 Lei Yu and the Hainan leadership began cautiously to deregulate the trade in imported cars between the island and the mainland. The car trade in Hainan began to grow rapidly during 1984, until September when Lei Yu was warned by his superiors to slow things down. Eventually, in November 1984 Lei Yu was summoned to Guangzhou, asked to explain his actions, and made the subject of an official investigation. Reporting in March 1985 the punishment was severe: un-resold vehicles on the island were confiscated; Lei Yu and others were dismissed and disciplined; Hainan's preferential policy in foreign trade was rescinded.

Despite the setbacks of Lei Yu's policy, Deng Xiaoping and other central leaders were apparently still committed to Hainan's rapid development.[23] In late 1986 and early 1987, Zhao Ziyang dispatched a number of senior investigative teams to Hainan, all of which recommended that Hainan should become a separate province and be granted SEZ status and functions. The proposal was approved by Zhao Ziyang, Hu Yaobang and Deng Xiaoping, who first revealed the idea publicly when talking to guests from the then Yugoslavia on 12 June 1987: 'We are setting up a larger Special Economic Zone, namely the Hainan Special Economic Zone'.[24] On 13 April 1988 the Chinese government formally established Hainan as both a province and a SEZ.

The decision was essentially to develop Hainan as a testing ground for central government to try bolder economic and political reforms. The leaders of the CCP believed that Hainan was expendable. It was such a small economy, accounting for only half a per cent of the nation's GNP, and its physical separation from the mainland meant that it would not do much harm to China as a whole if experimental reform on the island led to unpleasant results or even chaos. On the other hand, unlike the other four SEZs which were all small coastal cities, Hainan's experience of reforms could be more relevant to China as a whole. A comprehensive social-economic entity, with a per capita GNP at around the national average level and 80 per cent of its population engaged in agriculture or agriculture-related activities, it replicated some of the whole country's key features.

HAINAN'S COMMUNITIES

Hainan's economic geography may offer comparisons with many other provinces, but its political culture and social composition probably do not. With the exception of the western and non-Han-dominated autonomous regions of Tibet and Xinjiang, Hainan is one of the few areas of China where there have been and remain entrenched social as well as political conflicts between local and national interests.[25] In part this aspect of Hainan's political culture is a function not only of its quasi-colonial experience but also of the various communities, and the differences among them, that have emerged from the experience of the post-1949 years. In particular, there is a fundamental divide between those whose point of reference for Hainan, its politics and future is either Guangdong or Beijing, and those who regard Hainan as the primary reference point.

It is possible to identify five major and politically significant communities in Hainan – in addition to the Hainanese, these are the Old Mainlanders, the New Mainlanders, the Li and the Overseas Chinese communities – each of which has a relatively high degree of self-awareness and identity. Sense of community is reinforced by economic, political, social and physical location in Hainan. The parochialism of communities is necessarily not absolute, nonetheless the extent to which one of the island's communities is not involved in activities reserved for one of the other communities is quite remarkable. The existence of a mainlander-based ruling class through governmental affairs is perhaps less surprising than the virtual exclusion of Hainanese from senior political positions. More surprising still is the extent to which each community has its own home base and economic activity. For example, most Hainanese remain as land-based peasants and few are involved in the new industries that have emerged with reform. The Old Mainlanders have their social base in governmental agencies, the state sector and particularly state farms. The New Mainlanders are almost exclusively involved in the new industries and enterprises occasioned by the reform era, and live overwhelmingly in Haikou.

Old Mainlanders

About 30 per cent – 1.8 million people – of the 1995 population of Hainan Province are mainland immigrants. According to the 1990 census migration from the mainland accounted for one-third of population growth in Hainan during 1950–89.[26] As in the pre-1949 eras, so during the period of the PRC

Hainan has evolved through migration from the mainland. Since 1949 there have been two significant waves of mainlander migration to Hainan. The first came in the early 1950s with the establishment of the PRC. The second wave was forty years later as the impact of reform made Hainan attractive to the economically adventurous.

The early 1950s provided the migrants and their descendants who may now be identified as 'Old Mainlanders', though perhaps 'Early PRC migrants' would be a more accurate descriptor. During the early 1950s there were four major groups of migrants from the mainland to Hainan. The largest group were the ex-servicemen who were sent to or who stayed behind in Hainan – after both the Hainan Campaign of 1950, and the Korean War – to open up 'virgin soil' for tropical crops of strategic significance, rubber in particular and overwhelmingly.[27] The second group were members of the 'Southbound Work Team' and their families who were sent to serve as cadres in the new 'liberated area'. The third group were technicians and skilled workers, mostly from Shanghai and Wuhan, sent to develop industry on the island, the Shilu Iron Mine in particular. The fourth group were the Nationalist troops left behind in Hainan at the end of the final Civil War. During the 1960s thousands of school graduates were sent 'up to the mountains and down to the countryside' for re-education in Hainan, but most of them returned to the mainland when they were allowed to do so starting in the late 1970s.

The state farms and mining are the two key areas of economic activity for the mainland migrants of the 1950s. The first state farm in Hainan was established in 1952 by the First Forest Division of the PLA which set 8,000 soldiers and officers to grow rubber. By 1966 there were seventy-one state farms of this kind in Hainan, which in total employed more than 162,000 workers. They were further expanded and reorganised into seven divisions under the jurisdiction of the Production and Construction Corps of the Guangzhou Military Region during the Cultural Revolution. In the reform era these state farms have diversified: they have adopted a policy designed to develop a range of businesses other than simply the tasks of growing rubber trees and producing raw rubber. As at the end of 1992, there were 167 farms and 421 industrial enterprises with some half a million workers under the jurisdiction of the Hainan Agriculture Reclamation Bureau Corporation,[28] as well as their subordinate plants, research institutes, commercial companies, schools and hospitals. This conglomerate stretched across nineteen counties and cities, accounting for one-sixth of the total population and a quarter of the arable land of the island.[29]

The Hainan Agriculture Reclamation Bureau Corporation suffers from the syndrome of low efficiency common to state sector enterprises in China, even though all its economic activities are currently managed on the basis of contract. By the end of 1990, the group had overspent by 300 million *yuan* RMB, owed 88 million *yuan* RMB in salaries to its workers, and had overdrawn accounts of over 1 billion *yuan* RMB in the state banks. By 1993 the deficit had grown to 88 million *yuan* RMB, and the accumulated debt had climbed to more than 2 billion *yuan* RMB. In the mean time, the position of the state farms in the provincial economy had declined sharply. In 1978 state farms had provided 39 per cent of Hainan's industrial and agricultural output value and 28 per cent of its GNP. By 1993 these shares had dropped to 17 per cent and 11 per cent respectively.[30]

Old Mainlanders live mainly on the state farms and in the cities. They are predominantly workers in the state sector, working either on the state farms or in other former or current state sector enterprises. Necessarily their children attend schools associated with the state farms and heavy industrial enterprises, where they are taught by Old Mainlanders. They also, by definition, are to be found throughout the party-state system at all levels, government and tertiary education. However, a key tension in the 1990s has been that between Old Mainlanders and New Mainlanders, as the latter, often more qualified and experienced than the former, have challenged their established position in the party-state system and the professions.

New Mainlanders

The mainland migrants who came during the 1980s and 1990s were very different from their 1950s predecessors. Whereas migration from mainland China to Hainan during the 1950s to 1970s was by and large at the direction of the state, the migrants since the early 1980s have crossed the Qiongzhou Strait on a voluntary basis: drawn by the attractions of the market-place and the easy climate for politics compared to the mainland, and especially North China, rather than being allocated to Hainan by administrative fiat. 'Wealth and Freedom' is said to be their banner,[31] and one analysis of the New Mainland immigrants to Hainan puts the possibilities of economic and political freedom as the number one factor drawing them to the island.[32]

The first of these New Mainlanders started to come in 1983 when the central government first granted preferential policies to develop Hainan. However, most came after 1987 when central government announced the establishment of Hainan Province and Hainan SEZ. '100,000 qualified personnel flood into Hainan' was a sensational news headline in China during 1988.[33] For a number of years after the establishment of Hainan Province and the SEZ about 40,000 people migrated officially to the island from the mainland every year, more than half of them taking up positions in Hainan as entrepreneurs, technicians, managers or administrators.[34] Those cadres, professionals, entrepreneurs and graduates coming to Hainan through official channels have been extremely well placed to make the most for themselves from the rapid development of government and business.

The New Mainlanders form a significant elite group on the island, and certainly regard themselves in that light. A significant majority of New Mainlanders are college-educated, socially active and influential, and in many ways there are resonances between their profiles and behaviours, on the one hand, and those of the former British colonisers in Hong Kong, Singapore and

Malaysia, on the other. Most New Mainlanders would never dream of learning the local language and there is an observable tendency to regard native Hainanese as distinctly lower class.

In addition to those who have migrated formally, about 100,000 'blindly floating labourers' – those who have just crossed the Qiongzhou Straits with no guarantee of work – are estimated to have travelled to Hainan looking for work every year; 200,000 such migrants landed in Hainan in the first quarter of 1989 alone. Most migrants to Hainan were from Guangdong, Guangxi or Sichuan provinces. The number of migrants from Guangdong to Hainan was surprisingly large, accounting for 40 per cent of the migrants from the mainland in the period 1985–90.[35] However, a significant number of the New Mainlanders were also Democracy Movement activists who fled the aftermath of the Beijing Massacre in June 1989 in North China to seek refuge to some extent in Hainan.

The New Mainlanders are concentrated in Haikou, the provincial capital, taking positions in government, universities, research institutes and new enterprises. Given Hainan's policy of importing 'qualified personnel' many of the New Mainlanders have been able to secure desirable positions before leaving the mainland. The restructuring of Hainan government, the reopening of Hainan University, the restructuring and expanding of Hainan Teacher's College and Hainan Provincial Party School, and the establishment of new research institutes, new research centres and new firms have created golden opportunities for the New Mainlanders to seek positions, often in competition with Old Mainlanders and Hainanese.

The reopening of Hainan University is a particular source of conflict between New Mainlanders and Hainanese. New Mainlanders have led the recent redevelopment of Hainan University, claiming as they go that they are bringing qualified personnel to establish and staff a seat of learning in Hainan. This is untactful, to say the least, as the Hainanese community recalls that there was an earlier Hainan University, closed by the Old Mainlanders in the early 1950s. The earlier Hainan University had been established at the initiative of famous Hainanese officials and scholars, and Overseas Chinese of Hainanese origin as a private university – sourced with Overseas Chinese donations of money, equipment and books – and faculties of agriculture, medicine, humanities and science.[36] In January 1951 the Hainan Military and Political Committee turned Hainan University into a division of the Southern University, a cadre training school with its headquarters in Guangzhou.[37]

The Hainanese

There are some 2 million Han Chinese born in Hainan whose mother tongue is Hainanese: the Hainanese community as defined here. Despite almost universal claims to a Hainan identity from all of the province's communities, the politics of the post-1949 era have for many drawn a sharp line between mainlanders and the Hainanese community. The latter are predominantly to be found among the peasantry, but necessarily not among the rural proletariat on the state farms. Though there are Hainanese who live in the larger cities, especially Haikou and Sanya, these are more the locus of the mainlander communities. The Hainanese have been distinctly unwilling to be involved in the economic activities of the mainlander communities, so that somewhat counter-intuitively the new industries of the reform era have not for the most part been based on the absorption of native Hainanese labour.

Only a very small part of the peasantry has been involved in the reform era drive for economic development in Hainan. The contrast between the relative poverty of the countryside and the prosperity of Haikou and Sanya has been sharp enough to give rise to the complaint that the establishment of Hainan Province and SEZ has disproportionately benefited those living in the towns.[38] In 1992, 27 per cent of GDP, 48 per cent of financial income, 45 per cent of industrial output value, and 63 per cent of investment in fixed assets were generated in Haikou, which has less than 8 per cent of the provincial population. In 1993 Haikou managed to achieve one of the highest per capita GDP of all China's provincial capitals,[39] at almost 13,000 *yuan* RMB. At the same time, the per capita GDP of the province was just over 3,000 *yuan* RMB. About 420,000 peasants in the countryside even lived under the official poverty line, with an annual per capita income less than 300 *yuan* RMB.[40]

Urbanisation in Hainan has been and remains generally low, and lower even than elsewhere in China. In the 1950s urbanisation in Hainan was about 8 per cent of the total population, some 5 per cent lower than the national average. In 1990 Hainan's urban population still accounted for less than 20 per cent of the total when the national average was about 30 per cent.[41] Even Hainan's rapid economic development since 1980 has not been accompanied by urbanisation: the urban population has grown at a rate of less than 1 per cent every year since 1980, with the exception of 1987.[42] Moreover, in 1987 the rate was high because of administrative changes in the calculation of the urban population rather than socio-economic change. Sanya City and Tongza City were formally incorporated in 1987, with Sanya turned into a city at prefectural level, and Tongza established as a city at county level.[43] Given the rate of mainland migration into Hainan, most of whom become urban residents, it is clear that very few if any Hainanese have moved into the cities and towns as part of the process of modernisation.

Before 1988 Hainan's industry, with mining as its most important sector, was not a major factor in Hainan's urbanisation. There was no attempt to develop long-term settlements when industries or mines were developed. Workforces were imported wholesale from the mainland, and returned on completion of their assignments. A similar practice continued after 1988 as the industries established by the New Mainlanders brought with them skilled workers and even construction labourers from elsewhere in China, without involving Hainan villagers. According to one 1992 survey of Hainan's population, of some 300,000 labourers in Haikou, 25.4 per cent were from Sichuan, 22 per cent from Hunan, 11 per cent from Zhejiang, 8.8 per cent from Jiangxi, 7.6 per cent from

Hubei, 7 per cent from Anhui, 6 per cent from Henan, with the remainder (12.2 per cent) from Hainan and other provinces.[44]

At the same time, in Hainan, unlike Guangdong and Fujian, there has been little development of rural enterprises, and certainly not what might be expected in a SEZ. In 1992 when the average gross output value of rural enterprises in each county of the coastal mainland provinces was in excess of 3 billion *yuan* RMB, in Hainan the 100,000 or so rural enterprises generated a gross output value of only 2.5 billion *yuan* RMB, even though this was a 58 per cent increase on the previous year.[45]

One explanation for this lack of participation in Hainan's economic growth by the Hainanese community may well lie in its political marginalisation. The advent of provincial status for Hainan has not led to greater political expression for the Hainanese community. On the contrary, if anything their continued exclusion has been emphasised by the fact of provincial status. Few Hainanese hold positions of seniority in the institutions of the party-state, in the professions, or even in government. There are frequent tensions between the Hainanese and mainlander communities, exacerbated by linguistic differences.

The Li

The Li are a national minority and the original pre-Han inhabitants of the island. They inhabit the mountains in the central and southwest part of the island around Qiongzhong, Baoting, Baica, Cangjiang, Dongfang, Ledong and Lingshui counties – about half the area of Hainan. Constrained by poor natural conditions, the Li came to live a relatively primitive lifestyle with simple wooden tools for agricultural production and a low standard of living.

Under the PRC the rich but largely unexploited natural resources in traditional Li territory, including mines and forests, were commandeered by the state. Between 1967 and 1984 the Shilu Iron Ore Mine supplied more than 67 million tons of iron ore to state steelworks in Anshan, Wuhan, Beijing, Shanghai and Guangzhou.[46] The Guangdong Provincial Government set up forestry bureaux at Jianfeng Ling, Diaoluoshan and Bawangling to run the timber industry, and the area of tropical forest in traditional Li territory fell from more than 10 million *mu* in 1956 to 3.3 million *mu* in 1980.[47]

Before the 1990s the Li were engaged almost exclusively in subsistence agriculture – of the low-yield, Shanlan rice that requires less water and attention and is suited to mountain areas. The land in the Li areas is well able to support a number of economic crops – rubber, coffee, pepper, tea and cashew nuts. These were indeed all grown on large plantations, but through state farms and without the involvement of the Li. Similarly, industries on Li lands, mining in particular, have not involved the local community.

In the reform era, Li (and other national minority communities) have been permitted and even encouraged to develop economic crop production. However, this new policy has frequently resulted in increased tensions between the Li and the state farms rather than the intended easier working relationships. Land disputes became so serious that in 1980 the government of the Li and Miao Autonomous Prefecture organised 36 work teams with 840 cadres to handle the disputes. As a result, 68,356 *mu* of land including 1,461 *mu* that contained rubber trees, were handed over to Li communities by the state farms who also agreed to share a further 7,403 *mu* of rubber trees.[48]

Many of Hainan's tourism attractions are located in the Li areas, and there can be little doubt that the Li community has benefited from the development of tourist areas such as Sanya, Tongza, the Wuzi Range, Qizhiling, and Monkey Island in Lingshui. Through growing and selling tropical fruits, manufacturing and marketing nationality handicrafts, and providing housing and other services for tourists, many Li communities have been able to improve their living standards. Perhaps the most remarkable manifestation of the Li's new commercialism is the model Li village, built especially for tourists, alongside the Tongza–Haikou Highway, and including the presentation of Li culture and handicrafts.

Li leaders were involved with the CCP in fighting the Nationalists and the Japanese before 1949. In line with the CCP's national policy towards the non-Han communities, they were rewarded with senior positions in the early 1950s. An Administrative Committee of the Qiongya Autonomous Region for Minority Nationalities had been established by communists in 1949 before the mainland forces arrived in 1950, and Wang Guoxin, the then leader of the Li, served as deputy director. The establishment of the People's Government of the Hainan Li and Miao Autonomous Prefecture at Tongza in 1952 saw Wang Guoxin appointed Chairman, supported by numerous Li and Miao cadres at all levels of government throughout the prefecture.[49] When in 1958 Beijing and Guangdong moved to crack down on what they saw as manifestations of 'Hainan localism' there were some 2,119 Li and Miao cadres employed by the prefecture. Many lost their jobs and some – notably Wang Guoxin and Wang Yujin – were accused as 'nationalist separatists' and tortured to death during the Cultural Revolution. In the early 1980s when local government was localised through both elections and appointments, all the leading positions in the prefecture and its counties and cities went to a new generation of Li and Miao cadres, including Wang Yuefeng, Wang Xueping, Chen Shufeng, and Chen Liwen.[50]

Much to the concern of Li (and for that matter, Miao) cadres their Autonomous Prefecture was dismantled in 1988, as Hainan Province was being established. When interviewed, Li cadres have argued that while the earlier parallel operation of an Autonomous Prefecture and the Hainan Administrative Office might have caused problems for overall economic planning in Hainan, there was no justice in dismantling the Autonomous Prefecture at the same time as Hainan was being established as a province. They regard this development as a mainlander conspiracy to exploit their rich natural resources.[51]

Overseas Chinese

The final observable and self-identifying community on Hainan are the Overseas Chinese, of whom there are about 1 million living mainly in central and northeastern Hainan. The Overseas Chinese community consists of families that previously lived on the remittances sent them by family members from Hainan working abroad, usually in Southeast Asia; and the families of ethnic Chinese resettled in Hainan during the 1950s and 1960s from Southeast Asia, many of which were originally from Hainan, as the result of political problems in the region at the time. Hainan has long had strong overseas links particularly with overseas Hainanese in what is now Malaysia. More than 2 million Overseas Chinese living in over fifty countries are of Hainan origin, with particular concentrations in Hong Kong and Southeast Asia. According to one source, over 1 million Overseas Chinese living in Thailand are of Hainan origin, with 700,000 in Malaysia, 280,000 in Singapore, 200,000 in Hong Kong, and 150,000 in Indonesia.[52]

Many Overseas Chinese were forced to return to China by the suppression of Overseas Chinese communist activities in Malaysia and Indonesia during the 1950s and 1960s, as well as more general anti-Chinese riots in both those countries during the 1960s. Many of these 'returnees' and not just those originally of Hainan origin chose to settle in Hainan, attracted by the climate and the opportunities to grow tropical crops. They are to be found in considerable concentrations in Wenchang and Qionghai counties, where they account for 66 per cent and 60 per cent of the total population respectively, but also elsewhere notably Wanning and Qiongshan counties.[53]

Generally, the Overseas Chinese have been a most important source of foreign capital in the development of Southern China during the reform era. However, in the case of Hainan, the contribution of the Overseas Chinese to its development is somewhat paradoxical. Overseas Chinese involvement in the development of the economy of Hainan started well before the establishment of the PRC. Although Overseas Chinese investment and involvement has continued and grown through the 1980s and 1990s it has nonetheless remained muted, particularly in comparison to other parts of Southern China, such as the Pearl River Delta or the Fuzhou area.

The production of many important tropical crops – such as rubber, coffee, pepper, cocoa, pineapple, palm oil, sisal hemp and lemongrass – was first introduced by Overseas Chinese, who also founded the first modern factories, schools and hospitals in Hainan, and contributed to the establishment of a university in the 1940s.[54] By 1956 returned Overseas Chinese had started 2,325 farms to grow rubber, and there are now five large state farms run exclusively by returned Overseas Chinese, covering a land area of 430,000 *mu* and with a population of more than 60,000. In the period 1979–90, Overseas Chinese invested more than US$700 million in order to establish 1,100 enterprises on Hainan, accounting for 70 per cent of the island's total foreign capital enterprises. During the period 1984–90, 3,492 enterprises were established on the island through remittances by Overseas Chinese of Hainan origin.[55]

Many Overseas Chinese of Hainan origin were deeply involved in Chinese politics during the Republican period and suffered politically with the advent of the PRC. Those political disadvantages may explain why Overseas Chinese of Hainan origin have not invested in Hainan at the same kind of rate as their counterparts from Guangdong and elsewhere in Southern China. In addition, there are concerns about mainland colonialism in Hainan. Many complain that they cannot do business in Hainan in Hainanese, and that their fellow townspeople appear bullied by mainlanders in their hometowns. They have repeatedly complained to the provincial government that too many positions are occupied by mainlanders who do not speak Hainanese and have difficulties communicating with Overseas Chinese of Hainan origin. Not only are they upset that they cannot get things done during their visits to their native places in Hainan because the officials there do not now speak their language, but also they are angry that official delegations from Hainan usually consist of mainlanders who speak Mandarin rather than Hainanese.[56]

PROVINCIAL CONFLICT

As argued elsewhere, a major determinant of Hainan's post-1988 political instability has been the ambiguous nature of its relationship with the national party and government leadership.[57] However, another major determinant of political flux has been the developing conflicts between and among Hainan's communities. Tensions between mainlanders and natives are never far below the surface of political, economic and social life in Hainan. Those tensions are most obviously manifested in the composition of the provincial leadership and the personnel policies adopted for the new provincial structures of the CCP and provincial government since 1988. However, conflict is not simply bi-polar: there is as much mutual distrust, suspicion and resentment between Old and New Mainlanders as between mainlanders and natives, and there are tensions between the various non-mainlander communities. The discussions since the mid-1980s on the most appropriate economic development strategy for Hainan, and indeed the outcomes of that process, reflect these conflicts and their social bases.

Leadership in the new Hainan

At the declaration of Hainan Province in 1988 most key positions in the CCP, provincial government and business enterprises on the island were held by mainlanders who had come – or whose parents had first come – to Hainan in the early 1950s with the Southbound Work Team. Even though the localisation of politics has been a major trend, particularly at provincial level, in the PRC since the early 1980s,[58] in Hainan since 1988 this has counter-intuitively not been the case. On the contrary, at the highest levels of government, party leadership and the economy, the trend on Hainan is that one community of mainlanders has largely moved in on another, thereby serving to create another source of communal tension.

Since 1988 and the establishment of Hainan Province there have been two congresses of the provincial CCP. Each congress has elected its provincial party leadership: the secretary, deputy secretaries and the Standing Committee of the Provincial CCP Committee. In total there have been twenty-three members of the First and Second Standing Committees of the Committee of the Hainan Province CCP: seventeen were from the New Mainlander community, one was an Old Mainlander, three were Hainanese and two were Li.[59] At the same time there have been thirteen governors and deputy governors of Hainan Province. Of these eight have been members of the New Mainlander community, two are Old Mainlanders, one is a Hainanese and two are Li.[60]

Of the twenty-nine individuals in the provincial leadership since the establishment of Hainan Province only nine, including three Old Mainlanders, have lived in Hainan for any substantial period. It is reasonable to see all these appointments as a severe case of tokenism and that is certainly how many on Hainan regard them. Wang Yuefeng, Wang Xueping and Zhong Wen are all either from the Li-dominated area of Hainan or are indeed part of the Li community. Their appointment followed the abolition – amidst considerable local rancour in that area – of the Li and Miao Autonomous Prefecture in 1988. Chen Yuyi's appointment as Deputy-Governor is widely explained as compensation for his popularly assumed victimisation in the Hainan Car Scandal of 1985. Many Hainanese officials were reported extremely angry at that time and Chen's appointment was regarded as some kind of pacification.

The appointment of Wei Zefang to the CCP Standing Committee is particularly interesting in the context of tensions between mainlanders and Hainanese. Wei is a Hainanese who speaks extremely poor Mandarin. In 1992 Wei Zefang presented a report on the work of the provincial government to an inspection group of the central leadership of the CCP visiting Hainan. Unfortunately, so it is said, because of the thickness of his accent, none of the visitors understood him. The CCP Secretary of Hainan during 1991–3 was Deng Hongxun, who developed a ferocious reputation among Hainanese for being anti-Hainanese. At the time in his apology to his visitors from Beijing, Deng apparently explained that while he was more than willing to pay respect to Hainanese values and use local cadres, nonetheless their quality was low.[61]

Deng is popularly assumed to have deliberately selected Wei in order to introduce a new personnel policy barring local Hainanese from positions at or above that of departmental head in the provincial administration. Certainly that was one outcome of the incident. At the departmental level within the provincial government, almost all the directors thereafter have been mainlander appointments. As of 1995, thirty directors are from the mainland, and Hainanese head only six departments.[62]

A policy against localisation has been explicitly introduced at the county level. In 1989 shortly after the establishment of provincial status the Hainan government adopted a 'locality avoidance' cadre policy. Those appointed to specified positions at the same level in each locality must not themselves be from the same locality. The restricted positions are: the CCP secretary of the city or county; the mayor of a city government or the head of the county government; the deputy mayor of the city government or the deputy head of a county government with responsibility for personnel work; within the CCP structure, the Director of the Commission for Inspecting Discipline, the Director of the Organisation Department, and the Director of the Personnel Department; and within the county level government, the Director of the Public Security Bureau.[63] Unsurprisingly, the policy was not universally received with equanimity. One excited and indignant official in Wanning County wrote a letter to the provincial government demanding that in order to abide by the principle of 'locality avoidance' the CCP General Secretary and the Premier of China would have to be imported from abroad. In the same letter he also facetiously suggested that the provincial government import hundreds of cadres for the township and village levels in Hainan to replace the current 'unqualified' local cadres.[64]

Since the early 1980s it has been official policy that Hainan should import qualified personnel, particularly to senior positions, from the mainland because Hainan is regarded as having insufficient qualified personnel among the local population. Much to the chagrin of those already on Hainan, these New Mainlanders are to be attracted with higher salaries and housing benefits.[65] Even without such a policy, the dominant position of mainlanders in the Hainan administration is not a surprise. Unlike other provinces all the senior officials in Hainan were the direct appointment of central authorities when the province was established in 1988.[66] Given the traditions of China's politics it is more than usual to expect political leaders from the mainland to recruit their subordinates from their former staff. Moreover, since the removal of Feng Baiju and his colleagues in 1957-8, there have been few Hainanese in Hainan's leadership. In addition, language is an important impediment to the official career of Hainanese: Mandarin with a Cantonese accent may have become recently fashionable in China as a marker of wealth and even sophistication, but Hainanese Mandarin is regarded as an indicator of backwardness.

Hainan's development strategy

In terms of its economic development, Hainan Province was not established at an opportune moment, for the end of 1988 marked the beginning of three years' austerity in China. Nevertheless, the Hainan economy has managed to sustain impressive above-average growth, even allowing for the low point of departure. During 1988–93 the province's GDP growth rate averaged 14 per cent annually; the annual growth rate for national income has been 11 per cent; and the annual growth rate for local financial income has been 47.6 per cent. In 1994 GDP was 36 billion *yuan* RMB, an increase of 12.6 per cent over the preceding year, with Hainan's population reaching 7.11 million people. These economic achievements enabled 1.6 million people, some 80 per cent of the population, to rise above the poverty line.[67]

The major weakness of the Hainan economy, though, is its continuous dependence on the mainland, especially for capital. Because of its lack of an industrial base, Hainan has not been able to generate its own investment for development and has to depend on external sources to solve the problem of capital shortage. There was some expectation that Hainan's opening to the outside world might solve this problem. However, foreign investors responded much less favourably than mainland investors, mostly governments at all levels in other parts of the country. Foreign capital has accounted for only about one-third of total investment in fixed assets in Hainan since 1988. During 1988–93 a total of 6,484 foreign firms from 52 countries have been registered in the province, with contracted investment amounting to US$7.64 billion. At the same time, provinces from mainland China have registered 17,700 domestic-link enterprises on the island, with contracted investment totalling 49.5 billion *yuan* RMB.

Although there has been broad agreement within the government on the broad fundamentals of the provincial development strategy – the principle of 'small government, big society', the emphasis on market-oriented reform and integration with the international economy – there has been considerable disagreement within Hainan as to which sector of the economy represents the province's comparative advantage. Since 1988 the province's economic development strategy has changed direction several times. The leading sector has changed from industry, targeted at the establishment of Hainan Province; to agriculture, from late 1989 when the original expectation of industrial and external-oriented development disappeared with Western reactions to the Tiananmen Square incident of that June; to tourism in 1992 during Hainan's first property boom; to industry again, but with different emphases, as announced by Ruan Chongwu at the Second Provincial Congress of the CCP in July 1993.[68] Identification of agriculture, tourism or industry as Hainan's leading sector is neither a mere question of understanding nor a simple economic decision, but is politically charged, not least since the province's communities have their bases in different sectors of the economy. Interestingly from the perspective of political conflict, each change of emphasis in Hainan's economic development strategy not only has its proponents, but also creates fairly well-defined opposition.

Advocating agriculture

Hainan is still predominantly rural, and is even less industrialised than most inland provinces of China. After the depravations of the Sino-Japanese War and the Civil War, industry hardly existed in Hainan. In 1952 there were only thirty-five industrial firms with a total output value of 42 million *yuan* RMB. Little started to change until the end of the 1970s when the value of industrial output was still as low as 686 million *yuan* RMB.[69] Moreover, despite changes since 1988 the agricultural sector still accounted for 52 per cent of provincial national income in 1992, with the rural population accounting for more than 79 per cent of the total population and agricultural labourers 70 per cent of the total workforce.[70]

Instead of advocating a rapid industrialisation for Hainan – as was the original conception at the establishment of Hainan Province – a group of officials and economists have insisted that agriculture should be developed as the leading sector in the province.[71] Their argument is that Hainan's comparative advantage lies precisely in its tropical agriculture, unique in China. The island has a tropical monsoon climate, an annual average temperature of 22–28 degrees Centigrade, 1,750–2,650 hours of sunshine a year, and an annual average rainfall of 1,500–2,000 millimetres. In Hainan 98 per cent of land is usable, and the only weakness is the frequent incidence of typhoons.

There is a vast variety of plants and timber grown on the island, and Hainan is China's most important area for the production of tropical crops, in particular rubber, coconut, pepper, betel palm, coffee, cashew, lemongrass, sugarcane, palm oil and tropical fruits. Two-thirds of the national maritime waters come under Hainan's jurisdiction, totalling some 2 million square kilometres, with large and varied resources of fish. With little pollution (so far), rich biological bait, and long hours of sunshine, the natural conditions of the island are also favourable for aquatic breeding.

Although the advocacy of agriculture as the leading sector in economic development has benefits for a number of Hainan's communities – the Li, the Miao and even the Old Mainlanders, as well as the Overseas Chinese and the Hainanese, it is significantly the Overseas Chinese and the Hainanese who are its major proponents and beneficiaries. The Overseas Chinese have long been engaged in the encouragement of tropical crop production, though often without official support. The Hainanese, as a series of individual farmholds and villagers are more able to adapt to the new economic environment than the rural proletariat of the state farms. Opposition comes from the predominantly urban New Mainlander community, who are concerned that resources may be diverted from the pursuit of the economic opportunities that have attracted them to Hainan; as well as the Old Mainlanders – and particularly those on the state farms and their more conservative elements – whose dominance of the agricultural sector has been directly challenged by post-1988 developments.

Recent structural developments appear to have supported the arguments of those advocating an emphasis on the agricultural sector. Substantial land, capital and labour have been devoted to what have been variously described as 'high quality agriculture', 'eco-agriculture', or 'tourist agriculture'. The strategy to guarantee grain supply, which was a legacy of the subsistence agriculture of the past, is giving way to a strategy to maximise profits. In 1992, Hainan ranked first in China in terms of its per capita output value of agriculture, with the added value generated by agriculture in 1993 reaching 7.6 billion *yuan* RMB, almost three times that of industry, in which agriculture-based industry accounted for half.[72] Agriculture on Hainan had a particularly good harvest in 1994, when the price of dry rubber climbed from US$800 per ton in January to US$1,380 per ton in July, due primarily to the recovery of Western economies, and the automobile industry in particular.

It is also argued by the agriculture sector lobby that for the conceivable future Hainan's industry will continue to depend on the development of agriculture. Most of the province's industry is light industry, and the largest part is agriculture-based or agriculture-supporting. Since 1987 agriculture-based industry has accounted for over 65 per cent of the annual output value of light industry, which in turn was over 65 per cent of the annual industrial output value of Hainan. By maintaining its focus on agriculture-based industry, the province can try to turn the underdevelopment of its economy to its advantage. There is a considerable variety of food-processing and agriculture-based industries which produce sugar, rubber products, confectionery, liqueurs, beer, biscuits, cigarettes, soft drinks, tea, coffee, edible oils, dairy products, bean products, spices, canned food and handicraft articles.

A particular success has been the recent development of the coconut-processing industry which has been little short of spectacular. Starting from nothing there are now more than fifty products made from coconut available on Hainan. The coconut milk produced by the Hainan Tianren Coconut Milk Companies Group has become particularly well known internationally. The demand for Hainan coconut products both domestically and internationally has expanded so fast that the province, which previously exported millions of coconuts a year, now has to import a large number. In some factories 80 per cent of the total of processed coconuts are now imports from Vietnam.[73]

Capital and technology to develop advanced agriculture has been sought in Taiwan. By November 1994, a total of 127 Taiwan enterprises had become involved in agricultural development projects in Hainan, some 20 per cent of all Taiwan enterprises in Hainan.[74] In Sanya alone 38 per cent of Taiwan-funded enterprises were in the agricultural sector, renting 11,000 *mu* of land and introducing new technology and new varieties of economic crops from Taiwan and other countries. For example, the Sanheli Agriculture Development Company founded in Sanya by a Taiwan investor in 1988 has made an annual profit of more than US$1.5 million by growing fine varieties of water melon; and the Qianju Company founded in Sanya by a Taiwan investor has developed mango and banana production with strains introduced from Taiwan, the United States and Thailand.[75]

Touting tourism

The advocacy of tourism as a potential lead sector for the economy is easily understood. As in the promotion of the development of agriculture, Hainan's tropical location is a major advantage. It has beautiful scenery, a pleasant climate and privileged geographical position, and an exceptionally low level of industrial development. In time, particularly with the development of adequate airport facilities to deliver long-haul passengers direct from the holiday-making countries of Western Europe it clearly has considerable potential. In the mean time, and increasingly since 1988, it has been a focus of domestic tourism from the mainland. For China's new rich, foreign travel, let alone foreign holidays, are difficult for bureaucratic reasons and because of the lack of access to foreign exchange. Hainan is seen as an exotic and appropriate substitute, offering a very different lifestyle, if only for a short period.

Hainan is situated on the same latitude and has similar flora, climate and beautiful beaches as Hawaii. White beaches, blue seawater, bright sunshine, fresh air, and unique local customs are the charm of the tropical island. The tourism lobby argues that money brought in by the tourists is the best chance for original accumulation, given that Hainan's agriculture and industry are both relatively backward; that the development of tourism will be a strong stimulus to improve the infrastructure of Hainan, particularly transport, communications and other parts of the service sector; and that tourism will create a market for local produce and opportunities for employment in those labour-intensive sectors related to tourism.[76]

Those advocating the development of Hainan's potential for tourism point to its current success compared to original expectations. In his Hainan Provincial Government Work Report of 1988, Liang Xiang, the first Governor of the province, set a target of 600,000–800,000 tourists for 1992. In the event, the actual tourist numbers totalled about 2.5 million in 1992. Foreign exchange earnings from tourism in 1992 exceeded US$100 million, in addition to the 600 million *yuan* RMB earned from domestic tourists.

The rapid development of tourism holds out the prospect of substantial benefits to residents of tourist spots, and those involved in the emerging service industries in Hainan, including tourist agents, traders, hotel and restaurant enterprises and workers, transport workers of all kinds, and prostitutes. In terms of Hainan's communities, the tourism lobby includes all the non-Han peoples of Hainan and particularly the Li and Miao. In response to increased interest from domestic tourism that they have rapidly reconstructed their cultures and societies in forms that are readily accessible. Li and Miao tourist villages, complete with instant exotica such as stockades, sanitised thatched-hut villages, and regular on-the-hour performances of songs and dances, as well as shopping opportunities, have been built alongside the main central mountain highway that passes through the areas inhabited by the Li and Miao.

The tourism lobby also includes a sizeable number of New Mainlanders who have almost exclusively been the organisers of tourism and its new developments since 1988. They have been at the centre of the development of new hotels and entertainment complexes, particularly in Haikou and Sanya. Counter-intuitively, very few Hainanese have engaged in activities related to the emerging tourism industry, and on the contrary there are distinct rumblings of opposition. There are complaints about the pollution – social as well as environmental – that follow the exploitation of Hainan in the name of tourism. Prostitution has become a major industry – especially in Haikou and Sanya, where there is a regular and sizeable street night market – and it is frequently raised as an issue by Hainanese even though it appears that the prostitutes are all New Mainlanders.

Hainan has been identified as one of the seven major national tourism districts and the only nationally designated winter resort in China. Since the mid-1980s 123 tourist attractions in 5 different categories were identified and developed on the island, including internationally well-known landscapes of natural beauty, beaches, nature parks with rare animals, and historical sites. Transportation, accommodation and facilities for communications have been greatly improved to enhance the accessibility of tourist spots and make things easy for tourists. Hundreds of personnel, including managers, tourist guides, interpreters and service personnel, have been sent to Guangzhou, Shanghai, Hong Kong, Singapore and Thailand for training. There are now more than a hundred professional tourist agencies where there were only two in 1983, with most founded after 1988.

Moreover, Hainan has developed several 'tourism development zones' and 'tourist spots'. Luxury hotels have been built in a number of different places on the island, as have golf courses, a race track (for horses), swimming pools and other recreational facilities. Currently there are at least 33 major tourist projects under construction, each involving over 100 million *yuan* RMB. The largest of those projects include the Yalong Bay National Holiday Zone (involving 10.7 billion *yuan* RMB), Wuzi Island Tourist Development Zone (US$200 million), Guilinyang Tourist Zone (US$100 million), and Shimei Bay Tourist Development Zone (300 million *yuan* RMB). Plans have also been made to develop the Mulan Bay Tourist Zone, Wuzhi Mountain Tourist Zone, Wanquan River Tourist Zone, Tonggu Mountain Tourist Zone, Dongzai Port Tourist Zone, Nanli Lake Tourist Zone and Qizhi Mountain Tourist Zone.

The development of tourism has drawn with it other closely related activities, such as catering and the handicrafts industry. There is no doubt that tourism has been a strong stimulus to the catering trade in Hainan. Before the 1980s Hainanese food was but little known elsewhere in China, let alone abroad. The rapid expansion of tourism has led to thousands of new restaurants and the popularisation of Hainanese dishes – Wenchang Chicken, Jiaji Duck, Dongshan Sheep, Shishan Sheep, Lingao Hog, Hele Crab, Hainan Grouper, Sanya Sea Snake, and Wanning Bird's Nest – alongside the island's soft drinks, notably coconut and pineapple juices.

Insisting on industry

Those who reject the notions that tourism or agriculture should be the lead sector in Hainan's economic development in favour of industry argue from traditional wisdom about the centrality of the manufacturing sector, and that rapid industrialisation is the only way for an underdeveloped economy to catch up the advanced economies of the world.[77] This strategy has great appeal particularly to those who hope to achieve a higher degree of economic independence for Hainan, although it clearly disproportionately benefits the technocrats and industrial workers in the state industrial sector. It is necessarily a strategy of the Old Mainlanders, not least because of its requirement to mobilise substantial resources and to have close and reliable connections with the party–state establishment.

In fact a version of this strategy was a guiding principle elaborated in the *Hainan Economic Development Strategy* proposed in 1987 by a group of economists from the Chinese Academy of Social Sciences led by Liu Guoguang.[78] To their disappointment, industrial development in Hainan since 1988 has lagged far behind other sectors, particularly in terms of efficiency and returns. Instead of investing in the manufacturing sector in order to enjoy tax holidays and other preferential treatment, most external investors have put their money in property development, tourism projects and non-bank financial institutions.

On the surface Hainan Province is experiencing an extraordinary industrial growth. The value of industrial output increased more than 20 per cent annually between 1988 and 1993, with increases of 34 per cent and 36 per cent in 1992 and 1993 respectively.[79] A comprehensive industrial system has started to take shape in Hainan, producing more than 3,000 different manufactures and involving electricity, metallurgy, electronics, textiles, machinery, cars, chemicals, building materials, medicines, salt, sugar, rubber products, and food processing. However, as already indicated, most of Hainan's industry is labour-intensive, agriculture-based industry, rather than the high-technology industries originally proposed in 1987. Moreover, increasingly more industrial enterprises are running at a deficit, 20 per cent of the total in 1988 but 60 per cent by 1991.

These problems certainly indicate the difficulties of pursuing the original high technology industry strategy of 1987. Nevertheless, an alternative strategy favouring the development of heavy industry was adopted by the provincial government in the middle of 1993. In his report to the Second Congress of the CCP of Hainan Province, the Party Secretary and Governor of the Province, Ruan Chongwu, adopted a new development strategy that identified heavy industry as the province's major economic weakness to be rectified during the next five years. The key projects identified in Ruan's report included a refinery capable of producing 6 million tons of oil per annum and other petrochemical products; a steel works capable of producing 1.2 million tons of steel per annum; a cement plant capable of producing 800,000 tons of cement per annum; a natural gas chemical fertiliser plant capable of producing 800,000 tons of chemical fertilisers per annum; a cold rolled steel plate plant capable of producing 100,000 tons of steel plate per annum; and a sheet polyester plant capable of producing 60,000 tons of sheet polyester per annum.[80]

There is a certain logic to Ruan Chongwu's strategy. Hainan has a strong mining industry and there is potential for the development of related manufacturing sectors. Hainan is richly endowed in mineral resources, particularly oil, natural gas, iron, titanium and cobalt. The island has been a substantial supplier of iron ore to the iron and steel mills on the mainland. It is estimated that on the present annual output of about 4.5 million tons, the iron ore deposits in Hainan are enough for twenty years in the open cast mines and sixty years in the deeper mines. Hainan is one the most important sources of titanium and zircon in China. The proved and recoverable reserves of titanium and zircon in Hainan account for about 70 per cent and 60 per cent respectively of the national totals. An annual output of about 20,000 tons of fine titanium has been achieved since the late 1970s when two titanium mines began to operate along the coast of Qionghai and Wanning counties. Initial attempts or detailed plans have also been made to mine cobalt, zircon copper, gold, uranium and other minerals in Hainan.

More recently Hainan has become the base for the newer offshore oil and gas industries in the South China Sea, where the offshore oil and gas deposits are very promising. The Yinggehai Oil Field and the Beibuwan Oil Field have begun to produce petrol. The gas deposits of Yacheng, China's largest proven natural gas-field to date, are estimated at about 100 billion cubic metres. Since the end of 1992 the gas-field has been jointly developed by the China National Offshore Oil Corporation, Atlantic Ritchfield and the Kuwait Foreign Petroleum Exploration Corporation. Its annual production capacity is expected to reach 3.4 billion cubic metres, which will greatly ease energy supply bottlenecks in both Hainan and Hong Kong. Hong Kong will be linked to the Yacheng Gas Field by a 780 kilometre underwater pipeline, one of the longest in the world, currently under construction jointly by a consortium including the China National Metals Import and Export Corporation, Nippon Steel and other major Japanese steel makers. It is planned that after January 1996 the Yacheng Gas Field will supply 2.9 billion cubic metres of gas annually to Hong Kong and 500 million cubic metres to Hainan.[81]

Opposition to an industry-led development strategy comes unsurprisingly from the Hainanese community, but it is muted, not least since it is the question of social control rather than industrial development that is uppermost. Opposition is to mainlander influence, and has focused on questions of environmental degradation. Even without industrialisation, the destruction of natural forest in Hainan was substantial during the first four decades of CCP rule. The area of natural forest in Hainan, one of the eight largest forest areas of China, was reduced from 1.2 million hectares in 1950 to 298,000 hectares in 1986, a three-quarters reduction in thirty-seven years. Now only 8 per cent of the island is covered by natural forest, while the coverage was 50 per cent in the 1940s.[82]

Prospects for Hainan's politics

Economic reform in China has led directly to the establishment of a Hainan Province – a goal of many associated with the island for much of the twentieth century. However, more than a little paradoxically a not particularly integrated political system has emerged. In the provincial era Hainan has experienced one of the relatively well-known post-colonial phenomena and developed a politics of almost endemic communal conflict. Interestingly too, as in other systems where for various reasons political articulation is limited, environmental and social concerns – rather than explicitly political contestation – have become important public issues.

A resolution to inter-communal tensions and conflicts is not readily observable. Stable politics require coalitions among Hainan's communities, as well as mechanisms for mediating inter-communal rivalry. The experience of the post-1988 years indicates such coalitions are unlikely to emerge in the immediate future. The different communities on Hainan not only have different social bases and different agendas, but also find it difficult to compromise and cooperate, as the frequently changing policy environment of the post-1988 period demonstrates. At the same time, and despite the experience of former Yugoslavia, inter-communal rivalry need not result in either political paralysis or disintegration, particularly given rapid economic growth and modernisation.

A liberation narrative can clearly be useful in explaining Hainan's experience since 1949. Exploitation of the periphery by the centre is not straightforwardly the issue here. Were that simply the case then it would be possible to argue that colonialism were little more than a feature of a centrally planned economy, and that is not necessarily a sustainable argument.[83] The difference is the extent and scale of communal conflict in Hainan, and particularly its ethnic and possibly even racist undertones.

At the same time there are fairly obvious limits to using any colonial perspective in the interpretation of Hainan's development, even the presumably more appropriate concept of 'internal colonialism' developed after Lenin by a series of commentators.[84] The most important of these limits is that none of Hainan's communities – all of whom claim to speak for the province – is advocating revolution and independence. The arguments are about control and relative autonomy within the Chinese state, not about separation and the creation of entirely new political entities. Here a comparison with Taiwan – with similar mainlander–islander social and political conflict since 1949 – may well be instructive, for Hainan had developed from cultural integration, assimilation and compromise over several centuries even before 1949.

NOTES

1   The Tibet Autonomous Region was formally established in 1965, though formally announced much earlier. A number of smaller additional provinces and provincial-level cities had been created at the outset of the PRC in the early 1950s

when the provincial-level was not the immediate sub-central level of administration. Gradually between 1954 and 1956 the number of provinces was stabilised. In most cases these had already been provinces at some time before 1949. Ningxia, which was resurrected as a provincial level unit in 1958, had been a province from the Republican era until 1954.

2 Details on Hainan Province's economic development may be found in Feng Chongyi and David S.G. Goodman, *China's Hainan Province: Economic Development and Investment Environment*, University of Western Australia Press, 1995.

3 Feng Chongyi and David S.G. Goodman, 'Hainan Province in reform: political dependence and economic interdependence', in Peter Cheung and Jae Ho Chung (eds) *Provincial Strategies of Economic Reform in Post-Mao China: Leadership, Politics and Implementation*, 1997.

4 *Hainan Lizu, Miaozu zizhizhou gaikuang* [A Brief Account of the Hainan Li and Miao Autonomous Prefecture], Guangdong renmin chubanshe, 1986, pp. 58–62.

5 *Hainan Lizu, Miaozu zizhizhou gaikuang* [A Brief Account of the Hainan Li and Miao Autonomous Prefecture], Guangdong renmin chubanshe, 1986, pp. 44–5.

6 *Hainan Lizu, Miaozu zizhizhou gaikuang* [A Brief Account of the Hainan Li and Miao Autonomous Prefecture], Guangdong renmin chubanshe, 1986, pp. 51–4.

7 Zhu Yihui, 'Hainanren zhou xiang shijie' [Hainanese join the international communities], in Zhu Yihui (ed.) *Hainan mingren zhuanlue* [Famous Hainanese], Zhongshan daxue chubanshe, 1992, 1, p. 549.

8 For example, bus and screwdriver in English; *sabon* (soap) in French; and *mada* (police) in Malay.

9 For example, the belief in *Jin* – a magic which can make people ill or mad, or lead to death.

10 And now an extremely popular goddess on Hainan.

11 Quoted in Xu Shijie (ed.) *Hainan sheng* [Hainan Province], Shangwu yingshuguan, 1988, p. 115.

12 Zhu Yihui, 'Fayang Hainan ren de fendou jingshen' [Carry on the Hainanese tradition of fighting], in Zhu Yihui (ed.) *Hainan mingren zhuanlue* [Famous Hainanese], Zhongshan daxue chubanshe, 1992, 1, pp. 541–2.

13 Zhu Yihui and He Wensheng, 'Qiu Jun', in Zhu Yihui (ed.) *Hainan mingren zhuanlue* [Famous Hainanese], p. 13; see also, Jiang Zhuyuan and Fang Zhiqian (eds) *Jianming Guangdong shi* [A History of Guangdong], Guangdong renmin chubanshe, 1987, p. 275.

14 Merle Goldman, 'The Party and the intellectuals: phase two', in R. MacFarquhar and J.K. Fairbank (eds) *The Cambridge History of China*, 14, *The People's Republic, Part I: The Emergence of Revolutionary China, 1949–1965*, Cambridge University Press, 1978, pp. 446 and 460.

15 Office for the History of Armed Struggle in Hainan (ed.) *Qiongya zhongdui shi* [A History of the Qiongya Column], Guangdong renmin chubanshe, 1986, p. 298.

16 Li Zhimin and Wang Houhong (eds) *Hainan sheng qing gaiyao* [A Survey of the Current Situation in Hainan], Hainan chubanshe, 1992, p. 11.

17 Office for the History of Armed Struggle in Hainan (ed.) *Qiongya zhongdui shi* [A History of the Qiongya Column], Guangdong renmin chubanshe, p. 25.

18 Office for the History of Armed Struggle in Hainan (ed.) *Qiongya zhongdui shi* [A History of the Qiongya Column], Guangdong renmin chubanshe, pp. 213–14.

19 CCP Guangdong Provincial Committee, 'Resolution regarding the Hainan antiparty localist group and the mistakes of Comrade Feng Baiju and Gu Dacun', 19 December 1957.

20 Sun Yat-sen and Chiang Kai-shek were married to Hainanese sisters – Song Qingling and Song Meiling.

21 Hainan Party History Research Office, *Xin Hainan jishi* [A Chronicle of New Hainan], Zhonggong dangshi chubanshe, 1993, p. 132.

22 Xu Shijie (ed.) *Hainan sheng* [Hainan Province], Shangwu yanshuguan, 1988, pp. 337–8; Zhan Changzhi (ed.) *Zhongguo renkou – Hainan fence* [The Population of China – Hainan volume], Zhongguo caizheng jingji chubanshe, 1993, pp. 109–11.

23 Research Office of Hainan Party History, *Xin Hainan jishi* [A Chronicle of New Hainan], Zhonggong dangshi chubanshe, 1993, p. 565. In disussions with Hu Yaobang and Zhao Ziyang on 24 February 1985 Deng Xiaoping reportedly said that he would like to see Hainan catch up with Taiwan within twenty years.

24 'Zhongguo tequ sheng de jueqi' [The rise of a provincial Special Economic Zone in China], *Hainan Ribao* 20 August 1988.

25 On central–provincial relations generally in the PRC, see David S.G. Goodman and Gerald Segal (eds) *China Deconstructs: Politics, Trade and Regionalism*, Routledge, London, 1974; and Jae Ho Chung, 'Studies of central–provincial relations in the People's Republic of China', *China Quarterly* no. 142, June 1995, p. 487.

26 Li Zhimin and Wang Honghou (eds) *Hainan sheng qing gaiyao* [A Survey of the Current Situation in Hainan], Hainan chubanshe, 1992, p. 26.

27 Since the early 1950s Hainan has produced in excess of 80 per cent of China's total raw rubber output.

28 One step in the reform of government is the conversion of government departments previously concerned with economic activities into economic entitites. Some of these have become multi-enterprise conglomerates operating in and through the market-place rather than as previously through administrative allocation.

29 'Big farm group in Hainan is set for more growth', *China Daily* 14 June 1993.

30 Shi Fulin (ed.) *Hainan xintizhi:guojia yu shijian* [New Systems and New Practices in Hainan], Hainan chubanshe, 1992, p. 381; Liao Xun *et al.* (eds) *Hainan nianjian 1994* [Hainan Yearbook 1994], Hainan nianjianshe, 1994, 3, p. 13.

31 Liao Xun, 'Confusion from propertied socialist labourers', in *Tequ shehui jingji fazhan yanjiu* [A Study of Social and Economic Development in SEZs], Hainan chubanshe, 1994, p. 377.

32 Wu Ganlin, 'Decisive engagement on Hainan', in Jiang Wei (ed.) *Tequ sheng de guanli zhemen* [Administrators in the Provincial SEZ], Zhongguo jingji chubanshe, 1991, p. 10.

33 Liao Xun, 'Confusion from propertied socialist labourers', in *Tequ shehui jingji fazhan yanjiu* [A Study of Social and Economic Development in SEZs], Hainan chubanshe, 1994, p. 377; Wu Ganlin, 'Decisive engagement on Hainan', in Jiang Wei (ed.) *Tequ sheng de guanli zhemen* [Administrators in the Provincial SEZ], Zhongguo jingji chubanshe, 1991, p. 4.

34 Zhan Changzhi (ed.) *Zhongguo renkou – Hainan fence* [Population of China – Hainan volume], Zhongguo caizheng jingji chubanshe, 1993, pp. 86–91.

35 Zhan Changzhi (ed.) *Zhongguo renkou – Hainan fence* [Population of China – Hainan volume], Zhongguo caizheng jingji chubanshe, 1993, pp. 86–91.

36 Zhi Yuhui, 'Hainan wenhua fazhan' [The development of Hainan's culture], *Hainan daxue xuebao* [Hainan University Journal] no. 4, 1994, p. 17.

37 *Xin Hainan jishi* [A Chronicle of New Hainan], Zhonggong dangshi chubanshe, 1993, p. 27.

38 Liao Xun, 'Modernisation in the areas of minority nationalities', in *Tequ shehui jingji fazhan yanjiu* [A Study of Social and Economic Development in SEZs], Hainan chubanshe, 1994, p. 345.

39 Excluding the provincial-level municipalities.

40 Liao Xun, 'Let cities bring along the countryside', in *Tequ shehai jingji fazhan yanjiu* [A Study of Social and Economic Development in SEZs], Hainan chubanshe, 1994, pp. 78–83.

41 Zhan Changzhi (ed.) *Zhongguo renkou – Hainan fence* [Population of China – Hainan volume], Zhongguo caizheng jingji chubanshe, 1993, p. 113.

42 Zhan Changzhi (ed.) *Zhongguo renkou – Hainan fence* [Population of China – Hainan volume], Zhongguo caizheng jingji chubanshe, 1993, p. 111; Liao Xun *et al.* (eds) *Hainan nianjian 1993* [Hainan Yearbook 1993] 1, p. 66.

43 *Dangdai zhongguo de Hainan* [Hainan Today], Dangdai zhongguo chubanshe, 1993, 1, pp. 393, 404.

44 Quoted in Liao Xun, *Tequ shehui jingji fazhan yanjiu* [A Study of Social and Economic Development in SEZs], Hainan chubanshe, 1994, p. 315.

45 He Jiazheng, 'A survey of rural enterprises on Hainan', *Renmin ribao* [People's Daily] 20 May 1992.

46 *Hainan Lizu Miaozu zizhizhou gaikuang* [A Brief Account of the Hainan Li and Miao Autonomous Prefecture], Guangdong renmin chubanshe, 1986, p. 143.

47 *Hainan Lizu Miaozu zizhizhou gaikuang* [A Brief Account of the Hainan Li and Miao Autonomous Prefecture], Guangdong renmin chubanshe, 1986, pp. 127–8.

48 *Hainan Lizu Miaozu zizhizhou gaikuang* [A Brief Account of the Hainan Li and Miao Autonomous Prefecture], Guangdong renmin chubanshe, 1986, p. 135.

49 *Dangdai Zhongguo de Hainan* [Hainan Today], Dangdai zhongguo chubanshe, 1993, 2, p. 321.

50 *Hainan Lizu Miaozu zizhizhou gaikuang* [A Brief Account of the Hainan Li and Miao Autonomous Prefecture], Guangdong renmin chubanshe, 1986, pp. 86–8.

51 Interviews with cadres of government of the former Li and Miao Autonomous Prefecture, Haikou, December 1994.

52 *Dangdai Zhongguo de Hainan* [Hainan Today], Dangdai zhongguo chubanshe, 1993, 2, p. 353.

53 *Dangdai Zhongguo de Hainan* [Hainan Today], Dangdai zhongguo chubanshe, 1993, 2, p. 376.

54 Li Liangduan, 'Relations between overseas Chinese of Hainan origin and the development of Hainan: the past and the future', a paper presented at the workshop on *The Development and the Opportunities for Australia Haikou*, 9–14 May 1994.

55 *Dangdai Zhongguo de Hainan* [Hainan Today], Dangdai zhongguo chubanshe, 1993, 2, pp. 365–7.

56 Interview at New South Wales Hainanese Friendship Association, Sydney, March 1995; see also, Keng-Fong Pang, 'The structuring of new "Hainan-ren/Dalu-ren" boundaries in the Hainan Special Economic Zone', paper presented at American Association for Asian Studies Annual Conference, Washington, DC, 5–7 May 1995.

57 Feng Chongyi and David S.G. Goodman, 'Hainan Province in reform: political dependence and economic interdependence', in Peter Cheung and Jae Ho Chung (eds) *Provincial Strategies of Economic Reform in Post-Mao China: Leadership, Politics and Implementation*, 1997.

58 See, for example, David S.G. Goodman, 'Political perspectives', in D.S.G. Goodman (ed.) *China's Regional Development*, Routledge, London, 1989, p. 27.

59 Dong Fanyuan is both the only Old Mainlander and the only woman in this group. Born in Shanghai, she previously worked at Southern China Tropical Crops College, in Zhanxian. The three Hainanese are Wei Zefang, Zhong Wen and Chen Yuyi. Wei Zefang is a high school graduate who barely speaks Mandarin. Zhong Wen worked in the state farms system 1968–93 and was CCP Secretary of the Hainan Agriculture Reclamation Bureau during 1991–3. Chen Yuyi was Lei Yu's deputy during 1984–5 and was removed from office in July

1985 when central government changed the local leadership in the wake of the Hainan Car Scandal. The two Li are Wang Yuefeng and Wang Xueping. Wang Yuefeng was head of the Li and Miao Autonomous Prefecture to 1982, and Deputy Governor of Hainan Province during 1988–91. He was followed in both positions by Wang Xueping. The seventeen New Mainlanders are: Xu Shijie, former CCP Secretary of Guangzhou, from Guangdong; Liang Xiang, former Mayor of Shenzhen, from Guangdong; Liu Jianfeng, former Deputy Minister of the Electronics Industry, from Tianjin; Yao Wenxu, former Party Secretary of Zhanjiang, from Liaoning; Bao Keming, former Deputy Minister of Space Technology, from Shandong; Miao Enlu, former member of Guangzhou Party Committee, from Guangdong; Liu Guinan, former Head of the Propaganda Department of Guangzhou Military Region, from Guangdong; Li Zhimin, former Head of the Young Cadre Section of the Organisation Department of the Central Committee of the CCP, from Hebei; Deng Hongxun, former Deputy Party Secretary of Jiangsu, from Jiangsu; Duo Qinglin, former Deputy Party Secretary of Jilin, from Jilin; Wang Houhong, former Deputy Governor of Anhui, from Anhui; Pang Weiqiang, former Commander of Hainan Military District; Xiao Yushu, former Commander of Guangxi Military District, from Hunan; Cai Changsong, former Mayor of Changde, from Hunan; Wang Xiaofeng, former Deputy Governor of Hunan, from Hunan; Liu Xuebian, former Party Secretary of Shuihua, from Heilongjiang; and Ruan Chongwu, former Minister of Labour, from Hebei. Sources: *Xin Hainan jishi* [A Chronicle of New Hainan] pp. 937, 941–2; *Hainan nianjian 1993* [Hainan Yearbook 1993] 1, pp. 4–7; *Hainan nianjian 1994* [Hainan Yearbook 1994] 1, pp. 9–11; *Hainan Ribao* [Hainan Daily] 26 August 1988; *Hainan Ribao* [Hainan Daily] 6 September 1988.

60   The two Old Mainlanders are Liu Mingqi and Meng Qianping. Liu is an ex-serviceman who previously served as Mayor and Party Secretary of Sanya City. Meng worked at the Shilu Mine 1961–84 and was the head of the Hainan government in the interregnum between Lei Yu's dismissal and the establishment of Hainan Province. Chen Suhou, the only Hainanese in this group was Director and CCP Secretary of the Hainan Agriculture Reclamation Bureau 1988–90. Wang Yuefeng and Wang Xueping – also members of the CCP Hainan Standing Committee – are the two Li. The eight New Mainlanders are: Liang Xiang, former Mayor of Shenzhen, from Guangdong; Liu Jianfeng, former Deputy Minister of the Electronics Industry, from Tianjin; Bao Keming, former Deputy Minister of Space Technology, from Shandong; Wang Xiaofeng, former Deputy Governor of Hunan, from Hunan; Ruan Chongwu, former Minister of Labour, from Hebei; Xin Yuejiang, former Director of the Department of Education in Guangdong, from Hunan; Zhou Erkang, former Deputy Mayor of Shenzhen, from Zhejiang; and Mao Zhijun, Director of the General Office of the Hebei People's Provincial government, from Sichuan. Sources: *Xin Hainan jishi* [A Chronicle of New Hainan] pp. 937, 941–2; *Hainan nianjian 1993* [Hainan Yearbook 1993] 1, pp. 4–7; *Hainan nianjian 1994* [Hainan Yearbook 1994] 1, pp. 9–11; *Hainan Ribao* [Hainan Daily] 26 August 1988; *Hainan Ribao* [Hainan Daily] 6 September 1988.

61   This anecdote was repeated several times without prompting in interviews with various officials in Hainan during 1994 and 1995.

62   Informal advice provided by an official in the provincial people's government, 1 September 1995. Hainanese head the Provincial Workers' Union, the Water Conservancy Bureau, the Department of Education, the Department of Communications, the Committee for Overseas Chinese Affairs, and the Bureau of Agricultural Reclamation.

63   Chen Jiang, 'New move in Hainan: avoidance system for cadres', *Ban Yue Tan* no. 15, 1989.

64 Interview with an official from Wanning County, December 1994.
65 'Report on the work of importing qualified personnel in science and technology from outside Hainan' (1983) in *Xin Hainan jishi* [A Chronicle of New Hainan], Zhonggong dangshi chubanshe, 1983, pp. 560–1; 'Suggestions on making further efforts to do the work of importing personnel with expertise' (1987) in *Zhongguo gaige kaifang huihuang chengjiu shisi nian – Hainan zhuan* [China's Brilliant Achievements in Fourteen Years of Reform and Opening – Hainan Volume], Zhongguo jingji chubanshe, 1993, p. 416.
66 Xu Shijie (Hainan Party Secretary) reported in 1988 that 'All of the five leading bodies of our province are directly selected and organised by central authorities, because our province is a new one. The staff of some units which require expertise are selected and recommended by the authorities of the Central Party Committee and the State Council' in 'Report on the preparatory work for establishing Hainan Province and the preparation for the First Hainan Provincial People's Congress' in Research Office for System Reform and Policy Research Office, CCP Hainan Provincial Committee (ed.) *Fangzhen, zhengce, fagui, zhanlue: guanyu Hainan jiansheng banda tequ wenjian ziliao huibian* [Guiding Principles, Policies, Regulations and Strategies: A collection of documents regarding the establishment of Hainan Province and Hainan SEZ] 1988, 4, p. 79. The normal practice in other provinces is that the leading cadre for each of the five leading institutions at provincial-level is selected by central authorities, with deputies locally selected though later endorsed by central authorities.
67 Hainan People's government, 'Statistical communiqué of social and economic development in Hainan Province during 1994'; Liao Xun *et al.* (eds) *Hainan nianjian 1994* [Hainan Yearbook 1994] 1 p. 58; Liao Xun 'Buru gaoshu fazhan – liunianlai de Hainan jingji' [At the beginning of high speed development: Hainan's economy in the last six years], paper presented at the conference on *The Development of Hainan and the Opportunities for Australia* 9–14 May 1994.
68 For details see: Liao Xun, 'Tourism or industry: the choice of leading industry for Hainan' in Liao Xun, Fu Dabang, and Tang Yong (eds) *92 Hainan shehui jingji fazhan yanjiu* [A Study of Hainan's Social and Economic Development in 1992], Nanhai chuban gongsi, 1993, pp. 136–56; Fan Anxun, 'The stages of economic development in Hainan and the changes of leading industrial sectors' in Liao Xun, Fu Dabang and Zhou Liangxian (eds) *93 Hainan shehui jingji fazhan yanjiu* [A Study of Hainan's Social and Economic Development in 1993], Nanhai chuban gongsi, 1994, pp. 70–8.
69 Xu Shijie (ed.) *Hainan sheng* [Hainan Province], Shangwu yingshuguan, 1988, p. 218.
70 Liao Xun (ed.) *Hainan Yearbook* 1993, 1, p. 68.
71 For a recent restatement of these arguments, see Chi Fulin, 'Juyou quanju yinxiang de Hainan xiandai nongyue' [Modern agriculture on Hainan: a matter of overall importance], *Newsletter of China (Hainan) Institute for Reform and Development* no. 103, 8 December 1994.
72 Shi Fulin, 'Juyou quanju yinxiang de Hainan xiandai nongyue' [Modern agriculture on Hainan: a matter of overall importance], *Newsletter of China (Hainan) Institute for Reform and Development* no. 103, 8 December 1994.
73 Interview with an official of Hainan Provincial government, Haikou, May 1994.
74 'Tai shang dali touzi Hainan nongyue kaifa' [Business people from Taiwan devote huge investment to development agriculture on Hainan], *Hainan Ribao* 22 November 1994.
75 'Tai shang kaifa Hainan nongyue shitou kanhou' [Good prospects for agriculture developed by Taiwan business people in Hainan], *Renmin Ribao* Overseas Edition 27 June 1993.
76 Wang Zhimong, 'Tourism: the leading industry for the extraordinary economic

development in Hainan', in Liao Xun, Fu Dabang and Tang Yong (eds) *92 Hainan shehui jingji fazhan yanju* [A Study of Social and Economic Development in Hainan in 1992], Nanhai chuban gongsi, 1993, pp. 187–90; Zhao Xisheng and Zhang Ruxian, 'Leading industry in the Great SEZ: a study on current development of tourism in Hainan', *Hainan Jingji* [Hainan Economy] no. 4, 1993.

77   Liao Xun, 'The choice of the leading industry for Hainan: tourism or industry?' in Liao Xun, Fu Dabang and Tang Yong (eds) *92 Hainan shehui jingji fazhan yanju* [A Study of Social and Economic Development in Hainan in 1992], Nanhai chuban gongsi, 1993, pp. 136–56.

78   For details, see Liu Guogong (ed.) *Hainan jingji fazhan zhanlu* [Hainan's Economic Development Strategy] Jingji guanli chubanshe, 1988, parts 1 and 2.

79   Liao Xun (ed.) *Hainan Year Book* 1993, 1, p. 67; Hainan Provincial Statistics Bureau, 'Statistical communiqué of economic and social development in 1993', *Hainan Ribao* [Hainan Daily] 28 February 1994.

80   Ruan Chongwu, 'Jiashu fazhan shehuizhuyi shichang jingji ba Hainan jingji tequ xiandaihua jianshe tuishang xintaijie' [Accelerate the development of the socialist market economy and take modernisation in the Hainan SEZ to a new stage], speech of 12 July 1993, in *Hainan Ribao* [Hainan Daily] 15 July 1993.

81   Wang Yong, 'Undersea gas project in pipeline', *China Daily* 26 April 1993.

82   Xu Shijie (ed.) *Hainan sheng* [Hainan Province], Shangwu yingshuguan, 1988, p. 178.

83   David S.G. Goodman, 'Guizhou and the People's Republic of China: the development of an internal colony', in D. Drakakis-Smith and S. William (eds) *Internal Colonialism: Essays Around a Theme*, IBG Development Areas Research Group Monograph no. 3, Edinburgh University, 1983, pp. 107–24.

84   See, for example, and most significantly: A.G. Frank *Capitalism and Underdevelopment in Latin America*, Monthly Review Press, New York, 1969; A. Giddens, *Central Problems in Social Theory*, Macmillan, London, 1979; M. Hechter *Internal Colonialism: The Celtic Fringe in British National Development 1536–1966*, University of California Press, Berkeley, 1975; S.W. Williams 'Internal colonialism, core–periphery contrasts and devolution', *Area* 9 no. 4, p. 272.

REFERENCES

Feng Chongyi and David S.G. Goodman, *China's Hainan Province: Economic Development and Investment Environment*, University of Western Australia Press, 1995.

Feng Chongyi and David S.G. Goodman, 'Hainan Province in reform: political dependence and economic interdependence', in Peter Cheung and Jae Ho Chung (eds) *Provincial Strategies of Economic Reform in Post-Mao China: Leadership, Politics and Implementation*, 1997.

Hainan Lizu, Miaozu zizhizhou gaikuang [A Brief Account of the Hainan Li and Miao Autonomous Prefecture], Guangdong renmin chubanshe, 1986.

Research Office for System Reform and Policy Research Office, CCP Hainan Provincial Committee (ed.) *Fangzhen, zhengce, fagui, zhanlue: guanyu Hainan jiansheng banda tequ wenjian ziliao huibian* [Guiding Principles, Policies, Regulations and Strategies: A Collection of Documents Regarding the Establishment of Hainan Province and Hainan SEZ], 1988.

Hainan Party History Research Office, *Xin Hainan jishi* [A Chronicle of New Hainan], Zhonggong dangshi chubanshe, 1993.

Hainan Province Statistical Bureau *Hainan Sheng Tongji Nianjian* [Hainan Provincial Statistics Yearbook], Zhonguo tongji chubanshe, 1988–90.

Jiang Wei (ed.) *Tequ sheng de guanlizhemen* [Administrators in the Provinces and SEZs], Zhongguo jingji chubanshe, 1991.

Li Zhimin and Wang Houhong (eds) *Hainan sheng qing gaiyao* [A Survey of the Current Situation in Hainan], Hainan chubanshe, 1992.

Liao Xun *et al.* (eds) *Hainan nianjian* [Hainan Yearbook] 1993–5, Hainan nianjianshe, 1994.

Liao Xun, Fu Dabang and Tang Yong (eds) *92 Hainan shehui jingji fazhan yanju* [A Study of Social and Economic Development in Hainan in 1992], Nanhai chuban gongsi, 1993.

Liao Xun *et al.* (eds) *93 Hainan shehui jingji fazhan yanjiu* [A Study of Social and Economic Development in Hainan during 1993], Nanhai chuban gongsi, 1994.

Liao Xun, *Kaifang de chengben* [The Cost of Opening], Nanhai chuban gongsi, 1993.

Liao Xun, *Shen qu ji: tequ shehui jingji fazhan yanjiu* [A Study of Social and Economic Development in SEZs], Hainan chubanshe, 1994.

Liu Guogong (ed.) *Hainan jingji fazhan zhanlue* [Hainan's Economic Development Strategy], Jingji guanli chubanshe, 1988.

Liu Zhongyi and Ouyang Tong (eds) *Keji xingqing* [Develop Hainan with Science and Technology], Hainan chubanshe, 1993.

Office for the History of Armed Struggle in Hainan (ed.) *Qiongya zhongdui shi* [A History of the Qiongya Column], Guangdong renmin chubanshe, 1986.

Research Office for System Reform and Policy Research Office, CCP Hainan Provincial Committee (eds) *Fangzhen, zhengce, fagui, zhanlue: guanyu Hainan jiansheng ban da tequ wenjian ziliao huibian* [Guiding Principles, Policies, Regulations and Strategies: A Collection of Documents Regarding the Establishment of Hainan Province and Hainan SEZ], 1988.

Research Office for System Reform and Policy Research Office, CCP Hainan Provincial Committee (eds) *Hainan shehuizhuyi shichang jingji tizhi de jiben shijian* [The Hainan Socialist Market Economy in Practice], 1993.

Ruan Chongwu, 'Government Work Report for 1994', *Hainan Ribao* [Hainan Daily] 19 March 1994.

Shi Fulin (ed.) *Hainan xintizhi:guojia yu shijian* [New Systems and New Practices in Hainan], Hainan chubanshe, 1992.

Social and Economic Development Research Centre of Hainan Provincial Government, *Hainan sheng touzi zhengce* [Hainan Province Investment Policy], Sanhuan chuban gongsi, 1991.

Charles Wolf *et al.*, *Market-oriented Policies for the Development of Hainan*, Rand, Santa Monica, CA, 1992.

Xiao Yucai (ed.) *Zhongguo Jingji Tequ Shi Nian Congshu – Hainan Fence* [Ten Years of the Special Economic Zones in China – Hainan Volume], China's Special Economic Zones Data and Research Unit, Centre for Contemporary Asian Studies, Chinese University of Hong Kong, 1990.

Xu Shijie (ed.) *Hainan sheng* [Hainan Province], Shangwu yingshuguan, 1988.

Xu Shijie *et al.* (eds) *Dangdai Zhongguo de Hainan* [Hainan Today], Dangdai Zhongguo chubanshe, 1993.

Zhan Changzhi (ed.) *Zhongguo renkou – Hainan fence* [The Population of China – Hainan volume], Zhongguo caicheng chubanshe, 1993.

Zhongguo gaige kaifang huihuang chengjiu shisi nian – Hainan zhuan [China's Brilliant Achievements in Fourteen Years of Reform and Opening – Hainan Volume], Zhongguo jingji chubanshe, 1993.

Zhong Yechang, *Hainan jingji fazhan yanjiu* [A Study of Hainan's Economic Development], Zhongguo kexue jishu chubanshe, 1991.

Zhu Yihui (ed.) *Hainan mingren zhuanlue* [Famous Hainanese], Zhongshan daxue chubanshe, 1992.

Newspaper and journals

Hainan Jingji [Hainan Economy]
Hainan Ribao[Hainan Daily]
Kaifang Yu Kaifa [Opening and Development]
Touzi yu hezuo [Investment and Cooperation]

Liaoning Province

GENERAL

GDP (billion *yuan* renminbi)	258.40
GDP annual growth rate	11.20
as % national average	94.92
GDP per capita	6,354.07
as % national average	169.21
Gross Value Agricultural Output (billion *yuan* renminbi)	60.20
Gross Value Industrial Output (billion *yuan* renminbi)	459.90

POPULATION

Population (million)	40.67
Natural growth rate (per 1,000)	12.26

WORKFORCE

Total workforce (million)	20.09
Employment by activity (%)	
primary industry	31.20
secondary industry	38.50
tertiary industry	30.30
Employment by sector (% of provincial population)	
urban	28.33
rural	21.08
state sector	16.78
collective sector	19.74
private sector	4.14
foreign-funded sector	0.48

WAGES

Average annual wage (*yuan* renminbi)	4,269
Growth rate in real wage	5.20

PRICES

CPI annual rise (%)	24.30
Service price index rise (%)	34.10
Per capita consumption (*yuan* renminbi)	1,921
as % national average	110.59
Urban disposable income per capita	3,063
as % national average	87.61
Rural per capita income	1,423
as % national average	116.54

FOREIGN TRADE AND INVESTMENT

Total foreign trade (US$ billion)	10.23
% provincial GDP	34.12
Exports (US$ billion)	6.05
Imports (US$ billion)	4.18
Realised foreign capital (US$ million)	1,514.71
% provincial GDP	5.04

EDUCATION

University enrolments	171,284
% national average	180.36
Secondary school enrolments (million)	1.92
% national average	113.70
Primary school enrolments (million)	3.75
% national average	86.20

Notes: All statistics are for 1994 and all growth rates are for 1994 over 1993 and are adapted from *Zhongguo tongji nianjian 1995* [Statistical Yearbook of China 1995], Zhongguo tongji chubanshe, Beijing, 1995 as reformulated and presented in *Provincial China* no. 1 March 1996, pp. 34ff.

Liaoning Province

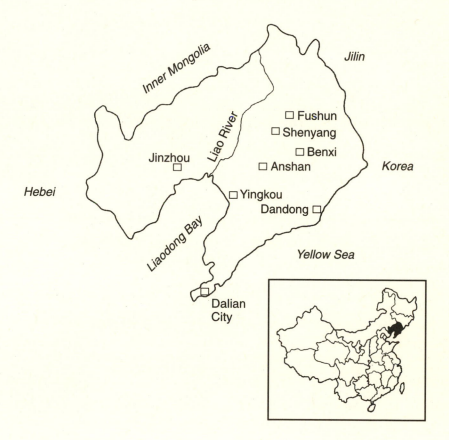

4 Liaoning

Struggling with the burdens of the past

Margot Schueller

Economic reform and integration into the world economy are challenging the political and economic elites of Liaoning Province in new and different ways. On account of its strategic importance, this southernmost of the three northeastern provinces of China was long said to have been cherished by the central government in Beijing like a 'king's daughter'.[1] Since reform was extended to the urban industrial sector in the middle of the 1980s, however, the province's large-scale heavy industry, once the glory of Liaoning, has been faced with great problems. The deterioration of the state sector's economic performance in Liaoning has coincided with the export-driven economic success of the southern coastal provinces' non-state-owned enterprises; not only Guangdong but also Shandong and Jiangsu are now ahead of Liaoning as far as the rate of economic development and performance is concerned.

Although Liaoning has tried to speed up its economic development, its unbalanced economic structure and inefficiency within the large state-owned industrial sector have remained a heavy burden. Social conflicts which arose during the process of transforming the loss-making enterprises into more profitable ones have put additional pressure on the political leadership. A sense of urgency for change with respect to long-standing problems and a desire to become competitive have gradually emerged and have highlighted the need for the modernisation both of Liaoning's 'hardware' and of its 'software', i.e. its political and economic elite. Adaption to the challenges of economic reform has been slow. Resistance from the old industrial sector, however, explains this only to a certain extent, as other factors have also been at work.

Compared to Guangdong's successful entry into the world market via Hong Kong and the large investment by the Overseas Chinese community in the South, Liaoning has lacked both access to foreign markets and Overseas Chinese with family ties in the province. Liaoning's slow integration into the world market has also been due to the relatively late introduction of the open door policies in Liaoning and to political tensions between sub-provincial entities and the province's capital. The rather inward-looking strategy of the state-owned enterprises' modernisation programme pursued by the provincial capital's bureaucrats has contrasted sharply with the outward-looking strategy which was adopted by the coastal cities of Liaoning Province in response to international demand.

This examination of the impact of reform on Liaoning starts with an overview of Liaoning's historical and strategic importance as a centre of heavy industry. Initially, this represented a major advantage for the province but during the process of economic reform it became a major obstacle to further development. The province's experience seems typical of all those provinces dominated by the planned economy and state-owned enterprises (SOEs), which was characterised by close allegiance to the planning system and the previous policy goals as well as considerable conservatism in implementing reforms.

The second section of this chapter analyses the underlying causes for Liaoning's recent dynamic development. Despite high adjustment costs in terms of technology, employment, welfare and from other social and political dimensions, the economy has undergone fundamental changes with major growth in the non-state sector. The last section of the chapter examines the impact on the province of the open door policy together with regional decentralisation, which transferred the authority to make decisions regarding economic development to local officials.

LIAONING'S PAST GLORY: THE STRATEGIC IMPORTANCE OF AN INDUSTRIAL BASE

Liaoning's border location made the province very vulnerable to the imperialistic ambitions of Russia and Japan in the nineteenth century. With central power continually weakening and after the defeat of Russia in the Russo-Japanese War of 1904–5, the province (known as Fengtian between 1919 and 1928) came under Japanese control. Using the South Manchuria Railway Company as an instrument to exploit the huge coal and iron deposits of the province, Japan's penetration of the three northeast provinces greatly restricted and conditioned the sovereignty of the Chinese administration. In the words of one famous scholar: 'De facto and increasingly from 1905, Manchuria was a piece of colonial property, probably even more effectively so than India or Java'.[2]

After a short while, the economic development of Fengtian became directly linked to the demand for products from Japan, which invested heavily in the construction of coal mines, iron mines and trunk railway lines, as well as in foreign trading, shipping companies and electric power stations. The first blast furnace was established in Benxi as early as 1915, and in 1917 the Anshan Steel Mill was founded. Mining operations were expanded to Fushun and other areas; textile, metal, chemical and foodstuff industries were established in the vicinity of the railway lines and in the port area around Lushun and Luda (Dalian).[3] The rapid industrialisation of the province led to an increase in its share in the national economy. By 1929, Fengtian accounted for a large percentage of coal and iron output, railway mileage, foreign trade and power capacity. It was not China, however, but Japan which was the major cause, controller and beneficiary of this development.[4]

After the annexation of Manchuria in 1931, Japan transferred capital and skilled labour to Manchuria on a large scale in order to launch an ambitious programme of rapid industrialisation. Besides increasing the capacity of extractive and heavy industry, a large communications network and hydro-electric power system was built. However, the Japanese development strategy neglected the agricultural sector almost completely, as the area's economic development was intended to serve Japan's military expansion and not any particular Chinese welfare needs.[5]

Besides determining the economic life of their colony Manzhouguo, the Japanese extended their influence to the whole of Chinese society. The teaching of the Japanese language was enforced and political opposition suppressed in a very brutal way, as shown by the Fushun Pingdingshan massacre. On this occasion, a large village was destroyed and its 3,000 inhabitants killed by the Japanese.[6] While resistance against Japanese influence was strong, it was not generally voiced openly. Trying to secure Japan's neutrality while expanding his military power, Northeast China's famous warlord Zhang Zuolin was nevertheless open to nationalist ideas. Increasingly in opposition to Japan, he supported the economic development plan of the Northeast China administration because he wanted to build a prosperous and 'independent' Manchuria. Zhang Zuolin, who became military and civil governor of Fengtian province in 1916, was able to extend his power to Jilin and Heilongjiang within three years and dominated Northeast China in the 1920s and 1930s. He was able to create a broad power base consisting of military and civilian elites known as the 'Mukden Clique'. However, his strategy of using Japan to his own ends did not work out; in fact, he himself was used as a tool in Japan's expansion into the northeast and he was ultimately assassinated by the Japanese in 1928.[7]

The Chinese administration's plan to strengthen Northeast China's economic development by building its own railway lines was hampered by strong competition from the Japanese-owned South Manchuria Railway Company. While Japan operated the Dalian–Mukden (Shenyang) line, the Chinese Railway company was not allowed to extend its network beyond the Yingkou–Mukden line, and was therefore kept in an inferior position.[8] Nevertheless, the railway lines established at that time permitted a large influx of labour from other provinces into Manchuria during the 1920s. The Fengtian civil governor Wang Yongjiang, senior Chinese official in Manchuria, supported this influx of labour as a means of developing the economy. Knowing that there was no assistance to be expected from the central government, Wang and the Provincial Bureau of Administrative Affairs worked out a 'Colonisation and Development Plan' with incentives for workers encouraging them to come to Manchuria and settle down there. By encouraging the growing of cotton and its processing, the Fengtian government successfully opened new avenues for agricultural production and established a textile manufacturing industry. By 1928, however, Zhang Zuolin's issuing of paper currency to finance his military actions had caused inflation to rise so much that the newly built industries began to suffer greatly.[9]

Zhang Zuolin's influence is still felt in Liaoning. In Shenyang's central district of Shenhe, the former mansion and home of Zhang Zuolin and his son Zhang Xueliang has recently been opened to the public as a museum. It incorporates various exhibition halls presenting historical events in Zhang Zuolin's life. Zhang Zuolin was eventually killed by the Japanese; his son, who later also became a prominent political figure, was deported to Taiwan by the Nationalist Party. The opening of the museum serves two goals. On the one hand, it reflects the increasing sense of regional identity in Liaoning, and on the other it is intended to attract investors and tourists from Taiwan to the province, people who might otherwise not come to the region as few Overseas Chinese investors in China have ancestral roots in the northeast.

Japanese influence on Liaoning's economic development has been enormous. As a legacy of Japan's occupation, the province came to possess a fairly highly developed industrial complex and transportation network but suffered from structural imbalances caused by the neglect of certain sectors and branches. While mining and other heavy industries constituted the dominant sectors, the share taken by the processing industry remained rather small. The weakness of the machine-building industry was very obvious and although the iron and steel industry was fairly well developed, equipment capacity was unbalanced.

Agricultural development had been generally neglected during the Japanese occupation, with crop cultivation remaining underdeveloped, causing a decline in productivity and insufficient supplies of industrial raw materials and foodstuffs. Furthermore, there was a high regional concentration of economic activities, with three quarters of the industrial production coming from three cities, Shenyang, Dalian and Anshan. In northern and western regions of the province, there were abundant mining reserves but a lack of industrial enterprises. These features of an unbalanced economy influenced the province's later development considerably.

The Party Centre's influence on Liaoning's political elite

Owing to Liaoning's strategic position and economic importance, the Chinese Communist Party's interest in the province was very strong. As early as 1923, the CCP Northeast Committee dispatched a number of members to Mukden and Dalian who helped to set up a CCP railway branch in Goubangzi and CCP branches in Mukden (Shenyang), Dalian and Tai'an. The next step in building an organisational structure was the foundation of the CCP Manzhou (Manchuria) Committee which was to lead the CCP organisation in the three Northeast China provinces. Liu Shaoqi and several other high-level Communist cadres were sent to Mukden to support the activities of the CCP Manzhou

Committee. They founded the *Jingyuan Xueguan*, an anti-Japanese propaganda team responsible for printing and distributing political propaganda. The CCP Manzhou Committee numbered 210 people at the end of 1928 and increased to 1,400 in 1931. After the Liutiaohu Incident, which set the final stage for the occupation by the Japanese, the CCP organised anti-Japanese protests and guerrilla activities along the railway lines.

In 1945, a quarter of the CCP Central Committee members, among them Peng Zhen, Chen Yun, Gao Gang and Zhang Wentian, led 20,000 cadres and 100,000 soldiers to Northeast China to organise the land reform and to fight in the civil war. In addition to CCP committees for Liaoning Province, Andong Province, Dalian City and Shenyang City, a Northeast Department of the CCP Central Committee was founded which had the task of organising military actions against the Guomingdang government. When Liaoning was finally 'liberated' in November 1948, the CCP organisational structure was remoulded and the East Liaoning Provincial CCP Committee and the West Liaoning Provincial CCP Committee were founded. The two committees – and indeed Liaoning Province – were united in 1954. In Shenyang, Luda, Anshan, Fushun and Benxi, the five largest cities in Liaoning, CCP committees were organised and subordinated to the Northeast Department of the CCP Central Committee. The number of CCP members also increased, reaching 140,000 by the beginning of 1949.[10]

On account of the province's strategic importance, the CCP's Central Committee exercised relatively tight control over Liaoning's political elites. After the liberation of the province by the People's Liberation Army under Lin Biao, Gao Gang, the deputy commander and deputy political commissar of the Northeast Military Region, became the top party government and military official, and came to represent a strong regional power in Northeast China. He used his close contacts with the Soviet Army to help bring about the rapid reconstruction of Liaoning's economy, not least by heading the first trade delegation to Moscow. Although the CCP's Central Committee supported his industrial policy for the First Five-Year Plan (FYP), the Central Committee tried to curb his power by calling him to Beijing together with other well-known local leaders in 1952. The following year, Gao Gang, by then holding some of the most powerful posts in the PRC, was accused by the Central Committee of attempting to build an 'independent kingdom' in the northeast and was consequently removed from his posts and expelled from the Party. Robbed of Gao Gang, Liaoning lost a strong representative of the province's interests.[11]

The allegiance of the province's political elite was very important for the realisation of the CCP's political programme during the Great Leap Forward (GLF). Liaoning was the first province to announce the amalgamation of the agricultural producers' co-operatives, a month ahead of Henan. The province's reports on the ease of the amalgamation reinforced Beijing's decision to push for communisation. During the 'Anti-Rightist Campaign' in Liaoning in 1957, around 25,000 people including party members were accused of 'leftist deviation'. During the GLF, Mao Zedong praised the Anshan Party Committee for its efforts in the anti-rightist struggle in July 1959 and Liaoning Provincial Party Committee's 'achievements' in August that same year. Just how far the setting of unrealistic goals and political submission went during the GLF is shown by the following slogans. In order to surpass Shanghai, the economic goal for Liaoning was set at '100 million *yuan* output value in one day'. In order to realise the technological revolution that was necessary for this, 'One revolution every two days' was initially called for and later 'Two revolutions a day'.[12] Despite these considerable ideological efforts, the leadership of the province was not able to achieve a breakthrough in realising the GLF's economic goals.

The GLF's goal of simultaneous development of agriculture and industry put the provincial CCP Committee under great pressure, as Liaoning relied heavily on food imports from other provinces. After being personally criticised by Mao Zedong, the local CCP tried to enforce regional autarky in food production, although this meant a complete change in its development strategy. Opposition within the provincial party was suppressed and large resources of capital and personnel were concentrated on the construction of water conservancy facilities and the fulfilment of *The Twelve Year National Programme for Agricultural Development (1956–1967)* ahead of schedule. The use of concentrated forces of peasants in the construction of large water conservancy facilities resulted in a shortage of labour during the harvest. In the light of this, Du Zhehang, provincial governor and secretary of the provincial party committee in charge of agriculture, attempted to redirect labour into other agricultural activities. According to Chan's analysis of the GLF in Liaoning, Du tried to pursue a more pragmatic policy which brought him into conflict with central orders. As a result, he was expelled from his posts. His political demise and the submission of Huang Huoqing, the new first secretary, to the contradictory goals of the GLF are taken by Chan as proof of how little independence in policy-making the Liaoning Provincial Party Committee actually had regarding a provincial development strategy. In the following decades, Liaoning's political elites showed a strong 'revolutionary enthusiasm' in enforcing mass mobilisation movements, or as Chan puts it, Liaoning 'became ultra-sensitive to the wishes of the centre, and felt obliged to implement all the central whims and policies at once'.[13]

Liaoning played a decisive role in the Cultural Revolution. By sending Mao Zedong's nephew, Mao Yuanxin, to Liaoning in May 1968, for instance, the people later called the 'Gang of Four' aimed at making the province a model for the Cultural Revolution. Mao Yuanxin, who took on the post of Vice-Director of the Liaoning Revolutionary Committee and secretary of the PPC, denounced the leading cadres of the Liaoning Provincial Committee as 'traitors, spies and capitalist-roaders' and ordered 30,000 high-ranking party officials to attend indoctrination classes. More than 100,000 cadres and 200,000 dependents were sent to the countryside as punishment or for re-education by the Revolutionary Committee. Mao Yuanxin put his comrades in key positions and established a close network with top personnel at Shanghai and Beijing's two famous universities Qinghua and Beida. The political left wing was very influential during the 1970s. In 1975, Mao Yuanxin even openly opposed Deng Xiaoping's reform policy, declaiming it as 'restoration'. Even after the purge of the 'Gang of Four' it needed a special order from the Central Committee in 1977 to reduce the political power of the provincial party's left wing.[14]

During the period of economic reform the Central Committee has exercised its influence on the province's assignment of leading cadres with the aim of bringing about ideological changes needed for adaptation to the new policies. The most recent reshuffling of the top provincial party leadership took place between 1990 and 1994. The province's governor Li Changchun (born in Jilin but with a family background in Liaoning) was replaced by Yue Qifen from Hebei. Yue was the first governor from outside the province for almost ten years. He was provincial governor from 1990 to 1994 and was then sent to Heilongjiang, another northeastern province shaken by structural adjustment and efficiency problems within the large state sector. Yue became the First Party Secretary of Heilongjiang in 1995 in an obvious act of promotion by the central government. The centre demonstrated its strong support for Yue Qifen later by publishing a book containing his speeches on economic reform in Liaoning.[15]

In Liaoning, Quan Shuren, the First Party Secretary (1986–93) and a native of the province, was replaced by Gu Jinchi from Hebei. Two newly appointed deputy party secretaries came from Hunan and Shandong and another from Liaoning. The fourth deputy party secretary, Wen Shizhen, has also been Liaoning's governor since 1994 and is again a native of Liaoning.[16] The replacement of prominent local figures by cadres from outside Liaoning at the beginning of the 1990s contrasted with the general trend of localisation among provincial cadres.[17]

Obviously, the centre wanted to resolve a deadlock in economic reform when introducing these 'outsiders' through the nomenclature system. And it was during Yue Qifen's term in office as provincial governor that strong criticism was openly voiced. In October 1993, for example, Yue Qifen gave an interview to the weekly national news magazine *Liaowang* in which he referred to various articles criticising the conservative attitudes of cadres and bureaucrats in Liaoning's SOEs and the missed opportunities for economic reform. In the interview, the governor acknowledged the critics' views – that Liaoning's products were not competitive, SOE managers neglected to promote the technical workers' initiatives and that conservative ideology was the main reason why Liaoning was falling behind Guangdong, Jiangsu and Shandong. Although certain changes had occurred in Liaoning in 1990 and 1991, not enough progress was made in solving these problems. Yue warned that 'some of our comrades are still reluctant to hear or read such news, but it is the harsh reality and if we don't face it we will not be able to make rapid advances.'[18]

PAST BURDENS AND NEW CHALLENGES

Liaoning's economy recovered rapidly during the First Five-Year Plan, thanks to assistance from the Soviet Union, financial support from central government and the Japanese legacy of an industrial complex and transportation network. In this period, an overwhelming share (94 per cent) of the central government's investments were directed at the development of the province's heavy industry, whose contribution to the national economy amounted to 71 per cent of iron production, 63 per cent of steel production and 58 per cent of steel products in 1957.[19] The steel works of Anshan and Benxi, the coal mines of Fushun and Fuxin, and the machine industry of Shenyang were of central importance for the development of heavy industry nationally. The provincial economy was concentrated in these large cities, the neglect of the agricultural sector leading to a strong urban–rural development bias.

Although the provincial economy suffered a number of setbacks during the GLF and the Cultural Revolution, economic development during the pre-reform period was more rapid in Liaoning than in most inland provinces and much faster compared to Jiangsu, Shandong and Guangdong. Yet, from 1979 to 1990, as Table 4.1 indicates, Liaoning's growth rates were conspicuously low compared to these other provinces, indicating that economic reform had worked against the comparative advantage of the province.

As Table 4.1 indicates, over the years Liaoning lost its dominant position in the national economy to other coastal provinces. Using an aggregated development index consisting of growth rates of twenty important indicators,

Table 4.1 Economic growth in Liaoning and other selected provinces, 1953–90 (%)

| | GVSP | GVIO | GVAO | GDP | Sector | | |
					Primary	Secondary	Tertiary
1953–78							
Liaoning	8.2	10.0	2.7	7.6	2.2	0.7	5.3
Jiangsu	7.3	1.7	3.3	5.2	2.5	12.3	3.9
Shandong	7.2	11.7	2.2				
Guangdong	6.7	10.6	3.5	5.2	2.7	10.5	4.5
1979–90							
Liaoning	9.0	9.1	5.3	7.6	5.1	6.6	13.6
Jiangsu	14.1	16.6	5.9	10.3	5.4	12.3	11.4
Shandong	12.8	14.6	7.1	9.6	6.7	11.1	10.2
Guangdong	14.8	23.4	7.1	12.3	7.4	13.7	14.4

Note: GVSP: Gross Value Social Product; GVIO: Gross Value Industrial Output; GVAO: Gross Value Agricultural Output; GDP: Gross Domestic Product

Source: Liaoning Daxue Jingji Yanjiasuo, *Liaoning Jingji Shichanghua Chengdu de Kaocha yu Jiangsu, Shandong, Guangdong san sheng bijiao*, 1993, p. 2

it is apparent that Liaoning's overall level of economic development dropped from the fourth rank nationally in 1978 to the twenty-first rank in 1992. The main problem confronting the province at the beginning of the 1990s was an inadequate basis for a modern economy: an unbalanced structure of production, little competitiveness and ideological restrictions towards adaptation to a market system.[20] Liaoning's unbalanced economic structure can be seen in a comparison of the shares of the Gross Value Industrial and Agricultural Output (GVIAO) and the contributions of heavy industry to the GVIO in 1957 and in 1993 (Table 4.2).

As early as 1957, GVIO had been 81.7 per cent of Liaoning's GVIAO, with heavy industry making up 75.8 per cent, indicating that Liaoning was one of the earliest industrialised regions in China. Until 1993 the agricultural sector's share decreased while that of light industry increased slightly. Although Liaoning's economic structure is evidence that the province has achieved the basic transformation from an agrarian society to an industrialised society, the industrial sector itself shows insufficient diversification. Inferior product quality, outdated equipment, the predominance of raw material industries within the heavy industrial sector and a very limited range of durable consumer goods supplied to the national and international markets are critical features of the province's economic system.[21]

The state sector: past advantage and current obstacle

The fact that Liaoning's economic development has fallen behind that of other provinces and that its economy has had such adjustment problems can be attributed to a number of interacting factors. The close integration of the province into the planned economy resulted in the setting up of a certain industrial structure shaped to the needs of the central plan. Economic control was exercised by direct supervision of major industries or by local governments directly managing enterprises. In Liaoning, a few thousand large and medium-sized enterprises belonging to central or provincial government

Table 4.2 Sectoral shares of Liaoning's GVIAO, 1957 and 1993 (%)

	1957	1993
GVIO	81.7	88.8
GVAO	18.3	11.2
Heavy industry	75.8	73.6
Light industry	24.2	26.4

Note: The shares of GVIO and GVAO are calculated on the basis of the aggregate value of GVIO and GVAO; heavy and light industry shares are calculated on the basis of GVIO

Source: Zhang Jinsheng, *Liaoning shehui jingji fazhan ji ge zhanlue wenti*, Liaoning University, Shenyang, 1995

made up the 'hardware' of the planning system. More than 60 per cent of this 'hardware' was outdated, built in accordance with the abundant natural resources, geographical location and favourable transportation made available during the First Five-Year Plan.[22]

During the 1980s, entry barriers for industry were reduced and SOEs came under pressure from increased competition inside and outside the province. The state sector's performance in efficiency and profitability deteriorated year by year. Return on investment for each 100 *yuan* of fixed assets decreased from 24.7 *yuan* in 1978 to 18 *yuan* in 1987 and to 8.1 *yuan* in 1992. At the same time, the losses suffered by state-owned enterprises grew from 340,000 *yuan* in 1977 to 3.79 billion *yuan* in 1992.[23] Looking at the regional distribution of industrial state-owned enterprises' losses in 1993, Liaoning's share of losses in GVIO amounted to 8.8 per cent, equal to the percentage share of Heilongjiang province. It was second only to Shandong province's share of losses (10.4 per cent).[24]

Problems were mainly located in the large and medium-sized SOEs in Liaoning, of which there were 1,263 in 1992. Although these enterprises represent only 4.8 per cent of the total, their share in GVIO and in profit and taxes was 70.7 per cent and 74.8 per cent respectively in 1992. There are only 144 enterprises under central government control at present, but their output was 48.847 billion *yuan* in 1992. While there were 1,117 enterprises run by the provincial government in the same year, they produced just 68,999 *yuan*, representing a central–local relationship of 40.8:59.2. The 373 large state-owned enterprises were of special importance within the industrial sector, producing 89,994 billion *yuan* GVIO, while the output of the 888 medium-sized and 20,681 small enterprises amounted to 27,853 billion *yuan* and 48,930 billion *yuan* respectively. In 1992, around 18 per cent of those large and medium enterprises seemed to be working well with no losses, efficient management and an average profit and tax delivery per capita of more than 10,000 *yuan*. About 60 per cent – 757 enterprises – possessed the basic conditions necessary to survive: their management structure was reasonably good and their products were competitive to some degree. This was despite the fact that they belonged to old industries and needed technological upgrading. The remaining 22 per cent of the enterprises were basically not able to survive because they had incurred high losses over a long period of time. These unsuccessful enterprises were characterised by outdated equipment, outdated technology, heavy debts, little or no profit-making capacity and an inability to undertake restructuring on their own.[25]

Liaoning's investment in the technological upgrading of state-owned units more than doubled from 6.84 billion *yuan* to 17.8 billion *yuan* between 1990 and 1993. Despite this investment, technological inferiority and worn-out equipment contributed to the enterprises failing to make profits. Chain debts were incurred on account of the poor quality of products and the resulting stockpiling of unsold goods.[26] The extent to which SOEs are threatened by inferior product quality is evident from the following example. At the end of

1994, Liaoning's largest iron and steel works, the Anshan Iron & Steel Works, ran into difficulties and even had to stop production because the amount of its unmarketable products had increased to 300,000 tons. Shanghai's Baoshan Iron & Steel Works, on the other hand, had so many contracts that it was unable to meet demand. At the beginning of 1995, the central government had to make emergency loans to pay workers' salaries in the Anshan Iron & Steel Works. According to estimates, an investment of approximately 50 billion *yuan* would be necessary to modernise such a huge enterprise, an investment volume that the province itself is not able to undertake.[27]

Apart from plant and equipment difficulties there is also a 'software' problem facing industries in Liaoning. The management and incentive structures of a planned economy with large SOEs produce a certain kind of value system and behaviour among local governments, managers and other employees of an SOE, which can be called their 'software' or behavioural pattern. Within the central economic plan, SOEs had to serve policy goals regarding employment and the production of certain goods. Since SOEs' productive function was linked to social services and lifetime employment, enterprises striving for greater efficiency by changing the capital and labour combination had to act against their workers' interests. With respect to SOE managers' attitudes, the larger the enterprise, the less incentive managers had to give up governmental protection from market changes.[28] Sheltering the SOEs from the discipline of 'hard budget constraints' and relying on SOEs for taxes and employment resulted in the rather substantial administrative involvement of government in decision-making within SOEs. To sum up, the challenge of reform for Liaoning was a need for diversification of the industrial structure, leading to a new balance between economic sectors and, at the same time, to changes in the distribution of economic wealth. Additionally, SOEs had to become more efficient and increase their competitiveness. However, the overwhelming presence of the state-sector, and the economic well-being of various groups in society strongly supporting SOEs, ensured that enterprise reform would prove to be very difficult.[29]

Enterprise reform

Liaoning's enterprise reform started in 1983 with the decentralisation of decision-making with respect to daily operations and the provision of workers' incentives, the responsibility passing into the hands of the managers of state-owned enterprises. In some medium-sized and small-scale enterprises a management contract system was introduced. The 1984 CCP Central Committee's decision on economic structural reform pointed the way for further reform measures aimed at increasing the power of enterprise directors to improve efficiency, productivity and profitability. Shenyang, Dalian and Dandong were chosen to experiment with the enterprise reform. The 'director responsibility system', a contract system similar to the one introduced in agricultural production, was at the centre of the reform. Basically it involved the separation of property rights between the local government as the enterprises' owner and the right to operate the enterprise by a manager within specified terms laid down in a contract.

By 1988, the contract system was reported to have become widely used in Liaoning, with 96.4 per cent of all large and medium-sized state-owned enterprises having introduced it – at least on paper. Contract terms usually referred to responsibilities for delivering a certain profit, development of input and output, asset management and operation objectives. Although the introduction of the contract system aimed at separating enterprise management and government function, an analysis of local state-run enterprises' decision-making powers at the beginning of 1992 revealed that the 1988 enterprise law and other reform policies had not been thoroughly implemented. Local government's control even persisted in such fields as organisational structure and employment.[30]

Indications of the further deteriorating state of some of the largest enterprises in Liaoning have increased and with them the pressure for new approaches to reform. In 1994, the province's new governor Wen Shizhen declared that 18 per cent of the state-owned enterprises, employing about 15 per cent of the provincial workforce and including many deficit-ridden mines, were in 'great difficulties or insolvent'. He listed another 49 per cent of the state-owned enterprises as 'profitless and unstable'.[31] As many large state-owned enterprises are concentrated in Shenyang and the pressure to solve their problems is constantly increasing, the city government found it necessary to adapt a new economic policy in 1994. Its decision to undertake 'experimental measures to establish a modern enterprise system' can be read as a description of the enterprises' difficult situation. The new policy involves twenty-two large and medium-sized state-owned enterprises in the experiment; two of those enterprises chosen as experimental enterprises belong to the central government and three to the provincial government. One of the most urgent policy goals was the clear division of property rights, an issue which obviously had been a problem in the experimental enterprises. The new policy document called for the transfer of enterprise management mechanisms to be carried out according to Company Law and for asset rights to be clearly defined by implementing the stock company system. The city government was required to encourage multiple ownership for these enterprises, including collective, individual and foreign investors' participation. The document set down special criteria to increase efficiency within the duration of the experiment, including labour dismissal and the introduction of the labour contract system even for state cadres.[32]

Although Liaoning was the first province to declare debt-ridden enterprises bankrupt in 1986, the time for allowing a large number of enterprises to go bankrupt does not yet seem to be ripe. The problems connected with bankruptcy are many, as can be seen from the following example. Up to the end of June 1994, fifty enterprises, nine of which were state-owned, went bankrupt and 13,500 people, 7,800 workers and 5,700 retired employees were affected by these bankruptcies. Because of the poorly developed social security system, it was difficult to provide these people with social security benefits. Problems existed on various levels. First, the pension and unemployment funds were very small – in 1993 the accumulated retirement fund amounted to 1.55 billion *yuan*, sufficient only for eight months' retirement support. The unemployment fund amounted to 250 million *yuan*, just enough for one year's unemployment pay. Second, the re-employment of workers affected by bankruptcy was very difficult because of their great number: there were about 1.6 million surplus workers. Those workers who were skilled had left the enterprises before bankruptcies were declared, leaving only unskilled workers in the plant.[33]

The extent to which SOE workers in Shenyang have suffered from the decline in their social position after being discharged by their employers has been the subject of an article in the Communist Youth League publication *China's Youth*. The journal claimed that the majority of the workers were not against the restructuring of the SOEs, but resented the way they had been treated. Once revered as 'loyal pioneers in the building of socialism', they found themselves sent home 'on leave' with a monthly allowance of 80 *yuan*, which is the minimum subsistence level for Shenyang. To support their families, they were forced to earn some extra money, often working as street-vendors or offering repair services. The article also referred to a survey regarding the reactions of displaced workers from SOEs. The documented attitudes ranged from anxiety and nostalgia for the past to total social withdrawal; in some cases workers' frustration led to acts of destructive theft.[34]

Since 1994, Beijing's tight credit policy has exacerbated the pressure on SOEs. To cut the number of workers on the payroll, SOEs in Shenyang first asked female and older workers to take prolonged leave while granting them only a small allowance. The increasing number of desperate SOE workers taking odd jobs as vendors in the streets of Shenyang contrasts sharply with the situation in other cities such as Beijing, where people from poorer provinces – by and large peasants – tend to do such work. Small-scale labour protests by discontented workers are reported to have already taken place in Shenyang, with several hundred workers demonstrating against the threat of unemployment.[35]

The year 1995 again saw a number of labour protests in Shenyang, none of which was reported in the official press. Workers' protests were not actually suppressed, but the demonstrators were guided to nearby sports halls and sports grounds to stage their protests out of sight of the public. As many loss-making SOEs were short of money to provide central heating in their residential buildings and coal-trading companies were not prepared to give these enterprises further credit, many of the workers' dwellings remained unheated in the early winter months.[36] During the spring festival in 1996 local government became quite nervous about the spectre of further labour-related unrest, and sent officials to visit unemployed workers' homes with gifts of money and food for the holiday. This 'good-will' measure was reported on Chinese television.[37]

In September 1994, the province launched a re-employment programme to provide jobs for redundant workers. While keeping the unemployment rate at 5 per cent, the provincial government declared that it would open up new areas of production for half of the expected 750,000 redundant workers within a period of four years. The remaining unemployed workers would have to find jobs on their own or get financial support from the government.[38] Despite the mounting pressure of unemployment, Shenyang City's Resettlement Office for Bankrupt Enterprises came to the conclusion that the task of resettling all laid-off workers will be impossible to fulfil.[39]

While it was the workers of SOEs who turned out to be the losers in the economic reform process, the social position of state cadres in these enterprises also changed drastically. A joint decision by the province's Department of Organisation and the Department of Personnel and the Committee for Restructuring the Economy had a major impact on the 650,000 cadres in Liaoning's SOEs, 410,000 of whom were state cadres. By delegating the autonomy to employ managerial and technical personnel according to production and management needs in the SOEs, the guarantee of lifetime employment which these cadres had previously enjoyed now vanished. Today these cadres, who account for nearly one-tenth of all employees in SOEs, have to be hired by the enterprise for different positions and can even be employed as ordinary workers.[40] One of the hardest-hit groups in the process of SOE restructuring were union cadres, who understandably became especially resentful towards the central government.[41]

The desperate state of the province's state-sector industry led to requests for more help from the central government at the National People's Congress in spring 1995. Deputies from Liaoning, many of whom were managers of large state-owned enterprises, urged the central government to grant preferential policies in order to support the industrial restructuring of the province. In April 1995, the central government formed a special group of experts with Vice-Premier Wu Bangguo at its head to transform and readjust the structure of the old industrial base. In June the same year, after inspecting many state-owned enterprises in the province, Wu Bangguo promised central government help in transforming Liaoning's industry. In July 1995, the provincial government decided to implement a modern enterprise system in thirty-five enterprises owned by the central and local government on a trial basis. Approval for five enterprises to go through the procedures of bankruptcy was given, two of which were the Dalian Glass Works and the Benxi Petrochemical Industrial Plant. The plan included the building of ten enterprise groups, exclusion of state-owned enterprises' social undertakings (such as welfare payments and housing) from productive undertakings, and a 're-employment project' to transfer 150,000 surplus workers to other employment.[42]

With the deterioration of the state sector's economic performance, pressure to liberalise and support the development of non-state industry and the service sector increased. On account of the strong economic dependence of the provincial and local bureaucracy on the SOEs, the role of the non-state sector was severely restricted up to the beginning of the 1990s. Changing the unfavourable political climate to bring about more rapid development of the non-state sector was a difficult task, but governor Yue Qifen was able to deal with this transition. Support for a more reform-minded policy in Liaoning also came from Deng Xiaoping on his famous journey to southern China and the CCP Central Committee's decision on building a 'socialist market economy', all of which brought about a general relaxation in the political climate.

The dynamism of the non-state sector

Before 1991 the non-state sector's contribution to economic development in Liaoning Province was rather small compared to the key role this sector played in other coastal provinces such as Guangdong.[43] During an inspection tour to the coal city Fushun in 1992, Yue Qifen emphasised that the 'software' problem was the main reason why the non-state sector had not been fully utilised in provincial development. 'Currently, the liberation of thought and the change in ideology are still the most important tasks for Liaoning', he claimed. Referring to the non-state sector, Yue pointed in his speech to the important role of township and village enterprises (TVE) for the acceleration of the province's growth. Depending on SOEs for a rapid accumulation of funds was no longer possible, he said: instead, the province should rely on TVEs to attain this goal. By developing TVEs, the economic gap between Liaoning and other provinces would be reduced, the adjustment of the economic structure hastened and the shortage of fiscal revenues facing the province relaxed. Although the growth rates of Liaoning's TVEs had increased in previous years compared to the more advanced regions, the gap in development between TVEs and other parts of the economy was still too large. In order to fill this gap Yue Qifen called for the advantageous local conditions in the counties and districts to be exploited, along with an increased reliance on the SOEs for raw material, personnel, markets and other resources.[44]

The provincial policies supporting the development of TVEs embraced fiscal incentives for the county governments on the one hand and an expansion of bank credits on the other. The volume of bank credits for TVEs increased continuously from 5 billion *yuan* in 1990 to 17 billion in 1994.[45] As they became heavily involved in the allocation of funds to develop TVEs and had a fiscal stake in the taxes remitted by TVEs, local governments showed a strong managerial interest in these enterprises. The strengthening of the county government's role in state-led growth, which Jean C. Oi has termed 'local state corporatism', also proved to be very successful in Liaoning.[46]

According to Yue Qifen, 1993 was the turning point in the non-state sector's development and in its overall importance for the provincial economy: the dynamic non-state sector accounted for 89 per cent of the GVIO growth rate and 70 per cent of the fiscal revenue in the same year.[47] In 1994 there was an increase in the non-state sector's share to 57 per cent; the collective sector constituted 33 per cent of the GVIO, individual-owned enterprises 14 per cent and enterprises of a different (largely foreign-funded) ownership structure 10 per cent. [48]

The dynamic development of the non-state sector compared to SOEs in the period 1989 to 1994 is shown in Table 4.3. SOEs achieved only meagre growth rates up to 1993 and even realised a negative growth in 1994. The poor performance of the SOEs prompted the party secretary Gu Jinchi to say to his colleagues at the provincial party congress in February 1994: 'We must seriously question whether it is correct for us to continue to assume that the emphasis on the development of state-run heavy industries in our province is a long term economic advantage to us'.[49] In line with Gu's belief, collective enterprises (mainly consisting of TVEs) have shown an impressive record in GVIO growth rates since 1991. The same holds true for enterprises which are individual-owned and foreign-funded.

The non-state sector continued to be the province's primary engine of growth for industry, but was also of paramount importance in the service sector during this period. By 1995, non-state traders accounted for 75.5 per cent of total retail sales of consumer goods.[50]

As has already been mentioned, the development of TVEs as the most important part of the collective economy was strongly supported by local government – that is, it was 'state-led'. It proved more difficult to develop individual-owned private enterprises, even at the beginning of the 1990s. Vice-Governor Zhang Rongmao criticised the fact that an unfavourable political climate still prevailed in the province with regard to the private sector in a speech held at the meeting of the Fourth Executive Committee of the Sixth Provincial Federation of Industry and Commerce in July 1992. Economic development in sectors other than the public sector was felt by some people to have a negative effect on development in the public sector, he said. The vice-governor also claimed that certain departments were forcing private enterprises and individual households to sell poor-quality and

Table 4.3 Liaoning GVIO growth rates: enterprises by ownership structure, 1989–94

Year	State-owned	Collective-owned	Other forms
1989	102.7	105.7	116.2
1990	100.4	101.0	104.0
1991	104.5	112.8	131.1
1992	109.5	123.0	133.1
1993	103.0	129.0	187.4
1994	96.2	128.2	183.0

Note: At comparable prices (previous year = 100)
Source: *Liaoning tongji nianjian 1995* p. 191

unmarketable commodities and that some departments were not giving preferential treatment to private enterprises which recruited workers from young unemployed people. These phenomena indicated that the task of eliminating the influence of 'leftist' concepts was still arduous, he said.[51]

Interviews with representatives of companies from the private sector reveal that bureaucratic interference in decision-making is still a problem, especially regarding the discharge of workers or obtaining of bank credits. In reaction to such interference, managers of these enterprises have tried to set up networks such as the Liaoning Branch of the Chinese Association of Young Entrepreneurs, with the aim of exchanging information and views. Founded in 1988, this association comprised 320 top managers by 1994. Although the organisation is subordinated to the provincial party, it seems to work successfully as a pressure group.[52]

DECENTRALISATION AND PROVINCIAL DEVELOPMENT

Besides the state-led growth of TVEs, sub-provincial competition has also played a key role in opening up the provincial economy and injecting new life into the economic development of Liaoning. According to Gong Ting and Chen Feng, decentralisation not only implies a redistribution of power to control economic and fiscal resources but also involves a broad reshuffling of political and administrative power. To measure these changes in the relationship between the centre and localities, Gong and Chen analyse the way in which the design and the functions of institutions have changed and whether institutional differentiation has taken place since the introduction of the open door policy. They come to the conclusion that because of decentralisation the centre's control has been reduced and localities have become more independent players actively searching for power and rights themselves.

Applying this approach to the relations between province and sub-provincial localities within Liaoning is useful because there has been a clearly observable change in the basic characteristics of the province's institutional framework. Within the province, competing localities empowered with economic decision-making rights have burgeoned, with some of them having enlarged their administrative authorities as well. The localities' determination in developing their local economy has played an important role in integrating the province into the world market and in injecting new dynamism into Liaoning's economy.

Competing territorial actors

In the mid-1980s, the centre's policy of allocating broader economic decision-making power to several selected cities and newly established economic zones had various goals: the role of cities in organising economic activities was to be increased, the local economy developed and economic management of large central and provincial enterprises delegated to lower administrative levels. However, while the establishment of new cities and metropolitan regions made a re-allocation of administrative authority necessary, no change in the administrative structure, was intended when giving special treatment to certain core cities.[53]

These cities were withdrawn from the economic grip of the provincial authorities and placed directly under Beijing's control by listing them separately – and regarding them as separate economic management units – in the state plan. Their economic power was the same as that of the provinces: they were entitled to formulate and implement plans independently regarding fixed assets, fiscal budget and credit, materials, wages, imports and exports, foreign currency, cultural activities, education and other planning items.[54] In Liaoning, two major cities, the capital Shenyang and the harbour city Dalian, were among the first seven cities chosen for preferential treatment by the State Council in 1984; by 1989, a further seven cities had been added to the list.[55]

By also allocating special economic power to Dalian City in 1984, the existing competition between the provincial authorities and the capital's authority was extended to a competition for resources between Shenyang and Dalian. On account of insufficient domestic capital for development, access to foreign investment, technology and skills became the key factors in the rivalry of these subprovincial localities. Schroeder has examined the intra-provincial competition for power in Hubei between the province and its capital Wuhan. According to his analysis, Wuhan tried to pursue its economic interests rather aggressively (though it was not very successful initially) by cutting itself off from Hubei, while Shenyang used a more balanced tactic, putting Liaoning first, 'even though it was breaking away from provincial bonds.'[56]

The relationship between the provincial government on the one hand and Shenyang and Dalian on the other was shaped by a conflict over competing claims to economic resources similar to the conflicts between other cities with a separate listing in the state plan and the provinces to which they were administratively subordinated. Central to this conflict was the attitude of the bureaucracy towards decentralisation; either it behaved passively or it interfered with the economic affairs of the city, evoking criticism even from the State Council. Many problems resulted from the fact that institutions were assigned economic but not administrative power. Cities with a separate listing in the state plan, for example, had both the right to formulate plans for the production of pharmaceutical products and the right to approve new pharmaceutical products, yet they were not permitted to issue licences for enterprises which enabled them to take up the production of those products. Gradually, however, the cities with special economic power acquired more administrative authority. Finally, in spring 1994, the State Council raised the administrative rank of six cities, among which were Shenyang and Dalian in Liaoning, and ten provincial capitals. They were given the status of 'cities of secondary provincial level', which implies independent economic and administrative power.[57]

In 1984, when Shenyang and Dalian were assigned the status of cities with a separate listing in the state plan, only Dalian was included in the centre's open door strategy. The city received the privileges of a coastal open city (COC) and was given the right to establish a state-level Economic and Technical Development Zone (ETDZ). Besides Dalian, two additional ports, Yingkou and Hulu, were also declared open ports.[58]

Although Dalian was empowered with special privileges regarding the open door policy, the construction of the EDTZ and its success in attracting foreign capital was initially rather disappointing. Besides the EDTZ's struggle to establish infrastructural facilities, ideological problems and different opinions on the concept of the EDZT hampered progress. The EDTZ's management committee explicitly referred to the local government as having conservative political ideas, a 'left-wing influence' which prevented the economic development they would have liked to have seen. These conservative ideas centred around such questions as the degree to which Dalian should open itself to the outside world and whether the transfer of foreign capital and technology would lead to capitalist thinking spreading into Dalian. Additionally, a hot debate arose concerning the issue of whether Dalian's EDTZ should be restricted to a simple export-processing zone or expanded into a comprehensive international metropolitan area with multiple functions.[59]

To incorporate the city's ambitious plans in a provincial open door strategy, the Liaoning government proposed a development plan with 'Dalian as the dragon's head, the port cities Yingkou and Dandong as its wings and Shenyang as well as other cities around the capital as the trunk of its body'. The opening of Liaodong Peninsula, which consists of seventeen districts and eight cities, was approved by the State Council in 1988.[60] Conversations with officials from the provincial government, however, revealed the absence of a detailed blueprint for a coordinated open door policy among these cities. Moreover, Dalian's EDTZ committee obviously aims at higher goals, striving to develop into 'an open window for the whole country'. Dalian's new mayor Bo Xilai wants Dalian to become the Hong Kong of the north; he sees the city's function as a gateway to the three northeastern provinces, a role similar to Hong Kong with respect to South China in the fields of finance, commerce, trade, tourism and the information industry.[61]

Dalian City, with its year-round ice-free harbour located at the southern tip of the Liaodong Peninsula, used the opportunity to open up its economy in a remarkable way. The city has once again become a hub of Japanese economic activity. Companies like Mabuchi Motors, Canon, Toshiba, Matsushita and Nissan have made large investments in Dalian. Low manufacturing costs, more favourable conditions for property utilisation than in South China, a relatively stable workforce and highly qualified technical personnel have attracted Japanese companies. Dalian has also improved its infrastructure, enlarging its telecommunication system, expanding the handling capacity of the harbour and building power plants to avoid power shortages. The geographical advantages of being close to Japan (just four hours away by plane) have been exploited by Dalian, which has set up flight services with eight weekly shuttle flights to Japan, thus making Dalian a low-cost manufacturing site within easy reach of the Japanese companies' home offices.[62]

Besides attracting foreign investors to the EDTZ, more than twenty large domestic SOEs from inland areas in Liaoning and from other provinces poured capital into the development zone to set up enterprises or engage in joint-venture projects. To finance the large-scale infrastructural facilities, Dalian has opened new channels and acquired investment from around forty large northeastern companies to found a trust and investment corporation. Up to the end of 1995, Dalian's EDTZ gave its approval for the setting up of 1,142 enterprises with a total capital of US$4.97 billion; the contracted foreign investment volume and the investment actually realised were US$2.8 billion and US$1.44 billion respectively.[63]

Although Shenyang was also given the status of a city with independent planning in 1984, the capital was not allowed to set up an ETDZ. To acquire financial resources for the modernisation of industry in the city, Shenyang lobbied Beijing for two years in order to get approval for the renewal of its Tiexi Industrial Area. The Tiexi scheme was then included in the national Seventh Five-Year Plan (1986–90) and financial support of US$2 billion was promised. A 3-kilometre area was designated as a high-technology zone within the 40 square kilometre industrial zone of Tiexi. In 1988, when the city was finally included in the open area of the Liaodong Peninsula, Shenyang received permission from the province to build its own ETDZ. It took the capital another six years, until 1993, however, to receive formal approval as a state-level ETDZ.[64]

The contribution of the ETDZ to the city's export volume rose from 25.6 per cent in 1993 to 40.6 per cent in 1994, indicating its important role in Shenyang's economic development.[65] Up to the end of 1993, 259 projects were approved for the ETDZ with a total investment of 6.6 billion *yuan*, including 203 foreign-funded enterprises involving foreign capital of US$332 million. Once the zone was upgraded to a state-level EDTZ in April 1993, foreign investment poured into the zone and more transnational corporations settled there.[66]

The ETDZ was regarded by the localities as a major channel open to the world market. As a result of foreign investment in technical and export products, the local authorities looked forward to the technological transformation and renewed competitiveness of old enterprises. Besides Shenyang, the port cities of Yingkou and Dandong also lobbied Beijing for approval as state-level ETDZs. Both cities received approval for state-level zones in 1992, which then became known as the Yingkou ETDZ and the Dandong Border Economic Cooperation Zone. With eleven large cities having successfully lobbied the provincial government to build provincial-level economic development zones and thirteen city-level development zones in districts run by the cities, the 'zone fever' spread virtually all over Liaoning.[67]

As a reaction to competitive pressure from Dalian, the capital successfully lobbied Beijing to be included in the scheme of state-level scientific development zones in March 1991. The Shenyang Science and Technology Zone had been founded by the provincial government of Liaoning and the Shenyang government in May 1988 and offered special investment conditions and preferential policies to attract both Chinese and foreign companies. With its high concentration of universities, research institutes and laboratories, the zone was designated as the leading site by the Shenyang authorities in its attempt to upgrade its heavy industrial base. By the end of 1995, multinational corporations such as IBM, NEC and the Goldstar Group had made investments of US$250 million.[68] In the meantime, Shenyang has also developed a very ambitious outlook: by the start of the twenty-first century, the city wants to have become a major industrial base and commercial centre in Northeast Asia. In order to attain this goal and transform itself into an international metropolis, Shenyang applied with success for the support of the United Nations Development Programme (UNDP) and invited experts from the USA, Japan, Finland, Thailand and the Republic of Korea to discuss the development strategy for Shenyang and especially for the city's ETDZ.[69]

A change in the retention rate of fiscal revenues was another important instrument for subprovincial localities like Shenyang and Dalian (as well as other cities in Liaoning) in their attempt to gain more independence. In her analysis of Wuhan's economic difficulties during reform, Solinger points to the low retention rate as one of the reasons for Wuhan's falling behind national norms. Even after 1984, Wuhan's profit retention ratio remained basically the same, moreover, the provincial government refrained from investing in Wuhan. According to various interviews carried out by Solinger, the retention ratio for cities with a separate listing in the state plan ranged from 16 to 30 per cent in 1988; the ratio for Shanghai was 18, for Tianjin 21, for Guangzhou 24 and for Shenyang 23 per cent.[70]

Since 1984, Shenyang has been able to expand its share in the fiscal (in-budget) revenue from 37 per cent to 63 per cent (in 1993). Furthermore, the city's extra-budgetary funds increased, making up 27.8 per cent of its fiscal revenue in 1993.[71] The available statistics on the distribution of fiscal revenue in Dalian refer to 1990. That year, Dalian's share in in-budget revenue amounted to 51.5 per cent, while the rest, with the exception of 2.9 million *yuan* or 0.05 per cent, had to be remitted to the central government. With regard to extra-budgetary funds, Dalian was able to retain a larger share of 67.3 per cent. Revenues delivered to the central government and the provincial government accounted for 28.6 per cent and 4 per cent. Compared to 1984, Dalian's access to fiscal revenues has increased considerably. In this year, the city was only able to retain 15.9 per cent of its fiscal (in-budget) revenues.[72]

The change in retention rates for the localities was part of a larger adjustment in central–local fiscal relations. In 1981, Liaoning was able to keep only 20.9 per cent of its fiscal revenue, whereas by 1993 this share had increased to 48.5 per cent. At the same time, the province's extra-budgetary funds, less than 10 per cent of which were delivered to the central government, increased from 3.97 billion *yuan* to 8.77 billion *yuan*. Compared to the in-budget revenue of 15.35 billion *yuan* in 1993, the important role of these extra-budgetary funds for financing the province's local development is self-evident.[73] Liaoning and other coastal provinces were able to set aside huge extra-budgetary funds which were not subject to central budgetary control. Local governments therefore increasingly became the driving force behind capital expansion.[74]

With the increasing number of decision-making institutions such as the twenty-eight state-level, provincial-level and city-level development zones, the science and technology zones, and other zones with special preferential policies, Gong Ting and Chen Feng's conclusion seems to be generally accurate for Liaoning: these new institutions have promoted horizontal linkages while vertical institutional relations have been complicated. Furthermore, these changes in the institutional design have been accompanied by a redistribution of fiscal revenues to the localities, enabling them to pursue their own local economic interests.[75]

Liaoning's integration into the world market

Central government's restrictive policies aside, one of the main reasons for the relatively slow opening of the province was that the provincial bureaucracy was more conservative than the reform-oriented leaderships of certain southern provinces. It was not until the end of the 1980s that provincial and local governments launched efforts to increase investments and exports by granting local areas greater flexibility in attracting foreign investors.[76] Subprovincial decentralisation has played a crucial role in restructuring the vertical hierarchy and in enabling local government to become more independent. Here, the various development zones had important functions for the dissemination of modern management knowledge and technologies, and access to foreign currency for domestic enterprises from the hinterland of Liaoning investing in the development zones.

Compared to the early entry of Guangdong and Fujian province into the world market, Liaoning opened its market rather late. Besides the heavy burden of inefficient state-owned enterprises, this time-lag in the opening of the economy was one of the major reasons for Liaoning's slower economic growth rates and other related economic problems. Because of the slow progress in foreign trade reform in Liaoning, not only Guangdong but also Jiangsu and Shandong moved ahead of the province at the end of the 1980s in terms of their growth rates of exports and absorption of foreign capital.[77]

Nevertheless, between 1989 and 1995 Liaoning's volume of foreign trade more than doubled, rising from US$5.3 billion to US$11 billion. Liaoning's exports accounted for 5.6 per cent of total national exports, ranking the province seventh in the country, behind Guangdong, Shanghai, Jiangsu,

Shandong, Fujian and Zhejiang. The foreign-funded enterprises, which contributed about a quarter of the province's total exports, played a crucial role in pushing up the export growth rates between 1994 and 1996, although this share is still much lower than the national average. The change in the export structure, with the finished product share amounting to 58 per cent, has also had a positive effect on export growth.[78]

Liaoning's ability to absorb foreign capital has gradually increased over the years, showing a significant improvement since the beginning of the 1990s. Between 1979 and 1992, the contracted value of direct foreign investment was US$3.8 billion, while from 1993 to 1995 more than the same volume of investment was contracted annually, making a total of US$12.3 billion. This trend also holds true for utilised direct investment, which amounted to US$1.3 billion during the period of 1979 to 1992, with a large increase in investment between 1993 and 1995, the total investment volume amounting to US$3.6 billion. In 1995, Liaoning's most important source of foreign investment was Hong Kong, although the province's main trading partners for exports were Japan and the USA, Hong Kong ranking only third.[79]

Liaodong Peninsula, and in particular Dalian City, has been very important for the province's integration into the world market. In 1995, Dalian's total export volume was US$3.46 billion, accounting for 42 per cent of the province's total exports and putting the city in the foremost position in the province. Although Shenyang's exports have also increased since the 1980s, its share of total exports has amounted to only 12 per cent.[80] Compared to the national average, Liaoning's economy had not integrated into international trade very much by 1994; its share of exports in Gross Domestic Product amounted to just 34 per cent.[81]

CONCLUSION

Liaoning's struggle with the burdens of the past seems to be typical for provinces dominated by a planned economy and state-owned enterprises. The elites of these provinces were characterised by close allegiance to the planning system and previous policy goals as well as considerable conservatism in implementing reforms. As Liaoning was of outstanding strategic importance as an industrial base and because of its historical role for the CCP, the allegiance of the province's political elite was very important in the past and still is today. The changes in the provincial elites' ranks proved to be very difficult, however. The Central Committee had to exercise its influence regarding the assignment of leading cadres, bringing in 'outsiders' to resolve a deadlock in economic reform.

In the 1980s, the province lost its dominant position in the national economy to other coastal provinces, indicating that economic reform worked against the comparable advantage of Liaoning. The fact that economic development in the province fell behind that of other provinces was partly due to Liaoning's close integration into the planned economy which resulted in the setting up of an industrial structure shaped to the needs of the central plan. With more than 60 per cent of the large and medium-sized SOEs possessing outdated equipment, inferior product quality and the predominance of raw material industries, reforming this old industrial base was an arduous task. Until the beginning of the 1990s, the provincial government concentrated most of its energy on the rebuilding of Liaoning's past glory, the state sector enterprises. Liaoning needed a diversification of its industrial structure and a change in the way enterprises were run. These changes, however, threatened the existing balance between economic sectors and the distribution of economic wealth. On account of the overwhelming presence of the state-sector and the economic well-being of various groups in society who strongly supported the state-operated enterprises, enterprise reform proved to be rather difficult. By 1994, the continuous deterioration of the SOEs' performance had made even Liaoning's first party secretary doubt whether the emphasis on state-run heavy industry was really of long-term economic advantage to Liaoning.

With the decline of fiscal revenues from ailing SOEs on the one hand and unemployment pressure on the other, the provincial government permitted the non-state sector to play a more important role in the economy. A change was necessary in the unfavourable political attitude towards the non-state sector, which had previously restricted this sector to playing a minor role in the economy. Decentralisation of economic rights to the county level and fiscal incentives were successful policies for the development of TVEs, which soon became an engine of growth.

Liaoning's difficulties in adapting to the agenda of economic reform were also due to the centre's opening policy and the provincial government's inward-looking strategy, resulting in its rather slow integration into the world market. Within this context, the decentralisation of economic decision-making power to lower administrative levels and the competition between localities turned out to play a crucial role for localities' determination in developing their economies. It has been shown in this chapter that this sub-provincial decentralisation was of utmost importance for the restructuring of the vertical hierarchy and in enabling local government to become more independent. Comparing the degree of Liaoning's involvement in inter-national trade and finance, the province is still far behind other coastal provinces such as Guangdong, Fujian or Jiangsu. Nevertheless, the rapid development of Dalian and other port cities along the coast of Liaoning Peninsula shows that the potential can successfully be tapped.

NOTES

1   Wang Yan, 'Jieyan dongnan yanhai ge sheng jingyan, jiasu liaoning jingji fazhan' [Borrow the experience of the southeast coastal provinces to accelerate Liaoning's economic development], *Liaoning Daxue Xuebao* 4, 1993, p. 56.

2   Gavan McCormack, *Chang Tso-lin in Northeast China 1911–1928*, Stanford University Press, 1977, p. 6.
3   US Department of Commerce, Office of Technical Service, Joint Publications Research Service, *Economic Geography of Northeast China*, Washington, DC, 1962, pp. 57–62.
4   McCormack, p. 3.
5   Ramon R. Myers, *The Japanese Development of Manchuria, 1932 to 1945*, University of Washington Press, Seattle, 1959, pp. 262–9.
6   Deng Liqun, Ma Hong and Wu Jie (eds) *Dangdai Zhongguo de Liaoning* [Liaoning in Today's China] 1, Beijing, 1994, pp. 21–4.
7   McCormack, pp. 251–7.
8   Arthur Rosenbaum, 'Railway enterprise and economic development: the case of the Imperial Railways of North China, 1900–1911', *Modern China* 2, no. 2, 1976, pp. 27–72.
9   Ronald Suleski, 'Regional development in Manchuria: immigrant laborers and provincial officials in the 1920s', *Modern China* 4, no. 4, 1978, pp. 419–34.
10 Deng Liqun, Ma Hong and Wu Jie (eds) 2, pp. 381–4.
11 Besides being the top Party government and military official of the Northeast Region, Gao Gang held the following posts before he was expelled from the party: Politburo member, one of the six chairmen of the Central People's Government Council, vice-chairman of the People's Revolutionary Military Council and chairman of the State Planning Commission. See F.C. Teiwes, *Politics and Purge in China, Rectification and the Decline of Party Norms 1950–1965*, M.E. Sharpe, New York, 1979, p. 166.
12 Deng Liqun, Ma Hong and Wu Jie (eds), pp. 126–44.
13 Alfred L. Chan, 'The campaign for agricultural development in the Great Leap Forward: a study of policy-making and implementation in Liaoning', *China Quarterly* 129, March 1992, pp. 61–5.
14 Deng Liqun, Ma Hong and Wu Jie (eds), p. 133.
15 Yue Qifen, *Liaoning jingji fazhan silu zhi tansuo* [Exploration of the Ideas behind the Development of Liaoning's Economy], Beijing, 1995.
16 The first party secretary of Liaoning Province, Gu Jinchi, is a native of Hebei, the two deputy secretaries come from Hunan (Cao Bochun) and Shandong (Wang Huaiyuan), while only one comes from Liaoning (Wang Guoguang). See *Who's Who in China, Current Leaders*, Beijing, 1989.
17 According to Gong Ting and Chen Feng, 'Institutional Reorganization and its Impact on Decentralization', in Jia Hao and Lin Zhimin (eds) *Changing Central–Local Relations in China: Reform and State Capacity*, Westview, Boulder, CO, 1994, p. 79; 43 per cent of the leading provincial cadres were local cadres in 1981. By June 1989, this share had increased to 70 per cent.
18 Wang An, 'Shengzhang jie jian' [The governor uses the 'arrows of the enemy'], *Liaowang* 11 October 1993, p. 17.
19 Deng Liqun, Ma Hong and Wu Jie (eds), p. 294.
20 Zhang Jinsheng, *Liaoning shehui jingji fazhan ji ge zhanlue wenti* [Strategic Questions Regarding the Social and Economic Development of Liaoning], Liaoning University, Shenyang, 1995.
21 Zhang Jinsheng, pp. 1–3.
22 Gao Shucheng and Song Hua, 'Dui Liaoning dazhongxing qiye de fenlei fenxi' [Analysis of Liaoning's large and medium-sized enterprise classification], *Liaoning jingji* 2.24, 1994, pp. 24–5; *Liaoning tongji nianjian 1993* [Liaoning Statistical Yearbook 1993], p. 228.
23 *Liaoning tongji nianjian 1993*, p. 234.
24 Harry G. Broadman, *Meeting the Challenge of Chinese Enterprise Reform*, World Bank Discussion Paper no. 283, Washington, DC, 1995, p. 14.

25   *Liaoning tongji nianjian 1993*, pp. 215 and 228. The data refer to large and medium-sized enterprises with independent accounting, GVIO on the basis of 1990 prices; Gao Shucheng and Song Hua, pp. 24–5; *Liaoning tongji nianjian 1993*, p. 228.

26   *Liaoning nianjian 1994* [Liaoning Yearbook 1994], p. 428. In April 1995, thirty factory directors and managers had to attend special courses on how to improve product quality. Enterprises failing to improve their quality standard within a specific period were threatened with a shut-down. *Xinhua News Agency* (XNA) Beijing, 26 April 1995 in BBC *Summary of World Broadcasts* (SWB), 4 May 1995.

27   Wen Shizhen 'Renqing xingshi, qingli silu, jiakai Liaoning jingji zhenxing' [Grasp the situation, clarify thought and invigorate Liaoning's economic development], *Liaoning jingji ribao* [Liaoning Economic Daily] 10 December 1994; *South China Morning Post* 13 June 1995.

28   Stephen Thomas, 'Chinese enterprise management reforms in the post-Tiananmen era', in Lane Kelley and Oded Shenkar (eds) *International Business in China*, London and New York, Routledge, 1993, pp. 45–62.

29   Regarding the relationship between economic growth and social change, see Andrew Watson (ed.) *Economic Reform and Social Change in China*, London, Routledge, 1992, here p. 6; XNA News Bulletin, Hong Kong, 20 February 1995.

30   Deng Liqun, Ma Hong and Wu Jie (eds), pp. 155–6; XNA 20 February 1995.

31   *South China Morning Post* 17 March 1995.

32   Unpublished paper on SOEs for internal circulation.

33   Zhang Ti *et al.*, 'Liaoningsheng qiye pochan zhong de wenti yu jianyi' [Problems of and recommendations for Liaoning's industry during insolvency], *Zhongguo gongye jingji yanjiu* 11, 1994, pp. 42–4. By April 1985, fifty-four debt-ridden enterprises had been declared bankrupt, twelve of which were SOEs. XNA 2 April 1995. SWB FE/WO 380/CNS 19 April 1995.

34   Foreign Broadcast Information Service FBIS-CHI-95-062 31 March 1995, pp. 33–5.

35   *Asian Wall Street Journal* 19 April 1995; *Lianhebao* Hong Kong, 8 May 1995, p. 7. SWB FE/D2298/CNS 9 May 1995.

36   Interviews in Shenyang, November 1995.

37   *International Herald Tribune* 21 February 1996.

38   XNA 28 September 1994. SWB FE/D2114/CNS 30 September 1994.

39   XNA 24 April 1995.

40   XNA 8 July 1993.

41   FBIS-CHI-95-062 31 March 1995, p. 34.

42   *South China Morning Post* 10 March 1995; *South China Morning Post* 13 June 1995 and *China Aktuell* April 1995; *Liaoning Ribao* 8 July 1995. SWB FE/D2365/CNS 26 July 1995.

43   *Zhongguo tongji nianjian 1992* [China Statistical Yearbook 1992]; calculations at current prices. According to calculations based on 1990 constant prices, the SOEs' share amounted to 71.8 per cent in 1991 but declined to 52.1 per cent in 1994: *Liaoning tongji nianjian 1995* [Liaoning Statistical Yearbook 1995] pp. 188–9.

44   Yue Qifen 1995, pp. 37–9.

45   *Liaoning tongji nianjian 1995*, p. 180.

46   Jean C. Oi, 'The role of the local state in China's transitional economy', *China Quarterly* 144, December 1995, pp. 1132–49.

47   Yue Qifen 1995, pp. 82–3.

48   *Zhongguo tongji nianjian 1995*, p. 379.

49   Consulate General of the United States of America, *Economic Overview of Northeast China 1993*, Shenyang.

50 *Liaoning Statistical Communiqué on 1995 Economic and Social Development*, SWB FEW/0428 WS1/1 27 March 1996.
51 *Liaoning Ribao* 18 July 1992. SWB 5 August 1992.
52 Interviews in various enterprises in Shenyang, November 1995; Gao Xiaolin 'Shidai huhuan qingnian qiye jiaqun de jueqi' [Call to the group of young entrepreneurs to rise], *Dangdai qiye*, Shenyang, 1994, p. 4.
53 Gong Ting and Chen Feng, pp. 72–4.
54 Wang Gousong, *Zhonghua renmin gong he guo zhengfu yu zhengzhi* [Politics and government in the People's Republic of China], Beijing, 1994, p. 141.
55 As early as the 1960s, Shenyang and five other cities (Tianjin, Wuhan, Guangzhou, Chongqing and Xian) were given the right to independent planning, albeit in a much narrower sense: see Wang Gousong, pp. 140–2.
56 Paul E. Schroeder, 'Territorial actors as competitors for power: the case of Hubei and Wuhan', in Kenneth G. Lieberthal and David M. Lampton (eds) *Bureaucracy, Politics, and Decision Making in Post-Mao China*, 1992, pp. 283–307.
57 Wang Gousong, pp. 142–3.
58 *Liaoning jingji tongji nianjian 1985* [Liaoning Economic Statistics Yearbook 1985], p. 18.
59 Interviews in Dalian, November 1995. Dalian Economic and Technological Development Zone Committee, *Fahui youshi, kaituo jinqu nuli ba Dalian kaifaqu jiancheng quan guo a liu de kaifang chuang kou* [Exploit Advantages, Develop Initiatives, Strive to Build Dalian into an Open Window for the Whole Country], 1995.
60 Deng Liqun, Ma Hong and Wu Jie (eds), pp. 159–60.
61 Interviews with various provincial departments, November 1995.
62 Preston M. Torbert, 'Windows on Liaoning Province', *China Business Review* November–December 1984, p. 20; Emily Thornton, 'Opportunity Knocks', *Far Eastern Economic Review* 8 December 1994, pp. 56–7.
63 *Liaoning nianjian 1995*, p. 94; Dalian Economic and Technological Development Committee 1995.
64 'Peking approves $2 billion plan for Shenyang', *Asian Wall Street Journal* 6 August 1986; by the middle of 1995, investment from central and local government in the Tiexi Industrial Restructuring Project is reported to have increased to a total of 10.34 billion *yuan*. XNA 28 July 1995.
65 *Liaoning nianjian 1995*, p. 96.
66 Management Committee of the Shenyang Economic and Technical Development Zone, *Shenyang Economic and Technical Development Zone*, Shenyang, 1994.
67 *Liaoning nianjian 1995*, p. 94.
68 XNA 9 December 1991; 24 March 1992; 17 October 1995.
69 Management Committee of the Shenyang Economic and Technical Development Zone, *Shenyang Economic and Technical Development Zone*, Shenyang, 1994.
70 Dorothy J. Solinger, 'Despite decentralization: disadvantages, dependence and ongoing central power in the inland: the case of Wuhan', *China Quarterly* March 1996, p. 20. Solinger cites Schroeder's statement on Wuhan's retention ratio of 20 per cent on average, which was much lower than other cities' retention rates of between 30 and 40 per cent.
71 *Shenyang nianjian 1994* [Shenyang Yearbook 1994], p. 554 and p. 321.
72 *Dalian shiqing* [Dalian City: Facts and Figures] 1986, p. 773; *Dalian nianjian 1992* [Dalian Yearbook 1992], p. 304.
73 *Liaoning tongji nianjian 1995* [Liaoning Statistical Yearbook 1995], p. 94. After the introduction of a new tax system in 1994, the province's (in-budget) share decreased to 27.2 per cent.
74 Wang Shaoguang, 'Central–local fiscal politics in China', in Jia Hao and Lin Zhimin, pp. 99–101.

75   Gong Ting and Chen Feng, pp. 76 and 83.
76   Stephen C. Thomas, 'Catching up: Liaoning Province is courting – and winning
      – foreign investment', *China Business Review* November–December, 1990, p. 8.
77   Liaoning daxue jingji yanjiusuo, *Liaoning jingji shichanghua chengdu de
      kaocha; Yu Jiangsu, Shandong, Guangdong san sheng bijiao* [A Study of the
      Degree of Liaoning Economy's Adaptation to the Market Principle: Comparison
      with the Provinces of Jiangsu, Shandong, and Guangdong], Shenyang, 1993.
78   *Liaoning Statistical Communiqué on 1995 Economic and Social Development.*
79   *Liaoning tongji nianjian 1995*, [1994 Yearbook] pp. 298–304.
80   China Statistical Information and Consulting Center, *The Collection of Statistics
      on China's Economic and Social Development*, Beijing, 1995.
81   *Provincial China* no. 1, March 1996.

REFERENCES

Bai Qinxian, 'Guangyu Liaodong bandao duiwai kaifang ruogan wenti de sikao'
    [Thoughts on some questions regarding the opening of Liaodong Peninsula to the
    outside world], *Liaoning daxue xuebao* 2, 1992, pp. 49–51.
Alfred L. Chan, 'The campaign for agricultural development in the Great Leap
    Forward: a study of policy-making and implementation in Liaoning', *China
    Quarterly* 129, 1992, pp. 52–71.
Dalian Economic and Technological Development Zone Committee, *Fahui youshi,
    kaituo jinqu nuli ba dalian kaifaqu jiancheng quan guo yi liu de kaifang chuangkou*
    [Exploit Advantages, Develop Initiatives, Strive to Turn Dalian into an Open
    Window for the Whole Country], 1995.
Dalian shiqing [Dalian City: Facts and Figures], 1986.
Dalian nianjian 1992 [Dalian Yearbook 1992], Dalian.
Deng Liqun, Ma Hong and Wu Jie (eds) *Dangdai Zhongguo de Liaoning* [Liaoning
    in Today's China] 2 volumes, Beijing, 1994.
Gao Shucheng and Song hua, 'Dui Liaoning dazhongxing qiye de fenlei fenxi'
    [Analysis of Liaoning's large and medium-sized enterprise classification], *Liaon-
    ing Jingji* 2, no. 24, 1994, pp. 24–5.
Jiang Changqi and Li Ming, 'Jiakuai Liaoningsheng qiye gufen zhidu gaige de
    shexiang' [Provisional plan for fastening the reform of the stock system in
    Liaoning's enterprises], *Liaoning daxue xuebao* 4, 1992.
Li Jingyu and Ma Shufang, 'Guangyu Dalian jianzao "beifang Xianggang" de jige
    wenti' [Regarding some questions of building Dalian into a northern Hong Kong],
    Zhongguo gongye jingji yanjiu 4, 1994.
Liaoning daxue jingji yanjiusuo, *Liaoning jingji shichanghua chengdu de kaocha; Yu
    Jiangsu, Shandong, Guangdong san sheng bijiao* [A Study of the Degree of
    Liaoning Economy's Adaptation to the Market Principle: Comparison with the
    Provinces of Jiangsu, Shandong, and Guangdong], Shenyang, 1993.
Liaoning sanshiwu nian [35 Years of Liaoning], Shenyang, 1984.
Liaoning jingji tongji nianjian [Liaoning Economic Statistics Yearbook], Shenyang
    (1984–92).
Liaoning tongji nianjian [Liaoning Statistical Yearbook], Shenyang (since 1993).
Liaoning nianjian [Liaoning Yearbook], Shenyang (since 1993).
Liaoning Statistical Communiqué on 1995 Economic and Social Development, in
    BBC *Summary of World Broadcasts* FEW/0428 WS1/1, 27 March 1996.
Management Committee of the Shenyang Economic and Technical Development
    Zone, *Shenyang Economic and Technical Development Zone*, Shenyang, 1994.
Gavan McCormack, *Chang Tso-lin in Northeast China 1911–1928*, Stanford Uni-
    versity Press, 1977.

Ramon R. Myers, *The Japanese Development of Manchuria, 1932 to 1945*, University of Washington Press, Seattle, 1959.

Arthur Rosenbaum, 'Railway enterprise and economic development: the case of the Imperial Railways of North China, 1900–1911', *Modern China* 2, no. 2, 1976, pp. 227–72.

Shenyang nianjian 1994 [Shenyang Yearbook 1994], Shenyang, 1994.

Ronald Suleski, 'Regional development in Manchuria: immigrant laborers and provincial officials in the 1920s', *Modern China* 4, no. 4, 1978, pp. 419–34.

Stephen C. Thomas, 'Catching up: Liaoning Province is courting – and winning – foreign investment', *China Business Review* November–December 1990, pp. 6–11.

Emily Thornton, 'Opportunity knocks', *Far Eastern Economic Review* 8 December 1994, pp. 56–8.

Preston M. Torbert, 'Windows on Liaoning Province', *China Business Review* November–December 1984, pp. 20–3.

US Department of Commerce, Office of Technical Service, Joint Publications Research Service, *Economic Geography of Northeast China* Washington, DC, 1962, pp. 57–62.

An Wang, 'Shengzhang jie jian' [The governor uses the 'arrows of the enemy'], *Liaowang* 11 October 1993, p. 17.

Wang Yan, 'Jieyan dongnan yanhai ge sheng jingyan, jiasu Liaoning jingji fazhan' [Borrow the experience of the southeast coastal provinces to accelerate Liaoning's economic development], *Liaoning Daxue Xuebao* 4, 1993, pp. 55–8.

Wen Shizhen, 'Renqing xingshi, qingli silu, jiakai Liaoning jingji zhenxing' [Grasp the situation, clarify thought and invigorate Liaoning's economic development], *Liaoning jingji ribao* 10 December 1994.

Yue Qifen, *Liaoning jingji fazhan silu zhi tansuo* [Exploration of the Ideas behind the Development of Liaoning's Economy], Beijing, 1995.

Zhang Jinsheng, *Liaoning shehui jingji fazhan ji ge zhanlue wenti* [Some Strategic Questions Regarding the Social and Economic Development of Liaoning], Liaoning University, Shenyang, 1995.

Zhang Ti *et al.*, 'Liaoningsheng qiye pochan zhong de wenti yu jianyi' [Problems of and recommendations for Liaoning's industry during insolvency], *Zhonguo gongye jingji yanjiu* 11, 1994, pp. 42–4.

Zhou Guangping, *Liaoning laogongye jidi gaizao* [Restructuring the Old Industrial Base of Liaoning], Shenyang, 1987.

Periodicals

Liaoning jingji [Liaoning Economy]
Liaoning jingji ribao [Liaoning Economic Daily]
Liaoning Ribao [Liaoning Daily]

Shandong Province

GENERAL

GDP (billion *yuan* renminbi)	387.20
GDP annual growth rate	16.20
as % national average	137.29
GDP per capita	4,465.69
as % national average	118.92
Gross Value Agricultural Output (billion *yuan* renminbi)	138.70
Gross Value Industrial Output (billion *yuan* renminbi)	822

POPULATION

Population (million)	86.71
Natural growth rate (per 1,000)	9.69

WORKFORCE

Total workforce (million)	45.46
Employment by activity (%)	
primary industry	55.90
secondary industry	24.20
tertiary industry	19.90
Employment by sector (% of provincial population)	
urban	11.36
rural	41.08
state sector	7.48
collective sector	19.82
private sector	5.35
foreign-funded sector	0.22

WAGES

Average annual wage (*yuan* renminbi)	4,338
Growth rate in real wage	10.20

PRICES

CPI annual rise (%)	23.40
Service price index rise (%)	24.50
Per capita consumption (*yuan* renminbi)	1,052
as % national average	60.56
Urban disposable income per capita	6,367
as % national average	182.12
Rural per capita income	2,182
as % national average	178.71

FOREIGN TRADE AND INVESTMENT

Total foreign trade (US$ billion)	9.62
% provincial GDP	21.41
Exports (US$ billion)	5.87
Imports (US$ billion)	3.75
Realised foreign capital (US$ million)	2,601.43
% provincial GDP	5.79

EDUCATION

University enrolments	156,879
% national average	77.48
Secondary school enrolments (million)	4.27
% national average	118.52
Primary school enrolments (million)	8.96
% national average	96.53

Notes: All statistics are for 1994 and all growth rates are for 1994 over 1993 and are adapted from *Zhongguo tongji nianjian 1995* [Statistical Yearbook of China 1995], Zhongguo tongji chubanshe, Beijing, 1995 as reformulated and presented in *Provincial China* no. 1 March 1996, pp. 34ff.

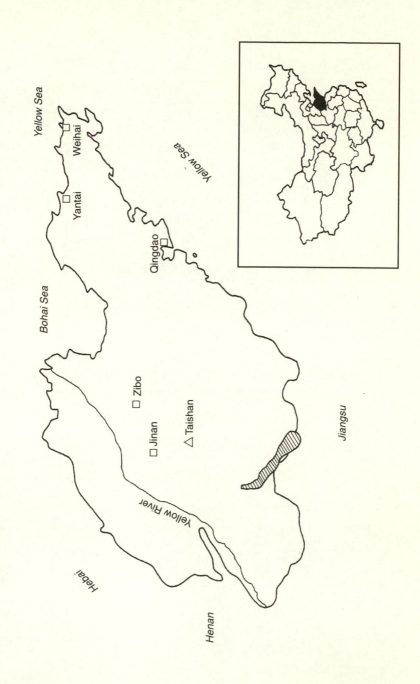

Shandong Province

5 Shandong

The political economy of development and inequality

Jae Ho Chung

Development is perhaps contagious as it radiates strong desires and incentives for growth and wealth. Development does not come cheap, however, as it always requires enormous material and human resources, and very often presupposes various changes in the established structure of interests – that is, reform. By challenging the established pattern of power, developmental reform is bound to create new problems and political confrontation. Developmental reform thus entails a complex process in which political conflicts interact with economic contradictions. The history of industrialisation provides examples of different institutions performing as the principal guide in this complex process of development – including factories, investment banks, and the state.[1] When the imperative to telescope the process of development is paramount, the role of the state is particularly crucial in mapping out core strategies including the dissemination of developmental ideologies, the effective allocation of capital, the prioritisation of key industries and regions, as well as the cultivation of technocratic elites and entrepreneurs.

The emergence of the state as the principal architect of development suggests that the origin of growth can be endogenous and dependency may not constitute a sufficient explanation for underdevelopment. Taking the state seriously also means paying close attention to the sorts of strategies it employs for the purpose of telescoping the process of development.[2] The state is no unidimensional authority, however, nor are developmental strategies the monopoly of central government since implementation is a key to developmental reform. The extensive literature on the East Asian newly industrialising economies (NIEs) rarely differentiates the roles played by central and local governments – all of which may be described as part of the 'state'.[3] Since most of the East Asian NIEs are small in size, their central governments were *de facto* the only state with sufficient power of its own, while local administration merely implemented the preferences of central superiors.

While the NIEs' experiences with target policies have been mostly sectoral and industry-specific, China's target policies have been predominantly regional, largely as a result of its physical size and political conservatism toward radical reform experiments. Unlike the generally mediocre impact of sectoral target policies in the NIEs, regional target policies have produced significant results in China.[4] Regional target policies have over time facilitated the rise of local power and local governments are playing an increasingly crucial role in guiding the developmental process by substituting for the shortage, if not the total absence, of bourgeois entrepreneurs and large business groups in China.[5]

In order for local governments to perform an entrepreneurial role, they should be able to translate varying local perceptions and interests into concrete local policies (as opposed to simply following the political preferences of the centre). In this respect, the abilities of local leadership constitute the most important factor. The local leadership's abilities specifically refer to two dimensions. First, they concern the strategic capacity to form and maintain a 'production alliance' with the central government, through which growth is promoted and its fruits – in the forms of increased tax revenues and enhanced regime legitimacy – are shared between the two. In order for such an alliance to start up, however, the central government should first create an environment favourable to development by means of granting highly preferential policies to a limited number of localities, which possess more potentials for the telescoping of development.

Second, under circumstances where the central government has only limited resources to support local efforts, local governments should cultivate entrepreneurial qualities vital to the strategic planning of development, particularly in the area of attracting domestic and foreign capital and technologies. As local governments become closely linked to foreign businesses, another production alliance is created, through which economic growth and technological advancement are promoted domestically and foreign capital obtains a widened access to overseas markets and other key resources (such as low-cost labour and raw materials). Thus, instead of the conventional format of a production alliance joining the local bourgeoisie, the state and foreign capital, the new formation currently emerging in China consists of the central government, local governments, and foreign capital.[6]

The formation of this kind of triple alliance is not a simultaneous but a sequential development because political leadership – both central and local – cannot commit all their time, efforts and resources to a multitude of strategic issues at once. In systems like China, therefore, one key issue that came up early in sequencing the developmental process concerned where to begin the establishment of the production alliance between central and local governments.[7] In the case of Guangdong, Beijing's initial policy support in terms of various regional preferential policies – for example, the special economic zone and Pearl River Delta development policies – facilitated the rise of reform-minded provincial leaderships which in turn came up with innovative local initiatives to obtain foreign capital and technologies. An identical sequence may be found in several other coastal regions, although recently many of the centre's grants of preferential policies came as *post-facto* endorsements of what localities had already been doing for some time at their own initiative, particularly in the inland regions.[8]

Both the sequencing strategy and regional target policies are designed to discriminate in favour of some areas against others, and such practices are very often inevitable in systems where key resources are highly limited and thus have to be closely managed. However effective they may be in promoting growth and creating local pace-setters, most regional target policies tend to create various political and social problems. One such problem concerns regional inequalities and both inter- and intra-provincial disparities.[9] How these sensitive socio-political problems are resolved will no doubt significantly affect the pace of development reforms. Perhaps, once again the triple alliance of central government, local governments and foreign capital may play a significant role, this time to alleviate regional disparities.

Central government may see immediate benefits in aiding poor localities as such efforts help to enhance its regime legitimacy and to garner political support for other key issues (for example, the succession issue). Local governments may also be fully aware of the virtue of reducing intra-provincial inequalities since less privileged localities are likely to constitute potential opponents of further development and reform. With appropriate frameworks of policy guidance and incentive provision, even foreign capital may find it useful to utilise disadvantaged areas since they offer highly attractive terms for foreign investment, notably cheap raw materials, and low-wage labour.

This chapter focuses on the political economy of reform and reaction in Shandong where innovative efforts were made to mitigate the tension between selective development and regional inequalities. The first section considers the province's general background, including an overview of its economic development during 1949–94. The second and third deal with the formation of a 'production alliance' joining Beijing, Shandong and foreign capital through the nexus of preferential policies, local innovations and external linkages. The fourth section investigates the origin and extent of intra-provincial inequalities in Shandong created by the region-specific target policies of the reform era. The fifth section examines a variety of measures taken by the province to mitigate regional inequalities without advocating equalisation.

A PROVINCIAL PROFILE

Located along the lower reaches of the Yellow River, Shandong is one of the 'cradles of human civilisation' and its history dates back several thousand years. Shandong's land area constitutes 1.6 per cent of China's total, while its population, 86.7 million as of 1994, is 7.2 per cent of China's total, making the province the third most populous and second most densely populated (population density of 553 people per square kilometre).[10] With 65 per cent of its total area as plains (mainly in the southwest of the province) with fertile soil, the province is well suited for agricultural production, particularly that of wheat, cotton and soybeans. With its coastline totalling more than 3,000 kilometres and including the Shandong Peninsula, the province is also well positioned for foreign trade. Shandong is richly endowed with a variety of natural resources, including gold, where it has China's largest estimated deposits, and diamonds, petroleum and copper, where it has China's second largest deposits. Shandong's petroleum accounts for more than one-fifth of China's total deposits and its Shengli Oil Field produces 20 million tons annually, the second largest producer in China.[11]

Shandong has historically been highly homogenous with an extremely small number of ethnic minorities (less than 0.5 per cent of its total population), which may have over time contributed to the well-known 'conservative' sentiment of its people. Shandong's history is filled with natural disasters, and there are traditions of lives being unbearable and in consequence very hostile attitudes toward anyone and anything that came from outside the province. Intra-provincially, there were regional rivalries between the southwestern plain region and the Jiaodong Peninsula region to the east, and many of the 'anti-outsider' and 'anti-western' revolts – including the Boxers' Rebellion at the turn of the century – originated from the western inland regions, most notably Heze.[12] Despite its anti-outsider sentiments, Shandong was rarely a resister in implementing central policy during socialist rule. Shandong's compliance may have had a lot to do with its geographical proximity to Beijing. Although physical proximity may not generally offer a very persuasive explanation as to provincial variations in implementation, the case of Shandong seems to be different. Several Chinese interviewees as well as scholars suggest that Beijing is geographically – and politically – close enough to the province to cast a significant shadow over the latter's implementation of policy.[13]

In economic terms, Shandong underwent significant changes since the early 1950s. As of 1979, Shandong's Gross Value Agricultural and Industrial Output (GVAIO) was RMB 45 billion *yuan*, almost fifteen times that of 1949. As of 1994, its GVAIO rose to RMB 961 billion *yuan*, over twenty times that of 1979.[14] During 1949–94, the share of Gross Value Industrial Output (GVIO) in GVAIO rose from 29 per cent in 1949 to 70 per cent in 1979 and to 86 per cent in 1994. Shandong's contribution to the national economy also changed over time: Shandong's share of China's national income was 6.9 per cent in 1952, 6.5 per cent in 1978, and 9.2 per cent in 1993. Shandong's share in total state fixed asset investment was 2.6 per cent in 1957, 4.4 per cent in 1978, and 5.8 per cent in 1994.[15]

Shandong's pace of economic growth was relatively slow in the early years of reform. As Table 5.1 indicates, it was in the 1990s that its pace of development took off to make Shandong one of the fastest developing provinces in China. In 1993, for instance, Shandong's annual rate of growth in Gross Domestic Product (GDP) was 20 per cent higher than in 1989, behind Zhejiang, Fujian and Hainan but equalling Guangdong.[16] For the period of

Table 5.1 Growth rates of four key indicators in Shandong, 1949–94

	GVAO	GVIO	GDP	Foreign trade
1949–78	3.9	13.5	9.0	N/A
1979–85	18.8	12.9	17.2	21.4
1986–90	14.2	26.8	17.4	7.9
1991–4	21.6	40.1	26.7	25.7

Source: Figures for 1949–78 were adopted from *Shandong tongji nianjian 1994* [Statistical Yearbook of Shandong 1994], Beijing, Zhongguo tongji chubanshe, 1994, pp. 11–13; and other rates were calculated on the basis of information provided in *Statistical Yearbook of Shandong 1995*, pp. 11–13

1979–94, Shandong's annual average rates of growth in GDP, Gross Value Agricultural Output (GVAO), GVIO and foreign trade far exceeded the national average in all four categories except for foreign trade where the national average came near that of Shandong.[17] In terms of national ranking among provinces, Shandong consistently ranked second on GVIO and GVAIO during 1990–3 and number one for GVAO in 1993–4, while it ranked only eighth on per capita GVAIO for the same period.[18] Shandong's foreign economic relations also made a big stride in the 1990s, occupying top-five positions among all provinces on exports, foreign funds utilised, and foreign direct investment during 1990–4.[19]

FIGHTING 'CONSERVATISM': PREFERENTIAL POLICIES AND THE STRATEGIC ALLIANCE BETWEEN BEIJING AND SHANGHAI

Compared to southern provinces like Guangdong and Jiangsu, Shandong's economic development proceeded rather slowly in the 1980s, although it clearly took off during the 1990s. What may account for its slow growth in the 1980s? One crucial reason lies in the well-known 'conservatism' of the Shandong people.[20] Shandong's conservatism has historical roots in that the prevalence of anti-outsider sentiments and its rich resource endowment have traditionally cultivated pervasive feelings of self-complacency and self-sufficiency which have in turn deterred the Shandong people from trying out new and innovative things for the better.[21] The following excerpt from *People's Daily* well illustrates the extent to which conservatism affected development in Shandong:

> Shandong people do not like to move around or contact with the outside world. . . . Shandong cadres like to talk about their conservatism. They say that Shandong is very rich and has many advantageous conditions and therefore it can develop without such foreign-related businesses like

'processing and assembling.' ... In fact, the Confucian tradition of 'cherishing the old' has exerted significant negative influence over Shandong's path of economic development.[22]

After the founding of the People's Republic, Shandong's conservatism was further reinforced by imperatives of bureaucratic careerism. Especially after the traumatic experiences of the anti-rightist campaign in 1957, local implementors approached central policy with extreme caution.[23] In China where personnel decisions for top provincial leaders are mostly controlled by the *nomenklatura* system, bureaucratic careerism – the tendency for career bureaucrats not to associate themselves too closely with controversial policies when there is even a slight chance that these policies will change at any time – is particularly pervasive. When advocating local interests against the priorities of the central government may be interpreted as following an incorrect ideological or political line and meet with severe punishment, bureaucratic careerism becomes the shared norms of local officials. Consequently, local officials always choose to play safe by staying away from controversial policies and carrying out such policies only when the centre's own preference has been firmly fixed.[24]

Shandong's caution-cum-conservatism was also well manifested during 1976–7 when it refrained from taking a side in two highly political campaigns of 'rectifying the party by taking class struggle as the key link' and 'criticise the decade-long abuses by the Gang of Four.'[25] Shandong's conservatism continued well into the post-Mao period. In 1979–83, for example, Shandong's pace of agricultural decollectivisation neither stayed too far ahead nor lagged too far behind, but very closely followed the national average. Only when Beijing pushed hard for its nation-wide implementation in late 1982, did Shandong opt for swift province-wide popularisation.[26]

Some evidence suggests that Shandong's relatively slow growth in the earlier years of the reform may be attributed to its conservative leaders and the lack of radical preferential policies granted by the centre. The first batch of Shandong's provincial leaders in the post-Mao era – Bai Rubing (1974–82) and Su Yiran (1979–85) – are known for their lukewarm attitude toward reforms.[27] Furthermore, Shandong remained under the strong influence of 'leftist' ideology and factions as late as 1985, and key provincial leaders were largely unwilling to implement reformist policies which had not yet proven effective.[28] Thus, bureaucratic careerism, radical ideologies, and fears of abrupt policy change were all combined to reinforce the province's conservatism toward reformist experiments. The longer these provincial leaders held on to such conservative attitudes, the more severely did the reform suffer.

Bureaucratic careerism has been fairly effectively tackled in the reform period by a series of decentralisation measures which provided local governments with genuinely expanded discretion in managing local affairs. In recent years, the success (and abuse) of such measures was such that some have even linked the rise of 'localism' with the prospect of China's territorial disintegration. Local initiatives in economic development were further promoted by the centre's provision of preferential policies applied selectively to a small number of localities. In retrospect, not only in Guangdong and Fujian but also in Shandong, the granting of radical preferential policies – as a crucial token of the centre's prioritisation of the reform imperative – has significantly mitigated the problems of conservatism.

First-batch preferential policies, 1984–7

In 1984 Beijing decided to expand the area of economic reform beyond the South China region. In April 1984, the State Council designated fourteen cities as 'coastal open cities' (COCs) which were allowed to implement preferential policies to attract foreign investment and promote export-oriented industries. Among these fourteen cities located in a total of ten coastal province-level units, only four provinces managed to have two of their cities designated as such: Jiangsu, Zhejiang, Guangdong and Shandong (which had Qingdao and Yantai designated as COCs). In 1984–5, the State Council also designated eleven Economic and Technological Development Zones (ETDZs) among the fourteen COCs, and this time only three provinces managed to have two of their cities designated as ETDZs: Jiangsu, Guangdong and Shandong (again with Qingdao and Yantai).[29]

The provision of these selective preferential policies was accompanied by changes in the provincial leadership in June 1985 when Beijing appointed Liang Buting as first party secretary and Li Chang'an as governor. Both Liang and Li were 'outsiders' whose appointments were considered a calculated move on the part of Beijing to inject some 'reformist spirit' into the conservative province.[30] As a protégé of Hu Yaobang, Liang was much more reform-oriented than his predecessors, occasionally pushing for reformist policies particularly in the area of foreign economic relations. Yet, Liang's contribution to Shandong's development was limited rather inevitably due to the overall policy environment at the time. As far as Shandong was concerned, the period of 1985–7 was still marked by uncertainties. Despite the designation of Qingdao and Yantai as COCs in 1984, no concrete follow-up support was provided by the centre. Rather, unfortunately for Shandong, the State Council's plan of extending the 'open policy' to the whole of the Shandong Peninsula region was shelved in 1985 in the midst of the Hainan scandal. Despite some support from the centre – particularly that of two Shandong natives, Gu Mu and Tian Jiyun, during 1985 – and indigenous efforts by Shandong (issuing provincial regulations on the preferential treatment of foreign capital in 1986) these initiatives were almost killed by the Anti-Bourgeois Liberalisation campaign of 1986–7.[31]

The limited scope of reform in Shandong during this period can also be illustrated with an example of organisational restructuring in the area of foreign economic relations. It was in 1984 that the Import, Export and Trade

Commission (ImExCom) was established within the provincial government. The principal function of ImExCom was to supervise provincial general foreign trade corporations formerly controlled by the Ministry of Foreign Trade. Despite the stipulations as to the delegation of foreign trade authority to the provincial government, the State Planning Commission (SPC) and the Ministry of Foreign Trade (later renamed Ministry of Foreign Economic Relations and Trade and abbreviated as MOFERT) continued to plan and regulate provincial foreign trade during 1984–6. It was only in 1987 that provincial foreign trade corporations were finally separated from the general foreign trade corporations under MOFERT's control. From 1987 on provincial foreign trade corporations were controlled solely by ImExCom under the provincial government.[32]

With the assumption of power in supervising provincial foreign trade in 1987, ImExCom was renamed the Foreign Economic Commission (FEC). The strengthening of FEC generated serious inter-agency conflicts over vested interest and lines of authority over the province's foreign economic relations. The most serious conflict of all was between FEC and another trade-related organisation called the Foreign Trade Commission (FTC) formerly under the functional control of MOFERT. The bifurcation of provincial foreign trade authority, and the resulting redundancy and confusion were hardly desirable, but the conflict could not be easily resolved due to the FTC's staunch opposition to merger with the FEC and to the inability (and unwillingness) of the provincial leadership to impose their will on the protagonists.[33]

Second-batch preferential policies, 1988–91

In 1988 many preferential policies were granted to Shandong and these contributed considerably to the mitigation of Shandong's conservatism. According to knowledgeable interviewees, a crucial decision was made at a State Council meeting held in December 1987 to designate Shandong as the key province in dealing with South Korea on a non-governmental and economic basis.[34] The decision was never put into formal writing (perhaps out of Beijing's political concerns with Pyongyang at the time) but Shandong was allowed by the central government to implement various preferential arrangements to cater for South Korean businesses. Such special arrangements included the opening of ferry routes between Weihai in Shandong and Inchon in South Korea (despite the absence of diplomatic normalisation), and the authorisation for the Shandong provincial authorities to issue entry visas to South Korean business people on their arrival in China.[35]

The long-expected 'opening' of the Shandong Peninsula finally occurred in March 1988 with the designation of the six cities of Qingdao, Yantai, Weihai, Weifang, Rizhao and Zibo and their forty-four counties. At the same time, the province's authority for approving foreign-invested projects was raised from US$5 million to 30 million.[36] In the immediate aftermath of the

State Council's decision to open the peninsula, Jiang Chunyun, who had succeeded Li Chang'an as governor, called for 'all-directional opening' toward socialist and capitalist countries alike. Jiang severely criticised the prevalent conservatism by saying 'without fundamental changes in ideas and attitudes toward opening, an outward-oriented economy would be impossible to achieve.'[37] In May 1988 the approving authority for 'processing imported materials' projects was delegated to the counties, while that for 'three foreign-invested firms' was decentralised to the prefectural cities. During the seven-month period of January–July 1988 alone, contracts for over 600 projects worth US$4.4 billion were signed, an amount that was twenty times larger than that for the same period in 1987.[38]

In February 1990, Shandong's open area was further expanded with the addition of Jinan and its nine counties, making the total number of Shandong's open areas seven prefectural cities and fifty-three counties.[39] The same year also witnessed a key institutional change with regard to Shandong's foreign economic relations. In 1990, the two foreign economic relations authorities – the FEC and the FTC – were finally merged to form the Foreign Economic and Trade Commission (FETC). As foreign trade and investment were becoming increasingly crucial for the overall development of the province's economy, Jiang Chunyun, provincial party secretary since 1988, allegedly intervened to unify the bifurcated foreign economic relations authorities. Fearing more severe factional infighting after the merger, the provincial leadership transferred the heads of both FEC and FTC to other organisations, and instead invited an outsider to head the newly formed FETC.[40]

Third round preferential policies, since 1992

With a renewed emphasis on reform and opening in early 1992, facilitated mainly by Deng Xiaoping's renowned southern tour, more preferential policies were granted to Shandong. In 1992, Qingdao was authorised by the State Council to set up a bonded zone. Bonded zones are granted the most favourable terms of trade and investment among all existing preferential arrangements.[41] In addition, in March 1991 the State Council authorised a handful of localities to establish so-called 'new and high technology industrial development zones'. Shandong once again obtained its share through this new preferential policy when Qingdao was authorised to set up a zone in 1992. Furthermore, Shandong joined another list of exclusive membership in 1992 by having Qingdao's Shilaoren District designated as one of China's eleven 'state tourism and leisure zones'.[42]

Another key event that provided a significant boost to provincial interests was the establishment of full diplomatic relations between China and South Korea in August 1992. While there were already extensive economic exchanges between Shandong and South Korea during 1988–91, the diploma-tic normalisation brought about an almost explosive expansion of the bilateral economic relationship, particularly in direct investments from Seoul. There was clearly the potential for an economically productive special relationship between Shandong and South Korea. Over 90 per cent of South Korea's Overseas Chinese were of Shandong origin and the geographical proximity led provincial leaders to pay special attention to the development of bilateral relationships: both Jiang Chunyun and Li Chunting – governor since 1995 – visited South Korea. By 1994 South Korea had become the second most important destination for Shandong's exports; and the third most important for its total investment in Shandong, after only Hong Kong and Taiwan.[43]

In March 1993, Dongying was designated by the State Council as an open area and Shandong's open area thus covered eight of its seventeen prefectural-level cities and fifty-six counties and 38 per cent of its population. In 1993, Weihai was authorised to set up an ETDZ to compete with Qingdao and Yantai. In 1993, thanks to Shandong's effective lobbying, Weifang, Weihai, Zibo and Jinan were all approved by the State Council to establish 'new and high technology industrial development zones', until then reserved to Qingdao.[44]

Could Shandong have developed as fast as it did without these highly selective preferential policies from the centre? The answer is probably not since the principal role of regionally targeted preferential policies was to confirm to the local recipients as well as to the prospective investors that the central government was serious about development and would actively support the select group of localities even if that meant impartiality and inequality to others. The creation and consolidation of the Beijing–Shandong developmental alliance were thus based upon an efficiency imperative, which seems to have worked out quite well in retrospect. At a national level, the Beijing–coastal region alliance has provided the key impetus for growth, but this alliance has also included another key participant in China's developmental process.

FOREIGN ECONOMIC RELATIONS AND THE STRATEGIC ALLIANCE BETWEEN SHANDONG AND FOREIGN CAPITAL

A full-scale 'opening' of Shandong started in 1988 with the provision of the second batch of preferential policies including the opening of the Shandong Peninsula. The goal of 'all-directional opening' was promulgated in 1988, with its initial strategic focus on the establishment of key linkages between foreign capital and six open cities of Qingdao, Yantai, Weihai, Weifang, Zibo and Rizhao. The development of an outward-oriented economy in these coastal areas was regarded as a key means of supporting inland areas in the longer run (through an eventual trickle-down effect) and, for this purpose, active solicitation of foreign funds was called for in developing township and village enterprises (TVEs), and small and medium-sized firms in cities as well as in renovating old and outdated large state enterprises.[45]

In order to attract foreign capital, Shandong made efforts in infrastructural development. By 1986 Shandong's electricity production was already the largest in China.[46] Shandong's railway and road construction are also well known in China. The total length of Shandong's first- and second-rate roads – 25,596 kilometres as of 1992 – was the longest in China and its 3,040 kilometres of railway was also far above the national average.[47] Jiang Chunyun played a pivotal role in providing policy support for the development of transportation linkages. One of Jiang's contributions in this respect was the establishment of various funds for the construction and management of key transportation linkages in the province. Some of these funds were financed by road maintenance fees levied on the owners of motor vehicles and tractors. Other funds were financed by central subsidies, bank loans, ministerial investments and foreign investment. In October 1992, the provincial transportation bureau set up the Shandong Provincial Transportation Development and Investment Corporation which would take charge of attracting external (both foreign and extra-provincial) investment in this sector. The construction of the Jiqing super-highway (linking Jinan and Qingdao) relied on five sources of funds: the World Bank, Beijing, domestic banks, the provinces, and several prefectures and cities in Shandong. The construction of Longkou harbour was also funded in significant part by investments from South Korea.[48]

Shandong's international linkages were closely linked to its agricultural development strategy, which has played a vital role in Shandong's recent success in reform.[49] First, effective decentralisation of policy-making authority to the county level since 1987 contributed significantly to the activation of local initiatives and avoidance of standardisation in rural production.[50] Second, Shandong's success is also attributable to its efforts to maintain steady investments in agriculture, including foreign investment. In 1994 alone, 169 foreign investment projects worth US$100 million were contracted in agriculture-related activities.[51] Third, the development of TVEs has also been closely interwoven with the strategy of vertical integration – supporting peasants to pursue the combined task of producing, processing and exporting their farm products without depending upon intermediaries.[52]

Shandong's path of enterprise reform – particularly in financing and renovating state enterprises – was also linked to the establishment of international linkages with foreign capital. In addition to such principal measures as 'stockification' (share-issuing), 'contracting out' and 'sale and merger', the utilisation of foreign capital to finance and renovate old state-owned enterprises has become increasingly popular in Shandong. As of 1993, for instance, 25 per cent of all industrial enterprises in the province at the township level and above were linked with foreign capital in one way or another, and the comparable figures for coastal cities like Qingdao, Yantai and Weihai were all well over 50 per cent.[53]

Shandong's linkages with foreign capital were further expanded in 1992. In the immediate aftermath of Deng's speech during his southern tour, Jiang Chunyun personally directed a series of surveys and investigation on outward-oriented economies and dispatched two vice-governors to four provincial-level units – Beijing, Dalian (as a central economic city), Fujian and Guangdong – to assess their experiences in 'getting linked up with' foreign capital. On the basis of these assessments, a series of 'work conferences on opening' were convened in March 1992, which were attended by provincial, prefectural and county party secretaries as well as other key local officials. At these conferences, the 'further liberation of ideas' was called for and more areas were subsequently opened up by the provincial authorities themselves. These new batches of province-approved zones included thirty-six 'export-oriented industrial processing zones', twelve 'opening and development comprehensive experimental zones', seven 'high-tech industrial development zones', two 'tourism development zones' and three 'tourism and leisure zones'.[54]

Shandong's provincial leadership, particularly that under Jiang Chunyun and Zhao Zhihao in 1988-94, repeatedly emphasised the need to further expand the province's interactions with the outside world. As a key result, a total of 64 cities and counties were opened up by 1994, thus making Shandong's open area the second largest in China after only Guangdong.[55] There are several principal indicators for the extensive external linkages Shandong has established over the years.[56] First, Shandong currently maintains economic relations with over 160 countries and, as of 1994, has established 'friendly relationships' with 61 regions and cities in 24 countries. Second, Shandong has more than 16,000 firms with foreign investments from more than 60 different countries. Third, Shandong has a total of 64 overseas offices in 17 countries. Some offices are managed directly by provincial government units, others by provincial enterprises, and still others by various city and prefectural governments.[57] Fourth, Shandong has a total of 87 overseas trading firms under the jurisdiction of various provincial, prefectural and city foreign trade corporations (examples include the Luxing Corporation in New York and the Hualu Corporation in Hong Kong).[58] Fifth, Shandong has a total of 115 factories located overseas with the total amount of investment reaching US$115 million (an average of US$1 million for each plant). Sixth, the total number of Shandong's firms with their own import and export authority rose to 351 by the end of 1994 (an increase of about 100 over 1993).[59]

REGIONAL DEVELOPMENT AND ITS COASTAL BIASES

Central government gave priority to a few select regions with the most development potential. As a result coastal regions have largely been the main beneficiaries of Beijing's regionally targeted preferential policies. Beijing's regional target policies in favour of coastal regions were also in line with the interests of foreign capital in constant search of areas offering low-cost labour, relatively good communications and transportation linkages, better-educated human resources, new markets, and so on. The outcome was generally the accelerated development of the coastal region at the expense of the inland region. In this respect, regional development in Shandong constitutes a microcosm of the national trend.[60]

In 1978–83, Shandong had no regional development strategy to speak of, not only because, as discussed earlier, the provincial leadership of this period was not geared toward the sort of reform then under way in some southern provinces, but also because it was more preoccupied with the implementation of agricultural decollectivisation. Shandong's regional development strategy was seriously considered for the first time in 1984 with the designation of Qingdao and Yantai as coastal open cities. During the subsequent period of 1984–7, the opening of the eastern region of the province was prioritised with its focus on those two COCs. During 1987–90, that focus did not change with the further opening and development of the eastern region receiving high priority in policy and investment support. Shandong's regional development strategy since 1991, however, has sought to further open up the province as a whole and to maximise the comparative advantages of its eastern and western regions.[61]

Generally speaking, up until 1990 Shandong's regional development strategy was largely to support a few key-point cities – most notably Qingdao, and Yantai, plus to a lesser extent Weihai – designated by Beijing as 'open areas' with certain preferential policies to promote foreign economic relations. According to interviewees in Jinan, a so-called 'two-three-six' strategy was researched in 1990–1 and proposed in 1991 by the Provincial Economic Research Centre, and formally endorsed in 1992 by the provincial government.[62] The first 'two' stands for 'two large chunks' of the province: the Shandong Peninsula development zone – covering the eight open cities of Qingdao, Yantai, Weihai, Rizhao, Weifang, Zibo, Jinan and Dongying, and geared toward an outward-oriented development strategy;[63] and the western inland regions – the nine cities and prefectures of Jining, Taian, Heze, Liaocheng, Dezhou, Zaozhuang, Linyi, Laiwu and Binzhou – heavily geared toward agriculture, animal husbandry, mining and energy development.

The 'three' component in the 'two-three-six' strategy stands for the 'three industrial concentration belts' located along the key railways in the province. The most important belt is the Jiaoji Railway with Dezhou in the northwest, the two central cities of Jinan and Jiaozhou, and Qingdao in the east. This belt prioritises the development of export-oriented agriculture, processing and high-tech industries including precision-machinery, pharmaceuticals and electronics, as well as service, finance and real estate businesses. The southern 'industrial concentration belt' is located along the Xinshi Railway linking Heze in the southwest with Rizhao in the southeast, and focuses on energy development (electricity and coal in particular), construction materials industries (cement, marbles and steel) and petrochemicals. The last belt, still in the stage of planning (and negotiation with Beijing), is to be located along the Delong railway linking Dezhou and Longkou in the northern part of the province and the Yellow River Delta Region concentrating on grain and cotton production, animal husbandry, and oil refinery.[64]

The final 'six' refers to six areas identified in terms of their levels of economic development and geographical location: the Jiaodong Peninsula including Qingdao, Yantai, Weihai and Weifang; the central area of the province covering Jinan, Taian and Laiwu; the northern part of the province with Zibo, Dongying and Binzhou; the northwestern area of Dezhou and Liaocheng; the southwestern area of the province including Zaozhuang, Jining and Heze; and the southeastern area of Linyi and Rizhao. Unlike the first two components of the strategy, this concept of six areas has not yet been officially endorsed by the provincial government.[65]

In almost all configurations of Shandong's regional development, one particular region always stands out in terms of the policy attention and developmental priority it has received over the years: the Jiaodong Peninsula (and the Shandong Peninsula to a lesser extent) was always the main beneficiary as well as the key pace-setter of reform in Shandong.[66] Most of the provincial officials interviewed also viewed this region as the backbone of Shandong's development. Furthermore, Qingdao is generally viewed as the 'dragonhead' in Shandong's developmental strategy, and Yantai and Weihai as the dragon's 'two wings'. While it is duly admitted that the province's infatuation with Qingdao has cooled down rather considerably after the city's designation as a 'central economic city' in 1987, the positive role Qingdao could play in spreading the ideology of development and in diffusing international linkages into the inland regions are nonetheless emphasised.[67]

Overall, Shandong's coastal region – the Jiaodong Peninsula region in particular – has over time benefited considerably from a variety of preferential policies granted by the central and provincial governments largely at the expense of the inland regions. According to Table 5.2, only

Table 5.2 Privileges of coastal and inland regions in Shandong, 1994

Preferential policies[a]	*Coastal region*[b]	*Inland region*[c]
State-designated COAs	6	2
State-designated ETDZs	3	0
State-designated NHIDZs	3	2
State-designated BZs	1	0
State-designated TLZs	1	0
Province-designated zones[d]	34	6

Notes: [a]COAs: Coastal Open Areas; ETDZs: Economic and Technological Development Zones; NHIDZs: New and High-tech Industrial Development Zones; BZs: Bonded Zones; TLZs: Tourism and Leisure Zones
[b]The coastal region encompasses seven cities (and their counties) of Qingdao, Yantai, Weihai, Weifang, Rizhao, Dongying and Binzhou
[c]The inland region includes ten prefectures and cities (and their counties) of Zibo, Linyi, Laiwu, Zaozhuang, Jining, Jinan, Taian, Heze, Liaocheng and Dezhou
[d]There are a total of sixty such zones as of September 1995

Source: Shandong Foreign Economic and Trade Commission, *Shandongsheng gelei kaifaqu fenbu qingkuangbiao* [List of Various Development Zones in Shandong], 20 April 1994

four state-designated open areas and development zones are located in the inland region while the coastal region claimed a total of fourteen (78 per cent). The provincial government paid a lot more attention to the inland regions in locating its own development zones. The inland region with ten prefectures and cities obtained twenty-six of sixty province-designated zones (43 per cent), while the remaining thirty-four were located in the coastal region with seven prefectural cities.[68]

Intra-provincial inequalities along the coastal–inland axis are quite apparent in many key dimensions of the province's economy as a whole. Table 5.3 provides such comparisons in the areas of agriculture, industry, foreign trade and foreign investment. With the notable exception of agriculture in which the inland region reached up to three-quarters of the coastal region, enormous disparities are found on all of the other three dimensions. Particularly in foreign economic relations, the three coastal cities of Qingdao, Yantai and Weifang accounted for 55 per cent of the province's total exports and 60 per cent of its foreign direct investment, while the percentages for the four inland prefectures were merely 12.6 and 6.3, respectively. Furthermore, as Table 5.4 indicates, all top five recipients of foreign direct investment in Shandong were coastal cities with the notable exception of Zibo in 1992 and Jinan in 1993–4, with Qingdao always leading the others and followed by Yantai and Weifang.[69] While the gap between Qingdao and the second city of Yantai decreased from 8.2 per cent of the total value of contracted direct foreign investment in 1992 to 3.8 per cent in 1994, the total share of the top five recipients remained almost unchanged at 76.2 per cent in 1992 and 76.6 per cent in 1994, indicating the difficulties the western inland region was facing in obtaining foreign capital.

A more appalling illustration of coastal–inland disparities in Shandong is found in the regional distribution of extreme poverty. As Table 5.5 shows, the eastern peninsula region has none of its counties designated as 'poverty-

Table 5.3 Coastal–inland comparison for selected economic indicators, 1994

	Per capita GVIO (yuan)	Per capita GVAO (yuan)	Share in Shandong's exports (%)	Share in Shandong's foreign direct investment[c] (%)
Coastal[a]	7,994	1,683	55.4	60.0
Inland[b]	2,370	1,247	12.6	6.3

Notes: [a]The coastal region is represented by three developed cities of Qingdao, Yantai and Weifang
[b]The inland region covers four backward prefectures of Heze, Liaocheng, Linyi and Dezhou
[c]The share is based on the contracted amount of investment

Source: Per capita shares and percentages in the province's total were calculated from the information provided in *Shandong tongji nianjian 1995*, pp. 29, 216, 266, 469, 475

Table 5.4 Foreign direct investment in Shandong by city, 1992–4

Rank	1992		1993		1994	
1	Qingdao	29.0%	Qingdao	18.7%	Qingdao	22.8%
2	Yantai	20.8%	Yantai	17.4%	Yantai	19.0%
3	Weifang	9.8%	Jinan	12.2%	Weifang	18.2%
4	Weihai	8.4%	Weifang	10.7%	Weihai	8.6%
5	Zibo	8.2%	Weihai	9.1%	Jinan	8.0%
Total		76.2%		68.1%		76.6%

Note: Figures are calculated on the basis of contracted investments
Sources: *Shandong tongji nianjian 1993* p. 484; 1994 issue, p. 414; 1995 issue, p. 475

Table 5.5 Regional distribution of poor counties, 1994

	State-designated	Province-designated
Eastern peninsula region[a]	0	0
Middle-belt region[b]	5	4
Western region[c]	5	5

Notes: [a]Eastern peninsula region encompasses five cities of Yantai, Qingdao, Weihai, Weifang and Rizhao
[b]Middle-belt region includes seven cities of Dongying, Linyi, Zaozhuang, Zibo, Laiwu, Taian and Jinan
[c]Western region covers five prefectures and cities of Dezhou, Liaocheng, Binzhou, Jining and Heze
Source: Zhang Feng, 'Shandongsheng fupin kaifa youguan qingkuang de diaocha' [Survey of Shandong's 'Poverty Alleviation'] in *Jingji yanjiu cankao* no. 653 (4 April 1995), p. 14

ridden' by the central or provincial governments.[70] The middle-belt region has a total of nine state- and province-designated 'poverty-ridden counties' and seven of them are located in the southern mountainous prefecture of Linyi which has long been known for its extreme poverty (the other two counties are located in Zaozhuang and Taian). On the other hand, the western region, which includes Heze, Liaocheng, Binzhou, Jining and Dezhou has ten 'poverty-ridden counties' distributed among all five prefectures: two in Heze, three in Binzhou, one in Jining, two in Dezhou and two in Liaocheng. In comparison with the eastern peninsula region where there are no 'poverty-ridden counties' and the middle-belt region where Jinan, Taian and Zibo are free of such counties, poverty is rather significantly concentrated in the western inland region.

'EQUALITY WITHOUT EQUALIZATION?': REMEDIES FOR INTRA-PROVINCIAL DISPARITIES

Shandong started its efforts to tackle intra-provincial disparities in accordance with the 1984 joint notification by the Party Centre and the State Council 'On helping poor areas to change their face'. Shandong's specific response was its 'Comprehensive plan for the development of the poor regions in Shandong for 1985–2000'. Concerted efforts were needed to alleviate poverty on the one hand and to reduce intra-provincial inequalities on the other. As of 1985, for instance, the province's per capita GVIO was RMB 703 *yuan*, but the comparable figures for the coastal (Qingdao, Yantai and Weifang) and the inland (Dezhou, Huimin, Heze, Liaocheng and Linyi) regions were RMB 991 *yuan* and 301 *yuan*, respectively.[71] After almost a decade, however, a similarly large gap (that is, a three-to-one ratio) is still observable with regard to the per capita GVIO for 1994: RMB 7,994 *yuan* for the coastal region and RMB 2,557 *yuan* for the inland region.[72]

Despite ambitious plans and policy stipulations, the task of poverty alleviation was largely overshadowed by the growth imperative throughout the 1980s. That is, the coastal region and the Jiaodong Peninsula in particular were the main beneficiary of preferential policies and privileges in the allocation of fiscal and material resources. For instance, total investment in the transportation sector in Liaocheng Prefecture – a lesser-developed inland region – during 1950–85 was only RMB 28 million *yuan*, about 2.8 per cent of Shandong's total investment in the sector for the year of 1985 alone. State basic construction investment in Liaocheng for the period of 1981–5 constituted only 1 per cent of the province's total, while the prefecture's share in Shandong's GVAIO accounted for about 5 per cent. Heze Prefecture was in a similar situation. State fixed-asset investments in Heze during 1949–83 was RMB 210 million *yuan*, an equivalent of only 20 per cent of the total investment in the province for the year of 1985 alone. The backwardness of industrial production in the inland region is another key source of regional disparities. As of 1987, for example, cotton production in the four western prefectures accounted for 78 per cent and 23 per cent of the provincial and national production, respectively. In its processing, however, these prefectures handled only 27 and 2.5 per cent of the provincial and national total.[73]

With the further expansion of 'opening' in Shandong during 1988–90, some attention was given to the goal of 'balanced development'. In March 1988, the provincial leadership stressed the need for closer linkages between the eastern and western regions and for technology transfer from the former to the latter. It also articulated a goal of supporting the western inland regions to export 10 or more per cent of their agricultural and industrial goods during the period 1988–97.[74] The need to extend the area of irrigation and road construction in these poor and underdeveloped regions was also emphasised. During 1985–92, a total of RMB 240 million *yuan* was provided by the provincial government to facilitate the construction of 10,000 kilometres of roads, over 400 bridges and 2,300 irrigation facilities. In the ten-year period 1984–93, RMB 600 million *yuan* was invested in building wells, constructing roads, and supplying electricity and potable water. Furthermore, the provincial government provided annual subsidies of RMB half a million *yuan* to nineteen state- and province-designated 'poverty-ridden counties' to help them build new roads.[75]

To assist these 'poverty-ridden counties' the central government established several channels of support and provided various funds after the 1984 joint notice by the Party Central Committee and the State Council.[76] The Ministry of Finance provided fiscal subsidies as 'funds for supporting underdeveloped regions' which amounted to RMB 15 million *yuan* annually. The central government also provided several regular bank loans for the development of poor inland regions. These loans included 'special loans for poverty allevia-tion'; 'loans for the old, minorities, remote and poor areas'; and 'loans for county-run enterprises'.[77] The central government supported the construction of road, irrigation facilities, and similar projects, through the practice of 'paying in goods for labour services' provided by local people. Since this practice started in 1987, the central government (through the State Planning Commission) has paid an annual average of RMB 35 million *yuan*.[78]

The provincial government, too, provided four different funds and loans for poverty-alleviation in the western inland region. These funds and loans include: 'fiscal-transfer funds for poverty alleviation' which started in 1985 and provided interest-free loans that averaged RMB 10 million *yuan* annually; 'loans for the dam regions' which started in 1987 and averaged RMB 5 million *yuan* annually; 'subsidies for the construction of transportation' provided since 1985 with an annual support of RMB 7.6 million *yuan*; and 'subsidies for the construction of electricity' supplied since 1985 with an annual provision of RMB 2.5 million *yuan*. In addition, since 1986 the provincial government also supplied a variety of material resources – such as petroleum, steel, cement, chemical fertiliser, automobiles and so on – at planned prices as opposed to market prices. In the case of chemical fertiliser, for instance, an annual average of 72,000 tons were supplied at planned prices to support agricultural production in these poor regions.[79]

With a total investment of well over RMB 1 billion *yuan* for 1984–93, Shandong claims that it was fairly successful in mitigating regional inequal-ities and alleviating poverty.[80] The total size of the province's 'poor population' decreased from 7.6 million in 1984 to 4 million in 1993.[81] The original fifteen poverty-ridden counties designated in 1984 had an average per capita income of RMB 237 *yuan* in 1984, which rose to over RMB 700 *yuan* in 1993. The size of the poor population in these fifteen counties also dropped from 4.8 million in 1984 to 1.2 million in 1993. Among the original fifteen counties, four counties in Linju, Linmu, Shangcheng and Liangshan managed to raise their status out of the league of the poverty-ridden. The newly designated nineteen 'poverty-ridden' counties (see Table 5.5 for their regional distribution) account for 15.7 per cent of the province's total population but only 4 per cent of the total county-level budgetary revenues, a fact which underscores the acute need for financial and policy support from the central and provincial authorities.[82]

In its efforts to alleviate poverty and mitigate regional disparities, the Shandong leadership has sought to extend international and inter-regional linkages into the inland areas of the province. The provincial leadership has used its own discretion to the maximum to authorise more than two dozen inland localities to enjoy various privileges similar to those granted earlier to the coastal development zones designated by Beijing. As Table 5.6 shows, Shandong established a total of sixty development zones which would have almost the same privileges as those enjoyed by the centre-designated zones (the only exception being bonded zones).[83]

Significant efforts were also directed at the extension of key transport linkages into the inland region to facilitate easier access to the coastal region as well as foreign capital. Such transport linkages include the newly opened super-highway joining Qingdao, Jinan and Dezhou; the northern Xinshi Railway linking Dezhou, Longkou, Binzhou and Dongying; and the Jingjiu Railway that is designed to pass Liaocheng, Jining and Heze.[84]

The provincial leadership has adopted a variety of innovative policies designed to link backward inland areas with more advanced coastal regions.

Table 5.6 Sixty province-designated development zones in Shandong, 1994

Province-designated		*Beijing-designated counterparts*	
36	Export-oriented Industrial Processing Zones[a]	8	Coastal Open Cities
12	Opening and Reform Comprehensive Experimental Zones[b]	3	Economic and Technological Development Zones
7	High-tech Development Zones[c]	5	High-tech Development Zones
2	Tourism Development Zones and	1	Tourism and Leisure Zone
3	Tourism and Leisure Zones[d]		
none		1	Bonded Zone

Notes: [a]Eight of these zones are located in non-coastal open cities of Zibo and Jinan but none is in the western inland region
[b]All but two (one each in Dongying and Binzhou) of these zones are located in the inland region
[c]All but two (one each in Yantai and Longkou) are located in the inland region
[d]The former two are located in the inland region (Taian and Qufu) and the latter three are located in the coastal region (Yantai, Weihai and Rushan)

Sources: Shandong Provincial Foreign Economic and Trade Commission, *Shandongsheng fazhan waixiangxing jingji huaqu budian zongti guihua fang'an* [The Overall Plan for Regional Zoning in the Development of an Outward-Oriented Economy in Shandong], 12 December 1992; and Shandong Provincial Foreign Economic and Trade Commission, *Shandongsheng gelei kaifaqu fenbu qingkuangbiao* [Regional Distribution of Various Kinds of Development Zones in Shandong], 20 April 1994

These measures for the promotion of domestic linkages were based in significant part on the realisation of only a modicum of success in the province's efforts to link inland areas with foreign capital.[85] One of the most important strategies of establishing domestic linkages is 'matching for cooperation' or 'pairing'. As early as 1985, the provincial government designated six eastern cities of Qingdao, Yantai, Jinan, Weifang, Zibo and Weihai to help develop the seven poor counties of Linyi Prefecture's Yimongshan region. In 1985–94, these cities located a total of 482 projects in the Yimongshan region with an added production value of over RMB 500 million *yuan*. Furthermore, by 1988 the same six eastern cities were 'paired up' with six inland prefectures and cities for economic cooperation and support.[86] In 1985–92, coastal and inland regions signed a total of 1,990 cooperative projects, among which 1,180 actually materialised.[87]

During 1990–4 the provincial government came up with another innovative scheme of intra-provincial linkages for economic cooperation. This scheme is usually referred to as 'four-directional matching' and links nineteen 'poverty-ridden counties' with territorial counterparts, provincial government organisations, and large state enterprises as well as with key provincial leaders (Table 5.7). Wendeng County of Yantai Prefecture, for example, has been linked up with Sishui County of Jining Prefecture, and Rongcheng is supposed to utilise low-cost labour in Sishui by encouraging its industrial enterprises to assign portions of processing work to the latter. Sishui county is also linked with the provincial planning commission and the Qilu Petrochemical Corporation which provide the county with monetary and material subsidies for industrial and infrastructural development. Vice-Governor Han Yuqun is also in charge of supporting the development of Sishui county.[88]

Finally, the exchange, circulation and education of local cadres constitute another key strategy implemented by the provincial leadership in its efforts to diffuse economic development into the backward inland region. Similar efforts are being made at the national level.[89] Sub-provincial level cadres are 'horizontally exchanged' between coastal and inland regions. Cadres from the inland areas are stationed in advanced coastal areas for a fixed period to learn from their experiences with reform. At the same time, cadres from the coastal region are assigned to the inland so that they can pass on their experiences with developmental reform and offer constructive suggestions as to developmental strategies inland regions may adopt. Well-known examples involving high-level cadres include the appointment of Zhang Huilai (formerly of Qingdao) as Dezhou prefectural party secretary and the transfer of Chen Yanming (formerly of Weifang) as Liaocheng prefectural party secretary.[90]

Provincial government officials often 'go down' – without giving up their institutional relationships with their original units – to serve as local government officials in backward inland areas. Examples include the transfer of Huang Sheng (formerly the secretary-general of the provincial government administrative office) to the mayoral position in Dezhou; and the assignment

Table 5.7 Select cases of 'four-directional pairing' in Shandong

Poor county	Provincial leader	Wealthy county	Bureau	Enterprise
Qingyun	Han Xikai	Huancui	Supply and Marketing Cooperatives	Qilu Petrochemical
Guan	Li Wenquan	Xixia	Water Conservancy	Qilu Pharmacy
Xin	Wang Yuxi*	Zhizhong	Transportation	Resources Import and Export Corp.
Sishui	Han Yuqun	Wendeng	Planning	Qilu Petrochemical
Mongyin	Zhang Ruifeng*	Rushan	Construction	Jinan Steel Mill
Pingyi	Li Chunting*	Fenglai	Building Materials	Shengli Oil Field
Dan	Wu Aiying*	Zhucheng	Post and Telecommunication	Light Industry Import and Export Corp and others
Zoucheng	Wang Yuxi*	Laixi and Jimo	Industry and Commerce	CITIC
Dongping	Chen Jianguo*	Laoshan	Economic	Qilu Petrochemical and others
Yangxin	Li Chunting*	Rongcheng	Agricultural Bank	Shandong Pesticide and others

Note: Among the total of nineteen, ten counties which have all of the four partners are shown here
*Indicates the rank of vice-governor or above

Source: Poverty-Alleviation Small Group Office of the Shandong Provincial Government, *Shenglingdao, tingju, qiangxian, dazhongqiyie lianxi yu duikou zhiyuan pinkunxian qingkuang yilanbiao* [List of Provincial Leaders, Bureaux, 'Strong' Counties and Large and Medium-Sized Enterprises Helping Poverty-Ridden Counties], September 1995

of a deputy-section chief of the provincial second light industry bureau to serve as a deputy-chief of Qufu county.

Academic and professional experts are also often invited to serve as administrators in backward inland areas. One notable example was the appointment of a former professor at the Chinese Academy of Agricultural Sciences to serve as a deputy-mayor of Heze. Additionally, coastal cities also station their technicians in inland areas to assist in the training of technical staff. Qingdao, for instance, has dispatched a total of 165 technicians to the western region since 1985.

GROWTH, INEQUALITY AND INTERVENTION IN LOCAL ECONOMIC DEVELOPMENT

Post-Mao economic reform has been highly successful mainly because it managed to motivate local governments – through more abundant local information and more direct interests in motivating growth – to participate in the promotion of economic development. De-ideologisation and decentralisation enabled local implementors to break out of the die-hard conservative crust and try out new and innovative ideas for local economic development. Preferential policies further consolidated the incentive relation between the central and local governments, and regionally targeted preferential policies favoured the emergence of a production alliance among the central government, foreign capital, and select local governments (which have quite successfully stood in for a local bourgeoisie and entrepreneurial classes in the process of development).

Yet such a production alliance has put almost one-sided emphasis on efficiency, thus producing a fundamental problem of regional disparities. In coping with this sensitive issue – which may in the long run threaten the political fortune of the regime as a whole – the central government has increasingly become willing to elicit the support of both local governments and foreign capital. Unlike local governments which saw immediate benefit in alleviating extreme poverty and mitigating inter- and intra-provincial inequalities, foreign capital has been lukewarm at best toward investing in backward inland regions with much less to offer than their coastal counterparts. As an alternative to foreign capital, the central and local governments have sought to create and consolidate 'horizontal linkages' among domestic capital and industries by way of various innovative schemes.

To what extent such schemes will be effective in reducing intra-provincial disparities remains to be seen. Despite Beijing's renewed determination – stipulated in part in the Ninth Five-Year Plan – sacrificing the pace of growth for the sake of more equality will be a very tough choice with significant political implications of its own. As the reform deepens, concerns with internal colonisation will be voiced. If the current situation is any guide, such a colonising process is perhaps already well under way. For instance, a majority of provincial leaders in Shandong are from the coastal region. Among the fifteen members of the fourteenth provincial party standing committee elected in 1992, eleven were Shandong natives and seven of them were from the coastal regions. The top provincial leaders such as Jiang Chunyun (Laixi), Zhao Zhihao (Longkou) and Li Chunting (Xixia) all come from the Jiaodong Peninsula, mainly Qingdao and Yantai.

It is far from clear what the inland regions can do on their own, particularly given that major policy frameworks are shaped mainly by the central and provincial authorities. The recent closing down of most of the development zones approved by sub-provincial authorities (particularly those in the western region) and the weakening of the fiscal authority of local governments with the implementation of the new tax-sharing reform tends to suggest a rather pessimistic scenario. One thing is clear, however: there are ever greater needs for central intervention – in the form of policies as well as functional grants designated specifically for industrial development and poverty alleviation in the backward regions of each province – although believers in the 'trickle-down' theory would argue the contrary. The dilemma as to whether to adopt a political or an economic logic of reform will continue to haunt the central and local decision-makers during China's economic transition.

ACKNOWLEDGEMENTS

Field trips to Shandong for this research were supported by a direct allocation grant of the Hong Kong University of Science and Technology. I thank John Fitzgerald and other participants of the Suzhou Conference for their helpful comments on an earlier version of this chapter.

NOTES

1 The *locus classicus* on this theme is Alexander Gerschenkron, *Economic Backwardness in Historical Perspective*, Harvard University Press, Cambridge, MA, 1962, pp. 12–20.
2 See Tony Smith, 'The underdevelopment of development literature: the case of dependency theory', *World Politics* 31, no. 2 (January 1979), pp. 251–9.
3 A notable exception is David Zweig, '"Developmental Communities" on China's coast: the impact of trade, investment, and transnational alliances', *Comparative Politics* 27, no. 3 (April 1995), pp. 253–74. For the need to 'unpack' the encompassing concept of state, see Gabriel A. Almond, 'The development of political development', in Myron Weiner and Samuel P. Huntington (eds) *Understanding Political Development*, Little Brown, Boston, MA, 1987, p. 477.
4 For the largely minimal impact of the industry-specific target policies, see Robert Wade, *Governing the Market: Economic Theory and the Role of Government in East Asian Industrialization*, Princeton University Press, Princeton, NJ, 1990, pp. 298–9; and World Bank, *The East Asian Miracle: Economic Growth and Public Policy*, Oxford University Press, Oxford, 1993, pp. 354–5. For an overview of regional policy in China's post-Mao development, see Terry Cannon, 'Regions: spatial inequality and regional policy', in *The Geography of Contemporary China: The Impact of Deng Xiaoping's Decade*, Routledge, London, 1990, pp. 39–59; and Susumu Yabuki, *China's New Political Economy: The Giant Awakes*, Westview, Boulder, CO, 1995, pp. 177–208.
5 For the entrepreneurial quality of communist cadres, see Ákos Róna-Tas, 'The first shall be last? Entrepreneurship and communist cadres in the transition from socialism', *American Journal of Sociology* 100, no. 1 (July 1994), pp. 40–69. And for the entrepreneurial role by local government in China, see Andrew G. Walder, 'Local governments as industrial firms: an organizational analysis of China's transitional economy', *American Journal of Sociology* 101, no. 2 (September 1995), pp. 263–301.
6 The original conceptualisation of 'triple alliance' is found in Peter Evans, *Dependent Development: The Alliance of Multinational, State, and Local Capital in Brazil*, Princeton University Press, Princeton, NJ, 1979. A different version has four groups of foreign capital, military, middle class and local bourgeoisie as

forming a 'rectarchical alliance'. See Fernando H. Cardoso, 'Associated-dependent development: theoretical and practical implications', cited in Stephen Haggard, *Pathways from the Periphery: The Politics of Growth in the Newly Industrializing Countries*, Cornell University Press, Ithaca, NY, 1990, pp. 17–18.

7 For the importance of 'sequencing' in reform, see Michel Oksenberg and Bruce J. Dickson, 'The origins, processes, and outcomes of great political reform', in Dankwart A. Rustow and Kenneth Paul Erickson (eds) *Comparative Political Dynamics: Global Research Perspectives*, HarperCollins, New York, 1991, pp. 248–9.

8 For the centrality of Beijing's preferential policies in Guangdong's development, see David S.G. Goodman and Feng Chongyi, 'Guangdong: Greater Hong Kong and the new regionalist future', in David S.G. Goodman and Gerald Segal (eds) *China Deconstructs: Politics, Trade and Regionalism*, Routledge, London, 1994, pp. 185–6; and Peter T.Y. Cheung, 'Relations between the central government and Guangdong', in Y.M. Yeung and David K.Y. Chu (eds) *Guangdong: Survey of a Province Undergoing Rapid Change*, Chinese University Press, Hong Kong, 1994, pp. 33–4. For the similar sequence in Shandong, see Jae Ho Chung, 'Shandong's strategies of reform and opening', paper presented at the 1995 annual meeting of the Association for Asian Studies, 6–9 April 1995, Washington, DC.

9 Quite a large number of studies are available on the issue of interprovincial inequalities and, for their list, see Jae Ho Chung, 'Studies of central–provincial relations in the People's Republic of China: a mid-term appraisal', *China Quarterly*, no. 142 (June 1995), p. 497 note 24. For a pioneering study on intra-provincial inequalities from both longitudinal and cross-sectional perspectives, see Dali L. Yang, 'Reform and intra-provincial inequality in China', unpublished manuscript, September 1993.

10 These figures and ratios are from *Zhongguo tongji nianjian 1995* [Statistical Yearbook of China 1995; hereafter *ZGTJNJ*], Zhongguo tongji chubanshe, Beijing, 1995, pp. 4, 60; and *Shandong tongji nianjian 1995* [Statistical Yearbook of Shandong 1995; hereafter *SDTJNJ*], Zhongguo tongji chubanshe, Beijing, 1995, p. 4.

11 See *Dangdai zhongguo de Shandong* [Contemporary China's Shandong], Zhongguo shehuikexue chubanshe, Beijing, 1989, 1, pp. 10–11; and Zhou Shunwu, *China Provincial Geography*, Foreign Language Press, Beijing, 1992, pp. 231, 235, 238, 241.

12 For the 'anti-outsider' culture in Shandong, see Zhang Yufa, *Zhongguo xiandaihua de quyu yanjiu: Shandongsheng, 1860–1916* [Regional Studies of Modernisation in China: Shandong Province, 1860–1916], Academia Sinica, Taipei, 1982, p. 136. For the historical significance of Heze and its difference from the rest of Shandong, see Zhang Zhenhe, *Luxinan shihua* [Historical narratives on the southwestern region of Shandong], Shandong renmin chubanshe, Jinan, 1983.

13 For the significance of physical distance from Beijing, see Kenneth Lieberthal and Michel Oksenberg, *Policy Making in China: Leaders, Structures and Processes*, Princeton University Press, Princeton, NJ, 1988, p. 338; and concerning its effect on Shandong in particular, see Peter Ferdinand, 'Shandong: an atypical coastal province?', in David S.G. Goodman (ed.) *China's Regional Development*, Routledge, London and New York, 1989, p. 159.

14 The process of 'telescoping' is indeed in operation as the post-Mao growth in GVAIO of twenty times or more was accomplished in only fifteen years (1979–94) as opposed to the earlier growth of fifteen times achieved in the thirty years of 1949–79.

15 *ZGTJNJ 1995*, p. 137; *SDTJNJ 1994*, p. 21; and *SDTJNJ 1995*, pp. 11, 86.

16   See *ZGTJNJ 1994*, p. 35.

17   The national averages are 9.8, 6.2, 14.9 and 16.5 per cent, while Shandong's rates are 19.7, 18.0, 24.1 and 18.2 per cent, respectively. See *ZGTJNJ 1995*, pp. 21, 23, 25; and *SDTJNJ 1995*, pp. 11–13.

18   Due to its relative weakness in per-capita terms, some refer to Shandong as a 'economically large province' (*jingji dasheng*) rather than 'economically strong province' (*jingji qiangsheng*). For the ranks, see State Statistical Bureau, *Quanguo zhuyao shehui jingji zhibiao paixu nianjian 1992* [Yearbook of the Ranking of Key National Social and Economic Indices], Zhongguo tongji chubanshe, Beijing, 1993, pp. 19, 31, 51, 153, 156; Ibid. 1993 issue, pp. 19, 31, 51, 156; and *ZGTJNJ 1995*, pp. 332, 378.

19   As of 1994, in exports, Shandong is led by Guangdong, Shanghai and Jiangsu; in foreign funds utilised, Guangdong, Jiangsu and Fujian precedes Shandong; and in terms of foreign direct investment, Shandong follows Guangdong, Jiangsu and Fujian. See *ZGTJNJ 1995*, pp. 552, 557.

20   Obviously, there are serious methodological difficulties associated with the task of empirically proving cultural effects on political or economic behaviour of the provinces. For such problems in general, see Chung, 'Studies of central–provincial relations in the People's Republic of China', pp. 489–90.

21   For Shandong's conservatism, see Ferdinand, 'Shandong: an atypical coastal province?', p. 157.

22   *Renmin ribao* [People's Daily], 15 May 1988.

23   Memories of previous campaigns played a key role in constraining the choices of local officials in responding to controversial central policies. For the impact of the anti-rightist campaign on provincial compliance during the Great Leap, see William A. Joseph, 'A tragedy of good intentions: post-Mao views of the Great Leap Forward', *Modern China* 12, no. 4 (October 1986), pp. 427–8.

24   For bureaucratic careerism in general, see Joel S. Migdal, *Strong Societies and Weak States*, Princeton University Press, Princeton, NJ, 1988, pp. 239–42. And for the prevalence of bureaucratic careerism in China, see *Renmin ribao*, 7 December 1978.

25   See Lewis M. Stern, 'Politics without consensus: center–province relations and political communication in China, January 1976–January 1977', *Asian Survey* 19, no. 3 (March 1979), p. 275.

26   See Jae Ho Chung, 'The politics of policy implementation in post-Mao China: central control and provincial autonomy under decentralization', doctoral dissertation, University of Michigan, 1993, Table 3.1 for data on various provinces, and Chapter 4 for a detailed case study of Shandong's decollectivisation.

27   Neither Bai (first party secretary in 1979–82) nor Su (governor in 1979–82 and first party secretary in 1982–5) supported agricultural decollectivisation in 1979–83. According to interviewees, they displayed very opaque attitudes toward the policy of household farming, which created serious confusion among the lower levels of administration and subsequently slowed down the whole process of the reform. For details, see Chung, *The Politics of Policy Implementation in Post-Mao China*, pp. 224–6.

28   Chinese used to call Shandong 'an area severely inflicted by the remnants of leftist ideologies' (*zuoqing yudu zhongzaiqu*). For the pervasive 'leftist' influence in Shandong in the 1980s, see Ferdinand, 'Shandong', pp. 155–6 and Research Office of the Shandong Provincial Party Committee, *Shandong sishinian* [Last Forty Years in Shandong], Shandong renmin chubanshe, Jinan, 1989, p. 140.

29   See *Zhongguo gaige kaifang dacidian* [Dictionary of China's Reform and Opening], Xiamen daxue chubanshe, Xiamen, 1993, pp. 855, 873.

30   Although born in Shandong, Liang hardly worked in the province as his functional affiliations were mainly with the centre and other provinces – the Communist Youth League, the State Office for Agriculture and Forestry, and Qinghai Province. As a native of Liaoning, Li also worked mainly in Beijing first as a factory engineer in 1968–73, then as vice-chairman of the Planning Commission in the Beijing People's Government, and as a vice-minister of the Seventh Ministry of Machine Building. See Wolfgang Bartke, *Who's Who in the People's Republic of China*, 3rd edn, K.G. Saur, Munich, 1991, 1, pp. 274, 333.

31   See Judd Howell, *China Opens its Doors: The Politics of Economic Transition*, Lynn Rienner, London, 1993, pp. 68, 72, 84.

32   Compared with Guangdong which had set up its first batch of provincial foreign trade corporations as early as 1980, Shandong's autonomy in managing foreign trade progressed very slowly. Even after 1987, the institutional relationship with the functional hierarchy (i.e. the MOFERT network) was not completely severed, however, since provincial foreign trade corporations were still required to pay up to 13 per cent of 'export rebates' (*zhekou*) to their respective general corporations. For this point, see Chen Lianwen, 'Shandongsheng waimao jingying tizhi gaige tansuo' [On the reform of Shandong's foreign trade management system], *Dongyue luncong*, no. 6 (1989), p. 19.

33   This section on organisational restructuring draws from interviews with officials from FEC in Jinan on 28 June 1994.

34   Interviews with officials from the Shandong Provincial Foreign Trade Commission on 29 June 1994. For a report on the official designation of Shandong as such, see *South China Morning Post*, 25 October 1988. Liaoning was also granted a similar designation in late 1988. See *The New York Times*, 25 November 1988 and *FBIS-China*, 6 March 1989, pp. 7–8.

35   The authorisation for Shandong to issue visas to South Koreans was also a very exceptional policy since, formally, there were no national regulations as to the citizens of the countries with which China had no diplomatic relations. See 'Guowuyuan guanyu yanhai diqu fazhan waixiangxing jingji de luogan buchong guiding' [Some supplementary regulations from the State Council on the coastal regions' development of 'outward' economies; the State Council document no. 22 of 23 March 1988] in the Special Economic Zone Office of the State Council (ed.) *Zhongguo duiwai kaifang zhinan* [Guide to China's Opening to the Outside], Yunnan renmin chubanshe, Kunming, 1992, p. 168.

36   Ibid. p. 164.

37   *Renmin ribao*, 14 May and 12 August 1988.

38   As of 1990, over 40 per cent of Shandong's area – though mostly coastal – was opened, making it the largest in China. See Zhao Haicheng, 'Lun Shandong jingji kaifangqu yu dongya diqu de jingji hezuo' [Shandong's open economic areas and economic cooperation with the East Asian region], *Tequ yu gangao jingji* [Economies of the Special Economic Zones, Hong Kong and Macau], no. 2 (1991), pp. 49–54.

39   Interviews with officials from the FEC in Jinan on 28 June 1994. The outsider inducted was Wang Yu'an, who had previously served as the director of the provincial planning commission before taking charge of FETC.

40   The first 'bonded zone' was established in Shanghai in June 1990, and in 1991 three other zones were established in Tianjin, Shenzhen and Shatoujiao. In 1992, nine more were set up in Dalian, Guangzhou, Zhangjiagang, Haikou, Xiamen, Fuzhou, Ningbo, Shantou and Qingdao. For the backgrounds and the details of the preferential treatment granted to 'bonded zones', see 'Zhongguo baoshuiqu de jianli yu fazhan' [The establishment and development of bonded zones in China], *Jingji yanjiu cankao* [Reference Materials for Economic Research], no. 424 (7 February 1994), p. 43.

41 Interview in Qingdao on 16 December 1994.

42 For the impact of Sino-South Korean normalisation, see 'Shandong bandao disanci hanshang touziri' [The third-time fever for investment in Shandong by Koreans], *Liaowang Weekly* (overseas edition), 16 November 1992, p. 16; and Jae Ho Chung, 'The political economy of South Korea–China bilateralism: origins, progress, and prospects', in Ilpyong J. Kim amd Hong Pyo Lee (eds) *Korea and China in A New World: Beyond Normalization*, Sejong Institute, Seoul, 1993, pp. 276–8.

43 Interviews with officials from the FEC in Jinan on 13 March and 28 September 1995; and *Zhongguo gaige kaifang shiwunian dashiji* [Chronicle of China's Reform and Opening in 1978–1993], Xinhua chubanshe, Beijing, 1994, p. 198.

44 See the text of Jiang Chunyun's speech in *Dazhong ribao*, 13 March 1988.

45 See 'Shandong jingji fazhan de aomi' [The secret to Shandong's fast development], *Qiushi zazhi* [Seeking Truth Magazine], no. 15 (1992), p. 22.

46 For a positive assessment made by Guangdong, see 'Guangdong zhengshi xianshi zaizhao youshi – yuelu liangsheng jingji fazhan duibi ji qishi' [Guangdong must face the reality and once again seek for its comparative advantages – a comparison of economic development in Guangdong and Shandong and its lessons] in *Guangdong tongji nianjian 1994* [Statistical Yearbook of Guangdong 1994], Zhongguo tongji chubanshe, Beijing, 1994, p. 21. I thank Peter Cheung for drawing this material to my attention.

47 See *Shandong nianjian 1993* [Shandong Yearbook 1993], Shandong renmin chubanshe, Jinan, 1993, p. 458; and Guang Xinwei and Zhang Haibo, 'Shandongsheng fazhan jiaotong yunshu de jingyan yu qishi' [Shandong's experiences in developing transportation and their lessons], *Jingji yanjiu cankao*, no. 289 (11 June 1993), pp. 42–3.

48 For reports that point out agricultural development as a key to Shandong's success, see 'The Secret to Shandong's Fast Development', p. 22; 'Shandong jingji gaoshu fazhan gei women de qishi' [Lessons from the rapid economic development in Shandong], *Qinghai ribao* [Qinghai Daily], 16 April 1993.

49 Zhan Wu, 'Shandongsheng nongcun gaige de qishi' [Lessons from Shandong's rural reform], *Nongye jingji wenti* [Problems of agricultural economy], no. 9 (1991), p. 23.

50 See 'Jiakuai nongye touzi tizhi gaige tuidong wosheng nongye shang xintaijia' [Accelerate the reform of the agricultural investment system and push our province's agriculture further ahead], *Shandong jihua jingji* [Shandong's Planned Economy], no. 5 (1988), pp. 19–20. The figures on foreign-invested projects are from *SDTJNJ 1995*, p. 474.

51 See Gao Changli, 'Shandong nongcun gaige yu xianyu jingji fazhan' [Shandong's rural reform and its county-level economic development], *Nongye jingji wenti*, no. 8 (1991), p. 18; and *Dazhong ribao*, 25 December 1992.

52 Sun Guangyuan, 'Shandongsheng gaohao guoyou dazhongxing qiye de shitiao luzi' [Ten ways to manage well Shandong's medium and large state enterprises], *Jingji yanjiu cankao*, no. 484 (1 June 1994), p. 20.

53 These sixty zones were approved and supported by the provincial authorities, but came to enjoy almost the same privileges as those enjoyed by the Beijing-designated zones. The list is from Shandong Provincial Foreign Economic and Trade Commission, 'Shandongsheng gelei kaifaqu fenbu qingkuangbiao' [Regional distribution of various kinds of development zones in Shandong], 20 April 1994. This number of sixty remains unchanged as of September 1995.

54 See the Special Economic Zone Office of the State Council, *Zhongguo duiwai kaifang diqu touzi huanjing he zhengce* [Investment Environments and Policies in China's Open Areas] (Kunming: Yunnan renmin chubanshe, 1993), pp. 142, 152–3.

55   The following data are figures as of 1994 and draw from the author's interviews in Jinan on 13 March 1995.

56   In Korea, for instance, Shandong maintains five offices: one managed by the province's Foreign Economic Relations and Trade Commission; another by the provincial tourism corporation; and the remaining three by Qingdao, Yantai and Weihai city governments.

57   For an earlier list of these firms, see Wang Yu'an and Lin Shuxing (eds) *Shandongsheng jingji kaifa: xianzai yu weilai* [Shandong's Economic Development: Its Present and Future], Jingji guanli chubanshe, Beijing, 1991, pp. 597–8.

58   In 1988, only about sixty firms had such authority. See Chen Lianwen, 'On the reform of Shandong's foreign trade management system', p. 15.

59   For the national trend, see Hu Angang, *Zhongguo diqu chaju yanjiu baogao* [Report on Inter-regional Disparities in China] (draft), October 1995; and Liu Qiusheng, 'Woguo quyu jingji fazhan de fenxi yu zhanwang' [An analysis and prospect for regional economic development in China], *Jingji yanjiu cankao*, no. 414 (23 January 1994), pp. 2–16.

60   Interview in Jinan on 27 June 1994. A Shandong source indicates that the first real regional strategy was conceived in 1988 when the goal of 'open the east, develop the west, and combine the two' (*dongbu kaifang, xibu kaifa, dongxi jiehe*). See Chen Guanglin, 'Shandong jingji fazhan de shige wenti – sishinian huigu conghengtan' [Ten questions of Shandong's economic development – a recollection of the last forty years], *Dongyue luncong*, no. 5 (1989), p. 6.

61   The following descriptions of the 'two-three-six' strategy draw from the author's interviews with officials from the Provincial Economic Research Centre and the Provincial Foreign Economic and Trade Commission in Jinan on 28 June 1994 and 13 and 15 March 1995. For a very brief description of the strategy, see Wang Yu'an and Lin Shuxing (eds) *Shandongsheng jingji kaifa*, pp. 70–1.

62   Among these three belts, the Jiaoji belt has been most prioritised since, as of 1990, localities situated along the Jiaoji Railway produced over 60 per cent of the province's gross industrial output value. See *Shandongsheng jingji kaifa*, p. 71. For a discussion of these three 'industrial concentration belts', see Ji Yangwen, Gu Yu'an, Dong Wenyan and Liang Zhencai, 'Dui Shandongsheng diqu jingji buju de gousi' [Thoughts on the regional economic arrangement of Shandong], *Jihua jingji yanjiu* [Studies of Planned Economy] no. 6 (1993), pp. 57–9.

63   According to some interviewees in Jinan, many in the provincial government argued that six is too many and four is probably enough (by merging the northern with northwestern areas, and the Jiaodong with southeastern areas). Author's interview in Jinan on 28 June 1994.

64   The Jiaodong Peninsula region covers four municipalities of Qingdao, Yantai, Weihai and Weifang. This is also the conventional coverage of the 'eastern' region of Shandong. The Shandong Peninsula region includes three additional cities of Zibo, Jinan and Rizhao.

65   Since the latter's designation as a central economic city, the provincial authorities have generally tended to give more support to Yantai and Weihai than to Qingdao in their regional planning. For instance, the first South Korea–China ferry route was given to Weihai in 1989 despite strong lobbying efforts on the part of Qingdao. In 1993, when Qingdao was finally granted its own ferry route to South Korea, the privilege had to be shared with Yantai. The information on the ferry route was provided by interviews in Jinan on 28 and 29 June 1994. For more on inter-city competition in Shandong, see Jae Ho Chung, 'A recipe of development in China's coastal cities: the case of Qingdao', unpublished manuscript, December 1994.

66 The coastal region is defined here as the localities bordering on a sea coast. Shandong's coastal region, therefore, includes seven municipalities of Qingdao, Yantai, Weihai, Weifang, Rizhao, Dongying and Binzhou. For a detailed comparison of different policy frameworks of these zones in Table 2, see Ma Hong (ed.) *Zhongguo jingji kaifaqu touzi guanli zhinan* [Guide to Investment and Management in China's Economic Development Zones], Zhongguo tongji chubanshe, Beijing, 1994, pp. 12–15.

67 Both Zibo and Jinan are 'open cities' in the Shandong Peninsula region with highly preferential terms of investment.

68 The yardstick for the designation differs for the state- and province-designated 'poverty-ridden counties.' As of 1993, the threshold for state-designated 'poverty-ridden counties' was the rural per capita income of RMB 440, while that for province-designated counterparts was RMB 600. These thresholds were raised annually to account for the rate of inflation: the threshold for the province-designated 'poverty-ridden counties' rose to RMB 740 and 850 in 1994–5, respectively. Interviews in Jinan on 27 September 1995.

69 See Chen Xiuying, 'Dui jiakuai kaifa wosheng jingji bufada diqu de jidian kanfa he jianyi' [On some views and suggestions regarding the development of underdeveloped regions in Shandong], *Shandong jihua jingji* [Shandong's Planned Economy], no. 4 (1987), pp. 28–9.

70 See *SDTJNJ 1995*, pp. 27, 266.

71 For Liaocheng, see Chen, 'On some views and suggestions regarding the development of underdeveloped regions in Shandong', pp. 29–30; and for Heze, see *Dazhong ribao*, 31 August 1992.

72 Zhang Feng, 'Shandongsheng fupin kaifa youguan qingkuang de diaocha' [Survey on Shandong's 'Poverty Alleviation'], *Jingji yanjiu cankao*, no. 653 (4 April 1995), p. 12.

73 This practice of *yigong daizhen* utilises surplus goods in paying for labour service by the local poor. During 1985–7, grain and cotton worth RMB 2.7 billion were provided by the central government, while foodstuff and low-grade industrial products worth RMB 10 billion were supplied during 1991–5. While in principle provincial governments were required to provide resources that would match the value of central support, Beijing almost always ended up contributing more to the pot. For instance, Ningxia's yigong daizhen projects were totally dependent on the centre's support. See Zhu Ling and Jiang Zhongyi, *Yigong daizhen yu nuanjie pinkun* [Paying Goods for Labour Service and Poverty Alleviation], Shanghai renmin chubanshe, Shanghai, 1994, pp. 20, 30.

74 In monetary terms, the difference between planned and market prices for 72,000 tons of chemical fertiliser amounted to RMB 57.6 million since the planned price for one ton of chemical fertiliser was RMB 1,400 while the comparable market price was RMB 2,200. Interview in Jinan on 27 September 1995.

75 The estimate of 1 billion is from Zhang Feng, 'Survey on Shandong's "Poverty Alleviation"', p. 11. The addition of all the aforementioned funds and loans for the period of 1984–93 produces RMB 1.18 billion for the central government support and RMB 215 million for the provincial support.

76 These data are from interview in Jinan on 27 September 1995.

77 Zhang Feng, 'Survey on Shandong's "Poverty Alleviation"', pp. 11, 15.

78 The designation by the State Council in 1993 of Dongying as another 'coastal open area' empowered to conduct its own foreign trade was the most recent outcome of such efforts. The move not only provided a significant boost for the scheme for developing the Yellow River Delta Region, but also motivated the northwestern region to concentrate on high-tech industries and export-oriented agriculture. See Li Youfeng, 'Bawo jiyu tuchu zhongdian jikuai huanghe sanjiaozhou waixiangxing jingji fazhan' [Grab the opportunity and accelerate the

development of an 'outward-oriented' economy in the Yellow River Delta Region], *Shandong jingji* [Shandong's Economy] no. 3 (1994), pp. 22–3.

79   See Ji Yangwen *et al.*, 'Thoughts on the regional economic arrangement of Shandong', pp. 57–60.

80   See Table 5.4 for the coastal region's predominance in attracting foreign investment. For problems and obstacles in inland regions' efforts to establish effective linkages with foreign capital, see Han Xinghua, 'Pinkunxian waimao fazhan houjing buzu de yuanyin ji duice' [Reasons and remedies for poor counties' inability to develop foreign trade], *Shandong duiwai jingmao*, no. 2 (1994), p. 31.

81   The six pairs are as follows: Qingdao–Heze, Yantai–Liaocheng, Weihai–Dongying, Jinan–Dezhou, Weifang–Linyi, and Zibo–Binzhou. Interview in Jinan on 26 September 1995. For the call for 'pairing' and 'matching for cooperation', see Zhan Deming, 'Shilun wosheng dongxibu jiehe de neirong yu cuoshi' [The measures of combining the eastern and western regions of Shandong], *Shandong jingji* [Shandong Economy] no. 6 (1989), p. 47.

82   *Zhongguo hengxiang jingji nianjian 1992* [Yearbook of Chinese Horizontal Economy], Zhongguo shehui kexue chubanshe, Beijing, 1993, pp. 275, 277.

83   The strategy of 'pairing' is becoming increasingly popular. At the national level, Shandong is paired with Qinghai. See *Qinghai ribao*, 16 April 1993. For the nation-wide practice, see Chung, 'Central–provincial relations', p. 3.30. Information on Shandong is from author's interviews in Jinan on 14 March and 26 and 27 September 1995.

84   Interviews in Qingdao on 14 December 1994 and in Jinan on 25 September 1995. Since July 1991, 127 cadres were exchanged among twelve coastal and inland prefectures and cities. For instance, Zibo sent eight officials to conduct surveys for the purpose of offering constructive suggestions to Huimin (now called Binzhou); and Qingdao dispatched eleven cadres to do a two-month research to produce a 'development work plan' for Heze. See Sun Dade, *Lun xiaokang* [On Comfortable Wealth], Jinan chubanshe, Jinan, 1993, pp. 77–8.

85   See *Dazhong ribao*, 31 August 1992; and Sun, *Lun xiaokang*, p. 78.

86   Such domestic linkages do have potential problems since coastal regions may not work as 'growth poles' but rather operate as 'magnets' attracting all the available resources of the inland regions. For these metaphors, I am indebted to David Zweig, 'The political economy of urban internationalization', unpublished manuscript, 1995.

87   See, for instance, David S.G. Goodman, 'Guizhou and the People's Republic of China: the development of an internal colony', in D. Drakakis-Smith and S. Williams (eds) *Internal Colonisation: Essays around a Theme*, IBG Development Areas Research Group Monograph no. 3. Edinburgh University, 1983, pp. 107–24.

88   The list of the members and background information are from *Shandong shengqing 1993* [Facts and Figures of Shandong 1993], Shandong shengqingshe, Jinan, 1993, pp. 49, 659–67.

89   By November 1993, the total number of various kinds of development zones in China dropped from 3,000 to 500 and over 90 per cent of those established by sub-provincial authorities were closed down. *Zhongguo gaige kaifang shiwunian dashiji*, p. 238. For the fiscal problems poor counties face under the new tax system, see 'Caishui jinrong tizhi gaige dui bufada diqu jingji fazhan de yingxiang ji duice' [The impact of the fiscal reform on the economic development of backward areas], *Jingji yanjiu cankao* no. 629 (20 February 1995), pp. 17–31.

90   For the dilemma between different logic, see Jeffrey J. Anderson, *The Territorial Imperative: Pluralism, Corporatism, and Economic Crisis*, Cambridge University Press, 1992, pp. 193–6.

REFERENCES

Chen Guanglin, 'Shandong jingji fazhan de shige wenti' [Ten questions for the economic development of the Shandong economy], *Dongyue luncong* no. 5 1989.

Chen Lianwen, 'Shandongsheng waimao jingying tizhi gaige tansuo' [A study of reform in the Shandong Province external trade economic management system], *Dongyue luncong* no. 6 1989.

Dangdai zhongguo de Shandong [Contemporary China's Shandong] 2 volumes, Zhongguo shehui kexue chubanshe, Beijing, 1988.

Peter Ferdinand, 'Shandong: an atypical coastal province?', in David S.G. Goodman (ed.) *China's Regional Development*, Routledge, London, 1989.

Ji Yangwen *et al.*, 'Dui Shandongsheng diqu jingji buju de gousi' [The results of advance in Shandong's regional economy], *Jihua jingji yanjiu* no. 6 1993.

Li Youfeng, 'Bawo jiyu tuchu zhongdian jikuai huanghe sanjiaozhou waixiangxing jingji fazhan', *Shandong jingji* no. 3 1994.

Special Economic Zones Office of the State Council (ed.) *Zhongguo duiwai kaifang zhinan* [The Direction of China's External Opening], Yunnan renmin chubanshe, Kunming, 1992.

Sun Guangyuan, 'Shandongsheng gaohao guoyou dazhongxing qiyie de shitiao luzi' [The condition of state enterprises in Shandong Province], *Jingji yanjiu cankao* no. 484, 1 June 1994.

Wang Yu'an and Lin Shuxing (eds) *Shandongsheng jingji kaifa: xianzai yu weilai* [Economic Openness in Shandong Province: The Present and the Future], Jingji guanli chubanshe, Beijing, 1991.

Zhan Wu, 'Shandongsheng nongcun gaige de qishi' [Rural reform in Shandong], *Nongye jingji wenti* no. 9, 1991.

Zhang Feng, 'Shandongsheng fupin kaifa youguan qingkuang de diaocha' [An investigation of conditions in poor and open areas in Shandong Province], *Jingji yanjiu cankao* no. 653, 4 April 1995.

Zhang Yufa, *Zhongguo xiandaihua de quyu: Shandongsheng* [Regions of Modern China: Shandong Province], Academia Sinica, Taipei, 1982.

Zhao Haicheng, 'Lun Shandong jingji kaifangqu yu dongya diqu de jingji hezuo' [Shandong's economic open areas and economic cooperation with East Asia], *Tequ yu gangao jingji* no. 2, 1991.

Periodicals

Dazhong ribao [Masses Daily]
Shandong nianjian [Shandong Yearbook] various years.
Shandong tongji nianjian [Shandong Statistical Yearbook] various years.

Shanghai City

GENERAL

GDP (billion *yuan* renminbi)	197.20
GDP annual growth rate	14.30
as % national average	121.19
GDP per capita	14,542.04
as % national average	387.25
Gross Value Agricultural Output (billion *yuan* renminbi)	14.00
Gross Value Industrial Output (billion *yuan* renminbi)	425.50

POPULATION

Population (million)	13.56
Natural growth rate (per 1,000)	5.80

WORKFORCE

Total workforce (million)	7.63
Employment by activity (%)	
primary industry	0.69
secondary industry	53.10
tertiary industry	37.90
Employment by sector (% of provincial population)	
urban	39.11
rural	17.18
state sector	26.36
collective sector	19.43
private sector	3.03
foreign-funded sector	1.90

WAGES

Average annual wage (*yuan* renminbi)	7,405
Growth rate in real wage	4.90

PRICES

CPI annual rise (%)	23.90
Service price index rise (%)	20.60
Per capita consumption (*yuan* renminbi)	4,162
as % national average	239.61
Urban disposable income per capita	5,889
as % national average	158.45
Rural per capita income	3,437
as % national average	281.49

FOREIGN TRADE AND INVESTMENT

Total foreign trade (US$ billion)	22.88
% provincial GDP	78.94
Exports (US$ billion)	9.16
Imports (US$ billion)	8.90
Realised foreign capital (US$ million)	2,582.17
% provincial GDP	11.28

EDUCATION

University enrolments	140,396
% national average	443.39
Secondary school enrolments (million)	0.66
% national average	117.44
Primary school enrolments (million)	1.15
% national average	79.38

Notes: All statistics are for 1994 and all growth rates are for 1994 over 1993 and are adapted from *Zhongguo tongji nianjian 1995* [Statistical Yearbook of China 1995], Zhongguo tongji chubanshe, Beijing, 1995 as reformulated and presented in *Provincial China* no. 1 March 1996, pp. 34ff.

Shanghai

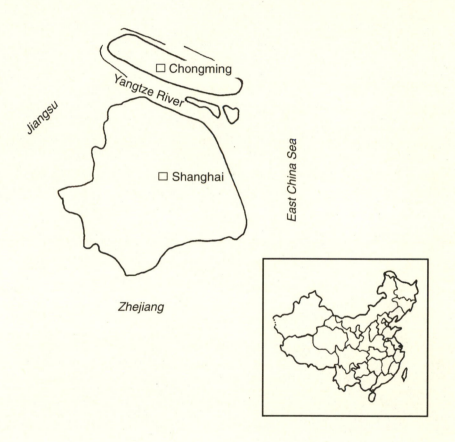

6 Shanghai

An alternative centre?

J. Bruce Jacobs[1]

Any person with only the slightest insight into contemporary world geography will choose Shanghai. Beijing is a typical Chinese-style walled capital city. Backed against the Great Wall, it sits facing south – upright, solemn, quiet and stable. Shanghai is the exact opposite. It looks towards the east, facing the vast Pacific Ocean. And behind it is the great, long Yangzi River which traverses and links numerous regions. In terms of a self-reliant China, Shanghai squats alone in a corner unimportant. But with respect to an open, contemporary world, it looks far and wide, swallowing and disgorging large quantities of goods with its special topography.[2]

Shanghai creates many images. It was the 'Paris of the East', 'the most sophisticated and the most cosmopolitan city in all of Asia' between the two World Wars,[3] a leading cultural, business and industrial centre. But it was also 'the most crime-ridden city in the world',[4] a city with grinding poverty and unemployment, and a city with considerable 'decadence' in terms of orthodox Chinese morality. Even today, the Chinese Communists have great ambivalence about pre-1949 Shanghai: it was a 'sink of iniquity', a 'modern city with lopsided development' and yet it was 'the cradle of China's modern industry and commerce', 'a window for the spreading of modern Western learning', and 'the forefront of the struggle against Imperialism and Feudalism in modern times'.[5]

Today, Shanghai – China's largest city – provides an alternative centre in two senses. First, Shanghai rivals Beijing. In the arts, the two cities compete quite explicitly to be China's cultural capital. But they also perform intensely different functions. Beijing is focused on the 'yellow' Chinese continent, whereas Shanghai looks out towards the 'blue' ocean.[6] Beijing is a very political city, while Shanghai is an economic centre. During the first four decades of the People's Republic, Beijing controlled and milked Shanghai to support the Centre and to build industry in the interior.

Shanghai also rivals Hong Kong as China's international economic and financial centre. At present Shanghai lacks Hong Kong's economic, financial, communications and legal infrastructure, yet politically Shanghai has proven relatively tame, while Hong Kong reeks of 'bourgeois liberalisation' and 'spiritual pollution'. Prior to and following the Beijing Massacre of June 1989, Shanghai remained relatively quiet while the people of Hong Kong protested vehemently. At that time, the Chinese leadership had all of its reform 'eggs' in the South China basket. Significantly, only after 1989 did the Centre grant the preferential policies which enabled Shanghai's subsequent growth. With election results periodically demonstrating Hong Kong's continuing dissatisfaction with China's policies, Beijing could easily make political decisions to strengthen Shanghai and suppress Hong Kong.

SHANGHAI IN HISTORY

Contrary to common understanding, Shanghai was not a Western creation. When Lord Amherst sailed up the Huangpu River in 1832, 'Shanghai was already a flourishing port, the harbour filled with the brown trapezoid sails of hundreds of junks. Here the merchantmen of Canton and the coastal ports met with the Yangtze traffic. The air was filled with bustle and the rhythmic chanting of coolies loading cargo.'[7] In fact, the area which is now Shanghai Municipality had a population in excess of 1 million throughout most of the Ming Dynasty (1368–1644), more than 2 million people in the eighteenth century and over 3 million as early as 1816.[8]

Shanghai was one of the five ports opened in 1842 by the Treaty of Nanjing following the Opium War precisely because it was an important port. The following year, in 1843, the British set up their territorial concession, while in 1848 and 1849 respectively the Americans and French established their concessions. In 1863 the British and Americans combined their concessions to form the International Settlement.[9] Yet, despite this foreign interest, Shanghai grew relatively slowly for the next half century. Although sources vary considerably about Shanghai's urban population, they agree that Shanghai's rapid demographic growth occurred only in the twentieth century.

Zhang Zhongli states that Shanghai's population in 1852 was only 270,000 and less than 500,000 in 1895. London (including its suburban areas) had a population of 2.38 million in 1841 and 3.93 million in 1871. In 1852 Hangzhou had a population of 1 million and both Suzhou and Ningbo had populations of 500,000. By the First World War Shanghai's population exceeded 2 million and had surpassed 3 million during the 1930s. In 1936, Shanghai had a population of 3.3 million, while Tianjin had 1.3 million and Guangzhou 950,000. Suzhou and Hangzhou both had about 500,000 people. Thus, in the fifty years from 1895 to 1945 Shanghai's population increased tenfold.[10]

Another source, using quite different statistics, gives a similar analysis. Zhang and Zhou state that Shanghai's population grew from 540,000 in 1852 to 1,280,000 in 1910, an average annual increase of only 13,000 persons and a rate of only 1.41 per cent. Yet, from 1910 to 1949 the population grew to 5,450,000, an average annual increase of over 100,000 persons and a rate of 3.78 per cent.[11]

Migrants from other parts of China accounted for most of this increase. During 1929–36, the average annual number of migrants arriving in Shanghai was 379,000 while an average of 258,000 departed, leaving an average annual net increase of 121,000. As a result, native Shanghainese accounted for only 20.7 per cent of the population in 1946 and only 15.1 per cent in January 1950.[12]

This large number of migrants came for economic and socio-political reasons. During periods of economic growth, Shanghai attracted poverty-stricken peasants while the comparatively favourable lifestyle and environment for economic production attracted landlords, capitalists, business people and the professions from other regions. Criminal elements also came to make a living.[13]

Socio-political reasons also stimulated migration to Shanghai. During periods of social unrest – especially during war – the city's population would increase markedly. Shanghai's role as a place of refuge owed to its foreign concessions. During the Taiping Rebellion (1855–65), the population of the foreign concessions increased by 110,000, while the Chinese city's population declined by 1,000. During the Japanese invasion, the population of the foreign concessions increased by 780,000 from 1936 to February 1942, while the Chinese city's population declined 670,000 during 1936–40. In the first three years of the Civil War (1945–48), Shanghai's population expanded by some 2.1 million persons, an increase of over 60 per cent. In this instance, Shanghai's geographical location as a key port away from the battle fronts accounted for its attraction.[14]

Social composition

These migrations naturally helped fix the social composition of Shanghai. Statistics from January 1950 roughly indicate the origins of Shanghai's present population. Native Shanghainese accounted for 15 per cent, while Jiangsu natives accounted for 48 per cent and Zhejiang natives for a further 26 per cent. Thus, almost three-quarters of Shanghai's population derived from these two neighbouring provinces. The next three largest groups, over 2 per cent each, came from Guangdong, Anhui and Shandong. Clearly proximity accounted for the large numbers of Jiangsu and Zhejiang natives, but other factors also had relevance. Although Fujian and Jiangxi were much nearer, Guangdong natives outnumbered Fujian and Jiangxi natives fivefold and sixfold respectively. According to a Chinese analysis, 'Guangdong was a traditional base for foreign trade' and most compradors were from Guangdong. When Shanghai was opened, 'a large number of compradors and businessmen from Guangdong poured into Shanghai. These people were comparatively affluent and could attract many relatives and friends from their native place to Shanghai for employment and residence. Thus, the population of people from Guangdong greatly exceeds the populations from Jiangxi and Fujian which are much nearer to Shanghai.'[15] Guangdong natives may also have moved to Shanghai as Guangdong had been an important Nationalist Party base. After the Northern Expedition and the establishment of the Nationalist government in Nanjing, with its base in the Southern Jiangsu–Shanghai–Zhejiang triangle, they would have moved north with the regime.

Native place clearly played important roles in Shanghai life.[16] But the broad provincial figures obscure much finer, yet very important geographical and social distinctions, especially between Southern Jiangsu and Northern Jiangsu (Subei) and within the latter region. As already noted, many Guangdong natives were involved in business including small business. Zhejiang natives, primarily from Ningbo, Shaoxing and Wenzhou, were also involved in business as well as in government. People from Wuxi in Southern Jiangsu gained fame as managers and entrepreneurs. All of these groups had middle to high status.

In contrast, two groups had lower social status. Native Shanghainese, often from the agricultural countryside, were perceived as 'country bumpkins'. The numerous migrants from Northern Jiangsu (Subei), a variegated region comprising most of Jiangsu province north of the Yangtze River, formed a poor underclass who tended to live in shantytowns on the periphery of Shanghai. One statistic suggests that perhaps 30 per cent of Shanghai's population (and over 60 per cent of the migrants from Jiangsu) came from Subei.[17] The Subei people tended to work in lowly, manual occupations. According to stereotypes, they worked in the 'Three Knives', cutting hair as barbers, cutting food as cooks and cutting softened corns off feet as bathhouse attendants. They also worked as rickshaw pullers, on the docks, in construction and as night soil and rubbish collectors.

During the Republican period two mutually reinforcing factors tended to keep these groups based on locality distinct – language and co-residence. These factors in turn meant that people tended to marry those from their native place. People from Northern Jiangsu almost became outcasts.[18] In recent years the social distinctions based on geographical origins have diminished. The shantytowns have been razed and Northern Jiangsu people, especially the younger generation, now speak Mandarin and Shanghainese rather than the Subei dialect. Yet some prejudice against Subei people continues to be a feature of Shanghai social life.[19]

Shanghai in PRC history

When the Chinese Communists came to power, Shanghai had two characteristics which would continue to have importance for Shanghai's roles in the People's Republic. First, Shanghai was a key industrial centre. In the mid-1930s, Shanghai accounted for about 40 per cent of China's industrial capital, 43 per cent of its industrial workforce and 50 per cent of its industrial product. The Japanese invasion of 1937 damaged Shanghai's industrial production, but in 1949 Shanghai still accounted for about one-quarter of China's industrial production.[20]

Second, Shanghai's population was relatively highly educated. In 1949, with less than 1 per cent of China's population, Shanghai had 2.0 per cent of China's primary school students, 8.2 per cent of its secondary students and 17.3 per cent of its tertiary students.[21]

The employment structure of the population in 1952 reflected these two factors. Although 48.7 per cent of the population worked in agriculture, forestry, animal husbandry and fishing, 28.3 per cent worked in industry while an additional 2.8 per cent worked in construction and 2.3 per cent in transport and communications. Nearly 10 per cent worked in commerce, food and service industries, while 3.1 per cent worked in science, culture and education, health and welfare. State organs and mass organisations employed an additional 2.2 per cent. Urban public services and the financial sector each employed close to 1 per cent of the workforce.[22]

Owing to its importance as an industrial centre and to its highly educated and skilled population, Shanghai continued to be both the destination and the source of considerable migration flows under Mao's rule (1950–76). The Chinese Communists organised substantial out-migration from Shanghai for two reasons: to fragment potential political opposition within the 'sink of iniquity' and to use Shanghai skills to establish industry in China's hinterland.

During 1951–4, even though 1,470,000 people migrated out of Shanghai, Shanghai still received substantial net in-migration. In 1951, migration added over 430,000 to Shanghai's population. But in 1955 the trend reversed and that year over 580,000 more people left Shanghai than moved to the city. In 1958, the regime strengthened control over migration and during 1958–76 out-migration greatly exceeded in-migration. Net out-migration during those years totalled over 1.2 million. The city lost over 700,000 during the three years (1969–71) when great numbers of cadres were 'sent down' and educated youth went 'up the mountains and down to the countryside'.[23]

A Chinese source illustrates the importance of Shanghai's contribution to industrial development in other parts of China. During 1950–57, more than 430,000 people were sent from Shanghai to help with construction. Interestingly, their main destinations were the three Manchurian provinces of Liaoning, Jilin and Heilongjiang,[24] China's other major industrial centre. During 1958–62, almost 240,000 employees and their dependants were sent to assist with economic construction in the three northwestern provinces of Shaanxi, Gansu and Qinghai as well as Shandong. In 1963–5 an additional 36,000 people were sent to the three northwestern provinces as well as to the southwestern provinces of Yunnan, Guizhou and Sichuan.[25] During 1966–79, 260,000 were sent over the entire country, in part to build the 'Third Front', though Anhui, Jiangxi and Shandong were especially important destinations.[26]

Despite these contributions to other regions of China, Shanghai may have gained more than it lost in terms of an educated population as a result of the migration flows under Mao. Certainly, migrants both to and from Shanghai had higher levels of education than did Shanghai's population as a whole.[27]

During 1950–57, before strong controls on migration were implemented, illiterates accounted for over 40 per cent of migrants to Shanghai as women and peasants going to live with relatives and seeking work accounted for a large proportion.[28] During 1958–65, the educational level of migrants to and from Shanghai was higher than that of Shanghai's population as a whole, but during this period of net out-migration, there was a net in-migration of people with tertiary education.[29] And, during 1966–76 the educational level of migrants into Shanghai's urban areas was higher than those leaving. (The reverse was true in Shanghai's rural areas.)[30]

These controls on Shanghai's population could not but affect Shanghai's development. In the words of a Chinese source:

> Shanghai is China's largest economic centre. Its industrial production, foreign and domestic trade, and scientific and cultural institutions are all very developed. Normal population flow is a normal phenomenon of development. But excessively large waves of population migration and excessively rapid processes of change can create abnormal changes in population size. The inevitable result is to increase the difficulties for municipal government facilities, to affect the planned development of the economy and other areas and to make the population problem even more complicated.[31]

With the end of the Cultural Revolution and the beginning of the economic reforms, Shanghai again experienced a net in-migration as many of those forced to leave Shanghai under Mao gained permission to return. During 1978–80, 260,000 of the 600,000 educated youth sent 'up the mountains and down to the countryside' from Shanghai during 1968–76 returned. From October 1978 to the end of 1981, about 125,000 young people came to Shanghai to begin employment in units where their parents had retired.[32]

ECONOMIC MODERNISATION[33]

Shanghai is currently booming economically, but this boom is relatively recent, beginning only in 1992 when the central government gave Shanghai 'policies' enabling it to begin shaking off the straitjacket of the 'planned economy' and to commence a substantial reform process. Building on its pre-1949 base, Shanghai has remained China's wealthiest provincial-level unit and an important, relatively efficient industrial centre. By 1988, with less than one-twentieth of the nation's fixed capital, Shanghai produced one-thirteenth of industrial product. During 1950–88, profits and taxes from Shanghai industry accounted for 11.7 per cent of the nation's fiscal income.[34]

Why did the central government keep the 'planned economy' straitjacket on Shanghai until 1992? At the heart of the question is Shanghai's crucial importance to central government revenues. Prior to the economic reforms, Shanghai provided one-fifth to one-quarter of central government revenue according to Shanghai economists.[35] (Shanghai has 1.1 per cent of China's population and 0.1 per cent of its area.)[36] Thus, when beginning reforms in the late 1970s, the centre could not afford to take risks with Shanghai and such other major contributors to central revenue as Jiangsu. Rather it experimented in Guangdong, which provided the centre with less than 1 per cent of its funds. The importance of Shanghai to central revenues was revealed during the Cultural Revolution when, despite the importance of the 'Gang of Four' in Shanghai, production in Shanghai was protected and the city remained relatively calm and one of the few places in China where goods were available.

Shanghai's importance to the centre as a 'cashcow' has continued into the reform period. Shanghai remains the single largest provincial-level contributor to central revenues and as late as 1992 was the source of over one-sixth of central government revenues. It is true that Shanghai also received considerable centrally funded investment, but the total accumulated central investment in Shanghai over twenty-four years (1950–83) was less than Shanghai's fiscal contribution to the centre in 1983 alone.

The corollary has been that Shanghai has also paid a much larger proportion of its revenues to the centre than any other provincial-level unit. From May 1949 to the end of 1988, Shanghai paid 83.5 per cent of its fiscal revenues to the centre, retaining only 16.5 per cent for services and the development of Shanghai.[37] As a result of its remaining in the 'planned economy' and ensuring the centre its revenues, Shanghai had poor roads, communications, housing and environment as well as a relatively slow growth rate. Shanghai lacked an underground rapid transit system, unlike Beijing which had two lines and Tianjin which had one line. Because Shanghai had given so much of its income to the centre, it had accumulated 'debts' to its population which, according to a senior Shanghai economist, totalled RMB¥40–50 billion. This sum would be required to build and repair public transport, roads, the port and housing. Unlike Guangdong, which had control over its local revenues, Shanghai had to go 'cap in hand' to the centre for major investment funds, a process that inevitably slowed Shanghai's growth.

The economic reform process in Shanghai

The crux of Shanghai's reform process, according to Shanghai people, has been the centre's 'giving' Shanghai 'policies'. Without a policy, Shanghai could not develop. With 'policies', Shanghai has been able to use its various capabilities to progress and develop. This very widespread belief suggests that the Chinese have reified the concept of 'policy' into something very concrete. In fact, a Shanghai vice-mayor recently stated this explicitly: 'policy is wealth'.[38]

The key policy changes for Shanghai occurred only in 1992, about fifteen years after the post-Mao reform process began in earnest. However, Shanghai did benefit from changes in 1988 and 1990. In 1988 the centre allowed Shanghai to use the financial responsibility system, thus enabling Shanghai to retain all fiscal revenues above a contracted amount which it provided to the centre. This increased Shanghai's fiscal income, though not by a large amount.

Shanghai's importance to China as a whole led to much more important policy changes in 1990 and 1992. Five factors contribute to Shanghai's importance. First, Shanghai is China's wealthiest area and a key industrial centre. Second, unlike Shenzhen, it has sufficient size to be China's economic powerhouse, a true 'Dragon Head'. Third, Shenzhen cannot become a major financial centre because it can never become distant from Hong Kong. Fourth, Shanghai's geographical location gives its proximity to both the north and south coasts as well as the Yangtze River Valley. No other Chinese city has such an advantageous geographical position. Fifth, Shanghai has China's most numerous and talented human resources in the fields of science and technology, economics and finance, and management as well as excellent, numerous quality workers.

These factors led to the decisions in 1990 to promote Shanghai and its Pudong region east of the Huangpu River. (The centre of Shanghai is in the Puxi area – literally west of the Huangpu River.) Following decisions of the Party Centre and the State Council, on 18 April 1990 Premier Li Peng announced that Pudong would be developed and opened to the outside. 'The development of Pudong and the opening of Pudong to the outside is a matter having important strategic significance for Shanghai and for the entire nation.'[39] Twelve days later, on 30 April 1990, Mayor Zhu Rongji announced ten preferential policies for the development of Pudong. These policies included such incentives as tax holidays and relief, encouragement for the establishment of service industries, a free-trade zone and land use for periods of from fifty to seventy years.[40]

Shanghai's opportunities accelerated in 1992 following Deng Xiaoping's 'Inspection Tour' of the South. Deng's favourable comments towards Shanghai fundamentally changed the course of reform in Shanghai:

> At present Shanghai has all the conditions to move a bit more quickly. In the areas of talented personnel, technology and administration, Shanghai has obvious superiority, which radiates over a wide area. Looking backwards, my one major mistake was not to include Shanghai when we set up the four special economic zones. Otherwise, the situation of reform and opening to the outside in the Yangtze River Delta, the entire Yangtze River Valley and even the entire nation would be different.[41]

Shortly afterwards, Shanghai benefited in two ways. First, Pudong obtained five more 'preferential policies' which Mayor Huang Ju announced on 10 March 1992. These new policies gave Shanghai Municipality more authority to make decisions regarding investment approval, allowed Shanghai to issues stocks and securities and permitted trading in Shanghai of stocks issued in other Chinese localities. They also authorised foreign department stores and supermarkets in Pudong, China's largest free-trade zone in Pudong, and the operation of foreign banks, finance companies and insurance companies in Shanghai. The purpose of these measures was to make certain Pudong 'has new impetus and vitality as a key area within

China for reform and opening to the outside during the next decade.'[42]

Second, tax rates for enterprises in Shanghai were lowered. Previously Shanghai enterprises had paid income tax rates of 55 per cent. With the addition of many other taxes such as an energy tax and an education tax, enterprises retained only 15–18 per cent of income and some retained only 8–9 per cent of income. The Shanghai Cigarette Company, according to a leading Shanghai economist, paid as much tax as the whole of Guangzhou Municipality![43] In 1992, however, the enterprise income tax was lowered to 33 per cent, thus allowing enterprises to keep an additional 22 per cent of income. This greatly increased the capital available in Shanghai. Further tax reform has again substantially increased Shanghai's fiscal income. In 1994 Shanghai had a fiscal income of RMB¥37.25 billion, a 40.6 per cent increase over 1993. Increases in consumption taxes and the VAT were especially important.[44]

The centre's 1992 gifts of 'policy' have clearly proved crucial to Shanghai's development. After the post-Mao reforms got underway in the early 1980s, Shanghai had a slower growth rate than the whole of China. As Table 6.1 indicates, since 1992 Shanghai's growth rate has exceeded that of China.

Initially, 'policy' stability concerned many people in Shanghai. On 11 May 1993, during a visit to Pudong, Party General-Secretary and State President Jiang Zemin felt it necessary to say, 'The Centre's policy to develop and open Pudong is firm and unvarying. It will not change'.[45] During a visit of 13–14 May 1993, CCP Political Bureau Standing Committee Member and Vice-Premier Zhu Rongji quoted Jiang Zemin's words and called them an

Table 6.1 GDP growth rates: China and Shanghai, 1978–93

	China (%)	Shanghai (%)
1978	11.7	15.8
1980	7.9	8.4
1983	10.2	7.8
1984	14.5	11.6
1985	12.9	13.4
1986	8.5	4.4
1987	11.1	7.5
1988	11.3	10.1
1989	4.3	3.0
1990	3.9	3.5
1991	8.0	7.1
1992	13.6	14.9
1993	13.4	14.9

Sources: *Zhongguo tongji nianjian 1994* [Statistical Yearbook of China 1994], Zhongguo tongji chubanshe, Beijing, 1994, p. 32; *Shanghai tongji nianjian 1994* [Shanghai Statistical Yearbook 1994], Zhongguo tongji chubanshe, Beijing, 1994, p. 24

'important statement'.[46] While on an inspection trip of Shanghai during 18–21 April 1995 celebrating the fifth anniversary of the opening of Pudong, Premier Li Peng noted, 'The basic policies of the Party Centre and the State Council concerning the development and opening of Pudong will not change'.[47] Privately, Li made oral promises which went much further, including a five-year extension of Shanghai's current preferential policies as well as new policies.

On 18 September 1995, following central government approval, the government announced the granting of five new preferential policies to Shanghai for the ensuing five years. In addition Shanghai was permitted to retain almost all of the policies granted during the previous five years. The new policies include enabling large foreign trade companies and a few joint-venture trade companies to operate in Pudong, and allow foreign banks with central government approval to operate RMB business in Pudong on a trial basis. Yet the central government also stipulated areas in which Pudong must adhere to the national system including the national fiscal and tax system, the central allocation of Pudong's foreign exchange credit and lending, and possible controls on capital construction.[48]

A central government official, Ge Hongshen, vice-chairman of the Special Economic Zones (SEZ) Office of the State Council, explained: 'As the newest among the country's major five SEZs, Pudong's development has only a five year history, while other SEZs existed for more than ten years. It would be fair to give Pudong more opportunities to catch up'. Ge also stressed Pudong's importance for the development of the Yangtze Valley and its national role.[49]

In summary, Shanghai's economic reform benefits from 'policies' rather than from funds granted by the centre. Policies permitting the establishment of the stock market, futures exchanges, the national foreign exchange centre established on 4 April 1994, and relatively liberal foreign investment policies have enabled Shanghai to attract capital from the whole of China and from abroad. The high demand, and thus high cost, of real estate in Shanghai also provides Shanghai with an enormous quantity of investment funds.

Sectoral changes

The Shanghai economy is primarily industrial, though the service sector is becoming increasingly important. Among China's provincial-level units in 1991, Shanghai had proportionately the smallest primary sector (3.89 per cent)[50] and the largest secondary sector (64.28 per cent).[51] The changing importance of the secondary and tertiary sectors provides a broad overview of changes in Shanghai's economic development strategies. Prior to 1956, the tertiary sector grew at a faster rate than the secondary sector. However, owing to the acceleration of industrial production, the secondary sector occupied an ever-increasing proportion of Shanghai's product. According to a senior Shanghai economist, 'Shanghai's economic development was decided by the secondary sector.'[52] In 1980, the growth rate of the tertiary sector began to exceed that of the secondary sector, 'but in total production, the secondary sector still remains decisive and definitely no basic change has occurred.'[53] In the words of another Shanghai economist, 'during the 1980s, tertiary industry was never really listed on the important agenda of Shanghai's economic development'.[54]

Perhaps these evaluations by senior Shanghai Municipal economists were too pessimistic. The December 1984 'Shanghai Municipality Economic Strategy' emphasised development of the tertiary sector to serve the entire nation. At that time the tertiary sector accounted for 21.9 per cent of Shanghai's product.[55] As Table 6.2 shows, Shanghai met the 'Strategy' document's goal of having the tertiary sector account for 30 per cent of product by 1990, but the original goal of 50–60 per cent of product by the year 2000 was revised downward.[56] According to former Mayor Huang Ju, Shanghai sought to have the tertiary sector account for 45 per cent of GNP in the year 2000 and 60 per cent in 2010.[57]

Within the industrial sector, considerable change is occurring. Shanghai now emphasises 'six pillars of industry': automobiles, iron and steel, petrochemicals, power station equipment, telecommunications, and household electrical. In crude terms, the proportion of light industry has declined while that of heavy industry has increased, a change most marked since 1992 (Table 6.3). Even though such sectors as food, textiles and chemicals continue to grow, their proportions of Shanghai's industrial output have declined while metals and machinery gain importance (Table 6.4). In 1993 production of automobiles and digitally controlled exchanges increased 47.0 per cent and 110 per cent respectively.[58] According to interviews, other important growth areas are power station equipment, household electrical goods, electronic meters, fine chemicals including pharmaceuticals, and communications

Table 6.2 The structure of the Shanghai economy by sector, 1952–93

	Primary sector (%)	Secondary sector (%)	Tertiary sector (%)
1952	5.9	52.4	41.7
1957	3.9	58.7	37.4
1970	4.7	77.1	18.2
1978	4.0	77.4	18.6
1980	3.2	75.7	21.1
1985	4.2	69.8	26.0
1990	4.4	64.8	30.8
1991	3.9	64.3	31.8
1992	3.2	63.6	33.2
1993	2.5	59.6	37.9

Sources: *Shanghai Tongji nianjian 1992* [Shanghai Statistical Yearbook 1992], edited by Shanghai shi tongji ju, Zhongguo tongji chubanshe, Shanghai, 1992, p. 33; *Shanghai tongji nianjian 1994* [Shanghai Statistical Yearbook 1994], edited by Shanghai shi tongji ju, Zhongguo tongji chubanshe, Shanghai, 1994, p. 28

Table 6.3 Percentage of light and heavy industry in Shanghai economy, 1978–93 (by value)

	Light industry	Heavy industry
1978	51.8	48.2
1980	55.3	44.7
1981	58.1	41.9
1985	52.9	47.1
1990	51.5	48.5
1991	50.1	49.9
1992	46.6	53.4
1993	42.1	57.9

Source: *Shanghai tongji nianjian 1994* [Shanghai Statistical Yearbook 1994], edited by Shanghai shi tongji ju, Zhongguo tongji chubanshe, Beijing, 1994, p. 28

Table 6.4 Changes in the structure of Shanghai's industry, 1990 and 1993

Industry	1990		1993	
	Value (RMB¥ billion)	Per cent	Value (RMB¥ billion)	Per cent
Food	11.32	6.9	17.09	5.1
Textiles	28.04	17.1	43.17	13.0
Light	9.09	5.5	14.64	4.4
Chemicals	27.24	16.6	44.08	13.2
Metals	29.09	17.7	77.94	23.4
Machinery	45.67	27.8	104.93	31.5
Other	13.83	8.4	30.80	9.4

Source: Professor Wang Yizhi, Shanghai Academy of Social Sciences

equipment. This industrial restructuring helps explain the special success of the Jinqiao Export Processing Zone in Pudong where industrial output increased from RMB¥1.2 billion in 1993 to RMB¥50 billion in 1994. In Jinqiao, high-tech projects account for 60 per cent of this production and half of the projects are foreign invested.[59] Excellent geographical location within Pudong has also contributed to the Zone's success.

The high cost of land and labour in Shanghai has forced Shanghai industry to restructure into high-technology and high-value industry in order to become profitable. Older, less efficient industries lose money and come under increasing competition from such areas as Southern Jiangsu and the Hangzhou area which have cheaper land and wages than Shanghai, yet have good quality labour forces. The completion of the new Shanghai–Nanjing and Shanghai–Hangzhou freeways will enhance the competitiveness of these areas.

The growth of the tertiary sector is especially pronounced in the financial area where Shanghai has also taken advantage of the centre's 'policy' gifts.

Table 6.5 Value of stocks and bonds traded in Shanghai, 1992–4

	1992 (RMB¥ billion)	1993 (RMB¥ billion)	1994 (RMB¥ billion)
Stocks	49.437	476.071	1147.016
Bonds	25.600 ·	37.461	3914.920
Total	75.037	513.532	5061.936

Source: Professor Wang Yizhi, Shanghai Academy of Social Sciences

The value of stocks traded in Shanghai in 1994 was 2.4 times that of 1993 and 23 times that of 1992, while the value of bonds traded in 1994 was 104 times that of 1993 and 153 times the value of 1992 (Table 6.5). Treasury bonds account for a very large proportion of the bond market.

Shanghai has recently established several futures exchanges which have also experienced substantial growth. The metals exchange, the largest, was established on 28 May 1992, followed by futures exchanges for agricultural producers goods (26 February 1993), chemicals (27 March 1993), petroleum (27 May 1993), grain and oil (30 June 1993) and building materials (18 October 1993). In 1994 the agricultural producers' goods, chemicals, petroleum and building materials exchanges were combined into a commodities exchange.[60] The value of futures traded has expanded rapidly (Table 6.6). The average amount traded each day in 1994 as compared to 1993 increased 21.8 per cent on the metals exchange, 9 times on the grain and oil exchange, 31 times on the agricultural producers' goods exchange, and 17 times on the building materials exchange, though the average daily value of futures traded on the petroleum and chemicals exchanges actually fell about 50 per cent in 1994.[61]

Since the policy changes in 1992, Shanghai has now become China's main centre for foreign financial institutions, supplanting Shenzhen.[62] The national

Table 6.6 Value of futures traded in Shanghai, 1993 and 1994

	1993		1994	
Exchange	Value (RMB¥ billion)	Trading days	Value (RMB¥ billion)	Trading days
Metals	388.905	175	682.083	252
Grain and oil	25.620	78	530.870	180
Agricultural producers' goods	.421	57	47.465	205
Building materials	1.294	20	257.818	235
Petroleum	24.946	112	27.279	228
Chemicals	5.887	113	2.448	115

Source: Professor Wang Yizhi, Shanghai Academy of Social Sciences

foreign exchange centre established on 4 April 1994, which arranges settlements between banks, had exchanged the equivalent of US$12.4 billion by 30 June 1994 and US$40.7 billion by the end of 1994 over a network encompassing twenty-three Chinese cities.[63]

The service sector has also grown in non-financial areas. Retail sales have increased especially rapidly since 1992 (Table 6.7). These increases primarily reflect growing per capita incomes in Shanghai (RMB¥3375 in 1991, RMB¥4273 in 1992, RMB¥5650 in 1993 and RMB¥7309 in 1994.)[64] Historically, when enterprises distributed goods according to the plan, many people had to go to Shanghai from the Chinese interior to buy goods. Now, enterprises have established sales networks with department stores in the interior and fewer people come to Shanghai to shop.

In the first half of 1995, a shift in the sectoral trends occurred as the secondary sector, which had been less than 60 per cent of GDP, exceeded 60 per cent. At the same time, the tertiary sector declined from 39.6 per cent of GDP in 1994 to 36.4 per cent. The industrial re-structuring discussed above and a series of price-fixing scandals which hit the futures markets in 1994 and 1995 and resulted in the closing of the futures markets in sugar, steel and Treasury Bonds account for this change.

SOCIAL IMPACT

In mid-1993, not long after the implementation of the 1992 reforms, Shanghai residents expressed concern about Shanghai's transport and infrastructure and the quality of its housing. Two years later, in mid-1995, Shanghainese exhibited much greater satisfaction with these two aspects of life. To some extent, these improvements have resulted from the reforms. But the reforms have also had negative social consequences including inflation and an increasing cost of living, inequality of incomes, unemployment, and a distinction between a registered population which is now ageing and has a negative growth rate and a non-registered transient (or 'floating') population seeking work. A small affluent group of 'new rich' now have access to a wide variety of new consumer products.

Table 6.7 Retail sales in Shanghai, 1990–4

	Value (RMB¥ billion)	Increase over previous year (%)
1990	35.13	0.1
1991	40.22	13.9
1992	48.94	21.7
1993	65.35	33.5
1994	77.07	17.9

Source: Professor Wang Yizhi, Shanghai Academy of Social Sciences

Transport and infrastructure

In mid-1993, transportation within Shanghai had become difficult, requiring long times to travel short distances. Road space had become so tight that trucks were forbidden to enter the city during daylight hours. Two years later transportation within Shanghai had improved dramatically owing to two important infrastructure projects. Although Shanghai authorities had long desired to complete both projects, they were unable to do so until the 1992 policy changes made more funds available to Shanghai.

The first important project is the elevated Inner Ring Road or Beltway. Completed with local government funds, the 48-kilometre Beltway connects Pudong in the east with Hongqiao in the west encompassing Luwan in the south and Zhabei in the north. It crosses the two new major suspension bridges which span the Huangpu River connecting Pudong with the rest of Shanghai, also completed with locally generated funds.[65] An 8-kilometre elevated road connects the northern and southern ends of the Beltway.

The second project, the 'Metro' or underground, has been financed with foreign investment and funds generated from real estate. The 16.1-kilometre first line is now open and runs from southwest of the Sports Stadium to the People's Park and then northwest to Shanghai Railway Station.[66] The second line, now under construction, will go to Pudong. Other infrastructure projects, planned and underway, include upgrading Shanghai's telecommunications systems and a second international airport in Pudong.

Housing

The economic reforms have enabled Shanghai to implement some housing policies which have gained widespread support among the city's population. For many years, the tiny housing space of the average Shanghainese caused many complaints. To some extent, this may have resulted from Shanghai's very high population density - nearly 12,000 people per square kilometre in the urban areas - 5 times the density of Beijing, almost 9 times that of Tianjin and 2.66 times more than China's second most densely populated city, Shijiazhuang.[67] In fact, Shanghai's living space per capita in its urban areas has improved over the years (Table 6.8) and it does not compare too unfavourably with most of China's major cities (Table 6.9). To reach the city's goal of 10 square metres per person by the year 2000, the city will have to construct 7 million square metres annually.[68] This target was reached easily in 1994 when 8.8 million square metres were completed.[69]

The new housing policy, based on a Singapore model, uses a public accumulation fund to fund new housing. Under the slogan, 'The Resident Should Own His Housing',[70] Shanghainese have been able to buy their own residence fairly cheaply, sometimes for as little as RMB¥10,000 (US$1,200) or RMB¥20,000 (US$2,400). The moneys received for the housing save the state (and its constituent work units) in two ways. First, moneys are set aside

Table 6.8 Living space per capita in Shanghai urban areas, 1952–93

	Space (square metres)
1952	3.4
1978	4.5
1980	4.4
1985	5.4
1990	6.6
1991	6.7
1992	6.9
1993	7.3

Sources: *Shanghai tongji nianjian 1992* [Shanghai Statistical Yearbook 1992], edited by Shanghai shi tongji ju, Zhongguo tongji chubanshe, Shanghai, 1992, p. 31; *Shanghai tongji nianjian 1994* [Shanghai Statistical Yearbook 1994], edited by Shanghai shi tongji ju, Zhongguo tongji chubanshe, Beijing, 1994, p. 33

Table 6.9 Living space per capita in urban areas of selected Chinese cities, 1993

City	Space (square metres)
Shanghai	7.3
Beijing	8.5
Tianjin	6.9
Shijiazhuang	7.9
Taiyuan	7.8
Shenyang	6.2
Nanjing	7.6
Hangzhou	8.0
Wuhan	6.5
Guangzhou	5.8
Chengdu	8.1
Chongqing	6.3
Xi'an	6.4

Source: *Zhongguo tongji nianjian 1994* [Statistical Yearbook of China 1994], Zhongguo tongji chubanshe, Beijing, 1994, p. 321

for maintenance; thus already constructed housing no longer drains the public purse. Second, the funds are used to build new housing. In mid-1995 several old friends quite excitedly told the writer, 'I have become a landlord!' Beginning in May 1991, Shanghai became the first place in China to use the public accumulation fund system and by the end of March 1995 the public accumulation fund had RMB¥5.34 billion.[71] About 4.5 million people and 30,000 work units (about 95 per cent) are participating in the public accumulation fund.[72]

Some ten variables are considered in determining the price of the housing. The base price is RMB¥902 per square metre, a very low amount. The purchaser receives a 1.2 per cent discount for each year of employment. A further discount of 2 per cent per year is given for the age of the house (with a maximum discount of 60 per cent for any house over thirty years old). Another 5 per cent discount is given 'to encourage employees to buy housing'. Residents buying their current housing receive another 5 per cent discount. A further 15 per cent 'space' discount is given if the housing is not new. The city is divided into six locations and discounts up to 50 per cent can be obtained for housing in the city's periphery. Housing located outside the Beltway receives discounts of 20 or 30 per cent. Chinese prefer housing facing south and this costs a premium (102 per cent) while housing facing north receives an 8 per cent discount. The storey of the housing also affects the price. Other preferences relate to area per person and the person's work status. A purchaser paying cash rather than instalments receives a further 20 per cent discount.

Each building establishes a repair and maintenance fund into which the purchasers pay 20 per cent and the government pays 80 per cent. The government also pays RMB¥500,000 for each elevator. Residents still pay a small management fee which takes care of general maintenance, gardens and repairs. However, the new owners are responsible for repairs within their flats. In addition to funds from the sale of housing, the public accumulation fund receives moneys from employees who pay 7 per cent of their basic salary, an amount also matched by the work unit. Thus, people save some RMB¥30–50 per month. People can use their contributions, but only for housing-related costs. To access the money they need to provide documentation that the funds are to be used to purchase or repair housing. The main stipulation when purchasing housing is that the new owner must occupy the residence for five years during which it cannot be rented or sold. After five years the housing fully belongs to the new owner who can sell it or rent it. Thus, in five years Shanghai will have an active real estate market.

Inflation and income inequality

Inflation (15–18 per cent per annum in 1995) has raised the cost of living. A kilogram of rice, which used to cost RMB¥0.34, now costs RMB¥3.20. A family of three will spend RMB¥1,200 per month on food. Water, gas and electricity cost RMB¥150–200 per month. The Shanghai government endeavours to keep inflation down by setting maximum prices for agricultural goods and by attempting to ensure an adequate supply of foodstuffs from the rural areas of Shanghai and other provinces. While the employed in Shanghai can cope with inflation as they receive relatively high incomes, inflation does present problems for Shanghai's less affluent population.

According to a survey of 30,000 urban Chinese families including 500 families in Shanghai, the average per capita income in urban Shanghai during

1994 was RMB¥5,566. The incomes of the top 10 per cent averaged RMB¥11,630 while the income of the bottom 10 per cent averaged RMB¥2,986. According to the survey, the average per capita expenditure on consumption was RMB¥4,668 leaving a surplus of 16.1 per cent of income. However, the survey indicated that the gap between rich and poor is widening.[73]

Two factors related to the economic reforms have contributed to this widening gap. First, the attempts to increase the efficiency of state enterprises have led to unemployment. Second, the industrial restructuring (discussed earlier), has also led to unemployment as old skills are no longer in demand. From 1990 to 1994 some 521,000 persons in Shanghai lost jobs in the state or collective sector of whom 327,000 have found new jobs.[74]

Since 1993, Shanghai has implemented a new system to lessen the burden on people declared redundant. People who 'leave their post' stay at home and receive the basic wage, normally about RMB¥200–300 per month. This functions as an unemployment benefit. However, since this payment cannot support a person in Shanghai, in 1995 the Shanghai Municipal government made it illegal to have a husband and wife both 'leave their posts'. If both work for the same unit, then one must be retained on a full salary. If they work for different units, the two units must coordinate to ensure no more than one 'leaves their post'.

The 'leaving their post' system employs both carrots and sticks. Employers are supposed to retrain those 'leaving their posts' and provide them with information. Employment advertisements frequently state those 'leaving their posts' will receive preference. Yet, the system also pressures employees to leave formerly permanent positions. In at least some work units the status of 'leaving their posts' terminates after three years and the employee is sacked.

A decreasing, ageing local population and an increasing transient population

The economic reforms have impacted on Shanghai's population in two contradictory ways, both with important social consequences. First, the local population (those with Shanghai population registration) has actually started to have negative population growth. At the same time this population has become aged and increasingly dependent. Second, Shanghai's prosperity has attracted large numbers of people from other places. While this transient (or 'floating') population performs many menial and dirty tasks to which Shanghainese are averse, this influx of outsiders is perceived to increase social disorder and crime.

In 1992, Shanghai experienced post-1949 China's first negative population growth rate (other than during the famine induced by the Great Leap Forward) when the 1991 rate of 0.11 per cent declined to –0.02 per cent. Since then the rate has decreased to –0.08 per cent in 1993 and –0.138 in 1994. Shanghai demographers attribute this negative growth rate primarily to the success of the birth control programme since the number of births has declined while the death rate has remained stable.[75]

A corollary of this declining rate of growth has been the spectacular ageing of Shanghai's population. In one decade (1982–92) the proportion of the population aged 65 and over increased from 7.43 per cent to 10.75 per cent, the median age of the population increased from 29.2 years to 36.0 years and life expectancy increased from 72.9 years to 75.4 years. The ratio of old to young (the proportion of the population aged 65 and over divided by the proportion of the population aged 0–14) has increased from 40.91 per cent to 60.52 per cent. If these trends continue, by 2010–20 over 30 per cent of Shanghai's population will be aged 65 and over and 10 per cent will be aged 80 and over.[76]

The social and economic consequences of this ageing process are serious. Already in the 1982–92 decade the proportion of the dependent population in Shanghai increased from 34.38 per cent to 39.86 per cent, necessitating each employed person to support more dependants. Furthermore, the capability and speed of workers decline after they reach the age of 50. A lonely and alienated aged population will affect the health and happiness of family members. And the government will discover it has an excess of schools but needs to fund facilities for the aged like activities centres, nursing homes and geriatric hospitals.[77]

As the post-Mao reforms have increased regional disparities and reduced controls over the population, tens of millions of Chinese have moved from poorer regions and rural areas with surplus labour to the wealthier regions and urban centres. The size of the transient (or 'floating') population in Shanghai has increased rapidly in recent years (Table 6.10). In the six years from 1982 to 1988 the numbers quadrupled;[78] according to another set of statistics the numbers more than doubled between 1988 and 1993.[79]

Table 6.10 Size of transient population in Shanghai, 1982–93

	Number
1982	500,000
1983	700,000
1984	1,020,000
1985	1,650,000
1986	1,830,000
1988	2,090,000*
1993	2,810,000

Note: *All of these figures except for 1993 are from Zhang and Zhou. *Shanghai jingji nianjian 1994* gives a 1988 figure of 1,246,000

Sources: Zhang Kaimin and Zhou Haiwang, 'Shanghai renkou fazhan ji qi fenbu de guoqu, xianzai he zhanwang' [The past, present and prospects for the development of Shanghai's population and its distribution], *Renkou* [Population] (Shanghai), no. 1, 1993 (cum. no. 32), p. 55; *Shanghai jingji nianjian 1994* [Shanghai Economic Yearbook 1994], Shanghai Academy of Social Sciences, 1994, p. 53

The 1993 transient population statistic of 2,810,000 derives from a 2 per cent survey conducted on 10 December 1993 by the Shanghai Municipal Public Security Bureau and the Shanghai Municipal Statistical Bureau. (In fact, many observers believe the actual statistic exceeds 3 million.) This unpublished survey provides at least nine insights into the nature of Shanghai's transient population.[80]

First, while people come from virtually the whole of China, most come from nearby provinces. About 31 per cent come from Jiangsu, 25 per cent from Anhui, 12 per cent from Zhejiang and 5 per cent from Jiangxi. Sichuan accounts for 4 per cent while all other provinces account for 2 per cent or less.

Second, the population is relatively young. Over half are aged 20–34. Nearly three-quarters are aged 15–39. Third, about 64 per cent are male. Fourth, the male and female transients have very similar age structures. Fifth, 80 per cent go to Shanghai's urban area and only 20 per cent to Shanghai's rural areas. Of those entering Shanghai's urban area, 80 per cent go to peripheral residential districts. Sixth, at the time of the survey, 21 per cent had been in Shanghai for 1–3 months, 13 per cent for 3–6 months, 20 per cent for 6–12 months, 16 per cent for 1–3 years and 13 per cent for more than 3 years.

Seventh, prior to coming to Shanghai, over 70 per cent had worked in agriculture, forestry, animal husbandry or fishing. Only 6 per cent had been workers, a proportion even smaller than the 7 per cent of pre-school-aged children. All other categories accounted for less than 5 per cent. Thus, the overwhelming proportion came from rural China. Eighth, about half (48 per cent) had junior secondary education, while 26 per cent had primary education. About 10 per cent had senior secondary education while almost 9 per cent were functionally illiterate. Finally, three-quarters came for economic reasons with 24 per cent of these in construction work, 36 per cent in other labouring work, 20 per cent in business, 10 per cent in the handicraft industry and 4 per cent in agriculture. About a quarter were in Shanghai for social reasons with about 80 per cent of these visiting relatives and friends.

While opinions differ, Shanghai social scientists generally believe that the city does not have a severe transient population problem. The transients provide labour for Shanghai's building and infrastructure construction boom. It has been difficult for the city to find sufficient people willing to perform physical labour and to provide menial services. The demand for physical labour has increased especially since the 1992 reforms. Even Shanghai farmers prefer to let outsiders till their land on their behalf. Shanghai is also protected by the prosperity of southern Jiangsu and northeastern Zhejiang, both of which have substantial construction and industry. If transients cannot find work in Shanghai, they often go to Jiangsu and Zhejiang seeking work. In the words of one senior economist, 'the situation would be considerably worse if Jiangsu and Zhejiang did not exist and Shanghai were adjacent to Sichuan!'

A substantial portion of the 'transient population' are already *de facto* permanent residents. In 1991 the number of such 'permanent residents' without household registration in Shanghai's urban area had reached 530,000. Their 'life and work is the same as the city's residents and they enjoy the city's public facilities. In fact, they have already become permitted city residents'.[81]

In 1994 and 1995 the Shanghai Municipal government instituted a series of regulations in order to control the influx of outsiders and regulate the domestic labour market. Occupations have been divided into three large categories. In the first category, employees must have Shanghai household registration. These jobs have been allocated to Shanghainese for security reasons and to ensure that local people obtain the choice jobs. Occupations in this category include elevator operators, child-care workers, nurses, store clerks, taxi drivers and the receptionists in hotels. The second category permits only a few non-Shanghai workers. The final category allows the employment of up to one-third outsiders and includes construction, textiles and private restaurants. In addition to reporting the type of work, employers wishing to hire non-Shanghainese must convince the labour management offices of the Shanghai Municipal government that they can provide housing and that the outsiders will be able to subsist in Shanghai. If the application is successful, the worker obtains a work permit.

There are also two kinds of residence permits. Individuals must apply for a Temporary Residence Permit if they plan to stay longer than three days and will not work or engage in business. If they plan to work, they must apply for a Permit to Live Elsewhere. According to Shanghai social scientists, less than half of the transient population has any of the above permits. Most rent housing or stay with relatives and friends.

Shanghai has also established a residence permit colloquially called the 'Blue Card', but officially called 'Blue Stamp Household Registration' in contrast to the red stamp on regular household registration. Blue Stamp Household Registration resembles the business migration programmes of some Western countries. Holders have normally been in Shanghai a long time and have invested substantial sums in Shanghai or own housing. Children in 'Blue Stamp Households' can attend schools in Shanghai. Blue Stamp Household Registration is almost the same as Shanghai household registration except that the household still retains its household registration in its original location. Numbering fewer than one thousand, 'Blue Stamp Households' have virtual dual household registration.

The new rich

Although many Shanghainese point to the substantial construction in Pudong, perhaps the most striking change since mid-1993 has occurred in retailing. Many new supermarkets and foreign department stores have opened, as have speciality shops which handle a particular prestige brand. These stores sell a wide variety of imported goods, which are not cheap by Chinese standards, but which sell for only about 10–15 per cent more than the price in Hong Kong. These stores target Shanghai's 'new rich' as their customers.

A survey by the State Planning Council found China's new rich include 'stock market traders, bosses of private businesses, the self-employed, entertainment stars, taxi drivers and managers in foreign-funded firms [as well as] [m]anagers, experts and technicians who take responsibility for profits and losses at State-owned companies, banks and technical research institutes'.[82] As noted earlier, Shanghai is China's wealthiest provincial-level unit and the gap between wealthy and poor is widening. Informal indices indicate Shanghai has many 'new rich'. Currently, Shanghai has 130,000 mobile phone subscribers (1 per cent of the population),[83] while 1.2 million people (10 per cent of the population) use pagers.[84]

Shanghai now has fifteen joint venture department stores. The most successful, such as Isetan (a joint venture between the Japanese store and the Huating Group), are 'mid-market'. The 'upmarket' stores have performed poorly indicating that Shanghai does not have the consumer base to support 'upmarket' stores. (Apparently the main 'upmarket' consumers are Hong Kong, Taiwan and local businessmen buying goods for their mistresses.) The mid-market stores plan to move slowly upmarket as they educate consumers. At present, Shanghai consumers are not particularly familiar with brand names, not knowing, for example, the differences between Esprit and Giordano. Some Shanghai consumers may lash out and spend RMB¥200–300 (US$24–36) for an imported T-shirt, but few will spend RMB¥10,000 (US$1,200) on a bag or RMB¥20,000 (US$2,400) on a suit.

Two surveys of Shanghai shoppers confirm the finding of the State Planning Council survey that many of the new rich 'have shown a reluctance to spend'.[85] Both Shanghai surveys targeted the 'new rich'.[86] The first survey was conducted in front of three major foreign-invested department stores. The second survey, targeting mainland Chinese working for foreign companies, was conducted in office buildings with large numbers of foreign firms. Each survey was conducted over three days and each questioned 1,000 persons. In both surveys, single females (without children) in their early and mid-twenties predominated.

In the first survey, about one-third of the respondents worked for state enterprises and about one-third worked for foreign firms. About one-third had salaries of RMB¥500–1,000 per month while another third earned RMB¥1,000–2,000 per month. Most were unwilling to spend more than RMB¥300 per month on clothes and over 70 per cent were willing to buy only one or two items of clothing a month. Over 70 per cent preferred to spend less than RMB¥300 per item of clothing. Close to two-thirds preferred to shop in foreign-invested stores as opposed to state or private stores. Seventh-eighths of those surveyed said they had bought goods with famous brand names, the most popular being Esprit, Pierre Cardin and Jeanswest.

The second survey analysed a more affluent sample. Almost seven-eighths worked for foreign firms. Three-quarters had monthly salaries over

RMB¥1,000 and about one-third had monthly salaries over RMB¥2,000. About 70 per cent spent more than RMB¥400 per month on clothing. Like the shoppers in the first survey, they bought only one or two items per month and preferred to spend less than RMB¥300 per item. Only 72 per cent said they had bought famous brand name clothes, but because many respondents had purchased several items, the second sample had bought six times as many brand name items as the first sample. The most popular brands were Esprit, Jeanswest, Puma, Goldlion, Giordano and Pierre Cardin.

POLITICAL CONSEQUENCES

Historically, Shanghai has been a key centre of Chinese politics. Much political activity took place within the protected foreign concessions while Shanghai's labour movement also provided a focus for political action. After 1949, Shanghai workers continued to be restive,[87] and the city served as the base of the 'Gang of Four' during the Cultural Revolution. However, in the post-Mao period – and especially in the 1990s – Shanghai's politics have been relatively quiescent. Two sets of factors explain this situation.

First, although Beijing and Shanghai are rivals, they also have a symbiotic relationship. Shanghai benefits from the centre's support in the form of preferential policies. The centre gains from increased tax revenues and the improved economic development of other areas in China. At the same time, the centre knows Shanghai will not cause problems for Beijing.

Although Shanghai has gained a new national leadership role since Deng Xiaoping's 'Inspection Tour' of the South, it does not try to compete politically with Beijing. While Beijing attempts to assert national leadership through top-down bureaucratic and authoritarian structures, Shanghai exerts its leadership through the market with the skills and knowledge emancipated by the centre's 'policy' gift.

The movement of personnel from Shanghai to the centre demonstrates the smooth working relationship. President Jiang Zemin, Vice-Premier Zhu Rongji and Vice-Premier Wu Bangguo succeeded one another as Shanghai Party Secretary from 1987 to 1995. (Jiang and Zhu also served as mayor during 1985–91.) Because of these personnel movements, some observers have suggested a 'Shanghai Gang' now operates in Beijing.

Shanghainese reject the concept of a 'Shanghai Gang' working on behalf of Shanghai. They note that people like Jiang Zemin and Zhu Rongji were outsiders who worked in Shanghai, but have now left and with their central responsibilities have central rather than Shanghai perspectives. And they certainly are not Shanghainese. Shanghai natives like Chen Yun and Qiao Shi never did help Shanghai and would be better described as members of a 'Beijing Gang'. Deng Xiaoping used to spend Chinese New Year in Shanghai every year, but he never assisted Shanghai until after his 1992 'Inspection Tour'. With the former Shanghai leaders now ensconced in Zhongnanhai, it may be easier for Shanghai's leaders to get past gatekeepers and transmit their messages to the centre, but their power in Beijing lies in Shanghai's importance to the national economy rather than in Shanghai's supposed *guanxi* with the centre.

The second set of factors explaining Shanghai's relative political quiescence relate to the achievements of Shanghai's political leadership. As noted earlier, the government has implemented a successful housing policy. It has demonstrated concern for the unemployed 'leaving their posts' and for the poor. People's incomes are rising and the new transport and infrastructure facilities are contributing to an improving quality of life. Public order is good and corruption relatively low. In the words of one Shanghai economist, the city's 'management efficiency is very high'. Thus, Shanghai's leaders have legitimacy. People – even those forced to leave their old housing – fundamentally agree with the 'Shanghai enterprise'. Shanghai's leaders have turned the city around and enabled it to reassert its role as a national leader.

The nature of Shanghai's current leadership increases its legitimacy. The top leadership consists of middle-aged technocrats. Natives of Shanghai and the surrounding region who speak Shanghainese predominate (Table 6.11). Although the mayor and vice-mayors have high visibility, the party remains the leading organisation. The pattern of promotion from mayor to party secretary, which Jiang Zemin, Zhu Rongji and Huang Ju all followed, reinforces this observation. Since 1987, only Wu Bangguo has served as party secretary without having first been mayor.

The three top leaders at present, Party Secretary Huang Ju, Mayor Xu Kuangdi and Executive Vice-Mayor Hua Jianmin are all engineers who have served in the Municipal Planning Commission. This planning experience may account for the annual convening of the 'International Business Leaders' Advisory Council for the Mayor of Shanghai' which includes the heads of such international corporations as IBM and Pacific Dunlop. Drawing on their vast resources, the international leaders present substantial briefing papers on specific topics like Urban Planning Human Resource Development, Air Transport and Telecommunications. According to a foreign observer in frequent contact with the Shanghai Municipal government, the mayors, vice-mayors and a large majority of bureau chiefs and section heads are very impressive. The quality of key personnel has improved greatly since the early 1980s.

This does not mean that the top leadership is united. Shanghai 'conventional wisdom' links Wu Bangguo, Huang Ju and Hua Jianmin to Jiang Zemin while Xu Kuangdi is supposedly close to Zhu Rongji. But, by and large, Shanghainese do not express much interest in politics. In the words of one senior economist with very high political connections, 'when Shanghainese are concerned with politics, they see the world'. They are concerned with China's relations with the United States, Japan's historical and present roles, the situation in Taiwan and issues of national independence. They are less concerned with machinations in Beijing and City Hall, and much more interested in the stock market.

Table 6.11 Shanghai leadership, end of 1995

Name	Position	DOB	Birthplace	Other
Huang Ju	Party Sec. 1995–	1938	Zhejiang	Mayor 1991–5; Exec. Vice-Mayor 1985–91; Politburo 1995– ; Engineer
Xu Kuangdi	Mayor 1995– ; Dep. Party Sec. 1994–	1937	Zhejiang	Vice-Mayor 1992–5; Dir. Shanghai Municipal Planning Commission 1991–2; Engineer
Wang Liping	Dep. Party Sec. 1992–	——	——	Dep. Sec. 1983–92; Mathematician
Hua Jianmin	Exec. Vice-Mayor 1994–	1940	——	Dir. Shanghai Municipal Planning Commission; Engineer
Zhao Qizheng	Vice-Mayor in charge of Pudong 1991–	1940	Beijing	Dir. Organisation Dept Shanghai Party Committee 1986–91; Nuclear physicist
Xia Keqiang	Vice-Mayor 1992–	1940	Zhejiang	Dep. Sec-Gen. Shanghai Municipal government 1984–92; Chemist
Meng Jianzhu	Vice-Mayor 1993–	1947	Jiangsu	Dep. Sec-Gen. Shanghai Municipal government 1992–3; Agricultural scientist
Jiang Yiren	Vice-Mayor 1993–	1942	Shanghai	Dep. Sec-Gen. Shanghai Municipal government; Senior engineer
Sha Lin	Vice-Mayor 1993–	1936	——	Dep. Sec-Gen. Shanghai Municipal government; Physicist
Xie Lijuan(f)	Vice-Mayor 1985–	1936	Zhejiang	Member of Jiu San Society; Physician

Note: This table includes ten of the top leaders of Shanghai: the Party Secretary, two of the four Deputy Party Secretaries, the Mayor (who is concurrently a Deputy Party Secretary) and seven of the eight Vice-Mayors. The missing Deputy Party Secretaries are Chen Liangyu and Chen Zhili (f). The missing Vice-Mayor is Gang Xueping, a Shanghainese.

Shanghai's immigrant culture, its cosmopolitanism, its relative wealth and its concern with economics rather than politics have created an impression both within Shanghai and in other parts of China that Shanghainese are different from other Chinese. In the words of one cultural observer:

> Virtually no place in China gives high marks to Shanghainese. Astute, arrogant, calculating, glib, free and undisciplined, stingy, exclusive, *holding leaders in contempt, lacking enthusiasm for politics*, an absence of collective consciousness, cold to people, miserly, selfish, trendy, ostentatious, fond of being unconventional, trivial, vulgar ... all of these added together are the Shanghainese in the mind of Chinese from other places [emphasis added].[88]

Some Chinese refer to Shanghainese as 'Domestic Overseas Chinese'. The relatively recent migrations of both Shanghainese and Overseas Chinese, their concern with the outside world, and their concentration on economics at the expense of politics reinforce the validity of this metaphor.

NOTES

1   I gratefully acknowledge that research grants from the Australian Research Council (ARC) enabled the field research. I express appreciation to many Chinese scholars at a variety of institutions, including the Shanghai Academy of Social Sciences and East China Normal University, for their many insights and materials. Last, but not least, I thank Ms Helen Tantau, Chief Representative in the Shanghai Representative Office of Batey Burn & Co. Ltd, for data and information on Shanghai's 'new rich'.
2   Yu Qiuyu, *Wenhua kulü* [Bitter Cultural Journeys], Zhishi chubanshe, Shanghai, 1992, p. 147.
3   Lucian W. Pye, 'How China's nationalism was Shanghaied', *Australian Journal of Chinese Affairs*, no. 29, January 1993, p. 117.
4   Frederic Wakeman, Jr, 'Policing modern Shanghai', *China Quarterly*, no. 115, September 1988, p. 408.
5   These terms come from headings in *Dangdai Zhongguo de Shanghai* [Contemporary China's Shanghai], Dangdai Zhongguo chubanshe, Beijing, 1993, I, pp. 10–28. With minor changes, I have used the English translations on p. 874.
6   The image of 'yellow' continent and 'blue' ocean comes from Su Xiaokang and Wang Luxiang, *Heshang* [River Elegy], Xiandai chubanshe, Beijing, 1988.
7   J.V. Davidson-Houston, *Yellow Creek: The Story of Shanghai*, Putnam, London, 1962, p. 13. I am indebted to Dr Antonia Finnane for this source. For an account of Shanghai's importance as a port during 1683–1840, see Linda Cooke Johnson, 'Shanghai: an emerging Jiangnan port, 1683–1840', in *Cities of Jiangnan in Late Imperial China*, State University of New York Press, Albany, NY, 1993, pp. 151–81, 248–59.
8   *Zhongguo renkou (Shanghai fence)* [China's Population (Shanghai Volume)], edited by Hu Huanyong *et al.*, Zhongguo caizheng jingji chubanshe, Beijing, 1987, pp. 32–6. The current boundaries of Shanghai Municipality date from 1958 when ten counties were transferred from Jiangsu Province to Shanghai Municipality. This increased the area of Shanghai Municipality tenfold. See ibid., pp. 31–2; Zhang Kaimin and Zhou Haiwang, 'Shanghai renkou fazhan ji qi fenbu de guoqu, xianzai he zhanwang' [The past, present and prospects for the

development of Shanghai's population and its distribution], *Renkou* [Population] (Shanghai), no. 1, 1993 (cum. no. 32), p. 54; *Shanghai jiaoqu nianjian 1949–1992* [Yearbook of Shanghai Suburban Districts 1949–1992], Shanghai renmin chubanshe, Shanghai, 1994, p. 23.

9 Zhang Kaimin and Zhou Haiwang, op. cit., p. 51.
10 Zhang Zhongli, 'A brief discussion of modern Shanghai's formation as an economic center', *SASS Papers (5)*, Shanghai Academy of Social Sciences Press, 1994, p. 116.
11 Zhang Kaimin and Zhou Haiwang, op. cit., p. 51.
12 *Zhongguo renkou (Shanghai fence)*, op. cit., pp. 49–50.
13 Zhang Kaimin and Zhou Haiwang, op. cit., p. 53.
14 Ibid.
15 *Zhongguo renkou (Shanghai fence)*, op. cit., pp. 50–1.
16 Bryna Goodman, *Native Place, City, and Nation: Regional Networks and Identities in Shanghai, 1853–1937*, University of California Press, Berkeley, 1995.
17 This is calculated from a statistic of 1,500,000 Subei people out of a total 1949 Shanghai population of 5,062,878 which Emily Honig cites in a series of four important articles: 'Pride and prejudice: Subei people in contemporary Shanghai' in Perry Link, Richard Madsen and Paul G. Pickowicz (eds), *Unofficial China: Popular Culture and Thought in the People's Republic of China*, Westview Press, Boulder, CO, 1989, p.143 note 1; 'The politics of prejudice: Subei people in Republican-Era Shanghai', *Modern China*, 15, no. 3, July 1989, pp. 270–1, note 2; 'Invisible inequalities: the status of Subei people in contemporary Shanghai', *China Quarterly*, no. 122, June 1990, p. 274, note 2; and 'Migrant culture in Shanghai: in search of a Subei identity', in Frederic Wakeman, Jr and Wen-hsin Yeh (eds), *Shanghai Sojourners*, Institute of East Asian Studies, University of California at Berkeley, 1992, p. 240, note 2. In each article Honig states that Subei people accounted for about 'one-fifth' of Shanghai's population, but this is clearly an arithmetic error. In a later work which incorporates and modifies the earlier articles, Honig retains the 'one-fifth' proportion and cites the figure of 1,500,000 Subei people in Shanghai, but casts doubts on the figure's validity; see Emily Honig, *Creating Chinese Ethnicity: Subei People in Shanghai, 1950–1980*, Yale University Press, New Haven, CT, 1992, pp. 40, 141 note 17.
18 For the formation of the Subei grouping, see ibid. and Antonia Finnane, 'The origins of prejudice: the malintegration of Subei in Late Imperial China', *Comparative Studies in Society and History*, 35, 1993, pp. 211–38.
19 See Honig's overlapping analyses in 'Pride and prejudice', 'Invisible Inequalities' and *Creating*, pp. 108–28.
20 *Dangdai Zhongguo de Shanghai*, op. cit., I, p. 386.
21 The Shanghai figures are available in *Shanghai tongji nianjian 1992* [Shanghai Statistical Yearbook 1992], edited by Shanghai shi tongji ju, Zhongguo tongji chubanshe, Shanghai, 1992, p. 400 and *Zhongguo renkou (Shanghai fence)*, op. cit., pp. 342–4. The national figures are available in *Zhongguo tongji nianjian 1992* [Statistical Yearbook of China 1992], Zhongguo tongji chubanshe, Beijing, 1992, pp. 702–3. The respective population figures appear in *Shanghai tongji nianjian 1992*, op. cit., p. 60 and *Zhongguo tongji nianjian 1992*, op.cit., p. 77.
22 *Zhongguo renkou (Shanghai fence)*, op. cit., p. 257.
23 Ibid, pp. 76–9. Table 3-5 on p. 77 gives annual figures for in-migration and out-migration during 1950–83. During 1956–76, 1957 was the only year with substantial net in-migration. A useful article on post-1949 migration is Zhang Kaiming, Shen An'an and Zhang Henian, 'Migration in Shanghai (1949–1986)', *SASS Papers (3)*, Shanghai Academy of Social Sciences, 1990, pp. 139–85.
24 *Zhongguo renkou (Shanghai fence)*, op. cit., p. 140.

25   Ibid., pp. 142–3.
26   Ibid., p. 146. On the 'Third Front', see Barry Naughton, 'The Third Front: defence industrialization in the Chinese interior', *China Quarterly*, no. 115, September 1988, pp. 351–86.
27   Zhang Kaiming, Shen An'an and Zhang Henian, op. cit., pp. 153–4.
28   *Zhongguo renkou (Shanghai fence)*, op. cit., p. 141.
29   Ibid., pp. 144–5.
30   Ibid., p. 148.
31   Ibid., pp. 80–1.
32   Ibid., pp. 149–50.
33   This section draws upon and updates J. Bruce Jacobs and Lijian Hong, 'Shanghai and the Lower Yangzi Valley', in David S.G. Goodman and Gerald Segal (eds), *China Deconstructs: Politics, Trade and Regionalism*, Routledge, London, 1994, pp. 224–35. A contemporary analysis with similar conclusions, but additional useful fiscal details, is Lin Zhimin, 'Reform and Shanghai: changing central–local fiscal relations', in *Changing Central–Local Relations in China: Reform and State Capacity*, Westview Press, Boulder, CO, 1994, pp. 239–60.
34   *Dangdai Zhongguo de Shanghai*, op. cit., I, pp. 400–1.
35   Shanghai contributed 17.6 per cent of central expenditure in 1953–57 and 33.2 per cent in 1958 according to Nicholas R. Lardy, *Economic Growth and Distribution in China*, Cambridge University Press, 1978, p. 135.
36   *Shanghai tongji nianjian 1992*, op. cit., p. 26.
37   *Dangdai Zhongguo de Shanghai*, op. cit., I, p. 617.
38   Xia Keqiang, 'Xu' [Preface], in *Pudong xinqu youhui zhengce yu caozuo chengxu* [The Preferential Policies and Operation Procedures of the Pudong New District], Shanghai shi renmin zhengfu Pudong kaifa bangongshi [and] Shanghai shi renshi ju Pudong xinqu banshiqu, Shanghai, 1992, p. v.
39   Text in ibid., p. 3.
40   'Shanghai Pudong kaifa shi xiang youhui zhengce' [Ten preferential policies for the development of Pudong, Shanghai], in *Shanghai Pudong xinqu zhengce fagui guizhang 1990.9–1992.6* [Policies, Regulations and Rules for the Pudong New District, Shanghai, September 1990–June 1992], Shanghai shi Pudong xinqu guanli weiyuanhui bangongshi, Shanghai, 1992, pp. 1–2. The text of these ten policies also appears in *Pudong xinqu youhui zhengce yu caozuo chengxu*, op. cit., p. 30 where it states the State Council has approved the ten preferential policies.
41   Deng Xiaoping, 'Zai Wuchang, Shenzhen, Zhuhai, Shanghai deng di de tanhua yaodian' [Important points of talks in Wuchang, Shenzhen, Zhuhai and Shanghai], in *Deng Xiaoping wenxuan* [Selected Works of Deng Xiaoping], Renmin chubanshe, Beijing, 1993, III, p. 376.
42   '1992 nian Zhongyang dui Shanghai Pudong xinqu xin zengjia de zhengce youhui he peitao zijin zushi' [New additional policies preferences and accompanying financial measures of the centre for Pudong New District, Shanghai in 1992], in *Shanghai Pudong xinqu zhengce fagui guizhang 1990.9–1992.6*, op. cit., pp. 3–5 and *Pudong xinqu youhui zhengce yu caozuo chengxu*, op. cit., p. 31.
43   Attempts to check this statement suggest it has some validity. In 1991 the profits and taxes of the Shanghai cigarette industry, i.e. the Shanghai Cigarette Company, totalled RMB¥1,581 million, see *Shanghai tongji nianjian 1992*, op. cit., p. 157. (See ibid., p. 155 for statement that the cigarette industry has only one 'unit'.) In 1991 Guangzhou Municipality had local revenues of RMB¥4,848.92 million and expenditures of RMB¥3,070.96 million, leaving a budget 'surplus' (paid to the centre) of RMB¥1,777.96 million, an amount only 11 per cent greater than the profits and taxes of the Shanghai Cigarette Company, see *Zhongguo*

chengshi tongji nianjian 1992 [Urban Statistical Yearbook of China 1992], Zhongguo tongji chubanshe, Beijing, 1992, p. 581. In 1991, the Shanghai Cigarette Company ranked ninth among China's industrial enterprises in terms of total profits and taxes, behind only Daqing Petroleum, four steel companies, two other cigarette companies and a petrochemical company, *Zhongguo gongye jingji tongji nianjian 1992* [Industry and Economics Statistical Yearbook of China 1992], Zhongguo tongji chubanshe, Beijing, 1992, p. 421.

44 *Wenhui bao* (Shanghai) 2 January 1995 and 4 February 1995.

45 'Jiang Zemin tan Pudong kaifa' [Jiang Zemin discusses Pudong development], *Pudong kaifa* [Pudong Development], no. 6 (June 1993), p. 4.

46 'Zhu Rongji shicha Pudong shi yaoqiu . . .' [During an inspection visit to Pudong, Zhu Rongji requests . . .], in ibid., p. 5.

47 *Renmin ribao* [People's Daily] 22 April 1995, pp. 1, 4. The quote appears on p. 1.

48 Jian Jiang, 'Pudong to have new initiatives for growth', *China Daily* (Beijing) 19 September 1995, pp. 1–2; Jian Jiang, 'New area privilege', *Shanghai Star* (Shanghai), 19 September 1995, p. 1.

49 Ibid.

50 Calculated from *Jiangsu zai quanguo de[,] shixian zai Jiangsu de diwei (1991)* [The Position of Jiangsu in the Nation and of Municipalities and Counties in Jiangsu (1991)], Jiangsu sheng tongji ju, [Nanjing], 1993, pp. 2–3. In 1991, the primary sector accounted for over 8 per cent of product in Beijing and Tianjin, and for 27.2 per cent nationally.

51 Calculated from ibid., pp. 2–3. Industrial product in 1991 accounted for over 50 per cent of total product in seven other provincial-level units: Heilongjiang (56.26 per cent), Tianjin (56.03 per cent), Liaoning (54.98 per cent), Shanxi (54.75 per cent), Jiangsu (54.23 per cent), Beijing (52.18 per cent) and Zhejiang (50.09 per cent). Nationally, the secondary sector accounted for 45.86 per cent of China's total product.

52 Wu Weiyang, '1992 nian Shanghai jingji zhanwang' [Shanghai Economic Forecast for 1992], in *1992 nian Zhongguo jingji zhanwang* [China Economic Forecasts for 1992], Guojia xinxi zhongxin, Beijing, 1992, p. 218.

53 Ibid., p. 219.

54 Yao Xitang, 'Strategy for Shanghai's economic development: changes in the 1980s become choices for the 1990s', *SASS Papers (4)*, Shanghai Academy of Social Sciences, 1992, p. 103.

55 'Shanghai shi jingji fazhan zhanlüe' [Shanghai Municipality Economic Strategy], in Yu Guangyuan (ed.) *Zhongguo diqu jingji shehui fazhan zhanlüe xuanpian* [Selected Articles on China's Regional Economic and Social Development Strategy], Zhongguo caizheng jingji chubanshe, Beijing, 1990, p. 14. The full 'Strategy' document, prepared by the Shanghai Municipal government (*Shanghai shi renmin zhengfu*) and the State Council's Investigation and Research Committee for the Reform and Revitalisation of Shanghai (*Guowuyuan gaizao zhenxing Shanghai diaoyan zu*), appears on pp. 11–19. The 'Strategy' document specifically lists the following service industries: commerce, finance, insurance, trusts, transportation, communication, science and technology, education, culture, journalism, travel industry, public utilities, real estate, service, medical, accountancy, law, information and consulting. Note that official Shanghai statistics give a somewhat higher figure than the 'Strategy' document, stating that the tertiary sector accounted for 25.1 per cent of product in 1984, see *Shanghai tongji nianjian 1992* [Shanghai Statistical Yearbook 1992], edited by Shanghai shi tongji ju, Zhongguo tongji chubanshe, Shanghai, 1992, p. 33.

56 'Shanghai shi jingji fazhan zhanlüe', op. cit., p. 14.

57 *Xianggang jingji ribao* [Hong Kong Economic Daily] 28 December 1992, p. 32.

58 *Shanghai tongji nianjian 1994* [Shanghai Statistical Yearbook 1994], edited by Shanghai shi tongji ju, Zhongguo tongji chubanshe, Beijing, 1994, pp. 2–4. These two products were highlighted in the Mayor's Government Work Report of 18 February 1994, see *Shanghai jingji nianjian 1994* [Shanghai Economic Yearbook 1994], Shanghai Academy of Social Sciences, 1994, p. 4.

59 Wang Yizhi, 'Patterns of the future economic development in China's coastal areas', 19 June 1995, unpublished paper, p. 3.

60 Information from Professor Wang Yizhi and *Shanghai jingji nianjian 1994*, op. cit., pp. 298–300.

61 Calculated from the data in Table 6.6.

62 For details of policy changes and comparative data, see Wang Yizhi, 'Waizi jinrong jigou de fazhan' [The development of foreign capital financial institutions], in *Zhongguo jingji da qushi 1995* [Major Trends in the Chinese Economy 1995], Shangwu, Hong Kong, 1995, pp. 192–7.

63 *Wenhui bao* 2 January 1995 and information from Professor Wang Yizhi.

64 Calculations by Professor Wang Yizhi dividing total salaries and wages by number of employees. These figures do not include 'grey' income outside of official salaries and they differ from survey data presented below.

65 For details on the construction of the elevated Beltway, see *Shanghai gaige kaifang fengyun lu* [The Impressive Record of Shanghai's Reform and Opening to the Outside], edited by Zhonggong Shanghai shiwei dangshi yanjiushi [Office of Party History, Shanghai Municipal Committee of the Chinese Communist Party], Renmin chubanshe, Shanghai, 1994, pp. 560–4.

66 For details on the construction of the first Metro line, see ibid., pp. 568–75.

67 *Zhongguo tongji nianjian 1994* [Statistical Yearbook of China 1994], Zhongguo tongji chubanshe, Beijing, 1994, p. 313.

68 *Wenhui bao* 24 March 1995.

69 *Wenhui bao* 27 January 1995; *Jiefang ribao* [Liberation Daily] (Shanghai) 26 February 1995.

70 *Wenhui bao* 24 March 1995. In Chinese, this slogan, *juzhe you qi wu*, closely parallels Sun Yat-sen's 'The tiller should own his land' (*gengzhe you qi tian*), usually translated as 'Land to the tiller'.

71 *Wenhui bao* 27 April 1995; *Jiefang ribao* 27 April 1995.

72 *Shanghai xinwenbao* [Shanghai Business News] 11 January 1995.

73 *South China Morning Post* (Hong Kong) 29 April 1995; *Shanghai Star* 2 May 1995.

74 *China Daily* 20 June 1995.

75 Zuo Xuejin, 'Shanghai renkou ziran biandong fu zengzhang de beijing yanjiu' [A study of the background to the Shanghai population rate of natural increase becoming negative], *Renkou* [Population] (Shanghai), no. 3, 1994 (cum. no. 38), p. 19. The 1994 figure was supplied from an unpublished report.

76 Shen An'an, 'Shanghai jinqi renkou laohua de tezheng fenxi' [An analysis of the characteristics of the ageing of Shanghai's population in the near future], *Shanghai laoling kexue* [Shanghai Science on Ageing], no. 1, 1995 (cum. no. 8), pp. 13–18.

77 Gu Xingyuan, Wu Zhuochun, Shu Yugang, 'Shanghai renkou fu zengzhang de chengyin ji shehui yinsu' [The causes and social factors of the Shanghai population's negative growth rate], *Renkou* [Population] (Shanghai), no. 3, 1994 (cum. no. 38), pp. 37–8.

78 Zhang Kaimin and Zhou Haiwang, op. cit., p. 55.

79 *Shanghai jingji nianjian 1994*, op. cit, p. 53.

80 Data from *Shanghai shi di wu ci liudong renkou diaocha* [The Fifth Transient Population Survey in Shanghai Municipality], conducted by Shanghai shi gong'an ju [Shanghai Municipal Public Security Bureau] and Shanghai shi tongji

ju [Shanghai Municipal Statistical Bureau], tabulated by Shanghai shehui kexueyuan renkou yu fazhan yanjiusuo [Institute of Population and Development Studies, Shanghai Academy of Social Sciences], unpublished.
81 Zhang Kaimin and Zhou Haiwang, op. cit., p. 55.
82 Wu Yunhe, 'Newly well-off spending little on the finer things', *China Daily* 11–17 December 1994.
83 *China Daily* 4 October 1995; *Shanghai Star* 6 October 1995.
84 *Jiefang ribao* 26 September 1995.
85 Wu Yunhe, op. cit.
86 Data from surveys of Shanghai shoppers conducted by Batey Burn in July and September 1994. I wish to express my appreciation to Ms Helen Tantau, Chief Representative – Shanghai, Batey Burn & Co. Ltd, for access to the survey results and for information on Shanghai retailing.
87 Elizabeth J. Perry, 'Shanghai's strike wave of 1957', *China Quarterly*, no. 137, March 1994, pp. 1–27.
88 Yu Qiuyu, op. cit., p. 143.

REFERENCES

Marie-Claire Bergere, *The Golden Age of the Chinese Bourgeoisie, 1911–1937*, translated by Janet Lloyd, Cambridge University Press, 1989.
Parks M. Coble, *The Shanghai Capitalists and the Nationalist Government, 1927–1937*, Harvard University Press, Cambridge, MA, 1980.
Joseph Fewsmith, *Party, State and Local Elites in Republican China: Merchant Organizations and Politics in Shanghai, 1890–1930*, University of Hawaii Press, Honolulu, 1985.
Bryna Goodman, *Native Place, City and Nation: Regional Networks and Identities in Shanghai, 1853–1937*, University of California Press, Berkeley, 1995.
Christian Henriot, *Shanghai, 1927–1937: Municipal Power, Locality, and Modernization*, translated by Noel Castelino, University of California, Berkeley, 1993.
Emily Honig, *Creating Chinese Ethnicity: Subei People in Shanghai, 1850–1980*, Yale University Press, New Haven, CT, 1992.
Emily Honig, *Sisters and Strangers: Women in the Shanghai Cotton Mills, 1919–1949*, Stanford University Press, 1986.
Christopher Howe (ed.) *Shanghai: Revolution and Development in an Asian Metropolis*, Cambridge University Press, 1981.
Neale Hunter, *Shanghai Journal: An Eyewitness Account of the Cultural Revolution*, Praeger, New York, 1969.
Lynn Pan, *Shanghai: A Century of Change in Photographs*, Hai Feng, Hong Kong, 1993.
Elizabeth Perry, *Shanghai on Strike: The Politics of Chinese Labor*, Stanford University Press, 1993.
Frederic E. Wakeman, *Policing Shanghai, 1927–1937*, University of California Press, Berkeley, 1995.
Frederic E. Wakeman and Wen-hsi Yeh (eds) *Shanghai Sojourners*, Institute of East Asian Studies, University of California, Berkeley, 1992.
Jeffrey N. Wasserstrom, *Student Protests in Twentieth-Century China: The View from Shanghai*, Stanford University Press, 1991.
Lynn Whyte, *Careers in Shanghai: The Social Guidance of Personal Energies in a Developing Chinese City 1949–1966*, University of California Press, Berkeley, 1978.

Sichuan Province

GENERAL

GDP (billion *yuan* renminbi)	277.70
GDP annual growth rate	11.40
as % national average	96.61
GDP per capita	2,477.17
as % national average	65.97
Gross Value Agricultural Output (billion *yuan* renminbi)	122.90
Gross Value Industrial Output (billion *yuan* renminbi)	404

POPULATION

Population (million)	112.14
Natural growth rate (per 1,000)	16.93

WORKFORCE

Total workforce (million)	62.57
Employment by activity (%)	
primary industry	64.60
secondary industry	15.80
tertiary industry	19.0
Employment by sector (% of provincial population)	
urban	9.79
rural	46.01
state sector	6.67
collective sector	8.87
private sector	2.43
foreign-funded sector	0.05

WAGES

Average annual wage (*yuan* renminbi)	4,028
Growth rate in real wage	8.90

PRICES

CPI annual rise (%)	24.60
Service price index rise (%)	21.30
Per capita consumption (*yuan* renminbi)	953
as % national average	54.86
Urban disposable income per capita	3,311
as % national average	94.71
Rural per capita income	946
as % national average	77.48

FOREIGN TRADE AND INVESTMENT

Total foreign trade (US$ billion)	3.10
% provincial GDP	9.62
Exports (US$ billion)	1.80
Imports (US$ billion)	1.29
Realised foreign capital (US$ million)	956.51
% provincial GDP	2.97

EDUCATION

University enrolments	198,407
% national average	75.77
Secondary school enrolments (million)	3.44
% national average	73.76
Primary school enrolments (million)	9.62
% national average	80.15

Notes: All statistics are for 1994 and all growth rates are for 1994 over 1993 and are adapted from *Zhongguo tongji nianjian 1995* [Statistical Yearbook of China 1995], Zhongguo tongji chubanshe, Beijing, 1995 as reformulated and presented in *Provincial China* no. 1 March 1996, pp. 34ff.

Sichuan Province

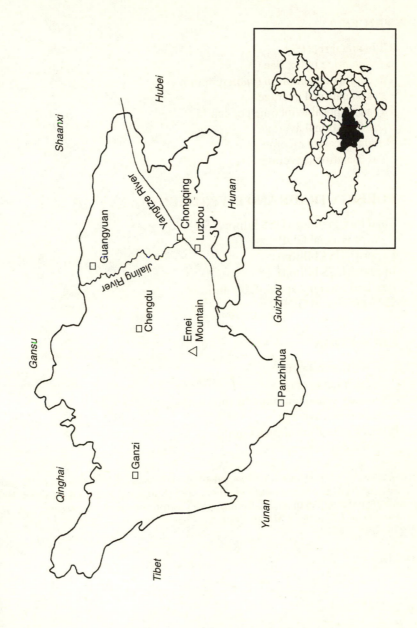

7 Sichuan

Disadvantage and mismanagement in the Heavenly Kingdom

Lijian Hong

Sichuan not only is China's most populous province, but also has – and has had consistently since the establishment of the People's Republic – one of the largest provincial economies. A particular source of economic strength has been its agricultural output. However, the development of Sichuan's economy – even before 1978 as well as during the reform era – has been hampered by both its natural and political settings. Remote and isolated, it has had difficulties in integrating its economy into the national mainstream. During the 1950s this was the result of a deliberately chosen unbalanced growth strategy that stressed Sichuan's role as a national provider of grains. In the late 1950s and 1960s, and indeed through the Cultural Revolution, the development of Sichuan was often determined more by the interplay between its political leadership and Beijing than by provincial concerns. Even during the 1960s and 1970s, when considerable investment was made by Beijing in Sichuan, it proved to be a double-edged sword. The industrial development, though large-scale, was often defence-oriented and non-productive. With the political changes that led to reform the province found itself left responsible for an inefficient as well as non-productive large industrial sector. The 1980s and 1990s have once again seen the province faced by the difficulties of integrating into a national economy characterised by an unbalanced growth strategy, though this time one driven by market forces rather than planned allocations. As in the 1950s, its relationships with Beijing and with other parts of China remain prime concerns for Sichuan's leaders.

THE PROVINCIAL SETTING

Sichuan occupies about 6.9 per cent of China's land area and is the largest of the Han Chinese provinces. Surrounded by mountains, Sichuan is somewhat remote but unlike other peripheral provinces, as Table 7.1 indicates, the province's aggregate economic performance is not too far behind the provinces of the more advanced coastal areas. Sichuan has a well-developed industrial sector with significant national concentrations of defence-related and nuclear industries. One of China's two space centres is located in the southwest corner of the province. The province is also one of China's four

Table 7.1 Economic performance of Sichuan in China, 1993

	National	Sichuan	% of national total	Provincial rank in China	National rank after	
Population (million)	1,185.17	111.04	9.37	1		
GDP (billion *yuan*)	3,138.03	195.87	6.24	4	Guangdong	(322.53)
					Jiangsu	(275.45)
					Shandong	(270.25)
National income[a] (billion *yuan*)	2,022.30	126.39	6.25	4	Guangdong	(179.36)
					Jiangsu	(169.70)
					Shandong	(168.56)
Capital construction investment of state-owned units (billion *yuan*)	461.55	22.19	4.81	5	Guangdong	(53.42)
					Liaoning	(26.95)
					Shanghai	(26.82)
					Shandong	(23.90)
Newly increased fixed assets of state-owned units (billion *yuan*)	275.89	13.59	4.93	6	Guangdong	(27.48)
					Shanghai	(19.74)
					Shandong	(17.48)
					Liaoning	(16.24)
					Jiangsu	(15.43)
Total investment in fixed assets (billion *yuan*)	1,245.79	58.06	4.66	7	Guangdong	(163.73)
					Jiangsu	(111.72)
					Shandong	(89.21)
					Zhejiang	(78.21)
					Liaoning	(71.09)
					Shanghai	(64.24)

Industry[b] (billion *yuan*)	5,269.20	282.59	5.36	7	Jiangsu (709.65), Shandong (597.01), Guangdong (523.74), Zhejiang (397.24), Liaoning (351.08), Shanghai (332.79)
Agriculture[c] (billion *yuan*)	1,099.55	87.64	7.97	3	Shandong (99.43), Guangdong (89.90)
No. of township enterprises (million)	24.53	2.42	9.87	1	
Gross value of output of township enterprises (billion *yuan*)	3,154	192.33	6.10	6	Shandong (472.50), Jiangsu (470.20), Zhejiang (275.90), Guangdong (220.20), Henan (192.33)
Grain production (million tonnes)	456.49	41.51	9.10	1	
Total value of retail sales (billion *yuan*)	1,359.26	80.80	5.94	4	Guangdong (139.97), Jiangsu (104.04), Shandong (99.38)
No. of institutions of higher education	1,065	61	5.73	3	Beijing (68), Jiangsu (67)
Scientific and technical personnel in state-owned enterprises (million)	18.12	1.39	7.67	1	

Table 7.1 continued

	National	Sichuan	% of national total	Provincial rank in China	National rank after	
Telephones (million)	26.13	1.05	4.02	9	Guangdong	(3.87)
					Jiangsu	(2.20)
					Shanghai	(1.54)
					Zhejiang	(1.53)
					Beijing	(1.47)
					Liaoning	(1.44)
					Shandong	(1.42)
					Hebei	(1.06)
Freight traffic volume (million tonnes)	11,157.71	753.80	6.76	2	Guangdong	(986.37)

Notes: [a]1992 figures
[b]Gross value industrial output
[c]Gross value of output from farming, forestry, animal husbandry and fishery

Source: *Statistical Yearbook of China 1994*, pp. 32, 35, 38, 60, 142, 330, 345, 361, 376, 463, 485, 496, 574, 603

major centres for the metallurgical, engineering, electronic and chemical industries.[1] While Sichuan is clearly one of the largest provincial economies in China, its large population means that its per capita economic performance – as Table 7.2 indicates – places it among the poorest provinces. At the end of 1993, the population of Sichuan reached 111.04 million, or 9.37 per cent of the national total, making it the most populous province in China.[2]

Sichuan was conquered by the Qin Dynasty well before it united the rest of China. Since that time the province has remained a central part of China during periods of strong central government and unity but has had a reputation and a tendency to local independence when central rule weakened or broke down. The strength of Sichuan was its agriculture and the industries and commerce which developed on that basis. The area around Chengdu in

Table 7.2 Economic figures per capita for Sichuan, 1993

	National average (yuan)	Sichuan (yuan)	% of national average	Provincial rank in China
GDP[a]	2,706	1,764	65.19	25
National income[b]	1,736	1,157	66.65	26
Capital construction investment of state-owned units	389.44	199.82	51.31	24
Newly increased fixed assets of state-owned units	232.79	122.41	52.58	24
Total investment in fixed assets	1,051.12	522.85	49.74	25
Industrial[c]	4,445.94	2,544.96	57.24	18
Agricultural[d]	927.76	789.24	85.07	20
Grain production (kg)	385	374	97.14	15
Residents' consumption	1,148	757	65.94	22
Scientific and technical personnel in total population (%)	1.5	1.2		25
No. of telephones per 100 persons	2.2	0.9		28

Notes: [a]National averages from Chen Yaobang (ed.) *Zhongguo xibu diqu kaifa nianjian 1994* [1994 Yearbook of Development of China's Western Region], Gaige Press, Beijing, 1994, p. 502
[b]1992 figures
[c]Gross value industrial output
[d]Gross value of output from farming, forestry, animal husbandry and fishery

Source: Figures based on *Statistical Yearbook of China 1994*, pp. 38, 142, 150, 154, 256, 330, 345, 376, 485, 603 (Sichuan's average, percentage and rankings separately calculated)

particular was highly developed and commercialised from early times. By the Han Dynasty, Sichuan had replaced southern Shaanxi as the 'granary of the nation' and assumed the soubriquet of 'heavenly kingdom'.[3]

During the late Qing, Sichuan's traditional agricultural production could not compete with the economic strength generated by the rise of modern industry and foreign trade in China's coastal areas. As Adshead has observed, Sichuan in modern times 'came to symbolise the inadequacies of traditional China and the radical incompleteness of Chinese modernisation' and 'represented the Chinese world at its worst'.[4] The mountains that once had protected Sichuan from civil war and other chaos now became obstacles to its modernisation.

During the Second World War Sichuan's economic development benefited, at least temporarily, from the relocation of coastal industries to Sichuan and the establishment of the wartime capital in Chongqing. In the 1930s and 1940s provincial economic development concentrated on the development of modern military, chemical, and metallurgical industries, as well as engineering and power generation. Chongqing became a new industrial centre of defence-related enterprises, steel production and the engineering industry.[5] The importance of Sichuan in wartime China can be seen from the province's contribution to the national economy. During the eight years of war, Sichuan provided one-third of the total grain produced by the Nationalist Party controlled areas and 30 per cent of national financial expenditure.[6]

Li Jingquan, Mao Zedong and radicalism

The communist movement in Sichuan started in the early 1920s. The 4th Front Red Army established a Sichuan–Shaanxi Revolutionary Base Area on the province's northern borders during the early 1930s. During the war, when a communist liaison office was set up in Chongqing, local party organisations were instructed not to make any trouble for the United Front between the Nationalist Party and the Communists, and were later ordered to disband.[7] In October 1949, Sichuan was liberated when the 2nd Field Army, led by two Sichuanese, Deng Xiaoping and Liu Bocheng, with cooperation from parts of the 1st and 4th Field Armies, entered the province. It was from these forces that the future provincial leadership was to be drawn: in particular the long-time provincial party secretary, Li Jingquan, who effectively governed the province from 1952 to 1967 and who was a radical supporter of Mao Zedong during the late 1950s and 1960s.

Li Jingquan relied heavily on personnel from the Jin-Sui Base Area where he and a sizeable proportion of the 1st Field Army troops had served during the Sino-Japanese War. This group was identified by local Sichuanese as the 'Shanxi Gang' or less respectfully the 'Potato Clique' because of their humble Shanxi origins. As well as tensions between 'insiders' and 'outsiders', there was tension between soldiers from the 1st and 2nd Field Armies, which also overlay tension between the provincial leadership in Chengdu (based on the

1st Field Army) and the city leadership of Chongqing (based on the 2nd Field Army). During seventeen years of Li Jingquan's rule, no party or government leaders from Chongqing, the largest industrial city in the region, was promoted to the provincial leadership. When the provincial leadership was reorganised in 1952, a native Sichuanese, Li Dazhang, who had also served in Shanxi, was appointed as the new governor. When Li Jingquan was promoted to be the secretary of the CCP's Southwest Bureau, he was replaced by another Sichuanese, Liao Zhigao, who had also been associated with the 1st Field Army.

Li Jingquan's radicalism and support for Mao Zedong provided Sichuan with a highly specific legacy. Economic development in Sichuan before the Cultural Revolution was very mixed, with first solid achievement, then disaster and the eventual development of a substantial non-productive industrial base. Achievement came early with the First Five-Year Plan, which brought political stability, economic order and considerable heavy investment. By the time the First Five-Year Plan was completed, national income in Sichuan had increased from ¥2.61 billion in 1949 to ¥7.31 billion. Total output value of industry and agriculture had increased from ¥3.19 billion in 1949 to ¥9.84 billion. The proportion of industry in total output value increased to 42.28 per cent. The total output value of heavy industry was 36.8 per cent of that for all industry.[8] Of total central investment, 81.4 per cent (more than ¥220 million) was for transportation and energy generation,[9] trends aimed at building Sichuan as a national strategic supplier. Indeed, during the period, Sichuan became one of China's major food suppliers and provided the central government with a total of 8.13 million tonnes of grain.[10]

These solid achievements were in stark contrast to the results of the Great Leap Forward where through unrealistic plans there was considerable waste of funds, materials and the energy of ordinary people. It is estimated that ¥1,100 million of investment in the steel industry, and ¥430 million of other projects led to unusable output.[11] According to an investigation conducted in 1963, a total of ¥60 million worth of materials had been lost in the previous years.[12] In agriculture there was an even greater disaster in Sichuan. The direct consequence of food waste and the surplus purchase of grain by central government was a widespread famine. Though the exact number of how many people died during the famine has never been published,[13] local historians believe that a total of more than 1 million people died of hunger during the Great Leap Forward.[14]

The 1960s saw Sichuan transformed into a defence-centred industrial base with the construction of the Third Front Project. The project was a direct response to China's deteriorating international relations and led Mao Zedong to advocate the dispersal of China's industry from the coastal provinces and its relocation in the interior. Sichuan received the lion's share of total investment in the Third Front Project: ¥36.25 billion, or 27.9 per cent. During an eight-year period several modern industrial centres were constructed in

Sichuan, including a conventional arms production centre around Chongqing; an aviation industry centre in Chengdu; a defence-related shipbuilding industry along the Yangtze and Wu Rivers; a nuclear industry in north Sichuan; a space centre in Xichang; an engineering industry corridor along the Chengdu–Jiangyou and Chengdu–Chongqing railways; a steel complex centred at Panzhihua; all joined by several railway lines connecting Sichuan with Yunnan, Guizhou and Hubei.[15]

Third Front construction concentrated on non-productive, defence-related industry. The result was that this industrialisation did little to improve people's living standards. In the Third Five-Year Plan period, for example, investment in light industry and agriculture were only 1.34 per cent and 0.55 per cent of the total respectively.[16] Nonetheless by 1970 the total provincial industrial output value surpassed that of agriculture – 42.16 per cent of GVIAO to 36.48 per cent[17] – an important indicator of local industrialisation. The change may be linked with the dramatic increase of investment in 1969 and 1970 as a result,[18] though Sichuan's economy became dominated by heavy industry: by 1976 it accounted for 53 per cent of GVIAO.[19]

Economic geography

Sichuan can be roughly divided into four parts: the western highlands, the central basin, the eastern hills and the southwest mountain and basin areas.

The western part of Sichuan is all highland. Mountains in this area are more than 3,000 metres above sea level.[20] The northern part of the highland is the extension of the Qinghai–Tibet Plateau, with an average of 3,500 metres to 4,500 metres in elevation. Most mountain peaks in this area are covered by snow all the year round. Low temperature and dry weather make animal husbandry and forestry more common than farming. Sichuan has the nation's second largest forest area of 7.46 million hectares. Most timber forests are in the western highlands, along the middle and upper reaches of the Yangtze River, with 80 per cent of Sichuan's timber reserves.[21] With more than 1,400 rivers in the province, Sichuan has a potential hydro-electric power resource of 91.66 million kilowatts, more than any other province.[22] Most of those rivers (75 per cent of the provincial total) are to be found in west and southwest Sichuan.[23]

The central basin, or the Red Basin as it is known by the outside world, is surrounded by mountains and hills. It is one of the largest agricultural basins in China with a total area of 160,00 square kilometres. The central part of the Basin is the Chengdu Plain, which had been one of the richest parts of Imperial China. From the surrounding mountains, the Yalong, Dadu, Ming, Tuo, Fu and Jialing Rivers run from north to south and the Wu River from south to north. All of them, and many more smaller rivers, join the Yangtze, which runs through the southern part of the basin. The climate in this area is sub-tropical. While the average temperature rarely falls below zero, the eastern part of the basin is warmer than the western. During the summer, the temperature in Chongqing can exceed 40 degrees. Generally the weather in the basin and southwest areas of Sichuan is favourable to agriculture and most areas allow double-cropping.

The central basin area, including Chengdu and Chongqing, is the most populous part of the province. While average population density in the province was 176 persons per square kilometre in 1986 (above the national average of 107) the eastern basin area had population density as high as 361 person per square kilometre. On the Chengdu Plain population density reaches 700 to 900 persons per square kilometre, compared to 16 people per square kilometre in the western and 4 people per square kilometre in the northwestern parts of the province.[24]

In terms of both agriculture and industry, the central basin area and its surrounding hills is the heartland of the province and the most developed part of Sichuan. It was this part of Sichuan that was traditionally referred to as a 'heavenly kingdom.' Since 1949, it has become an area that includes not only agricultural wealth but also modern industries: nuclear power, space, electronics, engineering, steel, chemistry and textile industries are all located here. In 1994, the gross value of agricultural and industrial output in Chengdu and Chongqing alone was ¥219.41 billion, 42.64 per cent of the provincial total of ¥514.62 billion. In Chengdu and Chongqing urban employment accounted for 38.17 per cent of the provincial total. Of the total 72.75 billion state-owned enterprises' employees, 37.49 per cent were in Chengdu and Chongqing. Total investment in fixed capital in these two cities accounted for 42.87 per cent of the provincial total.[25] These figures would be even more impressive if the major cities along the Chengdu–Baoji, Chengdu–Kunming and Chengdu–Chongqing railways were included.

In terms of industrial development, the central area has an excellent location. To the east, there are Sichuan's largest coal mines. To the south, the natural gas deposits are the second largest in China and 44 per cent of the national total. To the west, China's potentially largest hydro-electric power resource is not far away. Within the basin, agriculture is well developed with an advanced irrigation system. With the construction of the four major railways – the Chengdu–Baoji, Chengdu–Kunming, Sichuan–Guizhou and Chongqing–Xiangfan – and their branches, the central part of the province is easily accessible. Airlines connect Chengdu and Chongqing with almost all capital cities in China and some major cities in Asia. In addition, the Yangtze River forms the backbone of provincial waterway transportation, through Chongqing, linking Sichuan with central China.

The eastern part of Sichuan is a mountainous area. Local industries are mainly light industrial and textile. The food-processing industry is well known within China and accounts for a large part of the total annual industrial output. The eastern part of Sichuan is also a centre of the provincial energy industry. Coal mines are to be found in the northern, central and southern parts of East Sichuan. Natural gas extends from the south and central basin area into the heart of East Sichuan.[26]

The southwest part of the province is part of the Hengduan Mountain Range running from South Sichuan down into Yunnan. It is an area with rich mineral resources: iron ores account for 52 per cent of the provincial total, rich iron ores 86.6 per cent, copper 71.4 per cent, lead 74.9 per cent and zinc 80.4 per cent.[27] Symbiotic iron ores in this part of Sichuan are unique in China because of the large number of elements they contain. In the Panzhihua area, more than twenty elements (including vanadium, titanium, nickel and cobalt) are interspersed with iron. The large, high-grade titanium deposit found there accounts for about 90 per cent of the national total. The Panzhihua Steel Complex is one of China's major production bases of ferrous and non-ferrous metals and rare minerals; it produces more than eighty varieties of steel, and nearly forty different steel products.[28]

REFORM AND THE PROVINCIAL ECONOMY

The Cultural Revolution sharply reduced provincial agricultural and industrial production in Sichuan. In the worst years of the Cultural Revolution (1967 and 1968) Sichuan's gross value of agricultural production fell by 9.6 per cent and its gross value of industrial production fell 23.8 per cent compared to national figures of 9.6 per cent and 4.2 per cent respectively. Productivity per capita in state-run enterprises in 1966 was ¥6,282 but fell to ¥2,126 in 1968. By 1976 it had increased only to ¥4,912. State purchase of commodity grains in 1957 was 5.49 million tonnes. By 1976 and the end of the Cultural Revolution this had fallen to 3.64 million tonnes.[29] For the first time since the Great Leap Forward, this traditional grain exporter became a grain-importing province.

This was the situation that greeted Zhao Ziyang when he came to the leadership of the province in the late 1970s and presented Sichuan with the opportunity for taking a lead in introducing rural reforms in post-Mao China. Sichuan was the first province to abolish the egalitarian reward system created by the then agricultural model of Dazhai and introduce, or reintroduce, a contract system. The system was not new. Li Jingquan had mentioned in his report to the Eighth National Party Congress in 1956 that non-socialist methods of production would not be replaced by socialist ones for some considerable time,[30] but he conspicuously failed to develop policy accordingly. In early 1959, two local party secretaries, Deng Zili of Zigong Prefecture, and Zhang Fengwu of Jiangjin Prefecture, introduced new policies to abandon public canteens and to establish a contract system in rural areas. The implementation of these reforms were stopped soon after the Lushan Conference and prefectural party leaders Deng Zili and others were purged. The contract system in particular was outlawed as a political crime.[31]

A contract system was reintroduced in early 1978 by local party leaders in Guanghan County with the support of Zhao Ziyang, the then Party Secretary and Governor of Sichuan. To disguise their practice as socialism, contracts were reached between government and production teams – between the state and collectives, not individuals. The system was later introduced into other parts of the province, though not without resistance and criticism from remnants of Li Jingquan's 'Potato Clique'. Soon after, a similar system was introduced into rural enterprises.

A second reform in Sichuan that eventually undermined the foundations of Maoist order was the reorganisation of rural political power through the abolition of the people's commune. From the second half of 1980 Guanghan once again took the lead in dismantling the system of people's communes which had combined party, government and economic functions. With the introduction of the contract system, peasants came to have the autonomy to decide what they should plant as long as they completed the state quota. Neither government nor party organisation had any need or right to interfere in their production. Guanghan reintroduced a form of administration where party and government had separate organisations, and the management of local production was essentially the responsibility of a commercial company.

The reform of Sichuan's state-run enterprises began in the same year that party leaders in Guanghan County introduced their rural reforms.[32] Six enterprises in Chongqing and Chengdu were picked as 'experimental sites'. Under a new policy these enterprises were granted the right to retain more profit to pay bonuses to advanced workers, to expand production and to engage in production outside the state plan and market their products after the state plan was met. The new policy gave enterprises rights to deal directly with foreign companies and reserve part of the foreign exchange earnings to import new technology, raw materials, advanced equipment and other products necessary to improve their production. The new policy also gave factory managers the right to penalise those workers who brought heavy losses to the factory.[33] A modified new policy was soon extended to another 100 enterprises and a further 200 in 1980. In the same year, a more radical policy was adopted in several enterprises which allowed the factories to 'manage independently, pay tax rather than profit to the state and assume full responsibility of profit and losses'.[34] The result was encouraging. In the 403 experimental enterprises, industrial output value increased 29.9 per cent compared with that in 1978, productivity increased 12.72 per cent, profit increased 29.2 per cent, and the tax paid to the state increased 23.34 per cent.[35]

Politically, these reforms also indicated a new pattern of central–provincial relations in post-Mao China where local initiatives were more acceptable to the centre. Local reform was possible during this period because policy differences existed among the top leaders. While one faction in the centre needed support from provincial leaders, it still required a great political risk were local leaders to adopt an unofficial line. Should Deng Xiaoping have lost his battle with Hua Guofeng, Zhao Ziyang (and other reformers like Wan Li in Anhui) would probably have had to pay for such boldness.

Within the province, Zhao's reform ideas were not always shared by other provincial leaders, most of whom had worked with former Party Secretary Li Jingquan. Before Zhao's reforms were accepted by the centre, he was actually very isolated in Sichuan. Even Zhao himself accepted the introduction of the responsibility system with some caution and hesitation. He repeatedly stressed that various methods could be tried and compared, but not the contract system based on individual households, the redivision of land and the encouragement of individual farming.[36] Only after 1981 when rural reform swept China and the contract system between government and individual was practiced in other provinces, did Zhao admit that his hesitation had hampered the initiatives of local party and government leaders in Sichuan.[37]

REFORM AND POLITICAL DISADVANTAGE

While Sichuan continued to push its post-Mao rural and urban reforms, the rapid development of China's southeast coast, centred on the four special economic zones, gradually overshadowed its leading position in the reform era. A detailed study in 1993 compared economic development in three Chinese provinces: Sichuan, Shandong, and Hubei in central China. It shows that in 1978, Sichuan had the highest GDP among the three (¥24.48 billion in Sichuan, ¥22.91 billion in Shandong and ¥15.1 in Hubei). By 1990 GDP increased 367 per cent in Sichuan (¥114.4 billion), 482 per cent in Shandong (¥133.21 billion) and 424 per cent in Hubei (¥79.2 billion). National income per capita in 1978 was ¥238 in Sichuan, ¥321 in Shandong, and ¥332 in Hubei. By 1990 national income per capita had risen to ¥1,063 in Sichuan, ¥1,569 in Shandong and ¥1,496 in Hubei. Despite Shandong's higher population growth (18.63 per cent to Sichuan's 11.48 per cent) its economy was developing even faster.[38]

Another study (from 1993) shows that the annual growth rate in the gross value of industrial output in Sichuan was 11.8 per cent during 1953 to 1978, higher than the national average (11.4 per cent) and Guangdong (10.6 per cent). From 1981 to 1989, however, the growth rate in Sichuan was 12.2 per cent, lower than those of the national average (13.2 per cent) and Guangdong (20 per cent). The annual growth rate of national income in Sichuan in the period from 1952 to 1957 was 11.07 per cent, higher than the national average (8.88 per cent) and Guangdong (9.20 per cent). From 1979 to 1989, the growth rate in Sichuan was 8.3 per cent, lower than the national average (8.7 per cent) and Guangdong (11.6 per cent).[39]

The economic success of China's coastal areas is mainly the result of increasing investment, both Chinese and foreign. In comparison, Sichuan's decline has many explanations but lack of capital investment is certainly a major problem. Despite Sichuan's rich natural resource base and great potential, geographic isolation and lack of immediate benefit are seen as the main reasons for low foreign investment.[40] As Table 7.3 indicates, by the end of 1993, the number of foreign enterprises registered in Sichuan was 2.26 per cent of the national total, less than 10 per cent that of Guangdong. Foreign investment in Sichuan accounted for 1.98 per cent of the national total, or 5.75 per cent that of Guangdong. In terms of per capita figures, in 1993,

Table 7.3 Fourteen regions of China that attracted most foreign investment, 1993

	Number of foreign enterprises	National rank	Total investment (US$ million)	National rank	Actual foreign investment (US$ million)	National rank
National	167,507		382,388.77		38,959.72	
Guangdong	44,705	1	131,491.26	1	8,843.13	
Jiangsu	18,082	2	32,430.22	2	2,843.71	4
Shandong	12,561	3	23,733.78	4	1,882.67	5
Fujian	11,990	4	22,344.05	5	2,905.99	3
Zhejiang	8,085	5	14,368.79	8	1,031.75	7
Shanghai	8,056	6	29,796.18	3	3,178.03	2
Hainan	7,390	7	13,770.99	9	748.32	10
Liaoning	7,365	8	16,562.29	7	1,396.93	6
Beijing	6,516	9	18,404.89	6	817.31	9
Tianjin	6,004	10	7,003.41	14	623.68	11
Guangxi	4,365	11	10,775.15	10	897.56	8
Hubei	3,899	12	8,178.27	11	554.67	13
Hebei	3,798	13	7,708.15	12	396.54	14
Sichuan	3,787	14	7,558.65	13	571.41	12

Source: Statistical Yearbook of China 1994, pp. 530–1

Guangdong attracted US$133.84, while Sichuan attracted only US$5.14, where the national average was US$32.87.

At the same time, central investment in Sichuan, which had been the primary source for local economic modernisation in the previous years, has dropped continuously since the 1980s. Average state investment in Sichuan has decreased from 95.65 per cent of total investment during the Third Five-Year Plan (1966–70), to 89.83 per cent during the Fourth Five-Year Plan (1971–5), 75.44 per cent during the Fifth Five-Year Plan (1976–80), and to 42.53 per cent in the Sixth Five-Year Plan (1981–5), 53.12 per cent lower than in the Third Five-Year Plan.[41]

The decline of central investment in Sichuan was but a symptom of the change in central government's position with reform. A study by Wang Shaoguang and Hu An'gang has revealed that since the 1980s the state's financial capacity in China has dropped rapidly. From 1986 to 1991 the financial receipts of central government grew only 0.66 per cent for every 1 per cent growth in GNP. The proportion of financial receipts in GNP dropped from 31.2 per cent in 1978 to 14.7 per cent in 1992.[42]

To some extent, the decline of Sichuan is a structural decline. Sichuan has been severely disadvantaged by the national change in the strategy of economic development which has seen the focus of activities move from the Third Front to the coastal areas, and market forces replace central planning. The remainder of this section on the impact of reform on Sichuan is concerned with case studies that show the changing position of Sichuan in national political and economic development.

The Third Front Project

The fate of the Third Front Project in an era of reform provides a general example of the disadvantages that now face Sichuan. As mentioned earlier, the construction of the Third Front Project turned Sichuan into a highly industrialised province. However, the project also caused problems for Sichuan. The change in perception of the Chinese leadership's view of the world and their departure from the Maoist economic development strategy in and after 1978 have resulted in the decline of the Third Front Project. When the centre decided to transfer responsibility for the project to Sichuan, the provincial government was more than a little reluctant to accept, not least because there was little if any tangible wealth contained in the transfer.

Most enterprises in the Third Front Project had been designed for military production, and their economic efficiency had not been a relevant consideration at the time. In 1978 the realised output value for every ¥100 invested in fixed capital in Third Front Project enterprises was 30 per cent lower than the national average. Their capital-tax rate was 40 per cent lower than the national average and considerably lower than the coastal areas. The total value of fixed capital in the Third Front Project accounted for 56 per cent of the national total, but its gross value of industrial output accounted for only 39 per cent of the national total.[43] With the introduction of the market economy, this Maoist legacy was clearly likely to be more of a burden than an asset.

Although the Third Front Project had relatively high levels of technological inputs, its military-related technology is not easily converted into civil production. In a commodity production-oriented economy many enterprises may become uncompetitive in the market place. In any case after the 1980s and as a result of the transfer of substantial contemporary technology from the West to the coastal areas the Third Front started rapidly to lose its position as one of China's high-tech centres.

The sudden cessation of Third Front Project construction during the late 1970s left many of its constituent projects unfinished. As a result, many key projects are now having difficulties maintaining even a normal production.[44] The Project's construction was very much in the nature of a blood transfusion from the industrially advanced areas to those that were much poorer. When the process ceased before the whole project was completed, the poorer areas were not able to continue by themselves.

There are both profitable enterprises and loss-making enterprises to be found among the activities of the former Third Front Project. When the central government decided to transfer the Third Front Project to Sichuan, relevant departments of the State Council were willing to hand over only the non-profitable enterprises while maintaining control of the profitable.

After repeated negotiations, the central government agreed to provide special funds to Sichuan to assist in the reorientation of the industries of the Third Front Project. However, of more than 2,000 enterprises, the centre agreed to sponsor only 7 per cent. Of the total fund provided (¥2 billion), the central government provided only 40 per cent (in the form of a construction loan). For the other 60 per cent, enterprises must raise half by themselves (30 per cent of the total), while the other half was to be provided by provincial government and relevant departments of the State Council.[45] While provincial revenue decreased continuously after 1985, the provincial government had to spend millions of dollars to subsidise state-owned enterprises, many of them belonging to the Third Front Project.[46] For an already tight provincial budget, the Third Front Project represents a heavy financial burden. The Third Front Project was built with the strength of the entire nation, but Sichuan has had to take responsibility alone for the results of central government mismanagement.

The Three Gorges Project

In early 1992 a resolution to build the world's biggest dam – the Three Gorges on the Yangtze River – was passed at the Fifth Session of the Seventh National People's Congress. It is estimated that by the time the project is completed in 2008, Sichuan will lose the whole or part of 15 counties and cities, a total of 503 square kilometres of land. About 955,000 people will have to be resettled; 555 factories (including 4 modern industrial complexes and 11 medium-size factories, with a ¥712 million total value in fixed capital), 106 power stations, 595.4 km of trunk roads, 747.3 km of power lines, and 1,325.7 km of communication lines will be under water. The project is designed to provide protection against flood for the middle and lower Yangtze River valley area and to generate electric power for industrially advanced central and eastern China. Sichuan will have no direct benefit from the project.[47]

The idea of a dam at the Three Gorges on the Yangtze River had been raised by Mao Zedong shortly before the Great Leap Forward. Mao's ambition had an active response from the then provincial secretaries of both Sichuan and Hubei, but he himself seemed extremely cautious in moving to a final decision. In about 1960, Mao had a conversation with the then Party Secretary of Chongqing, Ren Baige. Mao asked Ren whether it was a good idea to build a dam on the Yangtze River which would generate electric power, prevent flood and encourage aquaculture. Ren replied in the affirmative, but suggested too much land might be submerged. Mao asked again if it was a good idea to have less grain, but more fish. Ren replied that it was a good idea, but that there would be many migrants who would be short of grain before they could afford fish. Mao is reported to have kept his silence.[48]

After the Cultural Revolution, when Lin Yishan, a main advocate of the project, tried to convince the then provincial Party Secretary Zhao Ziyang, Zhao replied diplomatically that people in eastern Sichuan had suffered heavily during the Cultural Revolution. They needed time to recover.[49]

However, the project became a topic of hot debate after Deng Xiaoping inspected the area in 1980. The project became an important component of an ambitious modernisation plan at the Twelfth CCP Congress. In early 1985 it was announced that a new province, Sanxia (Three Gorges) Province, was to be established which would include three prefectures from Sichuan (Fuling, Wanxian and Daxian) and two prefectures from Hubei (Yichang and Badong). A vice-governor of Sichuan, Xin Wen, was appointed to head the preparatory work. However, in the relatively liberal political environment of the mid-1980s Deng Xiaoping changed his mind under domestic and international pressure. In 1986 a central document decided to postpone the construction of the Three Gorges Project and in the same year the preparatory committee for Sanxia Province was abolished.[50]

The attitude of provincial political leaders in Sichuan toward the Three Gorges Project has been complex. Although Li Jingquan expressed his support during an inspection tour with Mao in 1958, other local cadres were more cautious. These different attitudes may also reflect the prolonged tension between provincial and Chongqing leaders of the CCP.

During the 1980s Sichuan showed no particular enthusiasm for building the dam, unlike Hubei, but it was interested in preparations for the proposed new province, since all three areas to be separated from Sichuan are poor parts of the province and cost the province a large amount in subsidies every year. While provincial leaders in Sichuan were active in preparatory work for the new province, they also urged their deputies to the National People's Congress to protest loudly against the dam project during the sessions. However, within Sichuan province, East Sichuan and Chongqing supported the project for different reasons.

The eastern area of Sichuan is one of the poorest parts of China. Ever since the 1950s both central and provincial governments have invested very little in the area because of the uncertainties surrounding the dam project. In 1991 national income per capita in the area was only ¥141.[51] In comparison, the figure for the national average was ¥1,401 in 1991, while the provincial average was ¥903 per capita.[52] When the decision was announced that central government would spend ¥18.5 billion on resettlement and local development, the project understandably won the support of local people in eastern Sichuan. An ¥18.5 billion future was irresistible compared to the ¥0.8 billion total investment during the previous thirty years. To get as much as they could for compensation, many local governments in the area greatly inflated their potential damage and worked out huge budgets to build new cities.[53]

For Chongqing, the situation is quite different. As mentioned earlier, despite Li Jingquan's support, Chongqing opposed Mao's idea to build a dam on the river in the 1950s. In 1983, Chongqing was granted provincial status in economic affairs and became one of the four separate planning cities (along with Wuhan, Shenyang and Dalian) under the direct leadership of the State Council. The aim was to rebuild Chongqing as a trade and industrial centre for the whole of Southwest China.[54] However, this economic independence did not give Chongqing any corresponding political or administrative independence. The province remained the direct supervisor of the city.

After Chongqing was upgraded, it suddenly found it became very difficult to get supplies of materials and market access for its products within the province and as such, many of its factories were facing closure.[55] The province made it clear that since Chongqing now had a new boss, it should ask its new boss and not the province, to solve these problems. Chongqing had to turn to the centre for help. After Xiao Yang was appointed leader of the city,[56] he showed a particular enthusiasm for building the dam and urged central government to build a higher dam than even the centre had originally planned.[57] Xiao's support of the centre's decision was considered a betrayal of Sichuan by local officials, especially those from the province: even local officials in Chongqing thought Xiao had gone too far. After Xiao left Chongqing the city immediately changed its attitude. At the Fifth Session of the Seventh National People's Congress in 1992 it was deputies from Chongqing who showed the strongest concern about the possible negative impact of the project on the city.[58]

One local leading person who has attended various National People's Congresses since the early 1980s said that before the Fifth Session, the centre warned the provincial leaders not to oppose the project at the forthcoming session of the National People's Congress. Among local leaders, Yang Rudai, the then provincial Party Secretary and a member of the Political Bureau, as well as a native Sichuanese, opposed the project. Governor Zhang Haoruo, a member of the 'Prince's Clique' from Beijing, supported the centre.[59] Finally, provincial leaders reached an agreement: while supporting the centre's decision, they would also use the opportunity to bargain. As a result, Sichuan agreed to support the project at the Fifth Session, while the central government, as a concession, agreed to increase investment to ¥18.5 billion in the Three Gorges area by way of compensation for Sichuan's loss. When the deal was agreed, Governor Zhang Haoruo expressed his support for the project, on behalf of Sichuan. Sichuan still loses much, but now at least it gets something in return.

The Fourteenth Congress of the CCP

During the era of Mao-dominated politics Sichuan had a strong political profile and presence in national politics. From 1958 through to the Fourteenth CCP Congress of 1992, Sichuan had seven provincial party secretaries of whom three – Li Jingquan, Zhao Ziyang and Yang Rudai – were all members of the CCP's Political Bureau. However, the election of the new leadership at the Fourteenth CCP Congress could well indicate the political decline of Sichuan in national politics with the rise of the East and Southeast China.

It is widely believed that Xiao Yang had been selected as the new provincial party leader who would succeed Yang Rudai both in the province and as a member of the Political Bureau because of his close relations with

Deng Xiaoping,[60] and because of his support for central decisions on many occasions. Local party workers have said subsequently that because Xiao Yang had a poor reputation in the province and might not get enough votes,[61] the centre had originally planed to promote Li Boyong, the then Deputy-Governor of Sichuan, to Governor with Yang Rudai remaining as the provincial Party Secretary until after a new provincial party congress was held in the wake of the Fourteenth CCP Congress. Then, Yang would retire and Xiao would be appointed by the Central Committee of the CCP as the new provincial Party Secretary and member of the Political Bureau without having to run the risk of an election.

These putative arrangements started to unwind when Li Boyong was appointed Minister of Labour and Xiao Yang was appointed Deputy-Governor of Sichuan before the Fourteenth CCP Congress. The centre decided that Xiao Yang should be elected to the Political Bureau at the Fourteenth Congress as a direct replacement for Yang Rudai. The decision proved a disaster not least for Sichuan. Xiao's performance at the National Party Congress elicited a strong negative response.[62] He was elected to the CCP Central Committee but only as its last alternate member,[63] and was consequently not eligible to be elected to membership of the Political Bureau. As a result Sichuan lost its seat at the centre of national politics. Xiao Yang is now Governor of Sichuan, but scandals and rumours have surrounded him ever since he took up the position, and those he had appointed in Chongqing were replaced after he left. Thousands of shareholders held a demonstration in front of the provincial government building in 1994 after a futures company supported by Xiao went bankrupt and the owner fled overseas.

To some extent, the decline of Sichuan in national politics and the rise of provincial leaders from the eastern seaboard at the Fourteenth CCP Congress serves as an indicator of a profound change in the political balance between regions, with the industrially advanced regions replacing an agricultural province, and the export-oriented east of China replacing the self-sufficient west. It was also an indicator of the changed relation between centre and province in post-Mao China, with fast growing South China wanting more say at the centre and to obtain political security for its economic development strategy.

REFORM AND SOCIAL CHANGE

The impact of reform and particularly changed economic development strategies has been considerable on Sichuan's place in China's national politics. The impact of reform on Sichuan's population has been equally as far-reaching. In the countryside the search for increased productivity and efficiency have led to the export of labour. In urban areas similar trends have resulted in considerable numbers of unemployed industrial workers. At the same time there can be no doubt that as all over China during the 1990s there are new social groups being both enriched and empowered by economic restructuring and the introduction of market forces.

Rural labour export

All over China since 1978 as rural reforms have increased productivity they have also released a large surplus of labour. Rural enterprises have limited funds and so are unable to absorb most of the surplus labour that is generated. At the same time neither central nor provincial governments are able to create sufficient new employment opportunities for all local peasants. Nation-wide the result has been that a total of some 120 million (at the highest estimate) domestic migrants are seeking their fortunes in various parts of China, attracted largely by the wealth generation capacities of the coastal regions and able to travel because of the relaxations in social control.

Among the migrants seeking work elsewhere in China were some 5.5 million people from Sichuan in 1993, accounting for 4.95 per cent of the total provincial population that year.[64] Large groups of Sichuanese migrants looking for work – often referred to as the 'Sichuanese Army' wherever they gather in substantial numbers – are now to be found in almost every capital city of China. Although the majority of them work as manual labourers in coastal cities, there are also high-tech engineers, technicians, university lecturers and government administrators. In Hainan, for example, it is reported that of the 460,000 permanent residents of Haikou, the provincial capital, some 20 per cent are from Sichuan. In Kunming, about 2 million Sichuanese (half the number of total residents) are actively engaged in various local economic activities.

In 1995 a large research project was carried out jointly by the Institute of Sociology of the Chinese Academy of Social Sciences and various local research institutions in Sichuan under the sponsorship of the United Nations, to investigate rural migration and its impact on local social and economic development. One of the project's constituent parts reported that the surplus labour force and the low levels of income were the two major reasons for the large extent of rural emigration. In terms of policy, the report suggests that government restrictions on land transfer made it impossible for peasants to increase their income by enlarging their scale of production.[65]

According to the report, in one village one-third of family members no longer engage in agricultural work.[66] In another village more than 90 per cent of emigrant workers were young people below 36 years of age. All of them had finished some level of education beyond the basic. Of those left behind, 59.74 per cent were female, and 88.31 per cent were either illiterate or had completed only primary school education.[67]

The large scale of emigration has reduced the population burden of the province and produced an important source of local financial income. It is estimated that in the first half of 1993 a total of ¥2.35 billion was sent back to Sichuan by Sichuanese working outside the province.[68]

While migrant workers increase their family income, improve the living standard of their family members and change their perceptions of the outside world, the large number of younger and better educated people leaving their villages, also has negative effects on the social, cultural and economic life of rural Sichuan. Research has found that while Sichuan has the lowest per capita area of cultivated land, lack of labour remained a common phenomenon in the countryside.[69] On the other hand, lack of talented people in the rural areas also makes it difficult to promote new agricultural technologies and techniques in the countryside.[70]

Unemployment of industrial workers

As already indicated, industrialisation in Sichuan was mainly a result of sustained central government investment in state-owned enterprises and industry, first during the 1950s but then more concentratedly during the 1960s under the Third Front strategy. As a result, like the other industrial key-points of the Mao-dominated era of China's politics, Sichuan's economy has a relatively large proportion of state-run enterprises (Table 7.4).

However, in common with state-owned enterprises throughout the PRC from the pre-reform era the efficiency of these enterprises is low. Moreover, the rate of investment to fixed assets in Sichuan is 58.2 per cent, lower than the national average of 67.5 per cent and ranking twenty-fourth of China's provincial-level units.[71]

Sichuan's state-run enterprises and their employees have suffered from the changed economic development strategy, the sharp reduction in central investment in the province, the competitive economic environment introduced by the market, and the lack of new funds and technologies. In 1993 the average annual wage of staff and workers in state-owned enterprises in Sichuan was ¥3,143 – compared to the national average of ¥3,592 and the twenty-fourth ranked of provincial-level units. It was only 54.4 per cent that of Shanghai (¥5,777) and 57.97 per cent that of Guangdong. Per capita consumption was ¥757, compared to a national average of ¥1,148, and only 28 per cent that of Shanghai (the highest) and 51.08 per cent that of Guangdong. At the same time Sichuan had one of the highest reported unemployment rates in China – 3.5 per cent, the third worst of provincial-level units[72] – and the real situation may be even worse.

In early 1993 a symposium was organised by the Sichuan Economic TV station to discuss the survival of state-run enterprises in the market economy. The participants were mainly directors, party secretaries and representatives of workers' unions from the big state-run enterprises in Chengdu.[73] From the beginning, the participants complained that the CCP and government had abandoned the working class and no longer cared about their welfare. One old worker from the Chengdu Meat Processing Factory complained specifically about possible infringements of health regulations. She pointed out that her factory was one of China's two largest modern meat processing factories built in the early 1980s. The central government permits pigs to be slaughtered and processed only in approved factories, but local leaders allow peasants to kill and sell pigs illegally without the necessary sanitation requirements being

Table 7.4 Seven regions with largest investment in fixed assets by ownership, 1993

Region	Total*	State-owned*	% of total	Collective-own*	% of total	Individuals*	% of total	Foreign or joint venture*	% of total
National	1,245.79	765.80	61.47	223.13	17.91	147.62	11.85	78.38	6.29
Guangdong	163.73	88.32	53.94	30.33	18.52	19.00	11.60	20.97	12.81
Jiangsu	111.72	39.78	35.61	45.59	40.81	17.75	15.89	6.67	5.97
Shandong	89.21	47.58	53.33	24.60	27.58	10.54	11.81	4.16	4.66
Zhejiang	78.21	25.46	32.55	30.51	39.01	16.51	21.11	3.74	4.78
Liaoning	71.09	47.58	66.93	9.19	12.93	3.67	5.16	8.11	11.41
Shanghai	64.24	41.34	64.35	11.76	18.31	0.83	1.29	6.16	9.59
Sichuan	58.06	37.61	64.78	9.21	15.86	7.26	12.50	1.83	3.15

Note: *Billion yuan

Source: Statistical Yearbook of China 1994, pp. 142–3

met. This kind of practice is referred to as 'hiding wealth among people' and lets enterprises make money from consumers and entrepreneurs without delivering anything to higher level governments by way of tax or revenues. In their balance sheets many sub-provincial local governments can thus show no increase in their revenue. The peasants involved (as suppliers in this case, but often as the source of recruits for the 'new' enterprise) make money, the state loses revenue, and workers lose their jobs. These kinds of practices and procedures suggest that the new generation of local leaders no longer have national or wider interests as their first priority.

The situation in an old industrial city like Chongqing may be even worse. Although it went unreported by the newspapers, local officials have said privately that several industrial demonstrations were organised in Chongqing during 1992–3 which involved thousands of workers from the defence-related industries. Many of them were underpaid or even had not been paid at all because their factories were unable to convert to civilian production and survive in a market economy. These demonstrations set off alarm bells for both central and provincial leaders. At the insistence of central government, the provincial party and government launched a campaign of 'sending sympathy activities'. In addition to calling for donations from society at large, they also asked banks and relevant departments of the central government to provide special funds to support unemployed workers.[74] In 1994 the government subsidy for the financial losses of state-run enterprises was ¥621.41 million.[75]

New rich

In contrast to falling living standards of workers in the state-owned enterprises and peasants in the remote areas, private business people seem to have been very successful in reforming Sichuan. Sichuan has a tradition of private economic activity and various kinds of private business never disappeared or were never rooted out even during the Mao-dominated era. Fresh vegetables, eggs and meat provided by peasants through free markets have long been the main sources of daily necessities for people in Chengdu. The post-Mao reforms, among other things, have also encouraged people in the pursuit of their self-interests. It is not surprising, therefore, that the first province to introduce economic reform also produced China's first private millionaires and even billionaires.

In the early stages of reform the way to wealth was relatively easy. Yang Yi'an became China's first private millionaire simply by providing more varieties of products (mosquito nets), better quality and better service than the same products produced by the state-owned enterprises. Most of those who came to engage in private business were people who had previously suffered an element of discrimination, such as those with a politically incorrect family background and released criminals. They needed little encouragement to jump from a skinking boat into the sea. In recent years, private entrepreneurs in Sichuan have become even more active and from more varied backgrounds.

Mu Qizhong is an example of the new breed private entrepreneur in Chengdu, and is considered one of the most successful private business people in China. Born to a famous local banker's family, Mu was severely discriminated against because of his family background. He was arrested during the Cultural Revolution because of his dissident ideas. In 1980, Mu resigned from the factory where he worked and began his new career as a private middleman. After many untold hardships, he became successful. In 1992 Mu exchanged China-made daily necessities for four Russia-made Tu-154M aeroplanes. The deal was possible because Russia had planes but no daily necessities, while many Chinese factories were unable to sell their products. Both sides had no hard cash. After repeated negotiations, the Russians agreed to deliver the planes without prepayment. Mu mortgaged the planes to apply for a bank loan and then used the bank loan to buy the Chinese-made daily necessities to sell them to the Russians. The whole deal is believed to be worth more than SF800 million.[76] It is so far the largest private international trade deal China has had since 1978, for in the absence of government support and cooperation the deal would appear almost impossible.

Although it is still difficult to provide a complete picture of the private economy in Sichuan, the statistics for 1994 show that employment in state-run enterprises was 7.27 million, 73.82 per cent of the total, and collective-run enterprise accounted for 2.15 million employees, 21.88 per cent of the total. Private enterprises employed only 0.42 million people or 1.26 per cent of the total. However, of the province's total of ¥77.39 billion invested in fixed capital, state-run enterprises accounted for 55.5 per cent, collective-run enterprises accounted for 17.2 per cent and private enterprises accounted for 27.3 per cent, between one-quarter and one-third of the total.[77]

NEW STRATEGIES FOR ECONOMIC MODERNISATION

Since the mid-1980s reform has basically concentrated on attracting foreign investment to China's ambitious economic modernisation programme, trying in the process to change the earlier Maoist economic structure. Preferential policies granted by central government, proximity to the overseas markets, and overseas Chinese connections, have all greatly helped the coastal areas to attract more foreign investment. These conditions do not exist in Sichuan and with the decline of central investment in the province and sustained financial deficits, Sichuan has had to raise funds from other sources in order to support its economic development. It has attempted to do this creatively and in a number of ways.

The increase of production costs in the coastal areas during the 1990s has presented Sichuan with the chance to attract foreign investment. Provincial leaders believe that labour costs in Sichuan are only one-third to one-quarter that of the coastal areas. It is estimated that the cost of production for the same item is roughly 20 per cent lower in Sichuan than in coastal China.[78] Unlike the east and southeast coastal regions where export-oriented light industry is the economic mainstay, Sichuan is seeking foreign partners in the areas of heavy industry, the aero and space industries, the automobile industry and the electronics industry. In recent years, Sichuan has held several large international trade fairs to sell its state-owned enterprises to foreign companies. To attract foreign investment, the provincial government has also developed its own preferential policies even more favourable than those of East and Southeast China. Major foreign companies like AT&T, McDonnell-Douglas, Coca-Cola, Honda, Yamaha, and many more (and smaller) Taiwanese and Hong Kong businesses have now established themselves in the province. Compared with the development of the coastal areas, however, progress is slow.

The Great Southwest Development Strategy

While maintaining the attempt to attract foreign investment and new technologies, Sichuan has also developed a strategy to strengthen its links with other provinces in China's western region. Sichuan felt itself disadvantaged in the 1980s by the changed national priorities and strategies of development. The feeling was reinforced when the centre published its new programme of development based on a theory of 'stages of development' according to which central government would give the first priority to the industrially advanced eastern region, to be followed at some later (undefined stage) by the central region once East China had developed. Sichuan and other poor provinces in Southwest and Northwest China were left hanging until some undefined future in the next century for their 'priority' assistance to develop.

With the support of provincial party and government leaders, scholars from the Sichuan Academy of Social Sciences took the initiative to invite local administrators, veteran Sichuanese who worked in the central government, and scholars from Yunnan and Guizhou (and later also from Guangxi and Tibet) to form an 'Economic Cooperation Conference of the Great Southwest'. Since March 1983 this semi-official organisation has held meetings annually: participants have included provincial party and government leaders, as well as local academics.

The provincial-level units of China's west and southwest - Sichuan, Yunnan, Guizhou, Tibet, Gansu, Ningxia, Shaanxi, Qinghai and Xinjiang - have come together to form a strong lobby, with particular potential significance for Sichuan as it is likely to take the leading position in regional development. In 1993 GDP in Sichuan accounted for 41 per cent of the regional total, the gross value of agricultural and industrial output was 44.2 per cent of the regional total, financial income was 34.3 per cent, fixed industrial assets were 36.3 per cent, steel production was 59.8 per cent, grain production 48.9 per cent, and the scientific and technological population

36 per cent.[79] It is obviously to Sichuan's benefit for the centre to adopt a more balanced economic development perspective on relations between the coastal, central and western regions.

Apart from drawing the centre's attention to China's west and southwest, advocacy of the concept of the 'Great Southwest's Development' has also helped Sichuan to attract domestic investment from other provinces. It is reported that during the first finance and trade fair of the southwest region held in 1987, a total of forty-six deals were reached among six parties (Sichuan, Yunnan, Guizhou, Guangxi, Tibet and Chongqing) involving ¥2.27 billion. In the same year, mutual investment among the southwestern provinces and Chongqing reached ¥75.72 million.[80] By 1990, a total of 14,800 economic and technological cooperation agreements had been reached between Sichuan and other provinces, and between different regions within Sichuan. The total of contracted investment reached ¥2.7 billion, of which ¥1.25 had been invested in Sichuan.[81]

'Boat-borrowing' policy

In addition to its adaptive strategies, Sichuan has spent part of its already tightened budget to invest in the coastal areas in order to share the benefits of rapid economic development. By the end of 1990 Sichuan had established more than 700 'window enterprises' in Shenzhen, Hainan, Guangdong, Fujian and Shanghai with a total investment of ¥1 billion.[82] In Shenzhen alone, there were 200 enterprises run by Sichuan-owned companies with a total investment of ¥460 million. The industrial output value of these enterprises was believed to account for 10 per cent of the city's total in 1989.[83] In Hainan, enterprises from Sichuan are the most numerous, and third in the value of investment (after Guangdong and Beijing) when ranked by provincial source. In 1990 Sichuan's external 'window enterprises' produced a total output value of ¥0.3 billion, and exported US$50 million worth of goods. More importantly, ¥30 million was sent back to Sichuan.[84]

In a new tide of reform stimulated by Deng Xiaoping's southern inspection tour, provincial leaders urged Sichuanese to invest in Beihai, Guangxi.[85] Yang Rudai, the then provincial party secretary, summarised Sichuan's strategy as 'borrowing a hen to lay eggs and borrowing a boat to go overseas'. In 1992 a total of ¥10 billion was needed for capital investment in Sichuan. Yet it is believed that the province instead invested ¥7 billion in the coastal areas, including ¥3 billion in Beihai alone.[86] Sichuan has invested so much in Beihai that people jokingly talk about Beihai City as part of Sichuan Province.

This 'boat-borrowing' policy has its problems. Sichuan's investment in the coastal areas has caused a serious shortage of capital funds within the province. At its worst during 1992–3 some local governments did not even have enough money to pay peasants for their grain delivered to the state. Meanwhile, local government officials used various kinds of excuses to increase peasants' taxes, levies and other charges. When rumours spread that local leaders had used the funds that peasants paid for the construction of roads to engage in real estate speculation in Beihai, and then subsequently lost the money, thousands of angry peasants in Renshou County, Yang Rudai's home town, surrounded the CCP County Party Committee and government, and burnt down the building. Fearing a negative reaction from other parts of the province, Yang Rudai was said to have refused to use force: he went to the area and promised the peasants that he would take care of the matter personally and ensure that none of the demonstrators was punished.

Another heavy blow to Sichuan's 'boat-borrowing' policy was the central government's decision in late 1992 not to approve any loans for real estate development following the declaration of Vice-Premier Zhu Rongji's strict new financial policy. Officials claim that Beihai became a new hot spot in real estate speculation during Li Peng's inspection of the city. After pushing land prices up and skimming enough profits from the speculation, companies run by various departments of the central government and by sections of the 'Prince's Clique' quickly withdrew before policy changed. For latecomers like Sichuan, unaware of the sudden change in policy, most of its funds were trapped in the real estate speculation, causing an even more serious shortage of fund in its own province. Insiders said that Yang Rudai tried to negotiate with the centre and wanted it to relax its financial policy so that Sichuan could withdraw at least part of its investment in Beihai. Zhu Rongji was said to have refused Yang's request, fearing that any new financial deregulation would cause the whole system to collapse. Yang's opportunism and his failure to restore the funds invested in Behai is regarded by some people in Sichuan as the reason for the end of his political career.

The two lines and two wings strategy

Sichuan's failure in real estate speculation in Beihai, however, seems to have been compensated to some extent by a small shift in economic development policy. The decline of Deng Xiaoping's health and consolidation of the new central leadership has also affected the course of China's economic reform. At the Fifth Plenum of the Fourteenth Central Committe of the CCP, a new policy was adopted. The centre clearly stated that in the next few Five-Year Plan periods, China will focus its development on the central and western regions. Policies will be adopted to attract foreign investment to the inland provinces. The more advanced eastern region will be expected to support the economic development of the poorer parts of the central and western regions.

Central government will also support the modernisation plans of the old industrial bases in Northwest and Southwest China.[87] In Sichuan, in addition to investment in the Three Gorges Project, the central government will also invest in the southwest part of Sichuan around Panzhihua, a major complex of heavy industry since the early 1960s.[88] Provincial leaders in Sichuan have wasted no time in readjusting their own perspectives on economic development in response to these national adjustments. During the meeting of the

CCP Sichuan Committee, held immediately after the Fifth Plenum, provincial leaders proposed that in the next five to ten years Sichuan would focus on a strategy of 'two lines and two wings'. The 'two lines' refers to the development of industrially advanced areas along two railways: one from Jiangyou to Emei via Chengdu, and the other the line connecting Chengdu and Chongqing. The 'two wings' refers to the Three Gorges Project zone in the east of the province, and Panzhihua in the southwest.[89]

These new perspectives on provincial development are particularly interesting for several reasons. First, it seems that there will again be some investment by central government in heavy industries located in and under provincial governments in the coming years, though how much and under what circumstances is clearly a matter for further exploration. Provincial officials are confident that Sichuan will be able to exploit the situation to develop the backward areas of the province. Second, although Sichuan has been a strong advocate of balanced development between the regions, within the province economic development remains uneven with the emphasis on already developed industrial areas and with less attention paid to the less industrialised and minority nationality areas. Third, unlike the situation in the coastal region, most industries receiving support in Sichuan are likely to be those containing state-owned heavy or defence-related enterprises. The relationship between these enterprises and China's export-oriented market economy remains very much an open question.

NOTES

1 Pu Haiqing, 'Changkai tianfu damen, jiakuai sichuan fazhan' [To open wide the gate of the Heavenly Kingdom and speed up Sichuan's development], *Jingji tizhi gaige* [Economic Reform] no. 4, 1994, p. 31.

2 State Statistics Bureau, *Zhongguo tongjinianjian 1994* [Statistical Yearbook of China 1994], China Statistics Press, Beijing, 1994, p. 60.

3 Yuan Tingdong, *Ba-Shu wenhua* [Ba-Shu Culture], Liaoning Education Press, Shenyang, 1991, p. 33.

4 S.A.M. Adshead, *Province and Politics in Late Imperial China: Viceregal Government in Szechwan, 1898–1911*, Curzon Press, London, 1984, p. 105.

5 Yang Chao (ed.) *Dangdai zhongguo de sichuan* [Sichuan in Contemporary China] two volumes, China Social Sciences Press, Beijing, 1990, 1, pp. 11–12.

6 Chen Shisong (ed.) *Sichuan jianshi* [A Brief History of Sichuan], Sichuan Academy of Social Sciences Press, Chengdu, 1986, p. 279.

7 *Zhonggong Sichuan difang dangshi dashi nianbiao* [CCP Sichuan Local Party History Yearbook], Chengdu, 1985, pp. 1, 44, 90–1.

8 State Statistics Bureau, *Quanguo ge sheng, zizhiqu, zhixiashi lishi tongji ziliao huibian* [Historical Statistical Data of Various Provinces, Autonomous Regions and Municipalities], China Statistics Press, Beijing, 1990, pp. 693, 696, 716.

9 Gong Zhide (ed.) *Zhonggong Sichuan difang shi zhuanti jishi: shehui zhuyi shiqi* [Chronicle of Major Events in the History of the Sichuan Communist Party: Socialist Period], Sichuan People's Publishing House, Chengdu, 1991, p. 5.

10 Yang Chao, 1, p. 74. During the period, the total grain production in Sichuan was 21,305,000 tonnes (see Gong Zide, p. 67.) The grain supplied to the state accounted for 38.16 per cent of the total provincial grain production.

11   He Haoju (ed.) *Dangdai Sichuan jiben jianshe, 1950–1985* [Capital Construction in Contemporary Sichuan, 1950–1985], Sichuan Academy of Social Sciences Press, Chengdu, 1987, p. 15.

12   He Haoju, p. 19.

13   Cong Jin estimated that a total of 40 million died during the famine. See Cong Jin, *Quzhe fazhan de suiyue* [Years of Tortuous Development], Henan People's Publishing House, Zhengzhou, 1989, pp. 272–3. Bramall has a detailed study of famine in Sichuan in his book: Chris Bramall, *In Praise of Maoist Economic Planning: Living Standards and Economic Development in Sichuan since 1931*, Clarendon Press, Oxford, 1993, pp. 291–304.

14   *Yibin shizhi* [History of Yibin City], cited in Ding Shu, 'Chong Dayuejin dao da jihuang' [From the Great Leap Forward to the Great Famine] special issue of *Hua Xia Wen Zhai* no. 75, 6 January 1996.

15   He Haoju, p. 22.

16   He Haoju, pp. 416, 418–19. Percentages are my calculation.

17   *Historical Statistical Data*, p. 696.

18   He Haoju, p. 416.

19   *Historical Statistical Data*, p. 705.

20   *Zhonghua renmin gongheguo fen sheng ditu ji* [Maps of Provinces of the People's Republic of China], Maps Press, Beijing, 1974, p. 115.

21   Yang Chao, 1, pp. 4–5; Zhou Shunwu (ed.) *China Provincial Geography*, Foreign Languages Press, Beijing, 1992, pp. 361–2.

22   *Hongqi* Press (ed.) *Zhongguo sheng qing* [Provincial Situations in China], Gongshang Press, Beijing, 1986, p. 672.

23   Zhang Ji (ed.) *Sichuan Sheng Jingji Dili* [Economic Geography of Sichuan Province], Sichuan Science and Technology Press, Chengdu, 1985, p. 316.

24   *Hongqi* (1986), p. 670.

25   Sichuan Statistics Bureau, *Sichuan Statistical Yearbook 1995*, China Statistics Press, Beijing, 1995, pp. 55, 81. Percentages are separately calculated.

26   Zhang Ji, pp. 287, 299, 377.

27   Zhou Yuande, 'Anning River Valley is Sichuan's Second Largest Plain', private paper, p. 2.

28   Guo Zongzhen and Tang Zejiang, *Xi'nan Jingii qu gai kuang* [A Survey of Southwest Economic Region], Sichuan Academy of Social Sciences Press, Chengdu, 1989, p. 239.

29   Yang Chao, 1, pp. 184–5.

30   'Comrade Li Jingquan's Speech at the 8th National Congress of the Chinese Communist Party', in *Zhonggou gongchandang di ba ci quanguo daibiao dahui wenxian* [Documents of the Eighth National Congress of the Chinese Communist Party], pp. 165–71, People's Publishing House, Beijing, 1957, p. 167.

31   Zhang Fengwu was not 'disclosed' until December 1960. Deng was later 'conditionally' rehabilitated after the Enlarged Working Conference (the 7,000 Cadres Conference) held in January 1962. Gong Zide, pp. 149–50, 152–3.

32   In his speech to the Eighth National Party Congress, Li Jingquan also suggested a reform of the incentive system in enterprises which would allow enterprises to share profits with the state. To what extent Li's idea was put into practice remains to be studied. See Li Jingquan, p. 171.

33   David L. Shambaugh, *The Making of a Premier: Zhao Ziyang's Provincial Career*, Westview Press, Boulder, 1984, pp. 88–9.

34   Gong Zide, pp. 365–7; Yang Chao, 1, p. 202.

35   Yang Chao, 1, p. 202.

36   Gong Zide, p. 347.

37   Yang Chao, 1, p. 199.

38   Ma Lieguang (ed.) *Zhongguo ge shengqu jingji fazhan bijiao* [A Comparison of

Economic Development in Various Provinces and Regions], Chengdu University of Science and Technology Press, Chengdu, 1993, p. 127.

39 The Research Office of the State Council, *Zhongguo lao gongye jidi gaizao yu zhenxing* [The Reform and Development of China's Old Industrial Bases], Science Press, Beijing, 1992, pp. 10, 52.

40 Lin Lin and Li Shugui (eds) *Zhongguo sanxian shengchan buju wenti yanjiu* [A Study of Problems in the Distribution of Third Front Production in China], Sichuan Science and Technology Press, Chengdu, 1992, p. 18.

41 He Haoju, pp. 415–17. Absolute figures in these periods were: ¥12.38 billion during the Third Five-Year Plan, ¥12.45 billion during the Fourth Five-Year Plan, ¥9.45 billion during the Fifth Five-Year Plan, ¥6.70 billion during the Sixth Five-Year Plan.

42 Wang Shaoguang and Hu Angang, *Zhongguo guojia nengli baogao* [A Report on State Capacity in China], Liaoning People's Publishing House, 1993, pp. 28–9.

43 Lin Lin and Li Shugui, p. 149.

44 A total of ¥100 million had to be spent as a 'maintaining fee' annually at least to 1990. Wang Xiaogang 'Woguo sanxian gongye zhengce de tiaozheng' ['Adjustment of Third Front Industries in China'], *Zhongguo gongye jingji yanjiu* [Studies of Chinese Industrial Economics], no. 5, 1989, pp. 59–68, 80.

45 Wang Xiaogang, p. 60.

46 ¥1.26 billion in 1985, ¥0.9 billion in 1986, ¥1.31 billion in 1988, ¥1.58 billion in 1989-90 and ¥1.3 billion in 1991. *Statistical Yearbook of Sichuan 1992*, p. 307.

47 Jin Xiaoming, *Fengyu sanxia meng* [Winds and Rains in Dreams of the Three Gorges], Sichuan People's Publishing House, Chengdu, 1992, pp. 196–7.

48 Jin Xiaoming, p. 191.

49 Jin Xiaoming, p. 191.

50 Jin Xiaoming, p. 140.

51 Jin Xiaoming, p. 199.

52 *Statistical Yearbook of China 1992*, pp. 32, 37.

53 Wanxian County, for example, planned to rebuild a new city twenty times bigger than the submerged area and thirty times bigger than Fuling; in Jin Xiaoming, p. 200.

54 Document of the Provincial Party and Government of Sichuan, 'Guanyu zai Chongqing jingxing jingji tizhi zonghe gaige shidian de yijian' [Opinions on experiments in comprehensive reform of the economic structure in Chongqing], in Legal Committee of the National People's Congress (ed.) *Yanhai, yanjiang, yanbian kaifang falu, fagui ji guifan xing wenjian huibian* [Collection of Laws, Regulations and Legal Documents Regarding the Openness of Coastal Areas, Border Areas and Areas Along the Yangtze River], Falu Press, Beijing, 1992, p. 500.

55 'Woguo lao gongye jidi fazhan chizhi de yuanyin ji gaizhao yu zhenxing de xilu' [Reasons for the slow development of old industrial bases in China and ideas on their reform and revitalisation], *Jingji xuejia* [The Economists] no. 4, 1993, p. 75.

56 Xiao Yang, a native Sichuanese, graduated from the former East Germany. After returning to China in 1956 he worked in Beijing until he was appointed Mayor of Chongqing in the late 1980s. Local people regard him as a person from Beijing rather than as a native.

57 Chongqing became a separate planning city in 1983 and enjoyed economic power equal to Sichuan Province. Xiao Yang, a native Sichuanese, was the vice-director of the Beijing Foreign Trade Commission before being appointed Mayor of Chongqing. In 1988, he became the party secretary of the city. See: Documentary Study Office of the Central Party Committee (ed.) *Zhonggong di shisi jie*

zhongyang weihuan minlu [List of Members of the 14th Central Committee of the CCP], History of Chinese Communist Party Press, Beijing, 1993, p. 69.

58   Jin Xiaoming, pp. 134–5.
59   Returning from the former Soviet Union in 1954, Zhang had been working as a chemical engineer in the Chinese petroleum industry for many years before 1986. Before he was appointed Governor of Sichuan in 1988, he worked as Vice-Minister of Foreign Economic Relations and Trade. See: *Zhongguo renmin da cidian: xianren dangzhengjun lingdao renwu juan* [Who's Who in China: Current Party, Government and Army Leaders], Foreign Languages Press, Beijing, 1989, p. 927. Zhang's father was said to be a senior official working in the Ministry of Coal Industry of the State Council in the 1950s. His two brothers were leading officials in Tianjin and Hainan.
60   It is believed that Xiao Yang became a good friend of Deng's second daughter, Deng Nan, when he studied at the Central Party School as a member of the provincial third echelon in the early 1980s.
61   Partly because of the prolonged tension between leadership groups in Chongqing and Sichuan, partly because Xiao was considered by local cadres as Beijing's man. This is especially so after Xiao led Chongqing in support of the Three Gorges Project.
62   During the Congress, Xiao urged Sichuan deputies to write an open letter to Deng Xiaoping to express their gratitude to the paramount leader. It is also said that when the deputy party secretary Xie Shijie held a press conference during the meeting, Xiao, instead of sitting with Xie to demonstrate the unity of the provincial leadership, went and talked to correspondents outside the meeting room.
63   Reliable sources claim that the number of alternative members was expanded in order to include Xiao Yang.
64   Liu Maocai, 'Lue lun di sanci langcao yu zou xiang dongnan ya' [A Brief Discussion of the Third Wave and Marching towards Southeast Asia], *Jingji tizhi gaige* [Economic System Reform] no. 1, 1994, p. 5. The population of Sichuan was 111.04 million in 1993. Percentage calculation from *Statistical Yearbook of China 1994*, p. 85.
65   Xu Ping, 'Nongcun renkou wailiu he nongcun shehui jingji fazhan – P cun diaocha baogao' [Rural Population Migration and Rural Social and Economic Development – Research Report on Village P], unpublished paper, p. 32.
66   Xu Ping, p. 5.
67   Xie Shenzan 'Nongcun renkou wailiu he nongcun shehui jingji fazhan – Yongxing Xiang, Santai Xian diaocha baogao' [Rural Population Migration and Rural Social and Economic Development – Research Report on Yongxing Xiang, Santai County] p. 18.
68   Liu Maocai, p. 5.
69   Xu Ping, p. 32; Xie Shenzan, p. 18.
70   Xu Ping, p. 32.
71   *Yearbook of China 1994*, p. 174.
72   *Statistical Yearbook of China 1994*, pp. 107, 126, 256.
73   This writer was invited to attend the meeting. Governor Xiao Yang was also invited, but he was said to be indisposed.
74   Report from the *People's Daily*, 25 December 1995, p. 3.
75   *Sichuan Statistical Yearbook 1995*, p. 165.
76   He Bosheng (ed.) *Zhongguo baiwan fuwong* [Chinese Millionaires], Shaanxi People's Publishing House, Xi'an, 1993, pp. 112–13. Another source believes that the total deal was worth SF240 million. Lu Jun (ed.) *Dangdai zhongguo yiwan fuhao* [Billionaires in China Today], Yi Lin Press, 1993, p. 41.
77   *Sichuan Statistical Yearbook 1995*, pp. 46, 50, 81.

78 Pu Haiqing, p. 32.
79 Xin Wen, 'Sichuan jingji fazhan de zhanlue diwei he canyu guoji jingji hezuo de qianjin' [Sichuan's economic development in strategic perspective and the province's future participation in international economic cooperation], *Jingji tizhi gaige* [Economic Reform] no. 4, 1994, p. 44.
80 *Economic Yearbook of China 1988*, pp. VI–257.
81 Lin Lin (ed.) *Sichuan: Zhongguonei lu dasheng de kaifang* [Sichuan: The Openness of a Big Chinese Inland Province], Sichuan Science and Technology Press, Chengdu, 1992, p. 233.
82 Lin Lin, p. 234.
83 Li Guoqiang, 'Jiang Zemin dui Sichuan you xin zhishi, Sichuan shixing di erci da gaige' [Jiang Zmin has a new instruction for Sichuan and Sichuan starts the second major reform], *Guangjiaojin*, June 1991, p. 33.
84 Lin Lin, p. 234.
85 The following information was gathered from several interviews with local government officials, academics and managers of business companies in Sichuan during my visits to Chengdu in 1993–4 and 1995.
86 The following information is based on my interviews with local government officials during visits to Sichuan in 1993–4 and 1995.
87 *Zhongguo gongchandang di shisi jie zhongyang weiyuanhui di wu ci huiyi wenjian* [Documents of the Fifth Plenary Meeting of the Fourteenth Central Committee of the Chinese Communist Party], People's Publishing House, Beijing, 1995, pp. 46–7.
88 Investment will be used to start a second steel complex in the Panzhihua area at Miyi which will bring annual steel production to 10 million tonnes. From a report of the Panzhihua CCP Committee and city government regarding speeding up construction of a second steel complex at Panzhihua, p. 1. The total investment is believed to be greater than Sichuan will receive from the Three Gorges Project.
89 'A proposal of the Chinese Communist Party of Sichuan Province regarding the Ninth Five-Year Plan on the economic and social development of Sichuan Province and long-term targets to the year 2010', *Sichuan Daily* 4 November 1995, p. 2.

REFERENCES

S.A.M. Adshead, *Province and Politics in Late Imperial China: Viceregal Government in Szechwan, 1898–1911*, Curzon Press, London, 1984.

Chris Bramall, *In Praise of Maoist Economic Planning: Living Standards and Economic Development in Sichuan since 1931*, Clarendon Press, Oxford, 1993.

Chen Shisong (ed.) *Sichuan jianshi* [A Brief History of Sichuan], Sichuan Academy of Social Sciences Press, Chengdu, 1986.

Chen Yaobang (ed.) *Zhongguo xibu diqu kaifa nianjian 1994* [1994 Yearbook of Development of China's Western Region], Gaige Press, Beijing, 1994.

'Comrade Li Jingquan's Speech at the Eighth National Congress of the Chinese Communist Party', in *Zhonggong gongchandang di ba ci quanguo daibiao dahui wenxian* [Documents of the Eighth National Congress of the Chinese Communist Party], pp. 165–71, People's Publishing House, Beijing, 1957.

Dangdai Sichuan dashi jiyao Editorial Office (ed.) *Dangdai Sichuan dashi jiyao* [Major Events in Contemporary Sichuan], Sichuan People's Publishing House, Chengdu, 1991.

Audrey Donnithorne, 'Sichuan Agriculture: Depression and Revival', *Australian Journal of Chinese Affairs* no. 17, 1984, pp. 59–84.

Gong Zhide (ed.) *Zhonggong Sichuan difang shi zhuanti jishi: shehui zhuyi shiqi* [Chronicle of Major Events in the History of the Sichuan Communist Party: Socialist Period], Sichuan People's Publishing House, Chengdu, 1991.

David S.G. Goodman, *Centre and Province in the People's Republic of China: Sichuan and Guizhou, 1955–1965*, Cambridge University Press, 1986.

Gu Jiegang, *Lun Ba-Shu yu zhongyuan de guanxi* [On the Relations of Ba-Shu and Central China], Sichuan People's Publishing House, Chengdu, 1981.

Gu Zongzhen and Tang Zejiang, *Xi'nan jingji qu gaikuang* [A Survey of Southwest Economic Region], Sichuan Academy of Social Sciences Press, Chengdu, 1989.

Gui Yintao (ed.) *Sichuan Jindai shigao* [A History of Modern Sichuan], Sichuan People's Publishing House, Chengdu, 1990.

He Haoju (ed.) *Dangdai Sichuan jiben jianshe, 1950–1985* [Capital Construction in Contemporary Sichuan, 1950–1985], Sichuan Academy of Social Sciences Press, Chengdu, 1987.

Jia Daquan, 'Sichuan lishi gaikuang' [A Brief History of Sichuan], *Sichuan jingji nianjian 1986* [Economic Yearbook of Sichuan 1986], Sichuan Science and Technology Press, Chengdu, 1986.

Jin Xiaoming, *Fengyu sanxia meng* [Winds and Rains of the Dream of the Three Gorges], Sichuan People's Publishing House, Chengdu, 1992.

Wolfgang Kasper, 'Note on the Sichuan Experiment', *Australian Journal of Chinese Affairs* no. 7, 1982, pp. 163–72.

Li Guoqiang, 'Jiang Zemin dui Sichuan you xin zhishi, Sichuan shixing di erci da gaige' [Jiang Zemin Has a New Instruction for Sichuan and Sichuan Starts the Second Major Reform], *Guangjiaojin*, June 1991.

Li Shaoming (ed.) *Ba-Shu lishi, minzu, kaogu, wnehua* [History, Nationality, Archaeology and Culture of Ba-Shu] Ba-Shu Shushe, Chengdu, 1991.

Lin Lin (ed.) *Sichuan: Zhongguonei lu dasheng de kaifang* [Sichuan: The Openness of a Big Chinese Inland Province], Sichuan Science and Technology Press, Chengdu, 1992.

Lin Lin and Li Shugui (eds) *Zhongguo sanxian shengchan buju wenti yanjiu* [A Study of the Problems of the Distribution of the Third Front Production in China], Sichuan Science and Technology Press, Chengdu, 1992.

Liu Maocai and Wang Xiaogang (eds) *Liuyu kaifa zhanlue yanjiu: Changjiang shangyou diqu ziyuan kaifa yu shengtai baohu de zongti zhanlue gouxiang* [A Study of Strategy in River Valley Development: A Concept Plan for the General Strategy in the Development of Resources and Ecological Protection at the Upper Section of the Yangtze River], Chengdu University of Science and Technology Press, Chengdu, 1993.

Liu Maocai, 'Guanyu diqu fazhan zhanlue yanjiu de ruogan wenti – *Da xi'nan zhanlue yanjiu congshu xuyan*' [Some Issues about Regional Development Strategy: a Preface to *Studies of Strategy for the Great Southwest*], in Tang Zejiang (ed.) *Lun Daxinan zhanlue diwei jiqi kaifa* [On the Strategic Position and Development of the Great Southwest], Sichuan Academy of Social Sciences Press, Chengdu, 1986.

Meng Wentong, *Ba-Shu gushi lunshu* [A Study of Ancient History of Ba and Shu], Sichuan People's Publishing House, Chengdu, 1981.

Pu Haiqing, 'Changkai tianfu damen, jiakuai sichuan fazhan' [To Open Wide the Gate of the Heavenly Kingdom and Speed up Sichuan's Development], *Jingji tizhi gaige* [Economic Reform], no. 4, 1994.

Pu Xiaorong (ed.) *Zhonghua renmin gongheguo dimin cidian: Sichuan sheng* [A Dictionary of Places in the People's Republic of China: Sichuan Province], Shangwu Press, Beijing, 1993.

Steven F. Sage, *Ancient Sichuan and the Unification of China*, State University of New York Press, Albany, NY, 1992.

David L. Shambaugh, *The Making of a Premier: Zhao Ziyang's Provincial Career*, Westview Press, Boulder, 1984.

Sichuan Baolu fengyun lu [A History of the Railway Protection Movement in Sichuan], Sichuan People's Publishing House, Chengdu, 1981.

Sichuan Provincial Editorial Office, *Sichuan sheng Ganzizhou zangzu shehui lishi diaocha* [An Investigation of Tibetan Social History in Ganzi Prefecture of Sichuan Province], Sichuan Social Sciences Press, Chengdu, 1985.

Sichuan Provincial Statistics Bureau, *Sichuan Jingji Nianjian 1986* [Sichuan Economic Yearbook, 1986], Sichuan Science and Technology Press, Chengdu, 1986.

Sichuan Provincial Statistics Bureau, *Sichuan tongji nianjian 1992* [Statistical Yearbook of Sichuan 1992], China Statistics Press, Beijing, 1992.

Dorothy J. Solinger, *Regional Government and Political Integration in Southwest China, 1949–1954: A Case Study*, University of California Press, Berkeley, 1977.

Tang Zejiang (ed.) *Da xi'nan ziran jingji shehui ziyuan pingjia* [An Evaluation of the Natural, Economic and Social Resources in the Great Southwest], Sichuan Academy of Social Sciences Press, Chengdu, 1986.

Tang Zejiang (ed.) *Lun da xi'nan zhanlue diwei jiqi kaifa* [On the Strategic Position and the Development of the Great Southwest], Sichuan Academy of Social Sciences, Chengdu, 1986.

The Legal Work Office of the Standing Committee of Sichuan Provincial People's Congress (ed.) *Sichuan difangxing fagui huibian* [A Collection of Local Legislation and Regulations of Sichuan], Sichuan People's Publishing House, Chengdu, 1987–93.

The Working Committee of the Party History of Sichuan Provincial Party Committee, *Zhonggong Sichuan difang dangshi dashi nianbiao* [Chronicle of Major Events in the History of Sichuan Communist Party], Sichuan People's Publishing House, Chengdu, 1985.

Tong Enzheng, *Gudai Ba-Shu* [Ancient Ba and Shu], Sichuan People's Publishing House, Chengdu, 1979.

Wang Xiaogang, 'Woguo sanxian gongye zhengce de tiaozheng' [Adjustment of the Third Front Industries in China], *Zhongguo gongye jingji yanjiu* [Studies of Chinese Industrial Economics], no. 5, 1989, pp. 59–68, 80.

Xin Wen, 'Sichuan jingji fazhan de zhanlue diwei he canyu guoji jingji hezuo de qianjin' [Sichuan's economic development in strategic perspective and the province's future participation in international economic cooperation], *Jingji tizhi gaige* [Economic Reform], no. 4, 1994.

Yang Chao (ed.) *Dangdai Zhongguo de Sichuan* [Sichuan in Contemporary China], 2 volumes, China Social Sciences Press, Beijing, 1990.

Yuan Tingdong, *Ba-Shu wenhua* [Ba-Shu Culture], Liaoning Education Press, Shenyang, 1991.

Document of the Provincial Party and Government of Sichuan, 'Guanyu zai Chongqing jingxing jingji tizhi zonghe gaige shidian de yijian' [Opinions on the experiment with comprehensive reform of the economic structure in Chongqing] (1983), pp. 499–518, in the Legal Work Committee of the National People's Congress (ed.) *Yanhai, yanjiang, yanbian kaifang falu, fagui ji guifan xing wenjian huibian* [Collection of Laws, Regulations and Legal Documents Regarding the Openness of Coastal Areas, Border Areas and the Areas Along the Yangtze River], Falu Press, Beijing, 1992.

Zhang Ji (ed.) *Sichuan Sheng Jingji Dili* [Economic Geography of Sichuan Province] Sichuan Science and Technology Press, Chengdu, 1985.

Zhejiang Province

GENERAL

GDP (billion *yuan* renminbi)	266.70
GDP annual growth rate	20
as % national average	169.49
GDP per capita	6,210
as % national average	165.39
Gross Value Agricultural Output (billion *yuan* renminbi)	70.70
Gross Value Industrial Output (billion *yuan* renminbi)	582.80

POPULATION

Population (million)	42.994
Natural growth rate (per 1,000)	13.24

WORKFORCE

Total workforce (million)	26.94
Employment by activity (%)	
primary industry	44.40
secondary industry	19.35
tertiary industry	15.50
Employment by sector (% of provincial population)	
urban	13.80
rural	48.94
state sector	7.01
collective sector	22.44
private sector	6.98
foreign-funded sector	0.52

WAGES

Average annual wage (*yuan* renminbi)	5,597
Growth rate in real wage	6.60

PRICES

CPI annual rise (%)	24.80
Service price index rise (%)	31.00
Per capita consumption (*yuan* renminbi)	1,653
as % national average	95.16
Urban disposable income per capita	5,066
as % national average	144.91
Rural per capita income	1,680
as % national average	165.19

FOREIGN TRADE AND INVESTMENT

Total foreign trade (US$ billion)	8.99
% provincial GDP	29.05
Exports (US$ billion)	6.90
Imports (US$ billion)	2.90
Realised foreign capital (US$ million)	1,156.50
% provincial GDP	3.75

EDUCATION

University enrolments	87,428
% national average	87.19
Secondary school enrolments (million)	1.94
% national average	108.70
Primary school enrolments (million)	3.66
% national average	79.70

Notes: All statistics are for 1994 and all growth rates are for 1994 over 1993 and are adapted from *Zhongguo tongji nianjian 1995* [Statistical Yearbook of China 1995], Zhongguo tongji chubanshe, Beijing, 1995 as reformulated and presented in *Provincial China* no. 1 March 1996, pp. 34ff.

Zhejiang Province

Jiangsu

Shanghai

Anhui

Huzhou

Jiaxing

Zhoushan Islands

The Grand Canal

Hangzhou

Qiantang Jiang

Shaoxing

Ningbo

Jinhua

East China Sea

Jiangxi

Wenzhou

Fujian

8 Zhejiang
Paradoxes of restoration, reinvigoration and renewal

Keith Forster

During the reform era Zhejiang has paradoxically been a province where the rate of economic growth has been at the forefront of those experienced across the country, while sweeping social change, which has undoubtedly occurred as a result of reform and opening to the outside world, has taken place against a political backdrop of political conservatism, caution and obsession with ideological orthodoxy, all features which demonstrate a remarkable continuity with the Maoist years. Zhejiang presents the paradox of a rapidly advancing economy, a vibrant, more open society (although constrained within parameters which, while enlarging inexorably, are still basically determined by the ruling party) yet a stagnant political system whose only signs of life are sporadic and relatively inconsequential.

Overall, Zhejiang Province has made the first steps toward its rehabilitation into the mainstream of Chinese economic and social life. Ever since the Song Dynasty the province had prided itself on its economic, intellectual and cultural achievements. Zhejiang's status was shattered by events of the twentieth century, from the collapse of the Qing Dynasty in 1911, and through the years of militarism, invasion and civil war that followed. Then, during the Maoist period, Zhejiang's fate fell hostage to a communist leadership with little sympathies toward and understanding of this past glory. Since the mid-1970s, a strong sense of local identity, whether at the provincial or sub-provincial level, has re-emerged, helping to drive Zhejiang forward and out of the rut in which it previously found itself. A sense of purpose and optimism have replaced years of pessimism and doubt. Zhejiang society and economy have rediscovered their identity, and success has reinforced their legitimacy. Yet there remains a tension between the heavy hand of communist political correctness and the new-found freedoms of the market-place.

PROVINCIAL BACKGROUND

Zhejiang's status as a centre of economic and cultural power in the Chinese Empire dates from the twelfth century, when Hangzhou became the capital of the southern Song Dynasty.[1] At the end of the fourteenth century, in the early years of the Ming Dynasty, Zhejiang's population of 10.5 million made the province the most populous in China.[2] During the Ming and Qing Dynasties Zhejiang was one of the main suppliers of bureaucrats who staffed the imperial bureaucracy. It was also a centre of intellectual pursuits and education, and became what Ping-ti Ho describes as a 'talent-exporting province'. During the Ming Dynasty four of the thirteen prefectures in China, characterised as possessing 'unusual levels of academic success', were found in Zhejiang: Shaoxing, Ningbo, Jiaxing and Hangzhou. These prefectures were located in the north and northeast of the province, in what has been described as the core areas of Zhejiang.[3] In the Qing Dynasty the same four prefectures, as well as the northern prefecture of Huzhou, comprised five of the nine prefectures with the same intellectual achievements. Hangzhou contributed the greatest number of successful examination candidates of all prefectures in the country.[4] The two core counties of Shaoxing prefecture, in turn, produced many officials who staffed the lower-levels of the bureaucracy throughout the empire.[5]

In the mid-nineteenth century, the northern districts of Zhejiang, including the capital city, were devastated during the fighting occasioned by the Taiping Rebellion. For example, the population of Hangzhou prefecture was 2,075,211 in 1784, but 70 per cent less at only 621,453 in 1883. The population of Jiaxing prefecture was 2,933,764 in 1784 and 68 per cent less at 950,053 in 1883. The lasting effects of the rebellion meant that the population of Jiaxing county in 1928 was less than half of what it had been in 1838, prior to the Rebellion.[6] So great was the depopulation of north Zhejiang that peasants and other classes moved from less affected districts such as Shaoxing to work the depopulated land and to make their fortunes in other trades and professions. Most of the wooden buildings in Hangzhou were torched by the Taiping rebels, and virtually all the architectural legacy of Hangzhou's period as the imperial capital was destroyed. Even a century later, the effects of the Taiping Rebellion (and other wars and natural disasters) were felt demographically. In 1850 the population of Zhejiang had been 30,027,000, ranking it sixth in China, but in 1953 it stood at 22,865,747, which was 24 per cent less. The province's population ranking over this period had fallen to eleventh.[7]

During the late nineteenth and early twentieth centuries the Chinese Imperial state in Zhejiang came into a gradual but irrevocable conflict with the local gentry-merchant elite, which mobilised in a conscious effort to enlarge the scope of the public domain. While the state attempted to direct and incorporate the local elite's managerial skills for the benefit of the empire, increasingly, the elite resisted this control and strove for greater autonomy and authority within a political system which was experiencing decentralising tendencies as well as facing threats, both internal and external, to its very existence.[8] Elites in the core areas of the province were also influential members of the industrial, financial and merchant classes rising to prominence at the turn of this century in the emerging metropolis of Shanghai.[9] During the twenty-year rule of the Guomindang under Chiang Kai-shek, who was a native of Zhejiang, the province became a stronghold of Nationalist Party power in the Republic of China.

In this context, the Chinese Communist Party experienced great difficulties in establishing itself.[10] In the three decades prior to the defeat of the Nationalists in 1949, communist activity in Zhejiang was confined mainly to the mountains of East Zhejiang, where a guerrilla base area was established to fight against the Japanese in the 1940s, to the south of the province in the countryside outside the isolated city of Wenzhou, and to the hills in the west of the province bordering on Anhui province. This small-scale communist movement operated on the fringes of the outer-core districts as well as in the periphery areas of Zhejiang, and in the countryside away from commercial and administrative centres.

While the communist leadership in many areas of the province was composed of natives of Zhejiang, this was the result of the isolation of Zhejiang from the mainstream of the communist movement. At critical periods, such as during the anti-Japanese War in the 1940s in East Zhejiang, as well as in the Fujian–Zhejiang border area of the late 1930s and early 1940s, outside cadres were brought in to take charge of operations. Friction between outside and native cadres was to be a major issue in communist rule over the province after 1949. Just as the local landlord-capitalist elites had resented the rule of outside officials in the last years of Imperial rule, so the more sophisticated natives of Zhejiang were unhappy at seeing the fate of their province handed over to peasant cadres from Shandong province.

The personality traits which have been attributed to the people of Zhejiang may have exacerbated the parochial feelings toward outsiders which characterise most Chinese. In an interesting article on Chinese regional stereotypes, Wolfram Eberhard lists a table of provincial personality traits based on descriptions found in key historical works, as well as those drawn from a survey conducted in Taiwan in 1964.[11] It transpires that such descriptors as 'cunning' and 'commercially adept' have been used to describe Zhejiangese since Song times. The Taiwan survey added such adjectives as unyielding and obstinate, terms which some observers might care to apply even today to the people of Hangzhou. As Eberhard points out, the state of communications is the key factor in assessing the extent of sub-provincial stereotypes,[12] and in the case of Zhejiang it is little wonder that the people of isolated Wenzhou have developed a reputation for extreme parochialism, compounded by the fact that their spoken language is incomprehensible to the people of the rest of the province.

Zhejiang in the PRC

During the Mao-dominated years, Zhejiang plodded slowly along the highway to economic modernisation with a great deal of lead in its saddle bags. It was the object of suspicion by a rural communist elite,[13] suspicious of its culture and wealth.[14] Zhejiang was one of the major fiscal contributors to central budgetary coffers for redistribution to fund the investment reorientation away from the coast to the interior of China.[15] It was a grain surplus province for much of the period from 1949 to 1976.[16] Yet for all the kudos such contributions to national well-being should have brought Zhejiang, its provincial leadership was either incapable of, or, more to the point, seemingly unwilling to, cash in on these credit points to obtain policy considerations from the centre.

Zhejiang seems, in retrospect, to have been a province largely taken for granted by Beijing. After the pacification of remnant nationalist and bandit forces in the early 1950s, and the political and economic emasculation of the landlord and bourgeois classes by the late 1950s, Zhejiang became a province which did not require central subsidies, was ruled by a compliant leadership and, apart from the odd political hiccough, could be relied upon not to cause undue trouble for the central leadership. While remaining an economically important province, Zhejiang was somewhat marginalised outside the mainstream of the Chinese state. This was a new and undoubtedly galling experience for a province whose importance had been recognised for over 700 years.

Political elites and their outlook

Until the Cultural Revolution erupted in 1966 Zhejiang had been ruled by a Mao Zedong–Tan Zhenlin–Jiang Hua axis of Hunanese peasant leaders. Mao called the shots from the centre, while Tan (who was provincial party leader from liberation until the early 1950s but retained an interest in and great influence over provincial developments until 1966) and then Jiang (who ruled Zhejiang from 1954 to 1966) carried out Mao's ideological and policy preferences loyally and unquestioningly. Several examples will serve to illustrate this phenomenon. In 1956, when delegates to the provincial party congress caused great disruption to proceedings with their complaints about the work of the previous seven years, it was Tan Zhenlin who was dispatched to Hangzhou to bring them back into line and to save Jiang Hua from even greater embarrassment.[17] In 1957, when Mao reversed his position concerning the major domestic contradiction in China in the light of the Anti-Rightist struggle, Jiang Hua, at the provincial party congress held at the end of that year, was the first provincial leader to express public support for Mao's change of mind.[18] Precisely at that time, Mao was on one of the many visits he paid to Hangzhou before the Cultural Revolution.[19]

While there may have been a 'Hunan Clique' at the top of the provincial political hierarchy, at the sub-provincial prefecture and county levels of administration Zhejiang was ruled by outside cadres, who were overwhelmingly from Shandong. An examination of the tables of party and government leaders contained in over forty county gazetteers published since the mid-1980s reveals this domination in unremitting starkness. Very few native cadres held the post of county party secretary until the post-Mao period, although inroads into the monopolisation of deputy posts by outsiders were made in the Cultural Revolution. A central cadre on a tour of inspection in Zhejiang in 1956 commented on the total lack of local cadres in the county establishments which he visited.[20]

In the early years after the establishment of the People's Republic, when the CCP was still in the process of securing its rule in Zhejiang, the provincial leadership was highly alert to the issue of relations between outside and native cadres, and the implications for stable and successful government if these relations were not handled with some sensitivity to local feelings.[21] However, its failure on this front soon became apparent. At the provincial party congress in 1956, delegates expressed the depth of their resentment and dissatisfaction with the party authorities in no uncertain terms, forcing the leadership to acknowledge the correctness of the main thrust of the complaints, and to promise to address them. However, within eighteen months, in the aftermath of the Anti-Rightist struggle, the expression of such sentiments became politically impossible, and the most prominent native provincial leaders, who were alleged to have incited the opposition the previous year, were purged and disgraced as suffering from that dangerous disease known as 'localism'.

The pre-Cultural Revolution elite was to a large extent dislodged by the combination of local rebellion and outside military occupation during the decade of the Cultural Revolution. Army and air force troops under central command took control of the province in 1967, and the streamlined bureaucracy which emerged with the establishment of the provincial revolutionary committee in 1968 was dominated at the top by military cadres. This new clique suffered two reverses in the early to mid-1970s. First, in 1972, after the downfall of Lin Biao, the three most senior provincial military-party leaders were removed. Then, in mid-1975, all remaining military representatives, as well as rebels and most rebel-backed cadres, were removed from party and revolutionary committee leadership bodies in a major shake-up carried out by the centre. Their places were taken by rehabilitated cadres with previous experience in the province, and military cadres who had supported the 'conservative' faction in the Cultural Revolution. Rebellion and factionalism, however, persisted in Zhejiang politics right up until the end of the Cultural Revolution in 1976.[22]

The outlook of the provincial political elite between 1949 and 1976 stemmed from its overwhelmingly peasant, non-native origins, its ranks leavened by a sprinkling of petty intellectuals possessing pre-tertiary educational qualifications, and a handful of prominent native officials. In background and experience, Jiang Hua typified, in many respects, party leaders found in Zhejiang and in many other provinces across China. He was a Yao nationality from Hunan province. His wife (and the wives of many provincial leaders were prominent in various strata of the bureaucracy) became head of the provincial supreme court in 1955 and was secretary of the political and law group within the provincial party committee. Both Jiang and his wife had served Mao in a minor capacity as far as back as the late 1920s on the Jinggang mountains. Jiang has recently written about his ideological indebtedness to Mao Zedong,[23] and it is clear that his work as a revolutionary from a very early age gave meaning and substance to a life which in other circumstances would most probably have been uneventful indeed. It was Jiang who set the pattern for provincial compliance bordering on obsequiousness which characterised policy implementation in Zhejiang during the Maoist era, and which was partly responsible for Zhejiang's economic performance falling behind the national average.

Social composition

Ethnically, Zhejiang is overwhelmingly a Han nationality province. The population of minority nationalities hardly troubles the census-takers. Nevertheless, in 1984 the State Council approved the establishment of the Jingning She autonomous county in the southern and economically most backward prefecture of Lishui. In 1994 the total population of this county (no ethnic breakdown is provided) was only 173,500, out of a total provincial population of nearly 43.5 million. Thus, in terms of ethnic composition, Zhejiang does not face the challenges posed by the diversity of nationalities in other Chinese provinces.

Nevertheless, Zhejiang can hardly be characterised as having a fully integrated provincial identity. The mountainous terrain, backward communications and particularistic loyalties define identity in more narrow terms. The contrast between the southwest and northeast of the province, between the coastal and interior regions and, to a lesser extent, between town and countryside are great and show little sign of diminishing. One distinguishing feature of the province's demographic base has been the slow pace of urban development and urbanisation since 1949.

Between 1949 and 1984 the average annual increase in the non-agricultural population of cities and towns (that is, the portion of the urban population entitled to state grain rations) was only 2 per cent, only slightly above the total population increase of 1.9 per cent. In 1984, on the eve of the extension of the reform programme from the countryside to urban China, in the three categories of the proportion of non-agricultural population, city and town population, and urban non-agricultural population to total population, Zhejiang's ratio was only about three-quarters of the national average.[24] This, for a developed province, is somewhat surprising. One analyst has explained this anomaly as deriving from an administrative decision by the provincial authorities not to grant township status to towns which, by size, had qualified for such recognition.[25]

It is possible to see an anti-urban bias as a reflection of the rural background of the political elite which has ruled Zhejiang for much of the period since 1949. Certainly, throughout the Maoist years, Zhejiang's economy performed better in the agricultural than the industrial sector, a situation which has been completely reversed over the last twenty years. For example, in 1949 Zhejiang's GVAO comprised 4 per cent of the national total, while in 1978 it stood at 5 per cent. Between 1950 and 1978 the average annual increase in GVAO of 4.9 per cent was above the national average of 4.3 per cent. On the other hand, Zhejiang's proportion of national GVIO was 3.7 per cent in 1949, falling to 3 per cent in 1978. The average annual increase in GVIO from 1950 to 1978 was 11.6 per cent, nearly two points below the national average of 13.5 per cent. In per capita terms, Zhejiang performed even more poorly, with provincial GVIO standing at 25 *yuan* in 1949 (compared to the national average of 23), while in 1978 it stood at 338 *yuan* compared to the national average of 441 *yuan*.[26]

Before 1949, as mentioned above, the local commercial, educated, landed elite had pursued social mobilisation for its own economic and political benefit. The large-scale mobilisation of peasants and workers which characterised other parts of China where the CCP was active did not occur on the same scale in Zhejiang. Some peasants were introduced to mobilisational politics by communist cadres in isolated pockets of the province. Student activists made an attempt to arouse the patriotic feelings of citizens in cities such as Hangzhou, and in terms of nationalistic fervour they were undoubtedly no less committed than their fellow-citizens from other provinces. But the power of the Nationalist Party was concentrated in Hangzhou and other core areas of the province, and communist activities were easily crushed.

The series of political and social movements launched in Zhejiang by the CCP after 1949 were led in the main by this outside contingent of party cadres, with local cadres playing a subordinate and apprentice role to their more experienced superiors. Zhejiang's new rulers preferred to recruit and train a local elite of young activists imbued with correct ideas and a strong sense of organisational discipline, and who were beholden to the regime. Thus, a new ruling class was formed in town and village, whose standards of literacy and education took a remote second place to their willingness to obey orders and conform to the new orthodoxy. The socialisation of industry and commerce gutted the capitalist class. The Ningbo-Shaoxing financial and industrial class fled to Taiwan, Hong Kong or elsewhere overseas, or remained at home only to be taken over and absorbed into the new state industrial complex run by outsiders for the benefit of a greater national good. The old intellectual class was reduced to silence or the impotent mouthing of vacuous party slogans.

The case of Lu Xun's scientist brother Zhou Jianren, appointed provincial governor in 1958 to replace his disgraced predecessor, Sha Wenhan (also a Zhejiangese), illustrates the contempt in which the provincial rulers held the educated stratum. Zhou was chosen for the post only because the party leadership and central leaders in Beijing felt that it should make a gesture to appease local anger felt over the downfall of the educated, popular and capable Sha.[27] Zhou outwardly went through the motions, but inwardly smarted deeply from the humiliation imposed upon him. This secret CCP member allegedly lost all faith in the party, was appalled at what the first seven years of communist rule had brought to his home province, and seems to have spent much of his time in Beijing in order to avoid confronting the distressing political and social reality which he found in Zhejiang.[28]

Economic development

Zhejiang's lagging economic development during the Maoist era was not just the result of disadvantages imposed by central investment decisions, and sectoral and regional priorities which worked against a developed coastal province. The situation was exacerbated and compounded by an agricultural policy that favoured grain at the expense of industrial and cash crops (which provided the base of Zhejiang's developed light industry), and an industrial policy which pursued the build-up of heavy and base industries, which placed Zhejiang at a comparative disadvantage due to its lack of raw materials. The reduction in maritime trade, although partly imposed by a hostile environment, also worked to the province's disadvantage.

Within the province, before 1978 one-half of total investment in Zhejiang occurred in Hangzhou and at key points along the railway line south through central Zhejiang into Jiangxi province.[29] For example, eight key state industrial enterprises, funded by the centre, were built in the suburbs of Hangzhou in the 1950s. Clearly, strategic and defence considerations dictated this arrangement, but its effect was to neglect the development of the two port cities of Ningbo and Wenzhou, and to reduce their ability both to take advantage of their coastal location and to radiate economic influence into their respective hinterlands.

In 1949, Zhejiang's economy was almost entirely agriculturally based with what industry there was almost entirely devoted to the production of consumer goods. In 1952, after three years of economic recovery, heavy industry comprised only 4 per cent of GVIAO. Agriculture contributed two-thirds, with light industry making up 30 per cent (the national proportions in 1952 were 58 per cent agriculture, 27 per cent light industry and 15 per cent heavy industry). In the balance between light and heavy industry in Zhejiang, the latter contributed only 11 per cent. The composition of GDP was distributed two-thirds to the primary sector, 20 per cent to the tertiary and the remaining 10 per cent to the secondary sector.

Zhejiang's economic structure was basically at odds with the Soviet-inspired planned model based on heavy industry which characterised the greater part of the Maoist years. Consumer cities were considered parasitic, and industry was very quickly developed – often inappropriately, and at great cost to the environment and to the health of urban citizens who lived near these polluting plants.[30] The concept of self-sufficiency and economic independence at the provincial level encouraged, even forced, local leaders to develop a heavy industrial base. However, in Zhejiang this approach was both unsuitable and counter-productive. A high level of accumulation relegated consumer interests to second place behind the development of the industrial base, and the preponderance of investment was directed into building an industry at odds with the existing structure, and one which would have to rely on outside supplies of raw materials and energy sources to become viable.

Although a number of backbone enterprises were built during this period, the developmental strategy contained in this approach condemned Zhejiang to limp along at a below average growth rate compared to the rest of the country. By 1965, nevertheless, the shape of GVIAO had changed considerably since 1952. Agriculture's share had fallen to 45 per cent, light industry (in spite of the planning bias against it) had risen to 41 per cent and heavy industry comprised 14 per cent. The light/heavy industry share stood at 75:25. These proportions were quite different to the national average, where light industry and heavy industry split 50:50 in their respective contributions to GVIO, while in the breakdown of GVIAO agriculture contributed 30 per cent, light industry 35 per cent and heavy industry 35 per cent.[31] In terms of provincial GDP by sector, primary industry comprised 47 per cent, tertiary sector remained largely unchanged at 23 per cent, and the industrial sector had increased to 30 per cent. In the period 1953-65 the rate of growth for heavy industry was twice that for light industry, which in turn was over twice that for agriculture.[32]

A developmental strategy characterised by small and complete (or large and complete), which emphasised heavy industry, accumulation and agriculture (grain) was pursued during the Cultural Revolution, this time by a military provincial leadership completely unfamiliar with the province. The plan to industrialise Zhejiang continued, with the share of heavy industry in GVIO increasing to 40 per cent in 1978 and doubling to 26 per cent of GVIAO in the same year. Light industry's share of GVIAO actually declined to 38 per cent over the period 1965–78, while the share of tertiary industry in GDP fell back to 19 per cent, below the proportion recorded in 1952.

During the Cultural Revolution, the centre devolved a great deal of economic power to the provinces, which were allowed to build up their own processing industries according to a strategy which promoted independent and complete industrial systems.[33] On this basis, one would have expected the small-scale, collectively owned and consumer-based industrial structure of Zhejiang to have flourished. However, political factors played a strong countervailing influence. For example, in the southern city of Wenzhou, the average annual growth rate of GVIAO during the 'ten years of disaster' was a mere 1.85 per cent, and the growth rate for GVIO in the Third Five-Year Plan (1966–70) was only 90 per cent of that for the Second Five-Year Plan (1958–62), a period which had included the years of natural and human-made disasters.[34] In the mid-1970s Hangzhou experienced wild swings in industrial output as a result of chronic factionalism in its industrial enterprises.[35] At the provincial level, GVIO fell in 1967, 1968 and 1974, while GVAO dropped in 1967, 1971, 1973 and 1975.[36]

By 1976, nevertheless, Zhejiang had built up a heavy industrial base, but its power, transport and communications sectors were backward, its industrial structure unbalanced and its agricultural base weak. The major success of the last years of Maoist rule was the emergence of the collective (both rural and urban, but particularly the former) industrial sector, which was largely outside the state plan, was quite flexible, small in scale and responsive to market needs.

In the immediate aftermath of the Cultural Revolution the provincial authorities set about repairing the economy from the ravages of the ten years of disruption. In late 1977, at the provincial people's congress, a plan was put forward for the development of a relatively comprehensive industrial and economic system with the all-round development of agriculture, light industry and heavy industry (and an emphasis on heavy industry).[37] This plan, which was in line with a decision made at the national planning conference in 1970 and endorsed by the then military provincial leadership,[38] was endorsed at a provincial party congress the following year,[39] and seems to have been part of a national developmental strategy focusing on regional development.[40] This was not the first, nor was it to be the last, time that the development of Zhejiang was placed in a regional context, and subordinated to the interests of a larger economic unit.

In 1980 the Zhejiang provincial planning commission criticised this strategy, and commented that:

> In the past Zhejiang failed to seriously study its economic advantages and characteristics while endeavouring for industrial development. An unrealistic proposal was even made to build a so-called independent comprehensive industrial system in Zhejiang. With very poor coal and iron resources, we made extraordinary efforts to produce coal and iron. As a result, not only have the coal and iron industries not been developed but other industries with good potential in Zhejiang have not been well developed either.[41]

This statement was the first sign that a rethink was underway about the development path Zhejiang should pursue, and that instead of forcing the province to conform to a national pattern the starting point should be the actual, local, concrete realities. For, despite the best efforts of the previous thirty years, the structure of the economy of the province showed interesting divergences from the norm. This was due to the continued strength of the traditional structure, despite the best attempts to neglect or weaken it, as well as to the weakness of the state sector.

There were four aspects in which the economy of Zhejiang differed from the national average, and which, ironically, assisted it to advance so rapidly in the reform period.[42] First, the proportion of the non-state economy in the provincial economy was high. In 1978 village industrial output value comprised 16 per cent of GVIO, compared to 9 per cent nationally. Urban collective industrial output value at 23 per cent of GVIO stood 9 per cent above the national average. In the retail sector, the value of sales from state outlets, at 43 per cent of social consumer retail sales, was 12 per cent less than the national average, while sales from collective and private outlets in Zhejiang were 10 per cent and 2 per cent respectively above the national average. Budgetary revenue at 22 per cent of GDP was only two-thirds the national average of 31 per cent.

Second, there were few centrally run enterprises or large and medium enterprises. The great majority of industrial enterprises came under the aegis of the local plan, and their inputs were allocated and their activities coordinated by the province. A mere 1.5 per cent of state investment during the years 1953 to 1978 had been directed to Zhejiang. By 1978 the output of centrally managed industrial enterprises came to only 2.5 per cent of provincial GVIO at the village level and above, while the output of large and medium enterprises contributed 16 per cent to GVIO. These figures were 4 per cent and 27 per cent respectively below the national average.

Third, the scope of mandatory planning for the supply, production and distribution of enterprise goods was narrow. Because most enterprises produced consumer goods and small agricultural tools they were allowed some flexibility in business operations, and the influence of market forces was not insignificant in investment allocations. Some of these enterprises had the power to sell their products themselves and even to fix the prices of their products. Fourth, there was a strong consciousness of the commodity economy among these economic entities. In sum, then, it appears that the Chinese state was only partly successful in its attempts to reshape the economy of Zhejiang. Central neglect, especially in investment, misguided policy parameters, rash and subjective decision-making and sheer ignorance seemed to cancel each other out, and what remained was the objective existence of a stock of production factors waiting to be directed in ways which complied with local conditions.

ECONOMIC MODERNISATION

A great irony of the reform period is that while the economy has recorded sustained levels of extremely high economic growth (although in the recession of 1989 to 1990 industrial output actually fell for the first time since the Cultural Revolution) this has occurred despite great misgivings and differences among the provincial political elite about the direction of economic reform, which in turn has led to the failure until recent times to map out and implement a consistent developmental strategy. Indeed, economic development has at times seemed to have occurred despite, rather than because of, any leadership exercised by the provincial party and government authorities.

As Table 8.1 indicates there have been incredible rates of economic growth during the post-Mao years. Between 1979 and 1993 Zhejiang's GDP increased by an annual average rate of 13.3 per cent (compared to the national average of 9.3 per cent), and its GVIO rose by an average 23 per cent (compared to the national average of 14.2 per cent). During the same period,

Table 8.1 Annual rates of increase in major indices: Zhejiang and China, 1979–93

	1979–93	1981–93	1986–93	1991–3
Population	0.9	0.9	0.9	0.6
National	1.4		1.4	
GDP	13.3	13.1	12.1	19.9
National (GNP)	9.3		9.1	
Per capita GDP	12.3	12.1	11.1	19.2
GVIO	23.0	22.9	23.8	37.3
National	14.2		16.9	
GVAO	4.9	5.0	4.0	5.1
National	6.1		5.2	
Grain output	–0.1	——	–1.5	–3.3
National	2.4		3.3	
Cotton output	–1.5	–2.7	–4.2	–3.4
National	3.7		–1.3	
Coal output	–0.9	–0.2	–1.0	–0.4
National	4.2		3.5	
Freight (railway)	3.2	2.7	3.9	7.5
National	5.5		4.9	
Road	23.6	25.6	21.7	16.8
National	19.7		11.6	
Waterways	12.9	13.1	10.2	21.3
National	9.1		7.6	
Self-managed exports	34.5	25.1	21.5	25.3
National	16.1		16.3	
Social retail price index	7.5	7.9	10.2	8.6
National	6.4		9.0	
Social agricultural procurement prices	9.6	8.6	10.7	8.2
National	7.9		8.3	

Sources: *Zhejiang tongji nianjian 1994*, pp. 9–17; *Zhongguo tongji nianjian 1994*, pp. 9–17; *Jingji cankao yanjiu* 58, 26 August 1992, p. 32

however, the rate of growth of Zhejiang's GVAO was only 4.9 per cent (compared to the national average of 6.1 per cent).[43] Over the same period Zhejiang's share of national net material product (NMP) increased from 3.4 per cent to 5.7 per cent, and its share of national income rose from 3.6 per cent to 5.5 per cent. In terms of per capita national income, in 1978 Zhejiang's share was seven points less than the national average, while in 1988 it was forty-three points above the national average, a graphic illustration of its vastly increased standing in the Chinese economy.[44]

By international standards, in 1988 the economy of Zhejiang had reached the phase of transition from middle to late stage industrialisation. This could be measured in terms of per capita GNP, the 48.7 per cent proportion of secondary industry in GDP (it rose to 53.4 per cent in 1994),[45] the proportion of manufactured goods in commodity exports (26 per cent), per capita exports (US$10.09) and the shift of labour from agriculture to non-agricultural pursuits. From 1978 to 1988 the proportion of the workforce engaged in agriculture in rural areas fell from 92 per cent to 63.4 per cent, which equalled 51 per cent of the province's total labour force. This figure was 15 per cent below the national average and the annual average rate of transition was 10 per cent higher than the national average.[46]

Zhejiang has attained this level of economic development during the period of reform largely through an increase in the key inputs of capital and labour, with little impact from the application of science and technology. Economic growth had been powered along primarily by demand inflation, chiefly inflation in investment demand, with the engine of economic growth being located in the manufacturing sector. The heart of industrial manufacturing lies in rural and suburban Zhejiang, where the phenomenal development of the township and village enterprise (TVE) sector has occurred.[47] By the mid-1990s, the Zhejiang economy seemed to have reached the peak of crude, extensive, high-speed quantitative growth, and was facing the huge challenge of how to transform itself into a more intensive, technology-driven, qualitative and efficient economic unit.

Despite the achievements of reform, Zhejiang's economic strategy in the period has been characterised by a lack of unity among its leadership as how best to proceed – which has resulted in advances, sidesteps, halts and retreats – and caution in setting goals. The provincial leadership has endeavoured to keep the province in step with the beat of the central drum, even if the pace of that beat has varied from time to time or unpredictable pauses have occurred. The principal area of debate and controversy within Zhejiang concerning the reform programme has concerned resources policy, in the most fundamental meaning of the term. Should Zhejiang invest in basic materials and energy industries to supply the inputs to build up its weak infrastructural base, or should it concentrate on further developing and upgrading its existing industrial strengths, characterised as 'light, small, collective and processing'?

If it opted for the former course how would the diversion of funds and other inputs into these expensive undertakings affect the development of the provincial economy, the thriving TVE sector in particular? If it opted for the latter course, where would it acquire the resources required – from the domestic market, as in the past, or from the international market? The question then became to what extent should the provincial economy open itself up from its previous semi-closed posture, and would it make this major transformation independently or in the context of a regional strategy based around a major urban centre such as Shanghai?

Such questions occupied the minds of provincial politicians, bureaucrats and academics for the most part of the 1980s, and were only really settled by the intensity of the recession of 1989–90. By 1992 it was recognised that unless Zhejiang opened up further to the world market it would lack a cushion to protect itself from a future fall in domestic demand for its consumer products, and that putting all its eggs in the domestic basket was too risky a strategy. But this recognition was arrived at only after much soul-searching, discussion, hesitation and experimentation.

The rapid pace of economic growth provided a certain leeway for Zhejiang, in that with its GDP and GVIO increasing at incredible speeds, and provincial fiscal revenues benefiting from this upswing, further financial sources were now available to pursue a two-pronged strategy of continuing to develop the province's traditional industrial base while at the same time investing on a massive scale in badly needed infrastructural works such as ports, roads, railways, airports, telecommunications and energy projects. Tapping a variety of sources of funds both domestic and overseas, government and private, since the early 1990s Zhejiang has embarked on an ambitious programme to pull its backward infrastructure into the modern world.

Sectoral differences

Table 8.2 provides a historical snapshot of the overall trends in the restructuring of the Zhejiang economy since 1952. While the place of tertiary industry in GDP has remained remarkably stable, and actually fell during periods of economic radicalisation in the Great Leap Forward and Cultural Revolution, secondary industry's proportion has grown at the expense of primary industry. While the proportion of light industry in GVIO has fallen over the whole period it has increased during the reform period, as previous expensive and futile efforts to continue increasing the proportion of heavy industry have largely been abandoned.

Table 8.3 provides a more detailed breakdown of trends since 1978. The proportions of both secondary and tertiary industry have increased at the

Table 8.2 Zhejiang's economy: major sectoral proportions, 1952–94

	1952	1957	1965	1978	1983	1988	1994
GVIAO							
Agriculture	65.9	56.3	44.6	36.3	34.5	19.8	10.9
Light industry	30.4	35.8	41.5	37.9	41.5	51.1	57.6
Heavy industry	3.7	7.9	13.9	25.8	24.0	29.0	31.5
GVIO							
Light industry	89.3	81.9	74.9	59.5	63.4	63.7	64.6
Heavy industry	10.7	18.1	25.1	40.5	36.6	36.3	35.4
GDP*							
Primary	66.4	51.7	46.7	38.1	33.0	27.0	16.6
Secondary	11.3	21.3	30.4	43.3	45.0	49.0	52.1
Tertiary	22.3	27.0	22.9	18.6	22.0	24.0	31.3

Note: *The figures for the proportion of GDP by sector for 1993 contained in the 1994 edition of *Zhejiang tongji nianjian* are vastly different from those for the same year contained in the 1995 edition. Estimates for the composition of GDP for 1995 are 15% (primary) 53.4% (secondary) and 31.6% (tertiary), making it a 1/6, 3/6 and 2/6 split. *Zhejiang Zhengbao* no. 145, 1995, p. 9

Sources: *Zhejiang shengqing*, p. 1,012; *Zhejiang tongji nianjian 1995*, pp. 14–15

Table 8.3 Zhejiang's economy: key proportions, 1978–94

		1978	1980	1985	1990	1994
1	Composition of GDP					
	Primary industry	38.1	36.0	29.9	26.9	16.6
	Secondary	43.3	46.8	48.1	48.8	52.1
	Tertiary	18.6	17.2	22.0	24.3	31.3
2	Composition of GVIAO					
	Agriculture	33.2	31.5	24.0	19.0	10.9
	Light industry	40.2	42.7	47.5	52.8	57.6
	Heavy industry	26.6	25.8	28.5	28.2	31.5
3	Composition of GVIO					
	Light industry	60.2	62.4	62.5	65.2	64.6
	Heavy industry	39.8	37.6	37.5	34.8	35.4
4	Composition of GVAO					
	Crops	77.4	69.3	63.9	59.4	52.7
	Forestry	3.0	3.9	5.1	4.7	5.9
	Animal husbandry	14.3	20.9	21.7	23.7	21.5
	Fisheries	5.3	5.9	9.3	12.2	19.9
5	Sources of light industry raw materials					
	Agricultural products	72.8	71.8	67.4	73.3	71.3
	Non-agricultural products	27.2	28.2	32.6	26.7	28.7
6	Composition of heavy industry					
	Extractive	5.0	3.6	3.0	3.1	2.3
	Raw materials	22.1	27.6	25.5	35.1	34.9
	Processing	72.9	68.8	71.5	61.8	62.8
7	Freight					
	Railway	16.7	15.9	8.0	5.1	3.4
	Road	31.8	31.5	42.0	68.3	74.1
	Waterways	51.5	52.6	50.0	26.6	22.5

Sources: *Zhejiang tongji nianjian 1994*, pp. 9–17; *Zhejiang tongji nianjian 1995*, pp. 14–15; *Jingji cankao yanjiu* 58, 26 August 1992, p. 32

expense of primary industry. This has also occurred at the national level, but the growth in secondary industry has been much faster in Zhejiang than for China as whole. In 1978 secondary industry provided 49 per cent of national GDP (six points above that for Zhejiang) while in 1994 this proportion had risen only three points to 52 per cent, while in Zhejiang it had risen by nine points to the same percentage. The more rapid transformation of GDP in Zhejiang than for the country in general is also reflected in the fact that in 1978 primary industry contributed 28 per cent to national GDP (ten points below that in Zhejiang) while in 1994 that proportion had only fallen seven points to 21 per cent (compared to the twenty-one point fall in Zhejiang). The proportion of tertiary industry in GDP rose faster in Zhejiang than the national average, from being five points below the national average in 1978 to four points above it in the latter year.

After hitting a high point of 65 per cent in 1991 the proportion of GVIO provided by light industry had declined only marginally in 1994, while the proportion of heavy industry had fallen below the level attained in 1978. At the national level the picture is entirely different, with the proportion of heavy industry exceeding that of light industry by fourteen points in 1978, falling to a more balanced six point differential by 1993. Within GVAO all non-crop sectors have increased at the expense of cropping, making Zhejiang's agriculture a much more diversified industry. At the national level similar trends have occurred. However, with its long coastline and many islands, the fact that Zhejiang's fishing industry has developed at a faster rate than the country's as a whole should come as no surprise. The more surprising fact is the extent of its backwardness prior to the reform period.[48]

In terms of raw materials supplied to the light industrial sector, the proportion provided by the agricultural sector has remained remarkably stable at around 70 per cent (slightly higher than the national average). This is the source of the concern expressed since the mid-1980s about the shakiness of the agricultural base in the province. In the heavy industrial sector, the proportion provided by extractive industries has halved, and that provided by raw materials made a ten point leap between 1985 and 1990, entirely at the expense of the processing sector. The latter still provides about two-thirds of heavy industrial output in the province. At the national level the picture is quite different and reflects a more balanced distribution between the three sectors. Processing supplies about one-half of national GVIO, extractive industries around 10 per cent and raw materials 40 per cent. The contrast between the high levels of manufacturing and low levels of basic materials and energy industries in the province is striking, and is reflective of the unbalanced industrial structure of Zhejiang.

Table 8.4 reveals interesting patterns in ownership changes over the reform period. Categories 1 and 2 show virtually no change, although private investment has increased by 50 per cent over the period, compensating for a less than 10 per cent fall in the proportion coming from the state sector. However, private investment, which is mainly directed into housing, has more than halved its share from a high point of 36 per cent in 1990. In the distribution of agricultural net income the state has increased its share four-fold, almost entirely at the expense of the individual peasant. Thus, the continued complaints from farmers concerning excessive charges and fees do appear to have an objective foundation. These figures also confirm the increased ability of the state to extract revenue from peasants, despite the fact that agricultural taxes comprise an insignificant and shrinking proportion of provincial budgetary revenue.[49]

However, it is in the figures concerning industrial output and commercial sales where the most dramatic trends have occurred. The share of state industry in GVIO has fallen by forty-five points over the period. The proportion derived from urban collective industry has also fallen, and has been eclipsed by the rise of the TVE sector from an already solid base in 1978 to be the star of industrial growth in the province. The individual sector of the economy has also experienced rapid growth, particularly since 1985, when policies toward the

Table 8.4 Zhejiang's ownership proportions, 1978–94

	1978	1980	1985	1990	1994
1 Employees by enterprise ownership					
State	10.2	11.2	10.4	11.0	11.1
Urban collective	7.2	8.2	7.9	7.4	6.5
Other economic entities			0.1	0.2	1.4
Urban private and individual	0.1	0.2	0.5	1.2	3.1
Rural	82.5	80.4	81.1	80.2	76.7
Other industries					1.2
2 Investment in fixed assets by ownership					
State	52.8	48.1	38.7	42.7	48.3
Collective	36.6	26.3	30.6	21.3	36.0
Individual	10.6	25.6	30.7	36.0	15.7
3 Distribution of agricultural net income					
State taxes	4.2	4.6	12.9	11.0	15.8
Collective	11.5	10.8	9.3	7.6	11.9
Individual	84.3	84.6	77.8	81.4	72.3
4 GVIO by ownership					
State	61.3	56.4	37.2	31.2	16.1
Collective	38.7	43.0	60.4	60.1	56.0
(TVE)	(16.0)	(16.8)	(32.9)	(36.7)	(73.0)
Other		0.5	0.7	2.1	10.1
Individual		0.1	1.7	6.6	17.8
5 Social consumer retail sales					
State	41.3	39.1	26.4	27.6	24.0
Collective	53.5	56.0	47.1	31.1	17.7
Joint			0.1	0.6	0.5
Private	0.4	0.6	16.7	27.6	38.5
Peasant to non-agricultural population	4.8	4.3	9.7	13.1	19.3*

Note: *Defined as other economies

Sources: *Zhejiang tongji nianjian 1994*, pp. 9–17; *Zhejiang tongji nianjian 1995*, p. 16; *Zhejiang Ribao* 10 May 1995

sector were relaxed. In the commercial sector, the state has performed better and has managed to retain one-quarter of retail sales. The big loser has been the collective sector. By 1994 the private commercial sector had grabbed about 60 per cent of retail consumer market sales in the province.

The most dynamic element within Zhejiang's industrial sector has been the township and village enterprise sector. Between 1979 and 1984 output value grew at an annual rate of 32 per cent. In 1984 the sector contributed 36 per cent to provincial GVIO, and Zhejiang's TVEs 11 per cent to national TVE GVIO. In 1989 when TVEs came under some pressure from a leadership which was lashing out in many directions to find a scapegoat for the economic problems facing the country, the people of Zhejiang were reminded that in 1988 TVEs employed 5.4 million people (25 per cent of the rural labour force), contributed 50 per cent of GVIO, 33 per cent of provincial taxation revenue, about 20 per cent of provincial exports, and 20 per cent of peasant income.[50] By 1994 TVEs contributed an astounding 73 per cent of provincial GVIO and 67 per cent of provincial fiscal revenue. Output value and sales rose a staggering 74 per cent and 72 per cent respectively over 1993, and the sector contributed 98 per cent of the net increase in budgetary revenue for the year.[51]

Economic geography and strategy

The nature and disposition of Zhejiang's regional economy can be viewed from different perspectives, depending upon whether historical, geographic, transport or administrative divisions are considered paramount. Nevertheless, it is clear that the northeast districts today remain, as they traditionally have been, wealthier than their southwest counterparts and, despite their neglect prior to 1978, that the coastal areas are better off than the mountainous districts in the west. Figures for 1984 revealed that the six cities of the northeast – Hangzhou, Jiaxing, Huzhou, Shaoxing, Ningbo and Zhoushan – which comprised 43 per cent of the area of the province and contained 51 per cent of the population, contributed 72 per cent of provincial GVIAO and 77 per cent of GVIO. Per capita GVIAO was 2.5 times higher than that in the five southeast cities (prefectures) of Wenzhou, Taizhou, Lishui, Jinhua and Quzhou.[52] By 1993 the gap had narrowed somewhat, with per capita GDP in the southwest cities now 84 per cent that of the northeast. The gap in per capita GDP between the highest and lowest city in each zone was approximately the same, at about a margin of 60 per cent. In terms of the provision of basic health facilities, the northeast is better served than the southwest, with both hospital beds and doctors per 10,000 population about 60 per cent more available in the wealthier zone.[53]

Below the sub-provincial city (prefectural) level of administration is the county (or county-level city). Zhejiang's wealthy counties are rich by national standards. In 1995 the province contributed twenty-three out of the total of China's hundred economically strongest counties, second only to Jiangsu (the two provinces together supplied forty-eight of the total). Nineteen of these twenty-three counties are located in the northeast of the province.[54] At the other end of the scale are poor counties in the southwest of the province with very low levels of income. In 1994 for example, rich Shaoxing county had a per capita GDP of almost 10,000 *yuan*, while per capita GDP in Wencheng county in Wenzhou city, in the south, was less than 1,500 *yuan*. Shaoxing's population was 951,000, compared to Wencheng's 370,000, yet the latter county's local budgetary revenue in the same year was only just over 3 per cent of its richer northern counterpart.[55] In 1993, forty-six counties in the province suffered a fiscal deficit, up from eight in 1988, while the budgetary revenues of Xiaoshan (city) and Shaoxing (county) in northeast China placed them fourth and eighth respectively on the national scale of fiscally wealthy counties.

No matter which provincial and, flowing from this, intra-provincial regional economic strategy is adopted, in the short term at least there will always be winners and losers. This is undoubtedly why the issue has aroused such controversy within the provincial leadership during the reform period. Until the mid-1980s the question of regional economic strategy had been seen mostly in terms of Zhejiang's role in a domestic regional economic grouping, such as the ill-fated Shanghai Economic Zone.[56] Zhejiang's attempts to orient its economy toward the outside world was thus constrained by regional policy, with Shanghai clearly wishing to draw on its neighbour's labour and raw material resources, as well as its rapidly developing markets, located in the north and northeast plains of the province, to assist in its own modernisation. At discussions held in 1984–5 to draw up a fifteen-year development plan for the province, delegates from Shanghai suggested that it would be premature for Zhejiang to shift its focus to the international market-place.[57]

The discussions on the development plan also focused on intra-provincial regionalism. A researcher from the Institute of Economics under the provincial Planning and Economic Commission argued that while the four-division regional economic structure (an eastern zone centred on Ningbo, a northern zone centred on Hangzhou, Huzhou and Jiaxing, a southern zone centred on Wenzhou, and a western zone centred on Jinhua)[58] was viable for the medium term, ultimately a two-zone division based on Ningbo and Wenzhou made the most sense. The two port-cities would link Zhejiang to the outside world and to the interior of the province, via rivers, railways and highways passing through the two communication axes of Hangzhou and Jinhua. This, essentially, was the view which prevailed in the Seventh Five-Year Plan (1986–90) and was given a major boost by Zhao Ziyang's coastal strategy of late 1987, which called for a fundamental reorientation in economic strategy, and in particular emphasised the export potential of the fast growing TVE sector in the Yangtze River Delta region.

Zhejiang was one of the key targets of the two visits which Zhao conducted to eastern provinces in late 1987 and early 1988, when he inspected Jiaxing and Ningbo.[59] While Zhao was in Zhejiang he was accompanied by Party Secretary and Governor Xue Ju, and his deputy, Deputy-Secretary and Deputy-Governor Shen Zulun. In Ningbo, Party Secretary and future Governor Ge Hongsheng acted as host together, with the city's mayor. After Zhao's first visit the local authorities responded in early December 1987 with a commentary in *The Zhejiang Daily* entitled 'Strike out for the international market!' which argued that in the past Zhejiang had relied on the domestic market for both supplies of raw materials and as recipients of its manufactured goods. This approach, pointed out the commentary, could not be maintained indefinitely because interior provinces were striving to process their materials and would compete with Zhejiang on the domestic market. The only way ahead was to shift to the international market. However, the commentary added a rider, thereby giving voice to the caution for which the Zhejiang authorities have become renowned, when it warned that just as food could be consumed only one mouthful at a time, the road ahead could be trodden only one step at a time. The provincial newspaper then carried a number of articles describing success stories in this shift in orientation.[60]

At a meeting held by the provincial party committee in late December 1987 to discuss the documents from the Thirteenth National CCP Congress, Deputy-Governor Shen Zulun made a key report in which he expressed his whole-hearted support for this shift in the province's economic strategy.[61] Shen also tackled head on some of the most controversial issues in provincial developmental strategy. These included the importance assigned to the outward-looking economic strategy in engaging the world market. Shen observed sharply that when talking about extending lateral links, in the past, in practice this had been confined mainly to the domestic market and, at a mere 10 per cent of GDP, Zhejiang's export industry was clearly under-developed and neglected.

Shen then referred to the relative importance assigned to light industry and heavy industry in industry policy. He pointed out that some people wished to increase the proportion of and importance assigned to heavy industry relative to the light and textile industries, or even switch toward the heavy and chemicals industries. Shen disagreed with this view. He also dismissed the perennial desire of striving for internal balance (that is self-sufficiency) within the provincial economy, and pointed out that the approach of strengthening lateral links with other provinces was preferable.

Shen finally referred to the long-standing problem of low efficiency in the province's industrial enterprises. He pointed out cuttingly that the root of the problem lay not with the state of the equipment or technology (he provided statistics to refute the notion that these were out-moded) but rather in the management of the existing stock of capital and labour. At the provincial people's congress held in the following month, at which Shen replaced Xue Ju as provincial governor, Xue's government work report devoted one section to the outward-looking strategy.[62] *The Zhejiang Daily* editorial which summed up the congress session stated that the province had now made a strategic shift in economic strategy. [63]

The political downfall of Zhao Ziyang in 1989, coupled with the discrediting of his role in economic decision-making – which cast a temporary pall over the coastal development strategy – made an immediate impact on Zhejiang's development strategy. Shen Zulun's enthusiastic espousal of Zhao's strategic initiative most probably played a part in his forced resignation from the governorship in 1990.[64] Shen's replacement as provincial governor, Ge Hongsheng, who had been promoted to provincial deputy-secretary in mid-1988, then presided over another strategic shift of the provincial economy which was announced in February 1991 to coincide with the commencement of the Eighth Five-Year Plan. The strategy was summed up in the phrases 'laying a foundation, improving standards and raising economic efficiency'. Laying a foundation referred to agriculture, basic industries, infrastructure, science and technology, education and economic management, all areas which had been neglected during the previous decade, particularly in the latter half. Improving standards referred to the necessity to improve the utility rate of the existing stock of equipment by raising technological levels, employees' skills and product quality. Raising economic efficiency was defined as taking the road of 'high output with low input and low consumption, and paying attention to social and ecological benefits'.[65] Conservative growth estimates were a feature of a strategy which, without returning to the mistaken, unbalanced and inappropriate approach of the past, seemed to downgrade the importance of crude manufacturing (and therefore the burgeoning non-state sector) in the overall context of the provincial economy.

Ge was probably one of those people whom Shen referred to in his late 1987 speech as advocating a return to an emphasis on heavy industry. Shen and Ge shared certain similarities in that both were born in 1931, joined the CCP in 1948, and had worked in Zhejiang since 1949. Unlike Shen, who was a native of Ningbo, Ge came from Shandong. He worked in the power sector of state industry until the early 1980s before transferring to the provincial economic commission and then serving as party secretary of Ningbo until 1988. Shen, on the other hand, had spent most of his working life prior to the Cultural Revolution in the office of the provincial party committee. After his return to office in the mid-1970s he served in the localities before his promotion to deputy-governor in the major leadership shake-up of 1983.[66] Shen was appointed deputy provincial party secretary in 1987, a year before Ge's promotion to the same position.

It is unlikely that Ge shared Shen's enthusiasm for the outward economic strategy and, given his background and work experience, it was perhaps hardly surprising that in 1990 and 1991 he became a staunch advocate of the revival of state enterprises in Zhejiang.[67] His conservative, cautious approach was overwhelmed and made redundant, however, as a result of Zhejiang's unexpectedly enthusiastic support for Deng Xiaoping's call for resumed high-speed growth in early 1992.[68] Zhejiang's economy shifted immediately into overdrive, a rate which it has maintained virtually unabated ever since, although the provincial leadership has combined its enthusiasm for growth with constant exhortations about the socialist nature of reform.

With the issue of Zhejiang's outward orientation virtually settled, the role of the coastal open cities of Ningbo and Wenzhou has been clarified, with priority being given to the immediate development of the northern port. Massive infrastructure and heavy industrial enterprises are being built along the coast near Ningbo, with foreign investment prominent. For the Ninth Five-Year Plan now underway, intra-provincial strategy has been reformulated to divide Zhejiang into three economic zones: the first zone corresponding to the counties adjacent to the Hangzhou–Jiangxi and Jinhua–Wenzhou railways of southwest and southeast Zhejiang; the second to the coastal counties of Wenzhou and Taizhou cities in southeast Zhejiang, and the third to the north and northeast plains.[69] Zhejiang has thus been divided into a southern interior zone, a southeast coastal zone and a northern zone, which in effect places more emphasis on the backward regions of the province in order to reduce the large intra-provincial imbalances evident in economic development and standards of living.

Given the controversy surrounding Zhejiang's economic strategy, and the inbuilt conservatism of the majority of its political elite, it is little wonder that throughout the period of opening to the outside world the province has stepped into the international market with great caution and at a slower pace than its geographic position and economic status would lead one to expect. Zhejiang's economic development, perhaps more so than most other advanced Chinese provinces, has been essentially domestically driven, in terms of the sources of capital, resources, personnel and destination of its finished products. With regard to foreign trade Zhejiang has maintained a large surplus of exports over imports for the whole of the reform period. From 1978 to 1988 exports increased at an annual average of 21.8 per cent, and foreign currency earnings from overseas tourism rose by 17.4 per cent per annum.[70] However, in 1994 foreign trade, at just under 30 per cent of GDP, stands over 15 percentage points below the national average of 45 per cent.[71] The gap is particularly glaring with respect to imports which, at under 10 per cent of GDP in 1994, are less than half the national ratio.

Table 8.5 shows the trends in foreign trade and foreign investment in Zhejiang since 1979. Between 1979 and 1987 Zhejiang received the third lowest amount of foreign investment of all coastal provinces, and only 1.43 per cent of total foreign investment in China.[72] Comparing Zhejiang with China's front-runner in terms of integration with the world market, Guangdong, in 1986 the value of exports from Guangdong was 3.7 times those from Zhejiang, and from 1979 to 1986 Guangdong used 21 times more foreign capital.[73] By 1994 Zhejiang's realised foreign capital stood at 3.7 per cent of GDP, compared to the national average of over 8 per cent. Both in terms of

Table 8.5 Foreign trade and investment in Zhejiang, 1979–94 (US$ million)

Year utilised	Exports	Imports	Contracted items	Contracted value investment	
1979–83			3	22.24	
1984	736.9	55.5	19		11.6
1985	957.7	185.8	83	89.1	62.1
1986	1,156.1	133.6	57	52.7	49.4
1987	1,370.3	213.5	84	143.3	114.0
1988	1,620.2	399.5	202	268.1	188.0
1989	1,879.2	450.1	248	345.3	269.2
1990	2,259.6	290.8	296	247.9	162.3
1991	2,912.6	538.4	592	374.8	171.9
1992	3,702.7	953.2	2,343	3,240.9	409.7
1993	4,560.4	1,690.2	4,497	4,043.3	1,219.9
1994	6,319.4	2,138.8	2,537	3,177.4	1,370.7

Sources: *Dangdai Zhongguode Zhejiang* 1, p. 148; *Zhejiang tongji nianjian* (various years)

foreign loans and direct foreign investment the ratio to GDP in Zhejiang was well below the national average.

POLITICAL CONSEQUENCES

The major political consequences of this rapid economic growth in Zhejiang for the political elite have been felt in terms of greater pressure on them to perform. The upper echelons of party and government leadership ranks have changed greatly in terms of educational and working background, in response to the shift in the party's work from class struggle to economic modernisation. The poorly educated generalist cadre of a peasant and military background, who made a mark as an activist in one of the many political campaigns launched during the Maoist period, has given way to educated specialists trained in various fields of economic and technical administration.

Second, the party and government elite has become more localised, in that more natives of Zhejiang now hold leading positions in the leadership. At the Ninth provincial party congress held at the end of 1993, five of the thirteen members of the provincial party committee's standing committee were born in Zhejiang, including two of the four deputy-secretaries.[74] This compared with four of the eleven members of the eighth standing committee elected in December 1988, three of the twelve members of the seventh standing committee elected in November 1987, and a mere two of the sixteen members of the sixth standing committee chosen in May 1978. Yet a native of Zhejiang has still to fill the top party post in the province.

The major turnover in the provincial leadership occurred in 1983, when Tie Ying was removed as first party secretary along with leading party and government officials.[75] This shake-up was less thorough-going than first appearances would lead one to believe, and many of the younger, more specialised and educated 'expert and red' cadres who were promoted in that year failed their first big political test when the student movement of 1989 rocked the Chinese political establishment.[76] Not only did it bring down the Governor Shen Zulun, but also the heads of the provincial propaganda department and television service were replaced by more experienced warriors in inner-party struggle.

At the top of the provincial hierarchy, two of Jiang Hua's former subordinates, Wang Fang and Xue Ju, successively held the post of provincial party secretary from 1983 until 1988.[77] Despite their reformist credentials, albeit of the cautious variety, they undoubtedly carried the burden of their long association with Zhejiang, a lack of specialised knowledge of the workings of a modern economy (Wang was a public security official and Xue a party administrator), and in particular the legacy of their factional entanglements in the Cultural Revolution.[78]

In December 1988 the nexus with the Jiang Hua clique was broken when Li Zemin, a graduate in party history from People's University in Beijing and at the time party secretary of Shenyang, was appointed provincial party secretary. Li got off to a promising start when, in a sign of a more open approach toward government, in March 1989 the provincial people's congress held its first press conference.[79] Then at May 1989 session of the provincial people's congress, the press for the first time published the number of votes recorded as either abstaining or opposing government motions and reports.[80] These gestures, although insignificant in the context of other political systems and even in other Chinese provinces, were noticed and applauded in Zhejiang. However, in the aftermath of the events of mid-1989, Li quickly retreated to a much more cautious position in which he effortlessly seems to reconcile the espousal of economic reform with political and ideological orthodoxy.

Administrative structure

The major change to the administrative structure of the province in the reform period has been the increased importance given to the role of cities. Overall, Zhejiang has been slow to undertake urban economic reform, just as, but for different reasons, it lagged behind in rural reforms. However, the reasons behind the tardy and hesitant steps along this road had less to do with an ideological abhorrence for the principles behind the reforms, as to indecision and divisions within the provincial leadership as to what these reforms meant, how far they would go, and how to implement them.[81] In this respect the leadership in Zhejiang was not alone. While peasants were major proponents of changes to the former agricultural collective structure, and could see immediate economic benefits for themselves in reform, urban reforms threatened to tear away the security blanket which many urban residents had held tightly for many years. The risks seemed to outweigh perceived benefits.

To strengthen the role of cities over their surrounding territory the Chinese government encouraged administrative change. For example, in 1984 Jiangsu province abolished all its prefectures and replaced them with cities with jurisdiction over their surrounding counties.[82] Twelve years later, in 1996, Zhejiang still retains one prefecture in the backward region of Lishui, with a provincial government office to supervise its proceedings.[83] At the end of 1988 Zhejiang had a total of eighty-seven county-level administrative units, made up of twenty districts, thirteen cities and fifty-four counties. As of 1994 Zhejiang had eighty-seven county-level administrative units in the province, made up of twenty-three districts, twenty-three cities and forty-one counties.[84] Thus, administrative change could be characterised as slow but steady.

Groups and interests

The Chinese state continues to restrict the social expression of group interests, except in forms which do not challenge its monopoly on political power. This means that such activities, such as those carried out by the traditional transmission-belt mass organisations such as the Women's Federation, Communist Youth League and Trade Unions, are guided and controlled, as well as often sponsored, by the authorities. The savage attack on unauthorised organisations in the wake of the defeat of the student movement in mid-1989 testified to the complete lack of legitimacy which these groups possessed in the eyes of the state.

In the early 1990s Gordon White undertook a study of social groups in Xiaoshan city, which is a wealthy county-level city located adjacent to Hangzhou. He set out to discover to what extent civil society (as he defined it) had emerged in this locality, and concluded that the social organisations which he uncovered in Xiaoshan exhibited dualistic institutional forms, but the extent to which they were dependent on state sponsorship, approval and support (often financial) exceeded their social autonomy.[85] If this is the situation in Xiaoshan, it is possible to imagine the scope which is given to social groups in the more backward areas of the province, although at the time which the research was conducted it is possible that the after-shocks of the student movement were still being felt and that the state had moved to reduce the social space of such groups.

Moreover, groups of business people, entrepreneurs and the like pose little threat to communist political hegemony, and nor do they see themselves in this light. In 1989 what the authorities feared most was the participation of industrial workers in the student movement. Factory managers and party officials issued a series of threats, cajolements and inducements to keep the workers off the streets and on the job. In Hangzhou, workers sympathised with students and were interested spectators to the events which occurred in the city, but it was in their capacity as concerned citizens and parents rather than as organised labour. After the defeat of the student movement the provincial authorities moved quickly to praise workers who had defied the calls of students – some of whom picketed the front gates of major state enterprises – to leave their posts. However, a number of articles which appeared in the provincial press in the aftermath of the movement revealed the dangerous situation which the party had confronted in the factories of Hangzhou.[86]

Changing patterns of governance

Little political reform of substance has occurred in China since the Maoist days, and when Zhao Ziyang proposed the separation of party and government in 1987 he undoubtedly alienated powerful forces within the CCP. In 1995, however, there were signs that administrative reform in Zhejiang – which is reform of an entirely different dimension to political reform, concerned as it is with making government more efficient rather than more accountable – is extending a little further than would be expected, given the overall political climate in Beijing. The provincial government has instructed major departments and administrative bodies to issue performance pledges for

1995,[87] a democratic appraisal of cadres at the bureau and departmental levels in provincial government organs has been carried out,[88] and a report from Hong Kong has stated that the provincial people's congress will take on a more pro-active role in supervising public officials.[89] But with the provincial party secretary holding the additional post of chairman of the provincial people's congress (since 1993), it is unlikely that any increased powers to this body will be much more than cosmetic. The standing committee of the provincial people's congress held 'heated discussions' regarding the campaigns against 'spiritual pollution' in 1983 and 'bourgeois liberalisation' in 1987,[90] but generally it has been a rather tame body.

The composition of delegates to the provincial people's congress has changed little since the mid-1980s. Given the extent of economic and social change this is both surprising and revealing. Of the 887 delegates who were elected to the Sixth Zhejiang provincial people's congress in 1983, workers and peasants comprised 29 per cent, cadres 21 per cent, intellectuals 25 per cent, PLA and armed police 5 per cent and members of democratic parties and patriots (the United Front) 20 per cent. Women comprised 22 per cent, minority nationalities 3 per cent and CCP members 61 per cent. The average age was 49, those with secondary education and above totalled 84 per cent, of whom 36 per cent had completed tertiary education. Model and advanced representatives in their fields made up 30 per cent of delegates.[91]

Almost a decade later the composition of delegates elected to the Eighth Zhejiang provincial people's congress showed little change. The proportion of workers and peasants had remained the same at 28 per cent, that of intellectuals had increased to 33 per cent, while the proportion of cadres had risen to 34 per cent. The number of PLA delegates had fallen to 4 per cent (with 1 per cent of others making up the balance). The proportion of female delegates had increased marginally to 25 per cent, while the percentage of minority nationalities had fallen to 2 per cent. Returned Overseas Chinese made up nearly 1 per cent of delegates.[92] From these figures it appears that members of the United Front, who were counted separately in 1983, may have been included in the category of intellectuals in 1992. Nevertheless, it is revealing too that the largest category of delegates in 1992 came from the ranks of cadres, and it is possible that the total percentage of party members may have been even higher than the 61 per cent in 1983.

SOCIAL IMPACT

Old classes and new rich

The nature of Zhejiang's economy has meant that state enterprise managers, as a group, have perhaps exerted less influence over policy and society than in other provinces. Clearly, this stratum was fearful of the implications for their enterprises of the coastal strategy, in that the opportunities presented were reliant on market awareness and adaptability, product suitability and other qualities where state enterprises were inferior to the collective and other sectors.[93]

But socialism, if it means anything in China today, is explained in terms of the predominance of the non-private sectors in the economy. Many party officials, who have forged close links with state managers during their careers in the bureaucracy, have been powerful spokesmen for the state sector. In the early 1990s they may have well seen Ge Hongsheng as a defender and upholder of their interests. During his short term as governor Ge went to extraordinary lengths to promote the cause of state enterprises. In an interview with a *People's Daily* reporter in April 1991 he expressed great confidence in the project to revive the state industrial sector, stating that the key point was not the question of ownership but that of leadership and management.[94]

At the annual session of the provincial people's congress in January 1993, a session marked by an unusually defiant mood among the normally placid delegates, Ge was voted out of office. It appears that there was a high level of dissatisfaction with his conservative, traditional approach to development combined with his ideological orthodoxy. Even Hangzhou's traffic problems, which were very bad that Chinese New Year, were sheeted home to the governor.[95] Ge failed to receive sufficient votes to continue in his post, despite the fact that the central Organisation Department had not nominated any alternative. With the number of candidates nominated for the posts of Deputy-Governor exceeding the quota, delegates nominated an alternative candidate for Governor. Suddenly and very unexpectedly, a newly arrived Deputy-Governor, Wan Xueyuan, found himself Governor of Zhejiang.[96] To what extent Ge's provincial origins were related to his downfall is difficult to determine, but it is clear that the people of Zhejiang do not want a return to the days when uneducated outsiders determined their fate and stifled their initiative.

The new rich in Hangzhou are found in the state bureaucracy and enterprises as well as among private entrepreneurs. The former have a social status and political clout which the latter can only purchase in surrogate fashion. One's individual status is closely related to the wealth and influence of one's work unit, which can bestow various kinds of material benefits in the forms of cash, expense allowances and desirable goods such as air-conditioners and scarce and exotic foods and medicines. An amusing ditty has been coined to describe this wealthy elite, which lives extravagantly and likes to flaunt its wealth: in the morning the wheel turns, at lunch-time the table turns, and in the evening the skirt swirls (signifying going to work in a motor vehicle, lavish dining at a restaurant, and dancing in an up-market nightclub).

Regional identities

The relatively weak level of integration of Zhejiang is related, as already indicated, to the poor state of intra-provincial communications. This is closely associated with the difficult terrain of the province, which is criss-crossed by rivers and dotted by mountain ranges. The present railway network in Zhejiang dates largely from pre-Liberation days. With the exception of the single-track Hangzhou–Changxing railway, which was built during the Cultural Revolution to bring coal from the province's largest coal mine to Hangzhou's iron and steel mill, nearly all the other lines date from pre-1949. It has only been in the past few years that the busy Hangzhou–Shanghai line has been double-tracked, while work to duplicate the line south to Jiangxi province and east to Ningbo is still in progress. In 1992 work commenced on the difficult Jinhua–Wenzhou line, and in 1995 Zhejiang tried, unsuccessfully as it turns out, to have a Wenzhou–Fuzhou line included as a priority item for state investment in the current Ninth Five-Year Plan.

The Zhejiang delegation to the National People's Congress in 1995 also lobbied the Ministry of Railways to have plans for a Wenzhou–Taizhou–Ningbo railway included in the province's investment priorities for the same period. The materialisation of these plans will do more than any political movement has done over the past fifty years to integrate Wenzhou into the economic and social life of the province, and to break down its feelings of neglect and isolation. The Wenzhou–Jinhua line will also link the southwest interior districts with a future major Chinese port, once the priority in port development shifts from Ningbo to Wenzhou.

Regional identity has been associated, in the reform era in Zhejiang, with regional patterns of economic development. The fifteen-year strategic programme, published by the provincial government in 1986, referred to four economic regions centred around cities. The first was based in north Zhejiang, and included Hangzhou, Jiaxing and Huzhou. It was viewed as a grain base, as well as the manufacturer of silk and textiles, processor of agricultural commodities for export and tourist centre.[97] The second zone, in the east of Zhejiang and centred on Ningbo, included Shaoxing, Zhoushan and part of Taizhou. Its strengths were identified as its ports, fisheries, fruit, fine arts, export commodities and trade, as well as the heavy and chemical industries.

The third zone, in the west of the province, and centred on Jinhua and Quzhou, would concentrate on the production of agricultural raw materials and minerals, crops, aquatics, textiles, foodstuffs, machinery, chemicals and construction materials. Finally, the fourth zone in the south, centred on Wenzhou, Lishui and part of Taizhou, would develop its transport and communications in order to extract and process local raw materials, rely on its favourable location on the sea to obtain further materials for processing, and open up its maritime and fishery resources as well as non-ferrous metal resources. It would concentrate on the export of labour, animal husbandry, aquatics, forestry and light industrial goods such as leather footwear, knitwear, electronics and meters, and so develop further its commodity economy.[98] It is highly likely that these distinct forms of economic development will, in the short term at least, strengthen the sense of regional identity which is so evident in Zhejiang, while longer-term processes at work will help undermine these and lead to a greater provincial integration.

CONCLUSION

A major feature of Zhejiang's hesitant and faltering advances along the reform path has been that when problems have been encountered the initial response has been to retreat, rather than to assess the situation and move ahead while resolving outstanding issues along the way. This seems to be a reflection of uncertainty within the provincial leadership as to how far down the 'capitalist road' Beijing is prepared to go, resulting in division within its ranks between those who favour a more adventurous push ahead and those who desire ideological and political justification and reinforcement for these changes. In his report to the ninth congress in December 1993, party secretary Li Zemin referred to the lack of unanimity within the provincial leadership when it was confronted with difficulties.[99]

Economic dynamism alongside cautious leadership and political conservatism has been a feature of the pattern of change in Zhejiang during the reform period. As recently as January 1995, provincial party deputy-secretary and executive Deputy-Governor, Chai Songyue, a native of Zhejiang, stated at the provincial economic restructuring conference:

> Reform is a pioneering undertaking. For what we regard as correct, we should just try it and go ahead developing in accordance with the criteria of the 'three conducives' [conducive to developing the productive forces of socialist society; increasing the overall strength of socialist society; and improving the people's living standards]. Even if there are different views with regard to a reform measure, we should try and review it in the course of practice. When a deviation occurs, we should promptly rectify it. We should not stand still whenever differences of opinion arise. This is an important point in the experience of reform over the past sixteen years.[100]

Here, Chai hit the nail on the head. Zhejiang's tardiness in implementing reforms has stemmed more from ideological and political differences within the provincial elite than objective factors related to its poor resource base or lack of central support. In fact central support, in the tangible sense of investment funds and preferential policies, has been greater than in any period since 1949.

The ultimate irony of Zhejiang's development since 1978 has been the shift to pre-1949 patterns in regard to the location of growth and the source of social and political influence. Ningbo, with its status as a separately listed city in the state plan, can now go ahead free, to some extent, of the shackles previously placed upon it by the provincial authorities. The same applies to Wenzhou. While it would be premature to talk of a reduction in the status and influence of Hangzhou in provincial affairs, the city desperately requires a better calibre of administrator who can plan its rational development while utilising the wondrous West Lake to best advantage. With native Zhejiang cadres now controlling local party and government bodies across the province the natural talent of the Zhejiangese for business has been allowed to flower once again.

The depressing aspect of the restoration, reinvigoration and renewal of Zhejiang has been that it has occurred without the cultural expressions which once marked the province as a major transmitter and upholder of Chinese civilisation. Political dogmatism, albeit of a more subtle variety, continues to thrive in Zhejiang, with every step forward along the road of economic reform accompanied by reiterations of ideological orthodoxy. The ultimate paradox in Zhejiang's revival is that much of what has occurred on the economic front would probably have occurred anyway, once the dead hand of Maoist policies in the province was relaxed, and that the communist rulers of the province have now found the most effective way to extract the maximum wealth from its sharp and assiduous inhabitants.

ACKNOWLEDGEMENTS

The greater part of the research for this chapter was undertaken in Hong Kong in the first half of 1995 while I was a Visiting Fellow in the Department of Management, Hong Kong Polytechnic University. I thank the department, and its head, Dr Peter Yuen, in particular, for the many considerations which I received during my stay. Thanks are due to Peter Cheung, Jae Ho Chung and Jane Ru for guidance to or the provision of source material drawn on in the chapter. Thanks also to James Cotton and especially John Fitzgerald for comments on the original version of this chapter.

NOTES

1   For a most revealing description of life in Hangzhou during the twilight years of the Song Dynasty, see Jacques Gernet, *Daily Life in China on the Eve of the Mongol Invasion 1250–1276*, Stanford University Press, 1970.

2   Ping-ti Ho, *Studies on the Population of China, 1368–1953*, Harvard University Press, Cambridge, MA, 1967, p. 10.

3   For a discussion of the inner and outer core and periphery areas (the four Zhejiangs), so delineated on the basis of their 'social ecology', see R. Keith Schoppa, *Chinese Elites and Political Change: Zhejiang Province in the Early 20th Century*, Harvard University Press, Cambridge, MA, 1982, ch. 2, Appendix B.

4   Ping-ti Ho, *The Ladder of Success in Imperial China: Aspects of Social Mobility, 1687–1911*, Columbia University Press, New York, 1962, pp. 227–32, 246–7.

5   James H. Cole, *Shaohsing: Competition and Cooperation in Nineteenth-Century China*, University of Arizona Press, Tuscon, 1986.

6   Mark Elvin, 'Introduction', in Mark Elvin and G. William Skinner (eds) *The Chinese City Between Two Worlds*, Stanford University Press, 1974, p. 4.

7   Ho, *Studies on the Population of China*, pp. 241, 246.

8   See Mary Backus Rankin, *Elite Activism and Political Transformation in China: Zhejiang Province, 1865-1911*, Stanford University Press, 1986; Schoppa, *Chinese Elites and Political Change*.

9   See Susan Mann Jones, 'The Ningpo Pang and financial power at Shanghai', in Mark Elvin and G. William Skinner (eds) *The Chinese City Between Two Worlds*, pp. 73–96.

10   See Zhonggong Zhejiang shengwei dangshi ziliao zhengji yanjiu weiyuanhui bian, *Zhonggong Zhejiang dangshi dashiji 1919–1949* [A Chronology of Major

Events in the History of the CCP in Zhejiang], Zhejiang renmin chubanshe, Hangzhou, 1990.

11 Wolfram Eberhard, 'Chinese regional stereotypes', *Asian Studies* 5: 12 (December 1965), Table 8, pp. 604–5.

12 Eberhard, p. 603.

13 See the interesting discussion of this issue in Wang Shan, *Di sanzhi yanjing kan Zhongguo* [Looking at China Objectively], Shanxi renmin chubanshe, Taiyuan, 1994, ch. 4.

14 For example, in May 1968 Jiang Qing excoriated the popular Shaoxing opera (*yueju*) for its alleged depraved custom of allowing men to play women's roles. See *Summary of China Mainland Magazines* 622, pp. 6–10.

15 Kjeld Allan Larsen, *Regional Policy of China, 1949–85*, Journal of Contemporary Asia Publishers, Manila and Wollongong, 1992, Table 8.2, pp. 195, 196.

16 Larsen, p. 253; Frederick C. Teiwes, 'Provincial politics in China: themes and variations', in John M.H. Lindbeck (ed.) *China: Management of a Revolutionary Society*, University of Washington Press, Seattle, 1971, pp. 162, 175, 186, 188. Teiwes ranked Zhejiang as a normal grain exporting province. However, its ranking for per capita grain output fell between the years 1952 and 1958.

17 'Qingsongji' bianjizu bian [Green Pines Collection Editorial Group] (eds) *Qingsongji – Jinian Yang Siyi: wenji* [The Green Pines Collection: Essays in Memory of Yang Siyi], Shanghai shehui kexueyuan chubanshe, Shanghai, 1991, pp. 107, 124.

18 For the details on these incidents, see Keith Forster, 'Localism, central policy and the provincial purges of 1957–58: the case of Zhejiang', in Tim Cheek and Tony Saich (eds) *New Perspectives on State Socialism in China*, M.E. Sharpe and Keith Forster, New York, 1997: 'Mao Zedong on contradictions under socialism revisited', *Journal of Contemporary China* no. 10 (Fall 1995), pp. 23–44.

19 See *ZJRB* (*Zhejiang ribao*), December 1983, and the table (incomplete though it is) in *Mao Zedong yu Zhejiang* [Mao Zedong and Zhejiang], Zhonggong dangshi chubanshe, Beijing, 1993, pp. 271–3. Mao also used the visits to convene several important national party meetings as well as to draft key documents.

20 Zhonghua renmin gongheguo guojia nongye weiyuanhui bangongting bian [Office of the State Agricultural Committee of the PRC] (ed.), *Nongye jitihua zhongyao wenjian huibian* [A Collection of Important Documents on Agricultural Collectivisation], 1, 1949–1957, Zhonggong zhongyang dangxiao chubanshe, Beijing, 1981, pp. 600–3.

21 See documents in Zhonggong Zhejiang shengwei dangshi yanjiushi, Zhejiang sheng dang'anguan (bian), *Zhonggong Zhejiang shengwei wenjian xuanbian (1949nian 5yue–1952nian 12yue)* [A Selection of Documents of the CCP ZPC (May 1949–December 1952)], Zhonggong Zhejiang shengwei bangongting, Hangzhou, 1988, pp. 5–7, 27–30, 62–4, 96–131, 291–301.

22 For a detailed study of the Cultural Revolution see Keith Forster, *Rebellion and Factionalism in a Chinese Province: Zhejiang, 1966–76*, M.E. Sharpe, Armonk, NY, 1990.

23 *ZJRB*, 26 December 1994.

24 Zhejiangsheng minzhengting bian, *Zhongguo renkou (Zhejiang fence)*, Zhejiang renmin chubanshe, Hangzhou, 1992, p. 191, Table 8.2, p. 194.

25 Larsen, p. 210.

26 Larsen, Table 9.3, pp. 222–3; Table 9.4, pp. 226–7; Table 9.13, pp. 264–5; Table 9.14, p. 267.

27 Huo Shilian, 'Hao zongli hao lingdao hao shuaibiao' (A good Premier, a good leader and a good teacher), Zhejiang sheng Mao Zedong sixiang yanjiu zhongxin, Zhonggong Zhejiang shengwei dangshi yanjiushi bian, *Zhou Enlai yu Zhejiang* [Zhou Enlai and Zhejiang], Zhonggong dangshi chubanshe, Beijing, 1992, p. 5;

Huo Shilian, 'Yidai weirende youliang zuofeng' [The fine work style of a first generation great man], Zhejiang sheng Mao Zedong sixiang yanjiu zhongxin, Zhonggong Zhejiang shengwei dangshi yanjiushi bian, *Mao Zedong yu Zhejiang*, pp. 30–1. Initially, Huo was appointed acting governor for several months.

28   Xie Dexian, *Zhou Jianren pingzhuan* [A Critical Biography of Zhou Jianren], Chongqing chubanshe, Chongqing, 1991, pp. 229–30, 235–6, 379.

29   Zhu Jialiang, 'Zhejiang diqu jingji buju zhanlüe tantao' [A discussion of the strategic disposition of Zhejiang's regional economy], *Zhejiang jingji yanjiu* no. 3, 1986, pp. 9–14. Examples include the Quzhou Chemical Works and eight major factories in the heavy industrial sector which were located in the suburbs of Hangzhou. Some of these plants produced equipment for the defence forces.

30   See Chun-Shing Chow and Hang Chen, 'Wenzhou: development in regional and historical contexts', in Yue-man Yeung and Xu-wei Hu (eds) *China's Coastal Cities: Catalysts for Modernization*, University of Hawaii Press, Honolulu, 1992, pp. 188–9.

31   *Zhongguo tongji nianjian*, 1980, p. 18.

32   Zhejiang sheng jingi yanjiu zhongxin bian, *Zhejiang shengqing* (The affairs of Zhejiang), 1949–1984 (Hangzhou: Zhejiang renmin chubanshe, 1986), pp. 1,009–14.

33   Barry Naughton, 'The decline of central control over investment in Post-Mao China', in David M. Lampton (ed.) *Policy Implementation in Post-Mao China*, University of California Press, Berkeley, 1987, pp. 51–80; Christine P.W. Wong, 'Material allocation and decentralization: impact of the local sector on industrial reform', in Elizabeth Perry and Christine P.W. Wong (eds) *The Political Economy of Reform in Post-Mao China*, Harvard University Press, Cambridge, MA, 1985, pp. 253–81.

34   Wenzhou tongjiju, *Wenzhou tongji nianjian*, 1994, p. 18. Figures based on 1980 fixed prices.

35   Keith Forster, *Rebellion and Factionalism in a Chinese Province*, chs 8–9.

36   *Zhejiang tongji nianjian* (Zhejiang statistical yearbook), 1994, (Beijing: China Statistics Press, 1994), pp. 160, 205. Of course natural factors play a major part in the swings in agricultural output.

37   *ZJRB* 31 December 1977.

38   *Dangdai Zhongguode Zhejiang* (Contemporary China's Zhejiang) shang, (Beijing: zhongguo shehui kexue chubanshe, 1989), pp. 102–6; Suisheng Zhao, 'From coercion to negotiation: the changing central–local economic relationship in mainland China', *Issues and Studies* 28, no. 10, 1992, p. 11.

39   *ZJRB* 7 June 1978.

40   Dorothy J. Solinger, 'The shadowy second stage of China's ten-year plan: building up regional systems, 1976–1985', *Pacific Affairs* 52, no. 2, 1979, pp. 241–64, esp. pp. 243–5, 257–61.

41   *Xinhua* 7 May 1980, in Foreign Broadcast Information Service, FBIS/091/O3.

42   'Jingji gaigezhong jihua he shichang guanxide bianhua ji qi qishi' [Changes in the relationship between plan and market during economic reform, and the message contained therein], *Jingji yanjiu cankao* [Economic Research Briefings], no. 58, 28 June 1992, pp. 29–43.

43   *Zhejiang tongji nianjian*, 1994, pp. 9–17; *Zhongguo tongji nianjian*, 1994, pp. 9–17.

44   Jingji fazhande xitong fenxi keti zu, *Zhejiang 1979–1988 jingji fazhande baogao* [Zhejiang 1979–1988 Economic Development Report], Hangzhou daxue chubanshe, Hangzhou, 1990, p. 6.

45   *Zhejiang Zhengbao* [Zhejiang gazeke], no. 145, 1995, p. 9. Estimates for 1995 are for this proportion to remain stable.

46 *Zhejiang 1979–1988 jingji fazhande baogao*, pp. 8–9; *Zhejiang tongji nianjian*, 1994, pp. 9–17.

47 *Zhejiang 1979–1988 jingji fazhan baogao*, pp. 11–15.

48 A recent report has claimed that the provincial fishing industry has fulfilled its targets for the Eighth Five-Year Plan one year ahead of schedule. *ZJRB* 15 June 1995. After many years' research, the province is presently considering a comprehensive report for the development of its coastal regions, including water resources.

49 In 1993 the agricultural tax contributed a mere 334 million *yuan* (or 2 per cent) to the total local budgetary income of 16.7 billion *yuan*. Budgetary outlays to support agriculture totalled 1.2 billion *yuan* in the same year. *Zhejiang tongji nianjian*, 1995, p. 317.

50 *ZJRB* 15 October 1989.

51 *ZJRB* 10 May 1995.

52 Zhu Jialiang, op. cit.

53 *Zhejiang tongji nianjian*, 1994, p. 397. The 1994 figures are not used as the figures contained in *Zhejiang tongji nianjian*, 1995, p. 387 seem suspect.

54 *ZJRB* 12 and 20 October 1995.

55 *Zhejiang tongji nianjian*, 1995, pp. 402–3, 404–5. Interestingly, both counties ran a local budgetary deficit in 1994.

56 See *ZJRB* 16 July 1986; 25 March 1987; see also Dorothy J. Solinger, 'Some speculations on the return of the regions: parallels with the past', *China Quarterly* no. 75, 1975, pp. 623–38.

57 See *Zhejiang jingji nianjian*, 1986, pp. 299–301. See also a series of articles debating these issues in the provincial journals *Zhejiang jingji* and *Zhejiang jingji yanjiu* for the years 1985 to 1986. The latter journal is published by the prestigious provincial economic research centre, which was established in 1983.

58 This division into four zones ignores the island chain of Zhoushan, which clearly should be considered as fifth zone. See *ZJRB* 16 April 1995.

59 *ZJRB* 26 November 1987; 7 January 1988. *ZJRB* 23 January 1988 carried the gist of Zhao's ideas, which were later reprinted in the 1989 issue of *Zhejiang jingji nianjian*, pp. 3–6.

60 See for example *ZJRB* 4, 8 and 9 December 1987; 2 and 4 January 1988.

61 *ZJRB* 30 December 1987; Shen's speech of 24 December 1987 is to be found in *Zhejiang jingji nianjian*, 1988, pp. 49–52.

62 *Zhejiang jingji nianjian*, 1989, pp. 22–3.

63 *ZJRB* 5 February 1988.

64 Other factors played a part in his downfall. See *Jiushi niandai* January 1991, p. 6.

65 *ZJRB* 21 February 1991, in *FBIS-CHI*-91-044, pp. 60–1.

66 See Keith Forster, 'The reform of provincial party committees in China: the case of Zhejiang', *Asian Survey* 24, no. 6, 1984, pp. 618–36; and 'Leaders of Chinese provinces', correspondence in *Problems of Communism* 34, no. 6, November–December 1985, pp. 85–7.

67 *ZJRB* for these years is replete with articles about and statements by Ge to this effect.

68 The first commentary in support of Deng's initiative was published in *ZJRB* 20 February 1992.

69 *ZJRB* 4, 21 and 29 April 1995. Strangely, there is no mention of Zhoushan in this regional strategy.

70 *Zhejiang jingji fazhan baogao*, p. 10.

71 *Jingji yanjiu cankao*, 645, 23 March 1995.

72 Dali L. Yang, 'Patterns of China's regional development strategy', *China Quarterly* 122, June 1990, p. 248.

73   Figures cited in Keith Forster, 'Catching up: Zhejiang Province', *China Access* no. 8, December 1992, p. 31. In 1986 the economies of the two provinces were of comparable sizes. See Fen Renyi and Shen Guoliang, 'Zhejiang, Guangdong jingji bijiao fenxi' [A comparative analysis of the economies of Zhejiang and Guangdong], *Zhejiang jingji* no. 1, 1988, pp. 40–4.
74   *ZJRB* 25 December 1993.
75   Forster, 'The reform of provincial party Committees in China: the case of Zhejiang', 'Leaders of Chinese Provinces', 'Tie Ying: Chairman of the Zhejiang Provincial Advisory Commission', *Issues and Studies* 20, no. 10, 1984, pp. 84–92.
76   See Keith Forster, 'Popular protest in Hangzhou, April/June 1989', *Australian Journal of Chinese Affairs* 23, January 1990, pp. 97–119, reprinted as 'The popular protest in Hangzhou', in Jonathan Unger (ed.) *The Democracy Movement in China: Reports from the Provinces*, M.E. Sharpe, New York, 1991, pp. 166–86.
77   See Keith Forster, 'Wang Fang: newly appointed secretary of the CCP Zhejiang Provincial Committee', *Issues and Studies* 19, no. 8, 1983, pp. 67–71; 'Xue Ju: newly elected Governor of Zhejiang', *Issues and Studies* 19, no. 10, 1983, pp. 82–7.
78   See Keith Forster, 'The repudiation of the Cultural Revolution in China: the case of Zhejiang', *Pacific Affairs* 59, no. 1, 1986, pp. 5–27.
79   *ZJRB* 23 March 1989.
80   *ZJRB* 6 May 1989.
81   See *Dangdai Zhongguode Zhejiang* 1, pp. 116–51.
82   Larsen, p. 211.
83   For details of administrative changes in the province since 1976 see *Zhonggong Zhejiang sheng zuzhishi ziliao* [Materials in the organisational history of the Zhejiang provincial CCP], Chiangzhu: Renmin in ribao chubanshe, 1994), pp. 1,012–45.
84   *Zhejiang tongji nianjian*, 1989, p. 3; *Zhejiang tongji nianjian*, 1995, p. 3.
85   Gordon White, 'Prospects for civil society in China: a case study of Xiaoshan City', paper presented to the conference Toward the Year 2000: Socio-economic Trends and Consequences in China, Asia Research Centre, Murdoch University, 1992.
86   My reading of *ZJRB* for the months June to September 1989.
87   *ZJRB* 25 March 1995.
88   *ZJRB* 26 April 1995.
89   *Southern China Morning Post* (SCMP) 8 June 1995. A later article, based on a *Xinhua* report, stated that the head of a county grain bureau had been fired for dereliction of duty following an investigation by people's congress delegates. See *SCMP* 15 June 1995. See also an article in *ZJRB* 6 October 1995 regarding the supervisory role of the People's Congress.
90   *ZJRB* 17 July 1983, 18 January 1987.
91   *ZJRB* 16 April 1983.
92   *ZJRB* 6 December 1992.
93   See the attitude expressed at a meeting of managers of state enterprises in early 1988. *ZJRB* 11 February 1988.
94   See *FBIS-CHI*-91-089, pp. 62–4; *FBIS-CHI*-91-077, p. 48.
95   Oral source. I can personally vouch for the accuracy of this observation, having spent that Chinese New Year in Hangzhou.
96   See a rather confused and somewhat inaccurate interpretation of the replacement of Ge in the electronic journal *Dignity*, no. 9408, 20 October 1994. *Xinhua* has recently made the first official mention of Wan's unusual election. See *SCMP* 15 June 1995. Another interpretation is that Wan's posting to Zhejiang in November 1992 as deputy-governor was precisely a move to prepare him for elevation to the governorship.

97   Hangzhou was designated a national tourism and recreational centre by the
      State Council in 1987.
98   *Zhejiang jingji nianjian*, 1987, pp. 52–60.
99   *ZJRB* 26 December 1993. See also Li Zemin's report on leading bodies in *ZJRB*
      25 May 1993.
100   Zhejiang People's Radio, 7 January 1995, in *FBIS-CHI*-95-009, p. 89.

REFERENCES

Cheng Chao and Wei Haoben (eds) *Zhejiang 'wenge' jishi (1966.5–1976.10)*
     [Principal Events of the 'Cultural Revolution' in Zhejiang (May 1966 to October
     1976)], Zhejiang fangzhi bianji bu, Hangzhou, 1989.
'Dangdai Zhongguo congshu' bianjibu bianji *Dangdai Zhongguode Zhejiang* [Con-
     temporary China's Zhejiang], Zhongguo shehui kexue chubanshe, Beijing, 1989,
     2 volumes.
Zhejiang 1979–1988nian jingji fazhan baogao *Zhejiang jingji yu shehui fazhan
     congshu* [Series on the Economic and Social Development of Zhejiang], Hangzhou
     daxue chubanshe, Hangzhou, various years.
Zhejiang sheng tongjiju bian *Zhejiang tongji nianjian* [Zhejiang Statistical Yearbook]
     1988–95, Zhongguo tongji chubanshe, Yichun, various years.
Zhejiang sheng zuzhibu, Zhejiang sheng dangshi yanjiushi, Zhejiang dang'anguan
     (eds) *Zhongguo gongchandang Zhejiang sheng zuzhishi ziliao (1922.4–1987.12)*,
     [Materials on the Organisational History of the CCP in Zhejiang April
     1922–December 1987] Liangzhu: Renmin ribao chubanshe, 1994.
Zhejiang zhengbao [Zhejiang government gazette].
Zhejiangsheng jingji yanjiu zhongxin bian *Zhejiang shengqing, 1949–1984* [The
     Affairs of Zhejiang], Zhejiang renmin chubanshe, Hangzhou, 1986. This volume
     is not to be confused with its abbreviated version published nine months later, and
     entitled *Zhejiang shengqing gaiyao* [An Outline of the Affairs of Zhejiang].
Zhonggong Zhejiang shengwei dangshi yanjiushi, Zhejiang sheng dang'anguan (bian)
     Zhonggong Zhejiang shengwei wenjian xuanbian [A Selection of Documents
     Issued by the Provincial Party Committee of the CCP] 4 volumes, Zhonggong
     Zhejiang shengwei bangongting, Hangzhou, various years.
Zhongguo gongchandang Zhejiang sheng weiyuanhui zhengce yanjiushi, Zhejiang
     sheng renmin zhengfu jingji jishu shehui fazhan yanjiu zhongxin (eds) *Zhejiang
     jingji nianjian* [Zhejiang Economic Yearbook] 1986–1991, Zhejiang renmin
     chubanshe, Hangzhou, various years.
Zhongguo gongchandang Zhejiang sheng weiyuanhui zhengce yanjiushi, Zhejiang
     sheng renmin zhengfu jingji jishu shehui fazhan yanjiu zhongxin (eds) *Zhejiang
     nianjian* [Zhejiang Yearbook] 1992–4, Zhejiang renmin chubanshe, Hangzhou,
     various years.
Zhongguo gongchandang Zhejiang sheng weiyuanhui zhengce yanjiushi, Zhejiang
     sheng renmin zhengfu jingji jishu shehui fazhan yanjiu zhongxin, Zhejiang sheng
     jingji tizhi gaige weiyuanhui (eds) *Zhejiang nianjian 1995* [Zhejiang Yearbook],
     Zhejiang daxue chubanshe, Hangzhou, 1995.
Zhongguo renmin zhengzhi xieshang huiyi Zhejiangsheng weiyuanhui *Zhejiang
     bainian dashiji (1840–1945)* [A Chronology of Major Events in Zhejiang over 100
     Years], in *Zhejiang wenshi ziliao xuanji* no. 31, Zhejiang renmin chubanshe,
     Hangzhou, 1986. Zhejiangsheng zhengxie wenshi ziliao weiyuanhui bian, *Xinbian
     Zhejiang bainian dashiji (1840–1949)* [New Edition of a Chronology of Major
     Events in Zhejiang over 100 Years], in *Zhejiang wenshi ziliao xuanji* no. 42,
     Zhejiang renmin chubanshe, Hangzhou, 1990.

Index

Note: page numbers in italics refer to figures or tables